INTERNATIONAL BUSINESS

THE ACADEMY OF INTERNATIONAL BUSINESS

Published in association with the UK Chapter of the Academy of International Business

Titles already published in the series:

INTERNATIONAL BUSINESS AND EUROPE IN TRANSITION (Volume 1)
Edited by Fred Burton, Mo Yamin and Stephen Young

INTERNATIONALISATION STRATEGIES (Volume 2)
Edited by George Chryssochoidis, Carla Millar and Jeremy Clegg

THE STRATEGY AND ORGANIZATION OF INTERNATIONAL BUSINESS
(Volume 3)
Edited by Peter Buckley, Fred Burton and Hafiz Mirza

INTERNATIONALIZATION: PROCESS, CONTEXT AND MARKETS (Volume 4)
Edited by Graham Hooley, Ray Loveridge and David Wilson

INTERNATIONAL BUSINESS ORGANIZATION: SUBSIDIARY
MANAGEMENT, ENTRY STRATEGIES AND EMERGING MARKETS
(Volume 5)
Edited by Fred Burton, Malcolm Chapman and Adam Cross

INTERNATIONAL BUSINESS: EMERGING ISSUES AND EMERGING
MARKETS (Volume 6)
Edited by Carla C.J.M. Millar, Robert M. Grant and Chong Ju Choi

International Business

European Dimensions

Edited by

Michael D. Hughes

and

James H. Taggart

First published 2001 by
PALGRAVE
Houndmills, Basingstoke, Hampshire RG21 6XS and
175 Fifth Avenue, New York, N.Y. 10010
Companies and representatives throughout the world

PALGRAVE is the new global academic imprint of
St. Martin's Press LLC Scholarly and Reference Division and
Palgrave Publishers Ltd (formerly Macmillan Press Ltd).

ISBN 0–333–94531–X

This book is printed on paper suitable for recycling and
made from fully managed and sustained forest sources.

A catalogue record for this book is available
from the British Library.

Library of Congress Cataloging-in-Publication Data
International business : European dimensions / edited by Michael D. Hughes and
James H. Taggart.
        p. cm. – (The Academy of International Business series)
        Papers from the 26th Annual Conference of the UK Chapter of the Academy of
International Business held at the University of Stirling in Scotland.
        Includes bibliographical references and index.
        ISBN 0–333–94531–X
        1. International business enterprises – Europe – Management – Congresses.
2. Personnel management – Europe – Congresses.   3. Subsidiary corporations –
Europe – Congresses.   4. Investments, European – Congresses.   I. Hughes,
Michael, 1947–   II. Taggart, J.H. (James H.), 1943–   III. Academy of International
Business. UK Chapter. Conference (26th : 2000? : University of Stirling)   IV.
Academy of International Business series (New York, N.Y.)
HD62.4 .I555 2001
658′.049′094 – dc21

                                                                          00–049147

10   9   8   7   6   5   4   3   2   1
10   09   08   07   06   05   04   03   02   01

Printed and bound in Great Britain by
Antony Rowe Ltd, Chippenham, Wiltshire

Contents

List of Figures

List of Tables

Preface

As the twentieth century was drawing to an end, the UK Chapter of the Academy of International Business held its 26th Annual Conference at the University of Stirling in Scotland. The conference, hosted by Professor Michael D. Hughes, was making its first visit to this university whose campus must be in one of the most beautiful settings imaginable. Nestling under the lower reaches of the Scottish Highlands, Stirling University looks down the valley of the River Forth towards Edinburgh across the battlefields of Stirling Bridge (1297) and Bannockburn (1314), both fought to secure Scotland's place as an independent member of the fourteenth-century European community of nations. The monument to the Scottish patriot Sir William Wallace towers over the campus on the summit of Abbey Craig, half a mile to the east. There is even an on-campus historical monument – Airthrey Castle – which houses the university's state-of-the-art IT services.

A more historical Scottish scene would be hard to conjure up, and it was appropriate that the conference assembled only four weeks before the first elections to the Scottish Parliament, prorogued since 1707. One of the new Parliament's key tasks *vis-à-vis* the business community will be to extent the already healthy internationalization process. On a *per capita* basis, Scotland is already among the world's most successful exporting countries, and in the last twenty years, trade with other members of the European Community has become increasingly important. It would not be overstating the case to suggest that Scotland's international business future will be tightly linked to the growth and development of the Single European Market (SEM) ideal. So Stirling was an appropriate choice of venue to consider European dimensions of international business.

JAMES H. TAGGART

University of Glasgow

Acknowledgements

The editors and publishers acknowledge with thanks permission to use copyright material from Professor Saul Estrin's ACE–PHARE research project no. 91–0381–R.

Our thanks to the administrative and secretarial team in the Department of Management and Organization at the University of Stirling who so ably supported the 26th Annual Conference of the UK Chapter of the Academy of International Business. Special mention should be given to Hazel Gentles, who acted as conference secretary and general editor for the proceedings and typescript for this volume in the Palgrave AIB series.

List of Contributors

George Anastassopoulos University of the Aegean, Chios, Greece

Mohamed Branine Senior Lecturer and MBA Director, University of Stirling

Ross Brown Research Unit, Scottish Enterprise

Trevor Buck Professor of Business Policy, Graduate School of Business, De Monfort University

Edwin Dott School of Management, Heriot-Watt University

Geert Duysters Associate Professor, Faculty of Technology Management, Eindhoven University of Technology

Grahame Fallon Senior Lecturer in Economics, University College, Northampton

Igor Filatotchev School of Business, University of Nottingham

Rebecca Guidice PhD Candidate, Washington State University

Neil Hood University of Strathclyde

Michael D. Hughes Professor of Management, University of Studing

Louise Hurdley Assistant Director, Ford Faculty, Business School, Loughborough University

Alan Jones Principal Lecturer in International Business, University College, Northampton

Xiaming Liu Lecturer in Business Economics, Aston Business School

Jim Newton Lecturer, Hong Kong School of Business

Peter Nolan Jesus College, University of Cambridge

Marina Papanastassiou Athens University of Economics and Business, Greece

Robert Pearce Reader in International Business, The University of Reading

Philip Raines Senior Research Fellow, European Policies Research Centre, University of Strathclyde

Bert M. Sadowski University of Technology, Delft, The Netherlands

Helen Sakho Associate Lecturer, South Bank University

Michael Sanderson Lecturer in Human Resource Management, Napier University, Edinburgh

Roger Strange Senior Lecturer in Economics, King's College London

James H. Taggart Professor of International Business Strategy, University of Glasgow

Ana Teresa Tavares Lecturer, University of Porto

Monir Tayeb School of Management, Heriot–Watt University

Emanuela Todeva South Bank University, London

Ash Vasudevan Manager of Strategic Alliances, CommerceNet

Yingqi Wei Lecturer in International Business, Department of Economics, Lancaster University

Mike Wright School of Business, University of Nottingham

Yuguang Yang Professor, Institute of the World Economy, Fudan University

List of Abbreviations

AEEU	Amalgamated Electrical and Engineering Union (UK)
AIB	Academy of International Business
AMC	American Motor Company (now Chrysler)
A–PJ	autonomy–procedural justice (model)
AT&T	American Telephone and Telegraph
BAG	Beijing Automobile Manufacturing Group
BJC	Beijing Jeep Company
BT	British Telecom (UK)
BUAMM	Beijing United Automobile and Motorcycle Manufacturing
CAPM	computer-aided product manufacture
CEE	Central and Eastern Europe
CEEC	Central and Eastern European countries
CEO	chief executive officer
CI	Continuous Improvement
CIM	Computer-Integrated Manufacturing
CNSIEC	China National Silk Import and Export Corporation
COMECON	Council for Mutual Economic Aid (USSR)
EBRD	European Bank for Reconstruction and Development
EC	European Community
EHQ	European headquarters
EMDC	East Midlands Development Company (UK)
ESRI	Economic System Reform Institute (FSU)
EU	European Union
FDI	foreign direct investment
FSR	former Soviet Republic
FSU	former Soviet Union
GAZ	Gorky Automobile Plant
GDP	gross domestic product
HQ	headquarters
HR	human resource
HRM	human resources management
IHRM	international human relations management
IIL	internationally independent laboratory
IJV	international joint venture
IT	information technology
JIT	just-in-time
JV	joint venture
LIL	locally integrated laboratory
MBO	management by objectives

MFA	multi-Fibre Arrangement
MNC	multinational corporation
MNE	multinational enterprise
MSFU	Manufacturing, Science and Finance Union (UK)
NDC	Northern Development Company (UK)
NN	Nizhny Novgorod (formerly Gorky)
NTB	non-tariff barrier
OEM	original equipment manufacturers
PDB	Polish Development Bank
PM	product mandate
PTO	public telephone operator
R&D	research and development
RHQ	regional headquarters
RPM	regional product mandate
RPS	rationalized product subsidiary
SEM	Single European Market
SIHRM	strategic international human resource management
SL	support laboratory
SME	small and medium-sized enterprise
SOE	state-owned enterprise
SRPM	sub-regional product mandate
TMME	Toyota Motor and Manufacturing Europe
TMR	truncated miniature replica
TNC	transnational corporation
TQM	total quality management
TVE	township and village enterprise (China)
USSR	Union of Soviet Socialist Republics
WCDA	West Country Development Agency (UK)
WOS	wholly-owned subsidiary
WPM	world product mandate
WTO	World Trade Organization

1 Introduction: Is There a European Dimension to International Business?

James H. Taggart and Michael D. Hughes

KEYNOTE

The opening address to the 26th Annual Conference was given by Professor Pervez Ghauri of the University of Groningen. Focusing on the theme of the conference, he mused on the meaning of 'international business' and how the significance of this term had altered subtly with new flows of research. For both academics and practitioners, there is an overriding need to acknowledge that there are different and equally effective ways of doing things in different companies and societies. The difficult but necessary task is to remove ethnocentrism from our analyses: the imperative of this is widely recognized, the process still has a long way to go. Many of the current ideas and concepts in international business seem to stem from US dominance in academic research and in numbers of home-based multinational corporations (MNCs). However, rapidly developing academic research in Europe, together with growing input from East Asia, suggests that there is no universal model or paradigm of international business. Ghauri's alternative is the adoption of a comparative management systems' approach and, as Editor of *International Business Review*, he is in a strong position to support such lines of research.

Ghauri also addressed the concept of globalization, probing whether it is an appropriate concept. It may well be, for example, that the process is really one of westernization or Americanization (Friedman, 1999). It certainly seems to be sector-specific in that globalizing/standardizing occurs in industries like electronics, airlines and finance. Globalization must involve more than the mere standardisation of products, especially where choices have to be made *vis-à-vis* aspects of adaptation. Perhaps, since firms are local everywhere, we should use the term 'glocalization', implying global brands with appropriate adaptation. It is not easy to identify a European perspective here since, although the European Union (EU) may be developing towards a single market for producers and consumers, there are many different ways of doing business. These, however, could be regarded as the Europe-specific outcome of the range of polarities between and within economies resulting from the process of globalization. Thus, the very existence of the EU may result in a degree of homogenization of business organization, which may result in a different and distinctive Europe. Lacking appropriate evidence, this could be a circular argument. Ghauri seems to conclude there is no single European perspective to globalization, but that there may be Europe-specific dimensions to the analysis.

EUROPEAN DIMENSIONS

This seventh volume of the Academy of International Business (AIB) series is broadly integrated around the theme of Pervez Ghauri's keynote speech, the European dimensions of international business. Accordingly, it is organized in a different manner compared to the previous six volumes. There are three parts, or sub-themes, with five chapters allocated to each. Part One concerns human resource management (HRM) – or, more broadly, people issues ranging from aspects of national culture to the international movement of scientists. Part Two focuses on the topic of multinational company (MNC) subsidiaries, in which there has been a rapid growth in the literature. The basic thrust of these chapters concerns the strategic and control aspects of operating in European countries. Part Three deals with emerging markets in Eastern Europe and European involvement in the vast emerging Chinese market.

Mohamed Branine's Chapter 2 reviews the arguments for and against internationalization of HRM and discusses the conceptual and practical difficulties in developing an international model of HRM. It approaches the topic via three different HRM paradigms: the matching model of strategic HRM, the multiple stakeholder model and the contextual model; these were initially developed at Michigan, Harvard and Warwick, respectively. The analysis is supported by evidence from China, Japan, Europe and the USA. Branine stresses the importance of national culture dimensions in evolving strategy and best practice in HRM, and concludes that there is a significant gap between practice and the prescriptive European and American models. This chapter is complementary to earlier work by Casson *et al.* (1998) which developed the corporate culture dimension of HRM, and offers interesting comparisons with Tayeb (1999).

Philip Raines and Ross Brown address in Chapter 3 the impact of workforce flexibility on foreign investment decisions. They use a comparison between the UK (where workforce flexibility is held to be an important determinant of successful attraction of FDI) and Germany (where inflexibility is supposed to be linked to underperformance in foreign investment attraction. Their findings suggest that workforce flexibility is not an important factor in the initial foreign direct investment (FDI) decision, but may have a greater influence on subsequent development decisions. They note that, on occasion, increased workforce flexibility may be induced by threat of closure or diverted investment, and conclude that differences in productivity may well be a more significant factor to MNCs considering both countries as sites of new investment.

Examining the role of expatriate managers in the global restructuring activities of MNCs, Helen Sakho in Chapter 4 draws on 25 detailed interviews within 20 European and American firms. She considers the specific roles and functions of senior expatriates in such processes. These managers tend to be carriers of business know-how, and they also act as protectors of corporate values and culture. Thus, they represent the core belief of the MNC at the point of contact with restructuring. Advances in information technology (IT) have helped MNCs in implementing corporate restructuring decisions, but this approach is still somewhat limited compared to the activities of skilled expatriates on the ground. Sakho's contribution breaks new ground in this series of books and makes a valuable contribution, despite a rather adventurous conclusion that, despite their high cost, senior expatriate managers continue to be vital to the implementation of MNCs' globalization strategies.

Monir Tayeb and Edwin Dott in Chapter 5 contribute an interesting case study analysis of three manufacturing subsidiaries of American firms operating in Scotland. They explore the implications of cultural similarities and differences between the two countries and how these affect managers within the firms. Three specific areas are analyzed: organizational culture and management style, human resource issues and labour relations and organizational control and parent–subsidiary relations. While they found that certain clashes occurred that related to differences in national culture, the consequent tensions were seldom sufficiently disruptive to cause real difficulties at the HQ–subsidiary interface. This reflects closely the findings of Taggart (1999) and goes beyond the propositions developed by Nicolaidis and Millar (1997).

Making their fourth contribution to this series, Marina Papanastassiou and Bob Pearce in Chapter 6 develop an interesting analysis about how the movement of scientists affects globalization of technology. Based on a questionnaire survey, they consider the movement of home-country personnel to subsidiaries, and the movement of host-country personnel to HQ or to other subsidiaries in the network. Their analysis covers movements of scientists in the UK, Belgium, Greece and Portugal. While much of the literature identifies technology as a centralized product created in the home country, these authors argue the alternative perspective that, in some cases, peripheral subsidiaries are deeply involved in creating new technological inputs for the network. The linkage with an earlier paper (Papanastassiou and Pearce, 1999) is clear, but there is also some resonance with the findings of Birkinshaw and Hood (1998).

The first chapter in Part Two of the book (Chapter 7) covers research carried out by Louise Hurdley and Neil Hood that attempts to conceptualize the regional economic impact of MNC strategy. Their enquiry revolves around two basic generic questions: 'Is the impact of MNC activity on economic welfare a good thing?' and 'If it is good, how can it be made even better?' The chosen research vehicle is the subsidiary strategies adopted by Japanese automobile manufacturing plants in the UK. While assessment of impact seems to be primarily with location of R&D and supply-chain management, yet the conceptual model produced looks simple, inclusive and robust. The regional economic impact of these Japanese firms seems more restricted than for the range of German subsidiaries in the UK carrying out a wider range of strategies (Taggart and Hood, 2000). There are also some interesting contrasts with the findings of Ali and Mirza (1998) for UK subsidiaries in Hungary and Poland.

James H. Taggart's Chapter 8 sets out to evaluate and validate the autonomy–procedural justice model of subsidiary strategy, using data collated from 92 manufacturing subsidiaries in Scotland and 120 in Ireland. This model uses the interactions between the level of autonomy held at subsidiary level and the degree of procedural justice (the feeling of being fairly treated) that exists in the subsidiary in relation to its dealings with HQ. The data provide strong empirical validation of the framework, but the real interest in this chapter lies in its focus on behavioural aspects of subsidiary strategy. The author claims that the model's dimensions and interactions are quickly recognized and understood by managers in the post-test interviews. This research indicates ways in which suitably motivated subsidiary managers may strategically reposition their subsidiaries over time, and yields useful lessons for corporate managers who wish to improve the overall operational responsiveness of networks of affiliates. The chapter also suggests ways in which policy makers may more usefully develop after-care programmes for inward investors to increase the local embeddedness of their populations of foreign subsidiaries. This research has interesting complementarities with Bartels (1998), but it is more obviously linked with Chapter 10 by James H. Taggart and Michael Sanderson. This is a case study analysis of two firms in the electronics industry, and uses the autonomy–procedural justice model as the prime analytical tool. It clearly illustrates that ability of subsidiary managers to negotiate with corporate headquarters in order to influence the development of the affiliate and the degree of bargaining power they possess. The chapter also indicates interesting research potential linked to subsidiary strategy in the EU as the euro-zone becomes more defined and distinct.

Chapter 9 by Ana Teresa Tavares and Robert Pearce focuses on the impact of European economic integration on structural change within MNCs, with particular regard to foreign subsidiaries located in Portugal. As a small peripheral economy, Portugal as reacted somewhat differently to EU accession and progressive economic integration. There has been a surge in FDI, and the chapter notes some consequential qualitative changes in the activities of MNC subsidiaries in Portugal. Perhaps the most notable conclusion to be drawn from the chapter's empirical data is the marked emergence of pan-European exporting strategies especially by US- and Asian-owned subsidiaries. High value-added affiliates are quite rare, and the most common type is the rationalized product subsidiary (narrow product range, broad market scope). With respect to US-owned subsidiaries, this chapter supports predictions made by Clegg (1996) and has strong parallels with Morgan (1997) in terms of restructuring.

The final chapter in Part Two (Chapter 11) is by Geert Duysters, Rebecca Guidice, Bert M. Sadowski and Ash Vasudevan. This reviews the literature on inter-alliance rivalry and applies it to the global telecommunications industry. Much of the literature on alliances has concentrated on their impact on the competitive advantage yielded to partners. The focus taken in this chapter is thus welcome in its alternative focus on competition between alliances, where the dynamics are quite different. In particular, inter-alliance rivalry may be characterized by difficulties in forecasting the likelihood of attack and the likelihood of response. The chapter identifies a number of research propositions linked to these and other probabilities and concludes with an insightful discussion of the implications of alliance-based competition, with a particular focus on bridging the conceptual underpinnings of alliances and competitive analysis. This chapter makes an interesting contrast with the findings of Faulkner (1998), and extends the conceptual thinking of Lu and Burton (1998).

Emmanuela Todeva's Chapter 12 on business networks in Eastern Europe is the first chapter in Part Three. Perhaps the main value of this chapter is that it focuses on a tightly defined notion of 'business network' as the regular and repetitive transactions that a firm maintains with buyers and suppliers within the value chain, including the complexity of relations between firms based on past contractual arrangements and present business links. Using a case study approach, the author establishes an interesting typology of transformed, failed to transform and newly established business networks. 'Transformation' in this context refers to (usually radical) change in dependencies in long-established relationships to take account of economic transition. Todeva links this typology to a range on imperatives that guide management action in relation to enterprise restructuring, but identifies time and resource constraints as the main barrier to optimal managerial decisions. This research is an interesting extension of perspectives advanced by Cook and Kirkpatrick (1996) at an earlier stage of economic transition in Eastern Europe.

A review of the most recent economic crisis in Russia, as it affects economic reform of state-owned industry, is the subject of Chapter 13 by Trevor Buck, Igor Filatotchev, Peter Nolan and Mike Wright. Comparisons are drawn with China by reference to a uniquely matched pair of case studies, and substantive enterprise-level differences are identified. China has achieved large inflows of foreign investment and know-how by vigorously promoting joint ventures (JVs) with overseas partners. In consequence, global product standards have been achieved in a wide range of manufactured goods. In contrast, Russia obstructed joint ventures with foreigners, thus reducing the flow on inward FDI. However, taking a more positive view of the future, the authors suggest that the economic setback may well make JVs potentially more attractive for foreign firms – but, clearly, much will depend on the attitude of the Russian administration. This chapter should be read in conjunction with earlier work by three of the authors (Buck *et al.*, 1996). A alternative perspective on joint ventures in China is set out by Dong *et al.* (1997).

Grahame Fallon and Alan Jones in Chapter 14 also focus on the Russian experience in a contribution that assess the obstacles to inward FDI. Competition between countries for such foreign investment is becoming increasingly intense, as more welcoming governments seek to join the globalizing economy. In addition, inward FDI helps to improve the competitiveness of indigenous firms through supply-chain linkages and leakages of technology and skills. Reflecting one of the findings in Chapter 13, the authors identify Russia's relative lack of success in attracting FDI compared to other countries in Central and Eastern Europe. Unlike Buck *et al.*, however, Fallon and Jones see little opportunity for improvement in the Russian situation, not only because of adverse infrastructural conditions and unhelpful economic policies, but also due to the basic attitudinal ambivalence towards inward FDI. This chapter gives an additional perspective on the Eastern European dichotomy on FDI identified by Hooley *et al.* (1998), that economic transition needs foreign investment but is not conducive to foreign investors.

The EU–China axis is the framework for Chapter 15, written by Xiaming Liu, Yuguang Yang and Yingqi Wei. Using the perceptions of Chinese managers in 51 EU–China JVs obtained in a series of personal interviews, a number of control and performance dimensions are explored. They conclude that overall control by foreign partners is positively associated with their equity shares but negatively related to the degree of local knowledge possessed by Chinese partners. There are also indications that performance may be linked to commonality of strategic objectives, cultural similarity, government support and mutual trust. These results provide a vital cultural contrast with research reported by Burton and Noble (1996), and perhaps explains some of the questions raised in Wu (1997) of the choice between licensing and joint venturing in China.

The silk industry has a history stretching over 4500 years, during which time China has been the major producer of raw silk, with export earning upwards of $4 bn. For several centuries now, Western Europe has been the world's major silk processor. Jim Newton and Roger Strange's Chapter 16 traces the history of the industry and the developing trade relationship between China and Western Europe. Technological developments and changes in the organization of production have significantly affected the nature of the Chinese industry, and in recent years it has massively increased its exports of processed raw silk to the EU. This has led to a clash of interests between retailers and manufacturers in the EU, with the former prevailing and tilting the balance of EU trade policy in this area. As might be expected, some of the issues raised in this chapter resonate with earlier research by Strange (1997). However, there is a fascinating sectoral contrast to be made via the work of Zhang and van den Bulcke (2000).

INTO THE NEW MILLENNIUM

The nature of the studies in this volume, their breadth of coverage and their depth of analysis seem to support Ghauri's view that it is facile to seek a purely European perspective on the process of globalization. That there is a variety of European dimensions is abundantly obvious, but constant and deep interaction between EU firms and those in other parts of the world suggest that these dimensions will always be deeply affected by other ways of doing things. Hofstede (1980) may well be right in suggesting long-term stability in his dimensions of national culture (power–distance, individualism–collectivism, masculinity–femininity, risk avoidance), but this cannot be generalized into an assumption of unchanging cross-border business practices and methods. The broad sweep of international business research in the last years of the twentieth century has demonstrated steady advance in the understanding and use of analytical dimensions. Individual models are parsimonious, but the population of useful paradigms is not. As Ghauri also noted, even the largest MNC is local everywhere.

The truth of this is clear in Scotland, home for AIB's 26th Annual Conference. Its businesses are regulated by EU authorities, they are buffeted by the Westminster parliament's refusal to enter the euro-zone at the present time, and they now have to contend with (or be supported by?) the new Scottish parliament. Scottish business is broadly in favour of membership of the euro, which will lead to an end of market segmentation by price discrimination. There is also a pragmatic view in many parts of the Scottish business community that the new parliament will form a bridge to full political independence in due course. The euro and independence would be the two sources of major change that Scotland's firms, particularly those engaged in international business, would be obliged to confront and factor into competitive strategy. The pragmatic way in which these potential changes are viewed are, perhaps, the best measure of the resilience of international business managers. What is true for Scotland is most likely to be true as well for Portugal, Greece, Norway, Ireland, Sweden and Finland. Not only will change impact discriminately on small peripheral economies, but they could see it as a source of incremental competitive advantage. There may well be no discernible European perspective to globalization, but the new millennium will invite increasing peripheral reaction to its European dimensions.

Part One

European Dimensions of Human Resource Management

2 International HRM: Americanization, Europeanization or Japanization?

Mohamed Branine

INTRODUCTION

In management circles, the concept of human resource management (HRM) is possibly the most frequently used and the least understood. Indeed it has helped to generate a new intellectual discourse among the teachers and practitioners of management. Attempts to spell out its theoretical and practical features have led to further confusion and ambiguity, raising debates over the credibility of the concept (see Blyton and Turnbull, 1992; Boxall, 1993, 1995; Legge, 1995). Relatively early notions such as those of Guest (1987) are still used as starting points in discussions of HRM. Guest (1987: 503), for example, defined HRM as 'a set of policies designed to maximize organisational integration, employee commitment, flexibility and quality of work'. It is assumed that operational plans and procedures will be implemented successfully when human resource policies are integrated into strategic plans; that when organizational commitment is combined with job-related behavioural commitment, high employee satisfaction and high performance will result; that when flexible organization structures are designed together with flexible job content and flexible working practices, effective utilization of resources will ensue; and that high standards of quality and a distinguished reputation will be attained when employment policies are in place to ensure the recruitment and retention of high-quality employees at all levels. However, the concept of HRM has been open to general and different interpretations and has been very much criticized (Keenoy, 1990; Blyton and Turnbull, 1992; Mabey *et al.*, 1998) and finally it seems that it has been taken for granted as a way or ways of managing people in organizations if not just as a new version of personnel management. Since the notion of HRM is now open to various speculations and different interpretations, what has been said about international HRM?

International human resource management (IHRM) has emerged in recent years as a significant field of academic research and study and has very often been associated with the management of employment in multinational companies, focusing mainly on expatriation (Desatnick and Bennett, 1978; Black, 1988; Adler, 1991; Brewster, 1991; Black *et al.*, 1993), and with the influence of national culture on HRM policies and prac-

11

tices in different countries (see Pieper, 1990; Brewster and Tyson, 1991; Hollinshead and Leat, 1995; Joynt and Warner, 1996). IHRM has been castigated in academic circles for being a construct of advanced Western management thinking that has been developed in business schools, marketed by management gurus and believed by naive practitioners to be helpful for managing their employees in times of change and uncertainty and in different organizational contexts. Hence literally labelled 'American models of HRM', especially the Harvard model, have been thought to include comparative and IHRM policies and practices (Beer *et al.*, 1984; Poole, 1990). In this context there has been a growing theoretical consensus on the main features of good HRM practice, despite the fact that there is no general agreement on the nature of HRM at either the local or the international level (see Sparrow *et al.*, 1994; Boxall, 1995; Hollinshead and Leat, 1995; Brewster and Harris, 1999). However the argument of whether what can be called 'good HRM practice' can be applied internationally has already been superseded by debates about convergence and divergence of management theory and practice (Sparrow *et al.*, 1994; Tayeb, 1988, 1996) and by explanations of how domestic differ from IHRM operations (Schuler *et al.*, 1993; Hendry, 1994).

The question of how multinational companies (MNCs) manage their human resources effectively in different cultural contexts has been asked by many researchers (see Evans and Lorange, 1989; Evans and Doz, 1992; Schuler *et al.*, 1993; Taylor *et al.*, 1996) but there have been no convincing answers to the question. There is no consensus about how employees are managed globally and there is no one definition of IHRM. Pieper (1990: 8), for example, argued that it is impossible to develop an international model of HRM because the concept itself 'seems to be more a theoretical construct than an applied reality' and there is a lack of theoretical framework for comparative analysis that enables us to compare the different aspects of HRM practices. Similarly, Kochan *et al.* (1992) argued that most of the explanations given to IHRM focused on the functions of HRM and lack a theoretical framework that is built on systematic research. In contrast, Adler and Ghadar (1990) suggested that it is possible to develop a model of IHRM that is defined in relation to the stage at which an MNC has reached, moving from domestic to international, multinational and global. Also, according to their management style (polycentric, ethnocentric or geocentric) MNCs adapt their HRM policies to the environment in which they operate. Others such as Schuler *et al.* (1993), Adler and Bartholomew (1992) and Welch (1994) linked the concept of IHRM to the company's international strategy and developed theoretical frameworks for the study of SIHRM. The framework by Schuler *et al.* (1993) is based on the view that there are a number of endogenous and exogenous factors which influence the choice that MNCs make between global and local human resource practices and policies. Commenting on this framework, Harris and Brewster

(1999: 4) stated that it 'demonstrates the complexity of HR decisions in the international sphere and the broad scope of its remit; going far beyond the issue of expatriation, to an overall concern for managing people effectively on a global scale'. It is therefore a useful model for the understanding of how MNCs operate in different countries.

Moreover, in an attempt to define and then develop a theoretical framework for the understanding of IHRM, Torrington (1994) suggested that one should know first what IHRM is not before attempting to define what it is. He explained that IHRM 'is not simply copying practices from the Americans, the Germans, the Taiwanese, the Koreans or the Japanese although this may be technically, operationally and financially appropriate', and that 'it is not a process of all managers learning the cultures of every country in which they have to deal and suitably modifying their behaviour when dealing with those nationals'. He added that 'the idea, implied by some writers, that international HRM requires all managers to move confidently between Argentina, Indonesia, Norway and Alaska with effortless adaptation is unrealistic' (Torrington, 1994: 4–5). Therefore he emphasized that the practices of HRM (i.e. the functions of recruitment and selection, industrial relations, training and so forth) are essentially national while the practice of IHRM requires managers to act locally and think globally because, he explained, 'in many ways international HRM is simply HRM on a larger scale; the strategic considerations are more complex and the operational units varied, needing co-ordination across more barriers' (Torrington, 1994: 6).

The points raised by Torrington (1994) are crucial for the understanding of IHRM because it has been widely assumed, as in Evans *et al.* (1989) and Schuler *et al.* (1993), that the internationalization of HRM is achievable mainly through MNCs which develop international managers with special qualities for their foreign assignments. The role of MNCs in developing IHRM should not be underestimated but it should be emphasized that IHRM does not take place only through them. Internationalization occurs whenever organizations from different societies adopt similar HRM policies and practices. However, if globalization of business strategy requires managers to act locally and think globally, will IHRM be the same anywhere? Is it possible to develop an international model of HRM that may be applied in different countries regardless of their national differences? In order to answer these questions one has to explain first the main models of HRM that have been promoted as 'international'.

MODELS OF IHRM IN THEORY

The conceptual debate raised above is very often related to models of HRM which were originally developed in the USA and then adopted rather than adapted in Europe, beginning with the UK. Such models are widely known as the Anglo–Saxon models of HRM (Sparrow and Hiltrop, 1994; Boxall, 1995). The following three models are the most apparent of the Anglo–Saxon perspective:

The Matching Model of Strategic HRM

This was initially developed at the Michigan Business School by Fombrun, _et al._ (1984). It emphasizes the strategic aspects of HRM and its main argument is that 'personnel policies and organization structures have to be managed in a way that is congruent with organizational strategy and organizational effectiveness depends on there being a tight "fit" between human resource and business strategies' (Sparrow and Hiltrop, 1994: 8). Fombrun _et al._ (1984) argued that HRM practices that have to be matched with strategy to produce appropriate employee performance are selection, performance appraisal, reward and development. The idea was taken further by Schuler and Jackson (1987) who, at the New York Business School, used Porter's (1985) model of generic competitive strategies of innovation, quality improvement and leadership cost, and suggested a set of 'needed role behaviours', which varied across a number of dimensions, for each strategy. After making assumptions about the personnel and industrial relations practices needed for effective strategy they identified planning, staffing, appraising, remuneration and training and development as foci for a set of strategic HRM choices that human resource managers can make in order to endorse appropriate, effective and strategically credible employment practices. However, the model has been the subject of many criticisms (see Hendry and Pettigrew, 1990; Boxall, 1992; Sparrow and Hiltrop, 1994).

The Multiple Stakeholder or the Harvard Model

This model of HRM was first enunciated by Beer _et al._ (1984) at the Harvard Business School, where IHRM was taught for the first time, and it was then echoed in Britain (see Poole, 1990). This model recognizes the importance of different stakeholder interests such as the shareholders, management, employee groups, government, the community and trade unions. According to this model the notion of HRM includes the policies and practices involving all management decisions and actions concerning employment. For an organization to achieve such desired outcomes as commitment, integration, quality, flexibility and cost-effectiveness the formation of four HRM policy areas (human resource flows, reward systems, employee influence and work systems) is required. The interests of the stakeholders and a wide range of situational factors such as workforce characteristics, business strategy, management philosophy, labour market, trade unions, task technology, laws and societal values affect these policy areas which have both immediate human resource outcomes such as commitment, competence, cost effectiveness and congruence, and long-term consequences such as individual and societal well-being and organizational effectiveness. The model allows for analysis of these outcomes both at the organizational and societal levels (Boxall, 1991). As this is much more pluralist than the Michigan model it has found greater acceptance in Europe (Poole, 1990; Hendry and Pettigrew, 1990; Boxall, 1991).

The Contextual Model or the Warwick Model

This model of HRM was developed in the UK at the University of Warwick's Centre for Corporate Strategy and Change. Studies of corporate strategy (Pettigrew, 1985; Hendry and Pettigrew, 1986) took a new direction with the increased interest in HRM in the late 1980s. It was argued that since the American models emphasized the importance of developing human resource strategies for successful corporate strategy it was appropriate to investigate the extent to which strategic decisions might transform HRM practices in British organizations (Hendry *et al.*, 1989; Hendry and Pettigrew, 1990; Whipp, 1991). Theoretically, it was initially developed from the Harvard model by utilizing and expanding on its analytical aspects. In line with the Harvard model' s description of the content of HRM, the Warwick model 'includes the need to consider the external business environment and strategy, and builds in a requirement to understand the culturally-unique role of the HRM function in terms of: 1) the definition of its responsibilities; 2) its perceived competence across a range of activities; and 3) the way the function is organized' (Sparrow and Hiltrop, 1994: 17). At Warwick University it was found that a combination of a number of important political and economic factors such as international competition, economic recession and government legislation, had forced many companies to adopt tough employment strategies for survival. For example, many companies resorted to strategies of labour reduction and flexible working practices which had been associated with 'new labour relations' and such policies as the decentralization of collective bargaining, the derecognition of trade unions, the empowerment of line managers and the introduction of performance-related pay. Overall, it was argued that external context issues can act on the inner context of organizations, although two organizations in similar circumstances may not respond in exactly the same way because they may follow different approaches of HRM to achieve similar objectives (Hendry and Pettigrew, 1990). Although the Warwick model encompasses a number of the Harvard model's situational factors within the inner context, such as task technology, factors relating to management's philosophy and workforce characteristics, it can be seen to differ on its consideration of HRM as a perspective on employment systems rather than as a single overall approach, as the Harvard model suggests.

The above models of HRM were developed in particular cultural and organizational contexts and it can be argued, therefore, that no one of them can be seen to be solely theoretically and practically international. Poole (1990) argued that the Harvard model of HRM was quite helpful for comparative analysis despite its being very general and prescriptive in its approach to managing employment. Indeed its authors were the first to draw attention to the importance of learning from other countries when trying to implement HRM policies outside the USA. They stated that 'looking at what managers in other countries do can also suggest alternative models for integrating people and organizations' (Beer *et al.*, 1984: 35). In launching the first issue of the *International Journal of Human Resource Management*, Poole (1990: 3) noted how several of the attributes of the Harvard Model 'reflect its North American origin' and suggested three necessary adjustments to make it more internationally relevant. These are: (1) the development of international business; (2) the empowerment of the different stakeholders and actors involved in the process of managing people; and (3) the clarity of specific links between corporate and human resource strategies. These key modifications, he argued, should strengthen international strategic choice of the four areas of HRM policy, as described by the Harvard model, which is valuable as a basic framework for international analysis of HRM. However there is still no convincing evidence for its existence in a global context to give it the credibility of being international in theory and practice.

In the absence of a commonly agreed and representative model of IHRM it can be argued that the most common policy principles and practices of HRM in economically developed countries can be interpreted as international since they have been implemented by MNCs in different countries. My attempt in this chapter is to investigate the extent to which there are common HRM policy principles and practices that do actually condition the ways in which employees are managed in Europe, Japan and the USA where models of HRM have been developed. Evidence is drawn from the literature on industrial relations, personnel management, organizational behaviour and management in general. It will be possible to conclude therefore whether IHRM is an Americanization, a Japanization or an Europeanization process, or something else.

MODELS OF INTERNATIONAL HRM IN PRACTICE

HRM in Europe

While a growing number of academics and practitioners believed that HRM was an American and Japanese product that could be consumed in other countries (see Hendry and Pettigrew, 1990; Poole, 1990) others tried to prove that HRM in Europe was neither Japanese nor American but European (see Brewster and Bournois, 1991; Brewster, 1993; Brewster and Larsen, 1993; Brewster and Hegewisch, 1994; Sparrow and Hiltrop, 1994, 1997; Brewster and Harris, 1999). The latter have gone beyond the description of national contextual variables that affect the way people are managed in different countries to explain that in a continent that is different in terms of culture, language, education, economic and political history and employee relations it is possible to envisage a *common system of managing employment*. It is argued that in order to be able to manage in Europe managers should understand, above all, the complexity of operating in a context of diversity because 'understanding the patterns of convergence and divergence in HRM practice across this diverse continent is one of the most important challenges that European managers face' (Sparrow and Hiltrop, 1994: 24).

One of the popular studies of HRM in Europe is the Price Waterhouse/Cranfield survey (see Brewster and Hegewisch, 1994) which found that the issues of HRM dealt with in Europe had been similar but the ways in which they had been carried out reflected national differences, that the different legislative and labour market influences which had pertained across Europe had influenced the ways in which HRM/personnel management departments had been organized and structured at national levels and that some models and concepts of HRM which had corresponded to the American models had not fitted well with the European practice. The survey found areas of common practice for a European model of HRM. These areas are: (1) the emphasis on promoting empowerment culture; (2) the need to improve horizontal management processes; (3) the use of information technology to help structure organizations; (4) the need for training and development; (5) the importance of communication; (6) the increasing use of flexible working; and (7) the link of pay to performance.

On the other hand it has been argued that despite the willingness to harmonize the different aspects of the community's economic and social systems there have been crucial areas of divergence mainly in employment relationships and terms and conditions of employment (Sparrow *et al.*, 1994). Such differences are shown in the practices of HRM. For example, the process of recruitment and selection in Italy is very often based on inter-personal contacts with family and friends while in France the use of graphology is very common. In contrast to Germany and France, where the law supports free and centralized collective bargaining and grants representation rights to all employees, the current trends of industrial relations in Britain limit the unions' collective bargaining power by deregulating the labour market and encouraging unitarist initiatives of employee relations. In France, the more restricted employer autonomy and the strong influence of state regulations are against the individualistic values of the Anglo–Saxon model of HRM. As well as the existing differences in indus-

trial relations and employee legislation there is the issue of national sover-
eignty which is perhaps the most important source of divergence 'because
of its effects on human behaviour and the consequent constraints on management action' (Torrington, 1994: 32).

Therefore such studies seem to confirm that a unified approach to management in a very diverse continent is yet to be established, but the use of
different approaches does not imply the existence of different objectives.
The same objective or even policy principle of HRM can be achieved
through different HRM practices as long as the drivers of that achievement
are similar. In Europe, common objectives such as economic recovery, high
economic growth, competition and full employment are the hidden factors
(drivers) towards the adoption of similar policies such as empowerment
of line managers, emphasis on quality and introduction of flexible working
practices. However the idea of a common purpose can be overshadowed
by national priorities and preferences, which are culturally or institution-
ally influenced.

HRM in Japan

The concept of HRM has also been seen as virtually synonymous with
best practice in the management of employment in Japanese companies
(Lincoln and Kalleberg, 1990). Describing that practice, White and Trevor
(1983: 5, also quoted in Briggs, 1991: 33) wrote:

> It consists of a stable work-force with a high level of commitment to the
> company: extremely co-operative in accepting change, extremely unwill-
> ing to enter into strikes or other forms of conflict, and generally putting
> the company's interests level with or even ahead of its own. The outcome
> is a high and rising level of productivity, and an altogether easier climate
> in which management can plan for change in products and processes.
> These results, it is argued, are produced by employment practices which
> emphasize the commitment of the company to its employees, which give
> them security, status and material benefits, and which develop their
> potential in a systematic, long term manner. Another feature which is
> often stressed is the way in which group cohesiveness and co-operation
> are fostered, rather than individualism and personnel initiative.

It seems from White and Trevor's description of Japanese management and
employment relationships that the main policy principles of the Japanese
system of HRM is to encourage employees' involvement and commitment
to the organization in which they work. Also, according to Ouchi (1981),
White and Trevor (1983) and Lincoln and Kalleberg (1990), the existence
of good working relationships which are inspired by traditions, working
autonomy through quality circles and pride in the firm after achieving high

standards of quality created employee motivation and led to organizational commitment. This is also supported by the emphasis on clear channels of communication and informality. Japanese managers very often wear the same kinds of uniforms, park in the same parking spaces, eat in the same canteens as their subordinates and spend a considerable amount of their time on the shopfloor with the workers.

The belief in the common objective between the employee and the employer is derived from feudal traditions and their expressions and use of language. For example, the Japanese word for company is *Kaisha*, which is correctly translated as our company. Employees see their prosperity and that of their companies as being inextricably linked. In representing the interests of their blue and white collar members company unions could play an important role in sustaining the pervasiveness of the corporate culture in their organizations. Employees' future prospects and quality of working life are seen to depend heavily on good relationships between the company and its union. Such relationships are strengthened by promoting union leaders to supervisory and managerial positions. However it is not clear whether the Japanese employees' work behaviour is a response to a deliberate management strategy or a result of inherited cultural values. In this respect Briggs (1991) drew evidence from different comparative studies involving Japan and argued that many Japanese employees were as dissatisfied with their work as many of their counterparts in Western economies. Therefore she concludes that the reason for organizational commitment is not just because people are given lifetime employment, continuous training and seniority-related pay but also because they are qualified to work for that organization only and they have no choice elsewhere and their income in terms of pay and benefits would suffer a great deal if they considered changing employment. It means that the expectations of the Japanese workforce are restricted to what they are being offered and therefore they seem to be obliged to be contented with their work as long as it is perhaps the only one in which they could do their best. Until recently it was commonplace that from the first day of taking up employment Japanese employees expected lifetime employment with its complementary benefits of social welfare, extensive training facilities and experience opportunities and various pay incentives related to seniority. These expectations contour employee work behaviour towards the achievement of organizational objectives. Since the separation of duty and personal feelings is ingrained within the Japanese culture organizational commitment does not mean non-existence of employee dissatisfaction. The reluctance of employees to show personal feelings produces a different conception of commitment. This point has been made by Briggs (1991: 41–2), who argued that 'it is not commitment in the Western sense that binds a Japanese worker to his or her company: loyalty is not fostered by any sense of obligation or by any specific employment practice'. Moreover, a number of Japanese best-management practices such as tough and careful recruitment and selection procedures followed by intensive and continuous vocational training, single status, strike-free agreements, performance-related pay, the emphasis on quality, functional flexibility, teamworking, clear mechanisms for consultation and communication and the provision of employment security, which are all synonymous with best HRM practices and policies in MNCs, have been reported as aspects of Japanization.

The Japanization of other countries' industries has attracted a raft of studies and publications (see Pang and Oliver, 1988; Oliver and Wilkinson, 1992; also papers in a special issue of the *Industrial Relations Journal*, 19(1), 1988 and *Employee Relations*, 20(3), 1998) but it is agreed that there is a difference between employment policies of Japanese companies from one country to another. What is practised in Japan is likely to differ from what is applied in other countries by the Japanese companies, depending partly on relevant national employment legislation, employee relations, levels of economic development and types of labour available. That means there are aspects of HRM related to Japanese practice in Japan and others to Japanization in other countries. The ways in which the Japanese manage in Japan are culturally influenced but Japanization does not always represent a Japanese culture. For example, the ideas behind Total Quality Management (TQM) and Just in Time (JIT) originated in cultures outside Japan and were then implemented as part of a Japanization process. Therefore it can be concluded that with the exception of a commitment to innovation, quality and flexibility in the approach to and resolution of employment issues there is little evidence to suggest that strategic awareness, the empowerment of line managers or individualism are characteristic of Japanese HRM.

HRM in the USA

Although the concept of HRM has been widely popularized as an American product there are a number of prominent scholars who have argued that there is a wide gap between the theory and practice of HRM in the American context, and that HRM is only one thread of a number of labour management strategies adopted by American managers (see Guest, 1990; Springer and Springer, 1990; Beaumont, 1992). It is argued that at the time when HRM was championed as an American product, many American companies had significantly powerful personnel departments in control of recruitment and selection, training and development, reward, performance appraisal and so on (Beer *et al.*, 1984, 1985; Kochan *et al.*, 1986). In this line of argument, Guest (1990) related the notion of HRM to the 'American Dream' in a 'land of opportunities' and argued that nothing about HRM was either new, or was even real, because the stories of success were 'like the myths of the cowboy and the Wild West which served to obscure the reality of the massacre of the Indians, so HRM can serve to obscure the assault on the union movement in the USA' (Guest, 1990: 519). It is also argued that the principal feature of HRM practice in the USA has been related to the way in which employee relations have been handled in notably large and successful organizations that had strong and established corporate strategies and cultures (Kochan *et al.*, 1986). Summarizing the main characteristics of HRM in the USA, Pieper (1990: 8) stated that 'HRM in the United States can be characterized as being confronted with a lack of well-educated labour. On the other hand it is scarcely regulated by state or federal law, hardly influenced by trade unions or shop stewards, and to some degree as a result it is flexible instead of bureaucratic.'

It is widely agreed that the practice of HRM in the USA is characterized by a tradition of unitarist, innovative and anti-union approaches to management. The legal environment for HRM in the USA is unique and closely related to history and culture (Springer and Springer, 1990). Historically, American management is associated with forms of strategic awareness which tend to link employment policies to corporate objectives. It is also widely believed that the promotion of good employment relationships needs to acknowledge the conflict of interest between employees and employers. The non-recognition of trade unions in many American companies is thus related to the emphasis on individual employee commitment to achieve organizational objectives. The aim of employment laws in the USA is to ensure that employers deal with individual employees on fair and objective terms and that the criteria which are used in making decisions are economic and market-oriented. The emphasis on high-quality products and services meant better quality management and highly committed employees. This act of 'empowerment is to encourage employees to become more personally involved in where the action is in improving the quality of products or service to customers' (Luthans and Hodgetts, 1996: 115). The large employer autonomy and the low level of state intervention in HRM issues are very consistent with the individualistic values of the country. American employers increasingly recognize the need to match the individual development and career progression of managers to the future needs of the organization (Hollinshead and Leat, 1995: 174). It is not surprising therefore that a high priority is attached to the rewarding of individual performance.

It can be concluded, therefore, that while strategic awareness, individualism, non-union recognition and empowerment of line managers are significant, the use of flexible working practices or extended family-friendly policies have rarely been reported as being at the heart of American HRM. There is no comprehensive proof that the American labour force has been divided into core and peripheral workers (Guest, 1990) as evidence of policies of flexible working practices. In contrast to Japanization, which differs from one country to another, the process of Americanization tends to be the same everywhere. American MNCs implement HRM policies that are similar to those being introduced in the USA.

CAN THERE BE AN INTERNATIONAL MODEL OF HRM?

From the foregoing examples of HRM policies and practices in countries whose economic performance could be identified with HRM outcomes it seems that in each country there are national employment policies which help to generate particular management practices. Such practices can indicate anything from conventional personnel management functions and industrial relations procedures to the development of HRM strategies for competitive advantage. It would therefore be a mistake to assume that different countries had to adopt similar practices in order to achieve their organizational objectives, as it would be equally wrong to think that each country has to devize its own (different) practices. There have been a number of contingency and comparative process theories which argue for or against the universality of management practices in general and HRM policies and practices in particular. Such theories are very often referred to as 'convergence and divergence theories.'

On the one hand there are those who emphasize cultural, economic and institutional differences as the main factors for divergence in management policies and practices. They argue that national cultures shape the ways in which organizations are designed and run because the degrees to which people look at their work as a central life interest or as an onerous task is affected by their cultural values, norms and beliefs, which have great impact on how they behave at work. The types of social relations and the power structure in family and society, the different norms and expectations related to leadership, interactive relations and perceptions of emotions are found to differ significantly between countries (Hofstede, 1980, 1991; Deal and Kennedy, 1982; Laurent, 1986; Schneider, 1988; Tayeb, 1988, 1996; Whitley, 1992; Florkowski and Nath, 1993). The second argument for divergence is that countries differ in their management systems according to their levels of economic development. Countries with similar levels of economic development may be likely to develop common managerial practices. It is argued, for example, that the difficulties encountered by managers in developing countries when trying to adapt Western theories occur mainly because those theories reflected the level of economic development of their inventors (Siffin, 1976; Glen and James, 1980; Hanaoka, 1986; Pang and Oliver, 1988). The third argument for divergence is that differences in institutions and legal systems are key factors for the existence of different employment policies and practices. It is argued that patterns of national distinctiveness such as a country's history, its national and regional institutions, its political system and its legislative procedures determine appropriate management systems (Lane, 1989; Child and Lu, 1990; Whitely, 1992; Florkowski and Nath, 1993; Brewster, 1995; Sparrow, 1995).

On the other hand there are those who argue for convergence, or the possibility of developing common practices and policies that can be applied in different countries. It is argued that management practice and organizational performance are shaped by the logic of industrialization and technological change rather than culture and environmental variables because technology imposes the need for similar work methods and structures (Kerr *et al.*, 1960; Farris and Butterfield, 1972; Hickson *et al.*, 1974; Form, 1979; Negandhi, 1979). They argue that it has become possible to share management information between countries, especially with the spread of MNCs and their use, for example, of similar techniques for job evaluation and employee appraisal which are constructed and instructed in a common language such as English. This has been made possible with the increased use of information technologies and international business meetings and conferences. It is the international characteristics of successful firms that led to the transfer of management. Multinationals are the creators of cross-cultural management policy and practice, and the main drivers for international convergence rather than divergence. Moreover, convergence can take place not only because of the transfer of technology and methods of work organization by MNCs but also because of historical legacies and myths of Western modernization. Economic dependency and cultural influence, as a result of colonial rules, led to the acceptance of Western management theories in many developing countries. There are examples of Mexican managers adapting American management (Boseman and Phatak, 1978) and Hong Kong managers having similar human resource policies as those of the British (Kidger, 1991) but it is uncommon to find American managers adapting policies which were originally Mexican or Filipino because of the belief in and the legacy of the efficiency of Western management systems.

It is possible to assimilate organizational structures, to rationalize processes and to standardize products and services between countries but, as Adler *et al.* (1986) pointed out, it is not simple to assimilate people's behaviour because of their culturally-based differences. A number of studies (Brewster, 1995; Jackson and Schuler, 1995; Budhwar, 1997; Budhwar and Sparrow, 1998) have shown that both 'culture-specific' factors such as national culture and institutions, and 'culture-free' factors such as size, age, nature, strategy and life cycle of an organization influence the practice and theory of HRM in an international context. In Europe, for example, there have been many advocates of convergence (see Thurley and Wirdenius, 1989; Brewster, 1993; Brewster and Hegewisch, 1994; Sparrow and Hiltrop, 1994, 1997) who argue for the development of a unified European model of HRM despite national differences. They argue that economic integration conducive to common strategies and practices of HRM will eventually happen in the European continent because such historically evolved differences will gradually disappear with the rise of new norms and values as a result of a new European economic order and technical advances. Since the European countries will face the same economic and human resource-based problems they will feel a greater need to integrate in order to provide common solutions to their problems. Further, the spread of MNCs across Europe will bring countries together, especially with increased mergers, take-overs and joint ventures (JVs). Thurley and Wirdenius (1989) argue that convergence is possible between the European countries only because their managers are different from those in the USA or Japan in terms of their shared values and abilities which are important in dealing with organizational change. In other words, the convergence is 'regional' rather than 'international'. However, despite some similarities in personnel management practices and in some policies towards the empowerment of line management, each European country adopts strategies according to its national industrial norms, values and legislation, its level of economic growth, its labour market distribution and its employee representation systems.

While MNCs and technological developments have played a significant role in internationalizing HRM practices, it is politics that has made that role possible. The drivers for convergence such as MNCs, the need for industrialization which involves the adoption of new technology and the internationalization of management education on the one hand, and the drivers for divergence such as national culture, the system of employee relations, national institutions and historical events on the other hand, are moderated by national and international political pressures. There is no one model of IHRM, as there are many national, regional and international practices and policies of managing employment which tend to be culturally influenced and politically driven.

CONCLUSION

The emergence of IHRM in recent years as a subject for study and research has been accompanied by a raft of literature from academics and practitioners but so far there is no one agreed definition of the concept or a convincing theoretical model for its international application. Whilst there are some practical differences there is some common ground regarding the basic characteristics of HRM such as the empowerment of line managers, the integration of employment policies into corporate strategy, the recognition of individual employee commitment and the introduction of flexible working practices. However, in none of the countries studied could employment practices be interpreted as promoting IHRM policies. It would be a mistake to assume that different countries had to adopt similar practices in order to achieve their organizational objectives, as it would be equally wrong to think that each country has to devise its own practices. It can be argued that divergence factors such as industrial relations systems, cultural norms and values, national institutions and historical trends could be super-seded by convergence factors such as economic pressures, educational and political influences, MNC operations and technological developments when there is a common understanding of the importance of human resources and the need to deal effectively with organizational change. Therefore it would be inappropriate to conclude that IHRM is an Americanization or a Japanization or a Europeanization process although most of the MNCs that dominate the world economy are American, Japanese and European because of the cultural and political pressures that influence the ways by which multinational companies manage their employees in different countries.

3 Does Workforce Flexibility Affect Foreign Investment Decisions? Germany and the UK Compared

Philip Raines and Ross Brown

INTRODUCTION

Throughout the world, the pressures to maximize manufacturing productivity have been increasingly felt by both countries and companies alike. With the increasing integration of the European economy, the opening up of cost-competitive production locations in Central and Eastern Europe and greater industrial competition from the Far East, many multinationals have focused on the scope to alter the flexibility of their workforces to adapt to changes in demand and supply conditions. Such flexibility is determined by several interdependent factors, among which the regulatory environment of different countries has featured prominently in recent years: in this respect, Germany and the UK offer contrasted examples of the pursuit of employment flexibility. For nearly two decades, the UK has undertaken an extensive deregulation programme so that the country now has the fewest employment protection constraints on employers in the EU. In contrast, the German labour market has been characterized by relatively high levels of regulation and a corporatist approach to industrial relations, placing greater restrictions on employer actions but resulting in higher levels of productivity among its workforces.

There is increasing evidence that companies may be sensitive to the different 'models' of workforce flexibility and employment regulations in both countries. In recent years, this has perhaps been most evident in the investment decisions of multinationals. The UK has been highly successful in attracting internationally mobile investment: not only has it been the main foreign direct investment (FDI) location in Europe, but it continues to be the world's second largest recipient of FDI after the US (UNCTAD, 1997). While the country's relatively low labour costs tend to be more frequently cited, foreign investors have often listed the importance of the UK's 'flexible' workforce as a key factour in their decisions (Montagnon, 1997). Moreover, the country's reputation has been heavily promoted by UK inward investment agencies in its marketing literature as one of its distinguishing advantages over other European locations, a claim that was reinforced by the UK's opt-out from the EU Social Chapter in the early 1990s (IBB, 1996).

Traditionally, Germany has also been a major destination for FDI – it has the second largest stock in Europe – but its inward flows have declined sharply in recent years, leaving the country with one of the lowest FDI–GDP ratios in Europe (UNCTAD, 1997). Investment inflows have also been dwarfed by massive outflows, prompting the so-called 'Standort Deutschland' debate over whether Germany industry is 'hollowing out' (Tüselmann, 1995). While it has been argued that German statistical collection methods may be exaggerating the 'crisis' (Döhrn, 1996), there is a rising volume of anecdotal evidence suggesting that Germany's reputation for high labour costs and labour market rigidities has not only dissuaded investors from locating but accelerated outward investment by German companies (Sadler and Amin, 1995; Flaherty, 1997; Kahraß, 1997). Yet in spite of its underperformance in terms of the *volume* of investment, Germany may have a comparative advantage with respect to the *quality* of investment. The country has been relatively successful in attracting R&D-based investment, which tends to place a higher priority on the productivity and skills level of the workforce as a determinant (Barrel and Pain, 1997; Ernst & Young, 1997).

The following chapter considers the relationship between employment regulation and foreign investment by examining how perceptions of differences in German and UK workforce flexibility have influenced foreign investment decisions. The chapter is based on a study undertaken in collaboration with researchers at the Rheinisch–Westfälisches Institut für Wirtschaftsforschung in Essen (Roland Döhrn and Markus Scheuer) and was funded by a grant from the Anglo–German Foundation for the Study of Industrial Society (see Raines *et al.*, 1999). In the next section, the chapter discusses the different components of workforce flexibility, the contrasted models of workforce flexibility offered by Germany and the UK and the theoretical relationship between flexibility and investment decision making. In the following section, the research method and study findings are outlined. The final section discusses the implications of these findings for the future ability of Germany and the UK to attract investment.

WORKFORCE FLEXIBILITY IN GERMANY AND THE UK

'Workforce flexibility' can be viewed as the ability of firms to adapt the organization of employment (collectively and individually) to existing and anticipated changes in markets, products and production processes (CEC, 1995). Against a background of mounting pressure on companies to maximize flexibility to increase plant productivity, companies have been experimenting with altering workforce compensation arrangements, the working conditions of their workforce and the quality of individual workers in order to reduce costs and raize productivity. In particular, companies have been exploring three types of workforce flexibility: 'numerical', 'temporal' and 'functional' (Beatson, 1995). *Numerical* flexibility can be defined as the employers' ability to modify the overall size and composition of the workforce. Its influence on production flexibility relates to the costs of companies changing the size and composition of their workforce in line with changing market conditions. It can also influence the cost of maintaining a 'peripheral' labour force, which includes the use of part-time and temporary employment on non-core business activities in which there are relatively low transaction costs involved in high personnel turnover. *Temporal* flexibility refers to the ability of companies to change production working time. Working time has become a more important aspect in strategies for raising plant productivity in response to the increasing need for firms either to maximize production output through continuous plant operation (resulting in a higher utilization of existing capital stocks) or to reduce and expand output in markets characterized by significant variation of demand (usually as a result of seasonality). Lastly, *functional* flexibility is set by the work capacity of the employees, as determined by their skills levels, task definition and overall productivity performance. It reflects the ability of workers to perform a wider range of tasks, adapt to changing job definitions and undertake responsibilities quickly and efficiently.

While each company's approach to flexibility will differ depending on a range of factors including company sector, size and location, several determinants are common to all efforts to increase flexibility. Employment regulation by governments is one of the major determinants in setting the type and extent of workforce flexibility. For example, with respect to numerical flexibility, restrictions exist on the freedom, timing and scale of dismissals, the levels of redundancy payments and the mechanisms for ruling on unfair dismissals. Non-standard employment contracts are becoming popular in certain countries and for certain types of work: regulation can determine not only the extent to which employers can use these different contractual forms (e.g. in avoiding claims of unfair dismissals), but also the costs of their use, mainly through employer liability for social security contributions. Similarly, working time issues consist of several areas where national regulation has been influential: ceilings on the length of working week, holiday and leave entitlements and night shifts.

Industrial relations institutions can also shape the ability of companies to alter employment conditions. In this context, what is often important to businesses is the level at which wage and employment issues are decided and whether individual companies desire autonomy in negotiating plant-specific agreements. In some systems, companies favour a stable, consensual industrial relations environment in which certain employment decisions are taken collectively, as this removes issues of potential conflict at enterprise level. In other systems, a higher priority is placed on the capacity of firms to adjust pay and working conditions at individual plant level, often resulting in weaker union representation and industrial relations that are anything but consensual.

The scale of these different types of flexibility and their determining factors vary across Europe. Germany and the UK offer good examples of contrasted policy approaches to comparable economic pressures and arguably to contrasting types of flexibility. *Germany* has had a highly stable approach to employment issues, distinguished by institutional consensus and collective agreements. Its 'co-operative model' is based on the provision of common and equal minimum standards in exchange for worker commitments to refrain from industrial actions to disrupt work. At national level, a legal framework sets the scope for negotiating wages and working practices – within this framework the collective bargaining system operates, in which sectoral associations of employers negotiate with trades unions on industry-wide agreements. At enterprise level, 'co-determination' exists though the statutory requirements for works councils – which have extensive rights with respect to ensuring the application of collective agreements and setting local pay and working conditions within those agreements – and worker representation on supervisory boards.

In contrast, the *UK* has been held up as the principal European example of decentralized and deregulated labour markets. In this 'competitive model', the regulatory framework governing employment protection at national level is markedly weaker and there are no industrial relations institutions comparable to the German system. In the period of Conservative government during the 1980s, the government maintained a stance of minimal intervention in employment issues and advocated a policy of settling wage and working conditions at enterprise level. Over the last two decades, government policy has been concerted in reducing union power overall, diminishing the remaining national institutions for bargaining and limited industrial relations to the enterprise level.

The differences between both countries are clear when examining the level of labour market regulation. Grubb and Wells (1993) concluded that Germany was more regulated than the UK with respect to the company's ability to vary the length of the working week, the setting of unusual working hours, dismissal procedures and the use of part-time and temporary employment. Similarly, with respect to working time, part-time and fixed-term contracts and workers' consultation procedures, Nickell (1997) found that the UK was one of the most liberal countries in Western Europe, while Germany was among the most regulated. As a result, workforces in the UK have traditionally been seen as having more numerical and temporal flexibility than German (and most other European) workforces (Beatson, 1995; Adnett, 1996). However, Germany has been associated with much higher levels of functional flexibility than the UK, particularly when labour productivity is used as a proxy indicator (McKinsey, 1998; O'Mahony, 1998).

How do these differences in flexibility affect the choice of one country or another as an investment location? Investments in new capital equipment can allow (and, indeed, often require) changes in the way that production is organized within plants. Companies investing in new machinery often maximize their value by increasing machine running time, leading to alterations in shift patterns and the organization of working time. Similarly, production flexibility is enhanced by investments in the workforce, allowing employees to undertake new responsibilities in their jobs, work in flexible teams and switch between different production tasks as required. Divestments can also be a part of efforts to increase overall production flexibility. In recent years, some industries – such as automotive and electronics manufacture – have been reshaped by the contracting out of parts of the production process. Increased sub-contracting can give multinationals greater flexibility with respect to market and product changes, effectively shifting some responsibility for productivity increases to suppliers.

Just as production flexibility and productivity can be determined by investment, FDI strategies are in turn influenced by productivity differentials and the scope for increasing workforce flexibility in plants. Where flexibility is a key factor in these strategies, investment would tend to gravitate towards locations where such flexibility can be increased at the least cost to the company. If *numerical* or *temporal* flexibility is critical, investors are likely to be more sensitive to national differences in labour protection frameworks and collective bargaining structures. If *functional* flexibility is to be maximized, the availability and cost of highly skilled labour will be particularly significant.

WORKFORCE FLEXIBILITY AND FOREIGN INVESTMENT IN GERMANY AND THE UK

To identify whether and how such processes have worked in the cases of Germany and the UK, the study examined a number of specific research issues: whether investment decisions have been significantly influenced by inter-European differences in workforce flexibility; whether the UK is perceived by multinational investors as possessing relatively more numerical and temporal flexibility and Germany is viewed as having greater advantages in functional flexibility; and whether the perception of workforce flexibility in the UK has positively influenced its ability to attract and retain relatively larger volumes of manufacturing investment than Germany.

To investigate these issues, the study undertook original survey work through a series of company case studies in Germany and the UK.

Structured, face-to-face interviews were held with senior executives and plant managers in investor companies. Individuals were questioned specifically about the influence on investment decisions and overall importance of the following labour market factors: different types of flexibility, labour costs, employment regulation and collective bargaining procedures. Altogether 46 interviews were conducted with manufacturing facilities in both countries, yielding a sample set of 31 multinational groups. Within the sample, 15 matched pairs – in which both subsidiaries and parents were interviewed – facilitated comparison between different parts of the same company. By adopting this approach, it was not only possible to study the views of investors with experience of labour markets in both countries, but also whether particular types of investment were placed in different locations. In addition, investors were selected from two sectors – engineering and chemicals – automotive in order to isolate sector-specific effects. Both are industries in which investment in the UK and Germany has been relatively extensive and in which improving employment flexibility has become a key issue.

In order to ascertain the importance of different location factors in both countries, analysis was made of the factors that influenced firms' decision to invest originally in either country. A list of ten factors was presented to interviewees who were invited to assess whether the factors had been 'very important', 'important', or 'not important' (Table 3.1). The answers were scored 2, 1, or 0, respectively, allowing a weighted average of the investment factors to be calculated. While such methods cannot provide very accurate estimations of the relative significance of different factors, they can indicate broadly which factors firms tend to value most. Where two firms in the same multinational group were interviewed – the parent and the subsidiary – only the answers for the parent were used to avoid double-counting.

Table 3.1 Importance of factors for initial investments

	Foreign investors in Germany	Foreign investors in the UK	All firms
Access to main markets	1.63	1.52	1.55
Access to essential materials/inputs	0.13	0.35	0.29
Quality of infrastructure	0.38	0.48	0.45
Labour market factors	0.63	0.69	0.68
Access to R&D resources/technologies	0.50	0.44	0.45
Government incentives/subsidies	0.13	0.75	0.57
Taxes	0.38	0.66	0.58
Government regulations	0.25	0.50	0.42
Trade barriers	0.13	0.22	0.19
Language/cultural factors	0.13	0.48	0.38

Table 3.2 Investment factors of growing importance or relevant to future decisions

	Total no. of mentions
Market/customer access	6
Access to essential raw materials/inputs	2
Physical/business infrastructure	4
Labour market factors	12
Access to R&D resources/technologies	0
Government incentives/subsidies	1
Taxes	4
Government regulations	5
Trade barriers	1
Language/cultural factors	1

As can be seen from Table 3.1, it is not surprising to find that market access was considered the most important investment factor by far, putting labour market factors into a distant second place. Looking separately at firms making foreign investments in Germany and in the UK, no significant differences appear in the ranking of the investment factors. However, the factors relevant for the allocation of later reinvestment among different *existing* sites of a multinational company are not necessarily the same as for the *original* investment. After the initial investment, market-related factors tended to fall off in importance. When asked which factors were of growing importance and would influence future investment, labour market factors were most mentioned when companies had to decide how to alter their existing investments – whether by enlarging or reducing production capacities or deciding where to manufacture newly developed products (Table 3.2).

To understand the role that labour factor differences between Germany and the UK play in investment decisions, companies were asked to rank different labour factors by their importance to the business using the weighted value system. In Table 3.3, it is clear that the most significant factors were direct wage costs, workforce flexibility and the use of skilled labour. Foreign investors in Germany valued workforce skills above all other factors, whereas those in the UK tended to place a great priority on wages and indirect labour costs (such as employers' insurance payments). This would tend to reinforce the traditional picture of Germany attracting investors with its highly skilled workforce and the UK's principal attraction being the low level of its overall labour costs. Interestingly, though, investors in both countries underlined the importance of the flexibility of the workforce, so much so that it is the one factor recognized by firms investing in both countries as critical.

Table 3.3   Importance of different labour market factors

	Foreign investors in Germany	Foreign investors in the UK	All firms
Availability of skilled labour	1.78	1.09	1.29
Direct wage costs	1.11	1.50	1.39
Indirect labour costs	1.00	1.23	1.16
Flexibility of the workforce	1.45	1.50	1.49
Level of regulations	1.00	0.87	0.91
Industrial relations	0.89	0.87	0.88

Table 3.4   Comparison of different labour market factors, Germany and the UK

	No. of companies favouring Germany	No. of companies favouring the UK
Availability of skilled labour	18	0
Direct wage costs	0	17
Indirect wage costs	0	16
Flexibility of the workforce	2	7
Level of regulations	0	10
Industrial relations	2	1

To examine attitudes to German and UK labour market differences in more detail, firms were asked about what they viewed as the relative advantages of each country (Table 3.4). Germany was overwhelmingly viewed as having higher levels of skills while the UK was seen as the lower-cost country. Industrial relations did not figure significantly in favouring either country. More surprisingly, though, a larger number of companies appeared to view the UK as having advantages in the flexibility of their workforce, a view strengthened by the similarly favourable view towards its more liberal system of employment regulations.

At first glance, the results suggest that the UK is perceived as having more flexible labour markets, but a more complex picture emerges when examining different components of flexibility. First, with respect to *numerical* flexibility and working time, few firms were able to identify significant differences between both countries. While most companies agreed that Germany's regulatory system was generally less flexible than that in the UK, it was consistently pointed out that there had been significant liberalization of German regulations in recent years. Moreover, exceptions to the existing regulations allowed companies to avoid major difficulties. Very few companies suggested that existing German restrictions in either fixed-term contracts or working time had affected their production operations to any extent, or that the differences between both countries had influenced their investment decisions (this only occurred in five of the 31 cases examined).

Second, the bulk of companies noted that they did not face significant restrictions in pursuing *functional* flexibility in either country. Where clear differences emerged was in one of the major components of achieving functional flexibility – comparative skills levels. The majority of companies considered Germany still to have greater skills level than the UK in their industry and linked this to a higher productivity performance in their German plants. Nevertheless, this did not necessarily mean that functional flexibility was systematically greater in German rather than UK companies within the same group. Flexibility was a product of the skills level of the workforce *and* the ways in which they were organized in production. In some case, UK plants could be 'trailblazers' for the group as a whole in the introduction of new working practices designed to maximize functional flexibility, in spite of lower skills levels. On occasions, this reflected the relative ease of introducing those systems in UK sites – especially where unions and regulations were weaker and particularly where a firm had recently been acquired and workforces were perhaps less 'entrenched' in particular working systems. Indeed, with respect to industrial relations, while many firms reported union and worker resistance to company efforts to change working practices in both countries, in very few cases did such conflict appear to influence management and investment plans.

From the evidence here, neither the UK nor Germany can be clearly associated with a particular type of flexibility. While the UK may have an (arguably) more liberal regulatory climate and fewer restrictions in achieving numerical and temporal flexibility than Germany, it does not appear to have given plants located there major advantages over those in Germany achieving these types of flexibility. The German regulatory and industrial relations framework allows considerably more scope for firms to negotiate comparable flexibility than UK plants in the same group. Similarly, although Germany continues to have higher skills levels and frequently better productivity than the UK, its advantage in functional flexibility is not as pronounced as might have been first assumed. Numerous examples were found of UK workforces willing to introduce new working practices, often before other plants in the group, though German workforces were often better able to adopt such practices more *quickly*.

As a result, flexibility differences between countries have not systematically favoured one country or the other. However, differences between *plants* have been significant, particularly where it involved follow-up investments. Differences in productivity – and the ability to influence productivity through workforce flexibility – were sometimes significant in the distribution of investment between existing plants. In one German-owned multinational producing automotive parts, the need to restructure the group had raised the importance of productivity as a factor determining plant survival. In order to reduce excess capacity, one plant had already been closed because of its poorer productivity performance – the UK plant realized that it could not compete with other plants in the group on a cost basis because of its relatively smaller size and, hence, had to improve productivity through increasing the flexibility of its workforce, allowing it to handle shorter and more complex production runs. A similar situation was found in a German-owned chemicals multinational which was considering how to restructure the group, again with a view to reducing excess capacity. As before, the UK plant was instituting a series of changes in working practices in order to improve its ranking ahead of a group review of plant productivity. Both these and similar firms tended to be multinationals where plants manufactured relatively similar, standardized products. Where excess capacity existed in the firm, there were pressures on individual plants to reduce costs and raize productivity as production could be transferred to other manufacturing units in the group. In multinationals where plants specialized in particular product areas, such obvious closure threats were less likely to emerge.

The threat of closure or diverted investment was used in a few instances to extract workforce concessions on issues of flexibility. Occasionally, the threat was explicit, as when one of the German automotive suppliers noted that the threat of shifting production from one of its smaller plants in Germany to an existing UK site forced the works council to agree to new shift and overtime pay arrangements. In other cases, though, the threat was not direct, but local management still reacted to fears of an imminent decision on restructuring within the group by reinforcing their flexibility. This was a factor in the case of another UK subsidiary of a German-owned automotive investor, where the local unions agreed to changes in working time in order to strengthen the plant's chance of survival. In this respect, the research confirms findings of other studies on the employment practices of other multinationals, especially in the automotive sectour. For example, US companies such as Ford and General Motors have made active use of differences in plant productivity to press for changes in working flexibility in their plants, often explicitly linking new investment (and improved chances of plant survival during a period of production overcapacity) to such changes (Mueller and Purcell, 1992; Wells and Rawlinson, 1994).

While labour factors did have a role in determining plant survival, the research found few clear connections between the type of investment made in Germany and the UK and any flexibility differences between both countries. There were very few examples of significant company functions being transferred to the UK by German investors or by UK investors to Germany as a direct result of labour market factors. Indirectly, though, the flexibility of workforces did assist some plants developing product specialisms within a group. For example, a UK chemical investor explained that European production of one of its healthcare products had been concentrated in its

German site to a large extent because of the ability of its German work-force to cope with the higher health and safety standards and more sophis-ticated equipment associated with its manufacture. Similarly, the UK subsidiary of a German-owned automotive supplier was able to reinforce its position as a 'lead centre' in one of the group's products as a result of its improved workforce flexibility and relative productivity.

CONCLUDING DISCUSSION

On the basis of the research findings, several conclusions can be made regarding the influence of workforce flexibility on the locational attrac-tiveness of Germany and the UK. First, at least for multinational compa-nies (MNCs) in the two sectors examined here, the extent of differences in the workforce flexibility available in Germany and the UK seems to have been exaggerated. Overall, all types of flexibility can be generated in both countries – though mainly temporal and functional flexibility, depending on a combination of individual company culture, industrial relations and the needs of the particular production process and workforce capabilities. Second, where flexibility improvements have been made, they have occurred in plants based in Germany as well as the UK, normally where the need to make productivity improvements is more pressing and local plant circumstances permit change. Significant national obstacles were not encountered, though the higher level of skills generally assist German plants in making flexibility changes more quickly than other plants in the group.

Lastly, FDI decisions in Germany and the UK – at least initially – have not been principally affected by differences in regulation or levels of flexi-bility. However, levels of workforce flexibility in different plants did have an influence on subsequent investment decisions, particularly where closure or scaling down was involved. Although investment in the UK has been par-tially influenced by its appeal of low production costs (notably wage levels and indirect labour costs), new investment decisions have usually been linked to the more important motives of access to particular customers and expansion into new national markets. Once sites have been established, firms placed a high priority on increasing workforce flexibility and plant productivity in their different locations. In this respect, neither Germany nor the UK present consistently major obstacles to firms being able to increase different types of flexibility.

As the evidence of some new investors into the UK – particularly from Japan and the USA – suggests that the appearance of more flexible labour markets has been a decisive location factour, it raises the issue of the force of *perceptions* in investment attraction. The experience of investors with production in both countries points to an ability to improve workforce flexibility within the existing structures of both the UK and Germany. New investors – unfamiliar with how German regulations work in practice – may be assuming that the appearance of regulation at macro level would greatly constrain individual company behaviour. In consequence, the UK's ability to use a reputation for labour market deregulation in promoting FDI may have been overstated. As a strategy for attracting – and perhaps more importantly, *retaining* – foreign investment, emphasis on the UK as a flexible, low-cost production base may be less effective in future, particularly as the experience of more companies in developing flexibility in Germany becomes more visible.

Indeed, what perhaps matters more to companies is not necessarily the ability to maximize particular types of flexibility but both the capacity for combining them together to augment productivity and the ease with which this can be done. In this respect, differences between the UK and German labour markets are perhaps marked in other ways. Productivity differences remain relatively entrenched in both countries. This appears to be less directly related to the regulatory or industrial relations approaches exemplified by both countries – the 'competitive' and 'corporatist' models – but more a reflection of the public sector commitment to raising skills. As noted earlier, and as frequently highlighted in the company interviews, Germany's national system for apprenticeship and skills training has played a major role in creating workforces whose skills allow changes to working practices – usually temporal and functional – to be made quickly. Again, it suggests that UK inward investment policy cannot rely on the use of deregulation as a long-term tool for encouraging investment, but should employ policies that seek continually to upgrade the productivity of workforces and the quality of business environments in order to more deeply embed foreign investments in local economies (Brown and Raines, 1999).

4 The Role of Expatriate Managers in Global Economic Restructuring: Some Key Components and Constraints

Helen Sakho

INTRODUCTION

This chapter explores the role, place and function of senior expatriate managers in the 'globalization' process. Senior expatriate managers are considered by transnational corporations (TNCs) to possess high levels of technical and business expertise, and are rewarded accordingly. They form the upper echelons of the core workforces of TNCs and are dispatched to foreign locations to implement corporate globalization strategies. The chapter is also about some aspects of the impact of new technology, and how this may affect expatriate managers, and the expatriation policies of TNCs. It reflects dimensions of recent research, and presents findings and some preliminary suggestions. The chapter points to a conceptual necessity to deconstruct the notion of 'expertise' in order to understand the specific contribution of expatriate managers to globalization; and to the possibility that these global managers may be playing an 'indispensable' role in the management of the new phase of capitalist development.

The chapter hopes to demonstrate that the expatriation of senior executives attached to TNCs cannot be fully explained without an understanding of the *nature* of the role that these managers are playing in the globalization process, and what components of this role are open to change.

BACKGROUND

It is commonly accepted that economic activity has, in the last 30 years or so, undergone fundamental restructuring and that it is the internationalization of capital by TNCs that has led to significant changes in the organization of production and labour. TNCs have been the main vehicles of globalization, a process aimed at facilitating the production and distribution of goods and services across increasingly open and inviting space, and one that allows trade and investment to go beyond substitutes and become increasingly inseparable.

The idea that there is an emerging group of highly mobile, highly rewarded and powerful people managing – *by way of transfer of knowledge and expertise* – new production and production processes around the globe, has been attracting growing interest in recent times. The literature on the movement of managers across national boundaries mostly concerns itself with constraints and problems associated with this type of movement. For example, some accounts focus on issues relating to dual-career families, stress and failure levels amongst the highly mobile (Smith, 1992; Scullion, 1994; Foster, 1997). Others approach the subject from a gender-specific perspective concentrating on the underrepresentation of women on international assignments (Adler, 1994; Harris, 1993; Hardill, 1997); or discuss expatriation from an organizational, and international business development viewpoint with emphasis on human resource management (HRm) (Foster and Johnsen, 1996; Foster, 1997; Welch and Welch, 1997, among others).

As mentioned earlier, most of these accounts point to an operational or ideological deficiency in the outlook of TNCs, such as a lack of involvement of human resource departments at the earlier stages of internationalization or the neglect of women and host-country nationals as potential international managers. The utilization of host- and third-country nationals is seen by much of the literature as a way towards achieving greater global success through the creation of cross-cultural teams which will also bring greater benefit to the host country, while cutting down costs. Consequently, there is a growing literature on remedial actions that need to be taken by TNCs to alleviate difficulties associated with the movement of expatriate managers and their families in order to maximize returns on high levels of investment involved in their relocation.

More recently, the possibility of technological developments having a substitution effect on costly expatriation has been identified by a number of researchers (see Salt, 1997; Koser and Lutz, 1998, for example) as an area where a gap in knowledge exists. This suggestion is of particular interest to this chapter, which explores such a possibility in some detail in relation to communication technologies. Expatriate managers are carriers of specialist expertise and corporate know-how, who are nonetheless regarded as extremely expensive. In other words, their value-adding potential may have the prospect of being transferred electronically, as effectively, at a cheaper rate.

RESEARCH STRATEGY AND METHODOLOGY

The data presented by the chapter are derived from in-depth, semi-structured interviews, using open-ended questions. The aim of the interviews was to gain an understanding of the meanings and interpretations attached to the specific role of expatriate managers in the global economy and the globalization process, and of how this role may be changing. Supplementary information is drawn upon from interviews with the international director of a leading management development institute.

The 25 participants were drawn from expatriate managers working in the UK for European (7) and American (13) TNCs, and human resource managers who are responsible for expatriates in the UK. All participants worked at senior corporate levels despite sectoral and organizational differences among the corporations they worked for. The interviews were secured on the basis of total confidentiality in relation to the identity and names of the TNCs and the managers. The following tables, however, present a general picture of their characteristics.

The TNCs

As can be seen from Table 4.1, the TNCs were drawn from a wide range of industries, with the common characteristic being their significance in the global economy, an indication of which is presented in Table 4.2.

Table 4.1   TNCs covered by industrial sectors

Industry[a]	No. of TNCs covered in each industry
Petroleum and refining	2
Airlines	1
Food	1
Aerospace	1
Metal products	1
Insurance	2
Securities	2
Soaps, cosmetics	2
Electronics	1
Entertainment	1
Pharmaceuticals	1
Chemicals	1
Motor vehicles, parts	1
Plastics	1
Medical	2
Total	20

Note:
a Industrial classification for companies is adopted from
   Fortune Global 500 (1998 edn).

Table 4.2 Ranking of TNCs by their total 1998 revenue in their sectors

No. of TNCs	Industry ranking
7	1
4	3
1	4
1	9
1	11
6	>11
Total	20

Source: Fortune and Hoovers, *Global 500* (1998 edn).

The Managers

In total, 25 managers were interviewed: seven were women and 18 men, with the women being concentrated in the human resource (HR) component of the sample. Only two of the women managers interviewed were working as expatriates in senior positions outside the HR function. The ethnic composition of the managers was as follows: 10 US, 11 European, and four host- and third-country nationals. All home-country and two third-country nationals were white. More than 90 per cent of participants were over 40 years of age, married and accompanied by their families.

ROLE OF EXPATRIATE MANAGERS

The specific role of expatriate managers, and their distinct contribution to TNCs, may be understood in relation to the gap they are considered competent to fill at a particular location in the division of labour in a given foreign location. The participants were asked to define such a role, identifying why it could not be filled by a local or a third-country national.

The Expatriate Contribution

Although a wide range of differing reasons and circumstances might necessitate the use of expatriate managers, an understanding that these managers carry special skills is explicit in both the literature on the subject and in *all* the respondents' accounts. The following three accounts are typical interpretations of what the expatriate contribution to foreign locations is:

> In a lot of emerging markets, where we are mostly engaged in joint ventures, the partner company provides country access, markets and we

supply technology and management skills. The *big* thing here is technical expertise and management skills. Our partners know how to build and operate a company using 35 000 local workers. They do not have any indigenous high quality technologists. So what they want from us is technology. We give them that in return for presence and access to market. Secondly, they want to know how to form and operate a company to modern international standards. My skill is to run that factory with 4000 people. That is the skill that the locals do not have. They need a small number of expats, people from the Centre, from the UK who know how to run things. We are going in there to help them develop those skills. (*General Manager of an oil TNC, joint venture, China*, respondent's emphasis)

One primary reason for expatriation is skill shortages, particularly in markets where there may be no concept of commercialization. Our longer-term strategy is to grow through alliances. Expatriates prepare and develop the locals via ideological spread. (*HR Manager of an airline*)

The expat needs two basic skills: one is technical knowledge and expertise, and the other is general business know-how. We do not use international assignments to train young lads at this level. If the business is going to be a world class business, it has to be run along our lines, it has to be a recognisable factory, anywhere in the world. We will train local workforces to our standards, and by our methods. So as far as we are concerned, it is an extension of our way of doing things. Obviously by putting in an expat, you are importing someone who has up-to-date knowledge of the business, which you can not get by hiring somebody locally, although it will cost *very much more*. (*Head of International Manufacturing of a motor vehicle and parts TNC*, respondent's emphasis)

What seems clear from these accounts is that expatriate managers need specific skills that incorporate product and market-related competence as well as a sound understanding of corporate culture and the corporations' ways of doing business in a global market. The two aspects need separate consideration in order to gain a more detailed understanding of reasons for the importance of expatriates to globalization strategies as well as their potential substitution by factors such as technology and/or host-country nationals.

'MANAGERIAL EXPERTISE' DEFINED

This part of the chapter reflects an attempt to establish more clearly how TNCs define global management skill and expertise. The managers were asked – through open-ended questions – to specify key components of managerial know-how, the expertise that could be distinguished from technical skills. The following three descriptions exemplify the responses:

These skills have to do with our core values, which are the rules wherever you are. When senior company people are put in charge, they become its face. We are a global company, and it is these values that matter a great deal to us. When we are criticized in a locality, we need sharp people who know these rules and can put things right. If we accept to work with local rules, there are places where we will never do any business. You have to have the skill to adapt these rules to your values and, *if need be*, to change, to shape the agenda. (*General Manager of an oil company – joint venture, China*, respondent's emphasis)

We would normally use our experienced managers, who have the necessary experience. We are happy to flavour our production locally, but our senior expats must be able to apply our core values to day to day decision making. A successful expat is one that combines technical expertise with our *core values*. (*Head of International Manufacturing of a motor vehicle TNC*, respondent's emphasis)

We are a global company, with a set of values, which ensure that we are ultimately the best in the market. These are very important to all our people. They are things like honesty, responsibility and openness. There are certain geographies which we do not trust, there we prefer neutral Britons to locals. (*HR Manager of an airline*)

In these examples, the managers describe the specific expertize required in an expatriate as being the ability to utilize their corporations' core values and philosophies in managing global operations and in shaping the local agenda. The corporate values are seen as a guideline that ensures cohesion between the core and the other geography. The expatriate manager is trusted to be an advocate for the TNC as well as being 'honest' and 'responsible' – attributes which the airliner HR manager believes might be rare in certain geographies.

The issue of creating consistency in organizational belief systems, particularly in acquisitions, comes up regularly in the managers' accounts. The expatriate manager is trusted to ensure that the core values of the parent TNC are understood and upheld by the workforces of the firms that it has taken over, as illustrated by the following response:

Take my own case as an example. My *main* marching order was to make sure that I incarnated our values and philosophies, and brought alive these in an organization growing in acquisition. It is a bit like making a melting pot happen. We as senior expatriates are charged with the task of taking wide-ranging values and make them consistent. As an expat, you walk in and you are first and foremost an establisher and protector of the company's values. (*HR Manager of a soap and cosmetics TNC*, respondent's emphasis)

PRELIMINARY SUGGESTIONS

What these examples illustrate is that notions of skill are commonly defined by criteria that go beyond technical expertise – as might be gained via the acquisition of formal qualifications or other training in engineering, or chemistry, for example. This appears to be the case in both manufacturing and services. The responses demonstrate that senior expatriates are carriers of more than technical knowledge. They are trusted with the task of managing the restructuring of the global economy. What is also clearly expressed is a trust in their ability to represent, shape and establish the core values and philosophies of a TNC. They are used by TNCs to spread to other locations values – documented or informally understood within the organization. Furthermore, what emerges is that high-level technical skills alone are not sufficient for a significant international assignment. The HR manager of an insurance TNC explains:

> In the case of these senior expats, both sets of skills are important. Sometimes you have to make adjustments if you do not have people who have both. If you are sending someone to train people and leave then that is fine. What does not work is sending someone with the technical skills who has none of the rest. They fail every single time.

What this chapter suggests is that the concepts and processes reflected in the managers' responses in the two preceding sections need to be placed in the context of fragmentation of production as a key feature underpinning the restructuring of the global economy. References to downsizing, jobless growth and the reinforcement of economic power relations are indicative of the ability of TNC managers to shape and implement such economic restructuring in other locations of production. Furthermore, it is this ability that may increasingly constitute the key skill required of these managers:

> In actual fact the role of the expat as the corporate glue and transferring the corporate culture around the globe has increased. This is so because as technical expertise can be increasingly replicated around the globe, so the expats don't necessarily have a technical function. Their role on the corporate cultural front is really important. From the point of view of the HQ, when they sent an expat to a foreign location, they want him to come back with first-hand knowledge of what is going on in the subsidiary, and this might impact on the development of strategic policies. (*International Manager of a leading management development institute*)

THE IMPACT OF TECHNOLOGY ON THE ROLE
OF EXPATRIATES

The impact of technology on expatriates merits separate and detailed consideration because, as mentioned in the Introduction, it has been gaining increasing attention as a factor that could facilitate international business at a distance, reducing the need for expatriates. The main focus of this section is to examine the extent to which technology can in fact replace expatriates and to draw attention to skills that only expatriates – particularly those in senior managerial positions – can provide.

The TNCs covered use the full range of electronic communication facilities that are now available, including electronic mail and video-conferencing. While all the TNCs considered the impact of new technologies to have been crucial and profound on their ability to run global businesses, what emerges from the respondents' explanations is that technology has had different consequences for the mobility of different groups of expatriates. The respondents were asked to consider the impact of new technology on expatriation.

The first impact has been to enable the managers to gain access to up-to-date information in an efficient and effective manner. Ease and speed of transfer of data seems particularly important:

Technology has basically taken the time lag out of different locations, and increased what we call 'real time'. You *could not* run a global business without it. You could not be out of contact. The business moves too quickly and you need on-line immediate access. So that if there is a problem in Japan, somebody elsewhere, anywhere in the globe, can pick the information and make a quick evaluation, quick decisions regardless of the day and the time. We communicate globally via e-mail, voice and video. But this is not related to expatriation *at all*. This is about the fast and efficient movement of data around the world. Decision making still takes an individual. (*Managing Director of a securities TNC*, respondent's emphasis)

Communications technology has transformed our networking and management of knowledge. I can tap into any other senior manager and talk through a problem anywhere in the world. (*Head of R & D of a soaps and cosmetics TNC*)

Secondly, communications technology seems to have facilitated the transfer of *some* knowledge and expertise, eliminating the need for physical presence, as the following two responses exemplify:

The impact of technology has been *tremendous*. It has meant that people in China can talk directly to people in Milton Keynes to solve a problem.

The problem and the solution can be shared on video. This means that we do not have to fly half a dozen people all the way, meaning lost time, lost production, lost money. (*General Manager of an oil TNC – joint venture, China*, respondent's emphasis)

It is nice to have the technological capacity. I can take my mechanics to a room and they can talk over a problem to the mechanics in South Boston. (*Head of Disposable Products of a metal TNC*)

A third outcome of the application of new communication technology is described by the managers as impacting on the amount and length of travelling:

The impact of technology has been absolutely profound. It has transformed our industry, although is not quite there yet, senior managers in the US can have their big meetings on a video conference call, which means they do not all have to get on the plane and go to New York for the day. (*Executive Director of a securities TNC*)

The impact has been extensive and important. We use telecommunication, e-mail and video-conferencing a lot. The impact on travelling has been on short-term assignments only. It has also impacted on the need for meetings and might have shortened the length of some assignments. (*HR Manager of a soaps and cosmetics TNC*)

So far, it appears from these accounts that new communication technologies have facilitated the more efficient and faster transfer of information. They have also impacted on the need for physical presence in some circumstances, and on the duration of some international assignments.

The following three responses, however, indicate the limitation of these technologies for the global activities of TNCs:

In terms of trouble shooting new technology works. But I do doubt if it will ever replace expats. You cannot replace sitting across the table with your Chinese colleagues, looking them in the eye and saying *no*. (*General Manager of an oil TNC – joint venture, China*, respondent's emphasis)

Expats are very, *very* expensive. But for us technology has affected the *speed* of developments. For us expat managers carry a mix of not only technical knowledge, but also actually up-to-date *company* knowledge including relationships and sub-relationships, be it in Poland, South Africa, or Peru. They need this knowledge, and this *cannot* be shipped down the e-mail. You need people who can take this knowledge and solve the problems of the locality. (*HR Manager of a vehicle and parts TNC*, respondent's emphasis)

Eventually technology may have a bigger impact, but not yet. We have *so many* opportunities still. There are so many places where we do not have market presence or distribution linkages. I think that certainly for the next decade or decade and a half, we will be relying on our expat managers. (*HR Manager of the same company*, respondent's emphasis)

What emerges from these typical responses is that the transfer of corporate values and culture and the maintenance of corporate trust in foreign locations require the physical presence of some (particularly senior managerial) expatriates. They may be extremely expensive to the corporations, but technology cannot be relied upon to influence local economies or to independently utilize corporate networks in other locations.

The following response sums up the impact of new technology and its key limitations:

The impact is two-fold: product development technology, which has impacted on some technical expat assignments. They may be shorter or in some cases cut out; secondly there is communications technology. The impact of this has been tremendous. We can video-conference globally which does cut the amount of travelling I did to the US. This is good for me, because I can travel more within Europe, where I am really based. Expats are very expensive. At a senior level talking about an average of $500 000 per annum. But because of the sort of things I mentioned about core values and the transfer of ideology, you *cannot* replace expat contributions with communication technology. This has made connections easier and faster, not traded them off. (*Managing Director of a chemicals TNC*, respondent's emphasis)

TOWARDS A CONCEPTUAL FRAMEWORK

Taken together, these responses illustrate that, first, expatriates cannot be treated as a homogeneous group, which carries out the same given (replaceable or otherwize) functions in the global economy. Secondly, they point to senior expatriate managers occupying a specific place in the global division of labour in terms of their dominant relationship to foreign production locations of production and their ability to influence the restructuring of local economies; and thirdly to the reality that there are certain things that new technology cannot replace. In order to understand what is capable of being transmitted electronically and is therefore open to the impact of technology, it is necessary to gain an in-depth understanding of what skills TNCs consider as indispensable expertise. These two dimensions – that is to say, the *nature* of the role of the senior expatriates and how this role is being sustained and *enhanced* – need to be considered as dynamically interacting in the context of globalization as the current form of capital accumulation.

What is important to an understanding of this interaction, moreover, is the distinction between managers and specialist professional workers and engineers, as these groups belong to different parts of the division of labour (Massey and Allen, 1988), the most pertinent point here being that the latter does not control the labour of others, or strategically reshape local economic relations. This distinction may also be the basis for understanding why technology might have enabled the transfer of expertise for some groups such as mechanics and engineers, but not for the managers interviewed.

Salt (1997:10), for example, comments:

> What is being transferred is expertise. We can think of the individual as a repository of expertise. Where skills are manual, then a physical presence is required. But with many 'brain skills' it is knowledge that is required and needs to be relocated. In a growing number of circumstances this can be achieved in a variety of ways, not necessarily requiring traditional forms of secondment, or indeed secondment at all.

Indeed this may be a plausible explanation for certain situations and certain tasks and functions such as the technical aspects of research and product development and design, and production process trouble-shooting. Furthermore, as indicated by the responses presented in this chapter, communication technologies might have impacted on the need for the physical presence of certain expatriates. It may have also impacted on the number and duration of meetings requiring physical presence. For managerial expatriates, however, communication technologies have created effective tools that can enhance performance, without eliminating or significantly affecting the need for physical presence in the geography they manage.

Globalization has necessitated new forms of international mobility. 'Highly skilled migration is a key element of globalization' (Castles and Miller, 1993:92). For those deemed to be highly skilled, such mobility – increasingly made easier by national governments in order to assist TNCs in the reorganization of their management arrangements (Salt and Singleton, 1995) – is determined by expansion opportunities developed by these corporations. Such migration takes place in order to ensure that TNCs' strategic position of control over production in foreign lands is secured, and is utilized effectively as decision making expatriates are connecting them to their base(s) through increasing reliance on technological advances.

These processes necessitate a contextual framework for the consideration of the expatriate intervention and its changing form or pattern. Such a framework will need to acknowledge the limitations (as perceived by TNCs) of alternative sources of labour, as well as technological constraints.

As Castells (1989:208–9) points out, what has emerged in the past two decades or so is a new techno–economic paradigm, the development of which has been crucial for the restructuring of capitalism.

> There is a growing concentration of knowledge-generation and decision-making processes in high-level organisations in which both information and the capacity of processing it are concentrated . . . Given the strategic role of knowledge and information control in productivity and profitability, the core centres of corporate organisations are the only truly indispensable components of the system, with most other work, and thus other workers, being potential candidates for automation from the functional point of view.

Although, as mentioned earlier, most accounts on expatriation seem concerned with operational difficulties of TNCs (cost, dual-career, cultural adjustment and failure rates are examples) more recent research points to the specificity of the role of expatriation within changing global relations of production. In a study of the movement of managers, experts and professionals from Western countries in Poland, Rudolph and Hillmann (1998), for example, point to the important role that these groups play in the management of the political economy of the new era in a former command economy. While the findings reflected in this chapter are not country-specific, they do point to similarities in the role being played. Expatriate managers may represent a growing cadre of 'globalizers' who occupy particular locations in the international division of labour, with a key task of shaping and creating new relations with and within local labour markets. Their most significant and currently indispensable attribute seems to be their ability to maintain the trust of their TNC in terms of spreading its culture and business ideology. Such trust is built up through the manager having a profound TNC-specific knowledge of corporate beliefs and of how the corporation works at the core, which is neither easily found in a local manager, nor creatable via new technology.

CONCLUSION

This chapter has considered the role and function of senior expatriate managers in the global expansion strategies of 20 global corporations. It has attempted to disentangle the notion of skill and global expertise that has been gaining growing importance and presented an analysis of what component(s) of such skill and expertise are, at this point in economic history, indispensable.

The key skill that the TNCs seem to seek in a senior expatriate, is their ability to establish, promote and protect the core values of the corporations in other geographies. Crucially, this incorporates the ability to contribute effectively to the reshaping of economic and cultural relations with others in different locations. In these terms, the greatest impact of communication technologies for these managers appears to have been a qualitative enhancement of their role through the faster and more efficient transfer of TNC-specific management information. Their physical presence – not easily replaceable by alternative local appointments either – will remain important to their ability competently to advance and safeguard corporate economic interests. Their cost does no seem to be a particularly decisive factor in the corporate calculations.

5 Two Nations Divided by a Common Culture: Three American Companies in Scotland

Monir Tayeb and Edwin Dott

INTRODUCTION

The question of implications of national culture for cross-border part-nerships, especially regarding parent–subsidiary relationships, has for a long time been a debating point among scholars and practitioners alike (see, for example, Harvey-Jones, 1988; Dowling, 1989; Schuler *et al.*, 1993; Caligiuri and Stroh, 1995; Ferner, 1997; Bae *et al.*, 1998). However, sur-prisingly, given the close political, social and business relationships between the UK and the USA, there have been very few empirical studies of American firms operating in the UK. The two cultures, although they are said to have certain similarities, not the least because of their common language and a certain degree of shared cultural heritage, are nevertheless very different from one another in subtle and not so subtle ways. These differences are bound to have implications for the management of UK–US joint ventures and wholly-owned subsidiaries from one nation operating in the other.

This chapter reports a case study of three American manufacturing firms operating in Scotland. Building on an earlier projects conducted by the first author (Tayeb, 1998), it aims to explore the implications of cultural differ-ences and similarities between the two nations for the management of these firms. The study focuses on three broad areas: inter-personal relationship and communication, human resources and labour relations issues, and or-ganizational control and parent–subsidiary relations.

THEORETICAL BACKGROUND TO THE STUDY

Parent–subsidiary relations with regard to human resource management (HRM), like other activities of a multinational company (MNC), are incor-porated into strategies which are then implemented at various levels. Broadly speaking, multinational firms have three strategic options to choose from: ethnocentric, polycentric and global (Perlmutter, 1969). These strategies would lead in turn to the firms having HRM policies which would resemble that of their home-country styles, or be similar to the host countries' indigenous styles or a company-wide style irrespective of home- and host-countries' styles.

The freedom to choose between the above strategies depends not only on the philosophy and preference of the company, but also on the local conditions. International firms might in practice be inclined to opt for a hybrid strategy and adopt, for example, an ethnocentric approach with respect to some subsidiaries and a polycentric one for others. The choice of strategy depends also on how the foreign subsidiary is set up. In a green field site, the expatriate managers have more room to exercise their choice. The Japanese multinational firms operating green field plants in many parts of the UK have been able to bring in many of their HRM practices to their brand-new subsidiaries. But if the subsidiary is created by taking over an already existing local company, the new firm is more likely to resemble other fellow firms in the country, initially at least until gradually the parent company organizational culture asserts itself (Tayeb, 1994).

A complicating factor is the specific areas of HRM practices. Rosenzweig and Nohria (1994) studied practices regarding time off, benefits, gender composition, training, executive bonus and executive participation in a large sample of foreign subsidiaries in the USA. They found that the degree of conformity to local practices diminished as one went down along these functions, with the time off showing the highest and the executive participation the lowest degree.

In the case study of the Scottish subsidiary of an American multinational company referred to above, Tayeb (1998) found that the company's HRM was influenced by major factors inside and outside it. The study showed clearly that the management of the workforce in a foreign subsidiary is a complicated affair. The choice between one of three major options – polycentric, ethnocentric and global – advocated by many scholars, is too simplistic a model for understanding what actually goes on in a subsidiary and between it and its parent organization. Moreover, the amount of influence of the factors identified in the study on the company's HRM was argued to be a dynamic one and could change over time and space.

The various points discussed above serve to remind us that multinational companies more often than not function under opposing pressures which they have to reconcile. As Tayeb (1996) argues, it is due to the very nature of relationships between the parent company and its subsidiaries that tension and conflict become inevitable, as there is both the need to maintain the integrity of the corporation as a coherent, co-ordinated entity, and at the same time to allow for responsiveness to their differentiated environments (Doz, 1976; Prahalad, 1976; Prahalad and Doz, 1987; Welch, 1994).

However, the appropriate mix of differentiation and integration depends on many factors and is often difficult to achieve successfully. Conflict can occur at a number of levels. Key areas are: conflict between head office and subsidiaries, conflict between subsidiaries and their host country, conflict within head office and communication difficulties between head office and subsidiaries. Decisions concerning such matters as organizational structure, production processes and technologies employed in a company which straddles many national boundaries are all fraught with conflict, tension and frustrations (Wilson and Rosenfeld, 1990).

The complexity of the structure of the international firm will have also a marked effect on the ease or difficulty with which information is transmitted across the organization. Perlmutter (1969) suggests that the key to understanding communication is to examine the relationships between head office and its international operations. The level of decentralization, the extent to which the international organization operates globally and the structure of the firm will all create potential problems for communication. In extreme cases, head office can be unaware of critical information, or may misunderstand completely the information coming from subsidiaries (Robock and Simmonds, 1983). Communication in the ethnocentric perspective, for example, can suffer from both blinkered thinking and the exercize of power. Head office strategies become in danger of institutionalization, precluding of certain attitudes and behaviours. In companies with polycentric strategies communication difficulties can arise from the duplication of effort between subsidiaries and from the inefficient use of head office experience (Heenan and Perlmutter, 1979).

THE BRITISH AND THEIR AMERICAN COUSINS

Before discussing the findings of the present study it is useful to take a brief look at the main aspects of the cultural background of American multinationals and their host country, in this case the UK. A qualification should, however, be made here straight away. Both the USA and the UK are multicultural societies, the former a nation of immigrants, the latter a nation of at least four distinctive cultural entities, Scots, Welsh, English and Irish, not to mention the sizeable ethnic minorities of Afro–Caribbean and Indian – Pakistani origins. What follows, therefore, is a general broad cultural pattern of the two nations, studied and observed mainly by outsiders.

Bakhtari (1995), after an extensive review of the relevant literature, concluded that Americans are, among other things, very informal and tend not to treat people differently even when there are great differences in age or social standing. They are direct and do not talk around things, they tend to say exactly what they mean. They are competitive, self-focused, goal-oriented and achievers, and like to keep scores, whether at work or at play. Americans value punctuality and keep appointments and calendars, and live according to schedules and clocks. They hold ethnocentric views and believe that their culture and values are superior to all others. They are independent and individualistic, place a high value on freedom and believe that individuals can shape and control their own destinies. In this connection, Hall (1989) also argues that the Americans are much more concerned with their own careers and personal success than about the welfare of the organization or the group.

In a similar exercise, complemented by an attitude survey among a small sample of the population, Tayeb (1988) found the British to be xenophobic, pragmatic, honest, self-disciplined, conservative and risk averse. They dislike uncertainty and change and value their own, and others', privacy. They are reserved and refrain from expressing their emotions in public, which may have something to do with their love of privacy. The unusual public show of grief in 1997 after the death of the Princess of Wales raised eyebrows in a number of quarters and prompted sociologists, psychologists and other observers to engage in lengthy debates and discussions in the media. The British are a class-conscious nation; almost everyone one speaks with places herself or himself in one class or another. Moreover, they tend to conform to the ways of the social class to which they belong, rather than standing out from the rest of the crowd – from their accent, ways of eating and drinking, sports and other recreational habits, to the schools and universities they go to and the professions they engage in. While the British are also highly individualistic, they cannot be said to be so obsessive with individualism as the Americans are. The British, particularly the Scots, have a distinctive cultural heritage characterized by, among other things, a caring for the community. Contributions to various charitable organizations, participation in ad hoc group activities to help a fellow citizen out of financial or legal troubles, and similar community-related affairs are all manifestations of this individualism tempered with collectivism.

Direct comparisons between the two nations bring their similarities and differences into clearer focus. According to Hall and Hall (1990), American and British communication styles are sharply different from one another, even though both nations have low-context cultures (see Hall, 1977, for a discussion of high- and low-context cultures). Americans, for instance, prefer directness and are more expressive in communication. This is so to the extent that they are uncomfortable with indirect communication and tend to miss non-verbal cues, which means that they often miss a build-up of tension in people, and as a consequence fail to realise something is wrong until a crisis develops. By comparison, the British are more reserved and use long-winded, indirect expressions. Hofstede's (1980) study, shows that both UK and US cultures are highly individualistic, have a small power distance, are relatively masculine and relatively weak in uncertainty avoidance, albeit to varying degrees.

As individualistic nations the British and the Americans are, in theory, endowed with a high level of entrepreneurial and capitalist spirit (Weber, 1930). In practice, however, the entrepreneurial and 'go-getter' spirit seem to be far less present among the British compared to their American counterparts (Wiener, 1981). It is important to note that nearly two decades after Wiener's study, a wide difference between the two nations still persists, judging by the real-life situation and also social anthropologists' and organisational psychologists' view that the British are less ambitious, more averse to risk taking, less individualistic and less entrepreneurial than Americans. Besides, deep-rooted cultural characteristics do not change over a decade or two even though Britain was, largely in the 1980s, subjected to what some call a 'business-friendly' and some others a 'loads-of-money' culture.

Although part of a wider definition of 'culture', labour relations ought to be mentioned at this point, as there appears to be significant differences between the two nations in this regard which are relevant to the present study. Unionism is strong in the UK, particularly so in Scotland, where employees have traditionally voiced their views through labour unions (Tayeb, 1998). Union membership is industry- and craft-based and cuts across firms and organizations. As a result there are likely to be several unions in the same factory or office, bargaining not just with the employers but also with each other. Most large plants are still organized by a cluster of separate, partly competing unions (Tayeb, 1988, 1993). Moreover, industrial relations in Scotland, as elsewhere in the UK, is characterized by a them and us attitude. In most cases, reflecting the class-differentiating structure of the society, the relationship between management and workers is ridden with mistrust and hostility, emanating from a conflict of interests between the middle-class and the working-class.

Trade unions in the USA are less militant and more pragmatic than those in Britain (Perlman, 1970; Wheeler, 1993). Moreover, the class-conflict overtones which underline the British industrial culture are far less pronounced in the USA, perhaps because Americans are not as class-conscious as the British (see, for instance, Wheeler, 1993).

In addition, a vast majority of American employees work in the non-unionized sector, and the power of employers in both organized and non-organized sectors is very great in both political and economic spheres. Also, the opposition of employers to unions has been especially intense since the mid 1970s (Wheeler, 1993). There are, however, laws which protect employees' interests, notably the minimum wage legislation.

THE STUDY

Given the differences between the two nations as noted above, the question arises as to what the practical implications are for management and other business activities between these two countries. How do differences in cultural values, expectations and behaviours affect managerial and organizational aspects of American companies set up in the UK, such as inter-personal relationships, industrial relations, communication and co-ordination? The present study is an attempt to address these questions.

Three American companies were selected from a list of foreign manu-facturing firms located in the Lothian region within the industrial belt of central Scotland in order to control for locational factors. The limited time and financial resources were also a factor in deciding on the number of par-ticipating firms and their exact location. Of the three companies, two are wholly-owned subsidiaries and the third is a franchisee with close manage-rial and organizational links with the American headquarters. All three companies are long-established organisations in Scotland and, with the exception of one that has currently only one American expatriate working on their management team, both the management and the workforce are very much British in composition.

After a series of preliminary exploratory interviews it was decided to conduct a semi-structured interview programme, concentrating on the fol-lowing broad areas of management: human resource issues and labour rela-tions, inter-personal relationships and communication and organizational control and parent–subsidiary relations. We also explored the effect of the American 'input', introduced largely through the parent-company policies and the expatriates posted in Scotland, into the participating companies, and the local impression of and reaction to this input. We asked the inter-viewees to give us examples of behaviours and actions and tell us about stories, events, incidences involving their American colleagues here and in the USA, as well as the more formal working arrangements in their company. We also asked them to tell us about the past, especially when the American expatriates used to work in their company, and compare those days with the times when there were no Americans present.

Also, because senior mangers were far more likely to be in direct contact with parent-company officials and expatriates and to have first-hand ex-perience of their American colleagues' ways of doing things, we decided to interview senior managers and directors. As was mentioned above, of the three companies one still had a working American expatriate who also held a senior position, and we were able to secure his participation in the study. All in all, in each company between four and five directors and senior mangers were formally interviewed. Informal discussions were also held with them over meals and coffee breaks.

The interviews were taperecorded and subsequently transcribed. Rele-vant company documents, organizational charts and literature were also consulted. The results from these interviews, however, are arguably biased as they take into consideration only the views of senior management. Table 5.1 summarizes the background information on each company and highlights their principal features.

Table 5.1 The sample

	Wyman–Gordon Limited	Oceaneering Multiflex	Ethicon Limited
Origins (Parent location)	Wyman–Gordon Limited Boston, MA, USA	Oceaneering International Inc., Houston, Texas, USA	Johnson & Johnson, New Jersey, USA
Method of founding	Acquisition	Acquisition	Franchise
Year established	1966	1984	1915
Year of last acquisition/franchise	1994	1994	1947
Why Scotland?	Government grants; appropriate geological site	Strategic location to serve the North Sea market	Corporate strategy of global expansion
No. of employees	320	100	1 800
Total no. in whole corporation	3500+	2000	80 000
Main product(s)	Forgings and extrusions (components for industrial use)	Sub-sea control umbilical cables	Medical sutures
Main market(s)	Energy: Power generation, oil and gas markets throughout Europe and Asia Aerospace: England	Oilfield markets in the North Sea, Europe and Australasia	Domestic and foreign national governments, NHS and UK private hospitals
Industry	Energy and Aerospace	Sub-sea offshore field development	Wound closure segment in the health care industry
Production technology	Small batch	Small batch	Small batch/cell manufacturing

FINDINGS AND ANALYSIS

Inter-Personal Relations and Management Style

Wyman–Gordon Limited (W–G)

At W–G it is believed that there are significant cultural differences between a US and a UK company. It was the US culture that was prevalent throughout the subsidiary in the early years of its establishment in Scotland. This was no coincidence because during those years until 20 years ago, the top management was predominantly American. Since then, there has been virtually no American management on the scene and thus the company has naturally adapted to local conditions, resulting in a gradual change-over to more of a British-cultured organization. This culture change has been witnessed by the present Managing Director who joined the firm 15 years ago, and by the Production Manager who joined 29 years ago, and are illustrated with the following examples.

First, it was noted that there was a strong can-do attitude prevalent at W–G; that is, things were done without due consideration to the consequences in a spontaneous manner. This was something of a *culture shock* for most locals, since it contrasts sharply with the cautious, traditional and procedural ways of the British. Secondly, the budgetary behaviour: W–G was perceived by the market as a top-quality and high-cost company and this was backed up with a requirement to fulfil that image. For example, all employees travelled first-class and salesmen were provided with big, expensive cars. This has all changed most visibly and all unnecessary costs have been cut. This change in the general attitude of management has had a spillover effect, changing ways not only at the subsidiary level but also throughout the whole US corporation. Furthermore, as was mentioned earlier, the management style at W–G was perceived to be very American in the earlier years. The 'them-and-us' attitude was less prevalent than in other typically British companies. This is further discussed under the section of labour relations.

Initially the US expatriate managers at W–G in the 1970s were sent with the objective of supervising and directly controlling the subsidiary. As the company grew with increasing profit levels, the Americans were sent more for training purposes. Whatever the purpose, mutual interaction was required between the US managers and the Scottish workforce. As the Production Manager recalls, the general behaviour and attitudes of the Americans were very different from what the Scots were used to:

> One American manager was sitting in his office; the then Production Control manager approached him with his proposed forge plan on a sheet of paper. The American read it, carefully folded the piece of paper into a paper aeroplane, threw it out the doorway, and said 'follow it'.
>
> Another American was sitting working at his desk. There was a wall-mounted telephone next to him which kept ringing continuously. This annoyed the American terribly as it was distracting him from his work, and so he wrenched the telephone off the wall and shoved it in his desk drawer.

Initially these behavioural differences caused tension and unease. However, this did not last long, as they soon became accustomed to and accepted each others' ways, learning from each other in the process.

Oceaneering Multiflex (OM)

At OM significant cultural differences between US and UK organizations were identified by the present American expatriate Sales Manager. With his 10-year experience working at the Scottish site, the American manager has found two significant aspects at work that differed from the ways to which he was accustomed back home.

First, it was found that the British and the Europeans in general are far more socialistic, structured and procedure-oriented in the way in which they organize themselves. By contrast, the Americans tend to be more unstructured, informal and spontaneous in their organization. While these cultures work well within themselves it can be very frustrating for the foreigner who is used to doing things in a different manner. For example, there are Scottish expatriates currently working in the US office, where they reportedly find that tasks are actually completed before they want them to be done. They find this most frustrating, as they would have preferred to ensure they were done properly and correctly, by following the procedures 'according to the book'.

While it can be equally frustrating for the American expatriates in the UK, the structured procedure approach of the Europeans can sometimes be used to the Americans' advantage. The Americans can rest assured that the European will always play by the same rules, and they, on the other hand, may not. However it was recognized that there were mutual feelings of frustration on both sides. As the Sales Manager asserted,

> it is difficult to get people in a culture in which they can find themselves worthy of the system, and not fit into the system merely by procedures. When you ask them to do something outwith that procedure then they are unsure, because they're outside their working environment with which they are comfortable.

Secondly, it was observed at OM that the British are very resistant to change. Their strong traditional values contrast sharply with the American ways: more ready to make changes and innovate. Indeed the Americans can be viewed by the British as having no tradition whatsoever, being too spontaneous and too ready to make changes to everything and anything, even if it doesn't need changing. This was reportedly the view taken by one of the Scottish Managers in the company who went over to work in the US office. The Americans view change as a necessary and inevitable means to future growth and improvement, especially, and logically, if the traditional ways are not producing profitable results.

Ethicon Limited (EL)

EL is different from the other companies in the study in some respects. As a franchised firm, it has had no inward investment from the USA and no direct American management. It is very much a Scottish firm in its own right. However, EL is equally answerably to their US head office and encountered some interesting cultural differences.

At EL it is felt that in the past the Americans have tended to be rather insensitive to the diversity of cultural differences within Europe; the Europeans were viewed as one cultural mass, and more so with the developments of the European Single Market. Furthermore, they would generally assume and expect all foreigners to speak English, and that the British were effectively Americans speaking with a strange accent. However, this perceived naivety on the Americans' behalf is now changing and the parent company, Johnson & Johnson, are aiming to restructure their global activities and encourage multicultural training of managers. Recently they have embarked on management training programmes in which managers are moved around to work in different countries. In the early 1990s a programme was held in Switzerland, where 20 000 or so managers of all nationalities were brought together, with the aim of breaking down cultural barriers and eliminating stereotypical beliefs among international colleagues.

At EL it is believed that the Americans are far more bureaucratic in their organizations compared to the average British firm. Their legal environment imposes tight controls and their employment laws require an excessive amount of paperwork from the US companies. This may be related to their judiciary system and their cultural ways of being almost obsessive with litigation; it is necessary to have signatures on all paperwork in order to ensure that one's responsibility is not abused. Thus, there is overkill in the amount of work in writing to suppliers for confirmation of areas of responsibility. This initially caused a certain amount of difficulty, when the Americans attempted to impose their mentality by expecting this type of bureaucracy to be followed in all subsidiary units abroad.

As a result, EL has more paperwork throughout the Scottish organization than the average British company does, although somewhat less so than in the USA. As Jamieson (1980) would agree, Americans tend to be very formalized, with many written rules and procedures, and yet at the same time they appear to be very informal and non-bureaucratic.

Labour Relations and Human Resource Issues

Wyman–Gordon Limited (W–G)
Whereas in the USA managers would normally make long-term wage agreements with the unions and very little contact between them thereafter, in the UK there is continuous communication between them, with management frequently informing and even consulting their trade unions. In the early 1970s this caused a fraught reaction, as the Americans tried to hold on to their threatened authority, as they saw it. This resulted in a

strike, as US managers tried to impose their ways in the working relations with the unions, causing conflict and tension. A compromise was arrived at whereby the parent company got their way with a three-year wage deal and the trade unions expected continuous discussion.

Today W–G has a strong unionized shop and deals with one labour union, the AEEU (Amalgamated Electrical and Engineering Union), and one staff union, the MSFU (Manufacturing, Science and Finance Union). These have a purely representative role and have no power as such in controlling the activities of W–G. There is continuous communication between them to discuss relevant matters. The relationship is very co-operative and is viewed as being beneficial on the whole. For example, the three-year wage contract with the AEEU has helped both groups extensively by giving stability to working relations. Inevitably, as with any domestic or international business, there are always minor tensions, and these primarily involve disputes for overtime.

First, working schedules differ: the British are generally more flexible with working times. In the USA it is common to work on permanent shift – either night, back or day shift. Workers can progress through these shifts by degrees within the company; they allow someone of seniority to claim a job in another area of someone else's shift which is approved regardless of capabilities or skills. This practice would not be permitted by UK labour unions, where a system of three-week rotating shifts is in operation.

Secondly, W–G used to have a 'hire-and-fire' policy, which was dictated from head office; loyalty was not seen as a key element in management style. The concept of redundancy pay is not known in the USA, and they still would argue that redundancy costs are too high and unnecessary. However, they are learning from the local management who are naturally more familiar with what is acceptable here.

There are both advantages and disadvantages to be found in any location, according to the Managing Director of W–G. In Scotland the subsidiary enjoys a shop-floor workforce with a high level of skills and who are more flexible in working times compared to their US counterparts. However the Scottish workforce 'can also be very resistant to change, and this intransigence forms a barrier to progress'. There is also present within W–G, as the Managing Director admits as an inevitable occurrence in such a large organization, a 'them-and-us' attitude between management and workers. This is an ingrained conception that the local people have – always having seen management as 'a body of people with no name to it'. The management is perceived as 'all about names and people who make decisions and they ought to stand up and say who they are and take responsibility'. Although W–G have always had a single canteen for all employees, there are other visible signs which support the distinction between management and the workforce, especially manual workers. For example they have distinctly designated car parks, with senior management car spaces placed in ascending order at the front entrance to the building; each has his/her own space which, based on an implicit understanding by all employees, goes with the position they hold in the company. Thus, as employees get promoted up through the organization, they respectively move up in their car park spaces. The car parks, as the Production Manager recalls, have been organized in this way since the beginning and were even reorganized to accommodate the new arrangements when the main reception was relocated a few years ago.

However, it may be argued that this 'them-and-us' attitude among management and employees, which is normally more pronounced in the UK industry culture, was significantly less marked at W–G owing to the American influence. A comparison was made between W–G, in 1969 when the current Production Manager first joined, and a British company in the Glasgow shipyards, where he previously worked. There the culture was strongly characterized by this rigid distinction of management and workers. The canteen was split in two, with a posh end for the management with tablecloths and napkins; workers had to address managers as 'sir'; foremen wore bowler hats and formal dress; and managers were God-like figures whom the workers never really saw. At W–G it was all much more informal – one canteen for all; people spoke on a first-name basis regardless of their ranks; managers would carry out informal shop-floor rounds and would stop to chat with workers. However the managers would not go as far as the Americans, who deliberately dress down to further eliminate barriers between them and workers.

Oceaneering Multiflex (OM)

OM has always been a non-unionized organisation, and there have always been very good working relationships between workers and management. The workforce has never expressed the need for union membership, and management does not see any long-term benefits from it either. Although there does exist a 'them-and-us' attitude to a certain extent, there is no hostility and they have never experienced any significant problems in working relations. These relationships are maintained through close communication between all levels in the organization, with frequent meetings taking place, employee participation greatly encouraged and managers taking regular shop-floor rounds. Many of the management team, including the General Manager himself, have got to their present positions through a history of promotions all the way from the shop-floor level up through the ranks. This means they are more in tune as to what the specific problems and needs of the workers might be.

The General Manager believes that the labour unions can be effective up to a point. In the 1970s and the 1980s, the unions for example the miners' union, proved their usefulness and their influential capacity. However, after the main problems are successfully dealt with, he feels that ridiculous issues begin to arise which have only negative affects on business and working relationships. On a wider level, the General Manager believes that within the UK labour market there is the need for a stretching of resources. There is the need to move away from the rigid demarcation tendency to a more flexible approach to working patterns. For example, there is believed to be a general attitude in the UK industry that an apprentice or a machine fitter cannot do any electrical work or scaffolding, an attitude he feels should be changed.

Ethicon Limited (EL)

EL has always been a non-unionized company and has never felt the need for unionization, as working relationships are claimed to be trouble-free. Positive relations between management and workers are maintained and very much built on a basis of trust. Barriers such as a 'them-and-us' attitude are eliminated by organizing regular social events in which employees from all levels participate. They also have one canteen for all and a common car park with no demarcations.

However, there are certain areas where there have been conflicting ideas on human resource policies between local management and their American counterparts. Two areas were identified as causing particular tensions. First, there have been different attitudes towards the notion of pension funds. The Americans tend to view these funds as an asset of the company, and so place senior management in charge of its administration. The British, on the other hand, believe that pension funds belong to the members themselves, and therefore place the funds in a trust owned by the members. These contrasting points of view initially caused problems and encouraged a 'them-and-us' feeling between them. This was overcome by having US corporate managers directly involved and working alongside the local management team as trustees. This way, the Americans were able to see how the system actually worked in practice and increased their confidence in the local management's ability to run their own affairs. As a result cultural perspectives were shared and business life was made much easier at EL.

Secondly, there was a problem for the Americans to understand the ranking within the British benefits system, in particular that of private medical insurance. In the USA they have no public health service, and therefore medical insurance is rated number one in the benefits list of priorities. It was thus difficult for head office to appreciate that medical insurance did not rank not nearly as high, since the UK has the National Health Service.

Organizational Structure and Parent–Subsidiary Relations

Wyman-Gordon Limited (W–G)

In an attempt to improve co-ordination and control, W–G has adopted a cross-functional matrix organization which cuts across its traditional product-based structure. This structure is 'fluid and flexible' and promotes responsiveness to changing markets and technology requirements (Ronen, 1986). It reportedly improves customer focus and integrates technology capabilities. This complicated structure which spans its world-wide operations has a direct effect on management style, as it can lead to a duplication of resources, resulting in a loss of economies of scale and synergies. There is therefore a strong need for effective and efficient cross-functional communication and co-ordination, as the degree of ambiguity and stress increases (Wilson and Rosenfeld, 1990). This is achieved through efficient telecommunications and extensive travelling. The Managing Director spends 60 per cent of his time travelling between the UK, the USA and the Far East, and communicates on a daily basis with head office (HO).

While sales and marketing functions are centred at HO, the Scottish plant is its own international division in the operational sense, as it is the only non-US manufacturing unit for the energy products line. This means that the subsidiary has a high level of autonomy to make its own decisions requiring only tacit approval from HO through informal discussions. These decisions include order-taking, make-or-buy, capital investment, market extensions and product pricing. This decentralized approach would appear to be appropriate for W–G's product-functional-based structure and reduce the potential for conflict between the parent and the subsidiaries.

Control from HO is limited in the form of setting guidelines, rules of business conduct, approval rates and HRM policies which can be modified to accommodate differences in the UK industry. As in any business, HO sets overall annual budget forecast figures which have to be met; however, it is up to local management as to how these are to be achieved. Furthermore, major capital investments over £50 000 require formal approval from HO, as does the recruitment of new personnel.

With regard to written procedures dictated by HO, these are restricted to mere guidelines to ensure quality standards are maintained in accordance with ISO9001 and ISO9002 regulations. Corporate policies on sexual harassment, racial discrimination and divulgence of insider information are expected to be followed globally. Health and safety rules, conditions of employment and structural policies such as accounting convention are handed out by head office, and are then modified to comply with UK laws. Job descriptions and 'rule books' are also issued to employees. However, flexibility and responsiveness to local conditions are given priority at W–G.

Communication between HO and all units occurs on a frequent basis to ensure efficient co-ordination, which is critical owing to the complex structure of the organization. Subsidiaries are required to report monthly, in the form of financial reports, bookings and profit repatriations. On a daily basis informal discussions are held at all levels, and formal discussions of strategic issues are held every three months. These meetings and reporting systems are important means of communication, which 'serve the function of sharing information, making and reviewing policy decisions, spelling out rules, dividing and co-ordinating work and responsibilities' (Ronen, 1986: 309).

Oceaneering Multiflex (OM)
OM enjoys a large degree of autonomy to operate, work and govern their own business. As with all international companies the numerous subsidiaries have to work within their own confines. Each division is accountable for their own financial figures and business plans for each year, and they must then be able to justify this within the whole corporate scene. Certain deadlines, financial restrictions and schedules are imposed upon OM by their US head office.

Additionally, corporate-wide performance is monitored and controlled through an interactive system based on Management By Objectives (MBO). All subsidiaries within each line of business set their own targets, which are then submitted to HO for approval and reconciliation with corporate strategy. Each division is then accountable for achieving these approved targets, informally referred to by staff as 'MBOs'. These are then broken down internally within OM, where each department submits their own goals and targets in line with the MBOs.

In the manufacturing department co-ordination and compliance with the MBOs are done through a Continuous Improvement (CI) system. Here, all resources are pooled together and participation from all levels takes place, from the shop-floor labourers to the engineering managers. These are in effect, 'quality circles' which take place on a weekly basis for each project. A project manager, who reports back to the General Manager, monitors the outcome of the CI meetings. The General Manager then submits a monthly report to HO with details of on-going work, financial status on each project, what price these are at and how profits are being maintained between dips in operations.

As for the degree of formalization, the General Manager described the organization as both informal, in that open dialogue is actively encouraged between all levels, and formal, although not particularly bureaucratic, in that there are numerous written procedures and specifications. OM has quarterly meetings for senior management reviews and there is regular communication on a daily basis between OM and the HO. Although informal communication channels prevail within OM, communication media, such as e-mail, act as a barrier to achieving more personal communication since it tends to cocoon people away in their offices. Written procedures mainly come in the form of the MBOs and ISO9001 quality assurance regulations to which they are accredited.

Ethicon Limited (EL)

As EL's parent company, Johnson & Johnson, has become increasingly global in its operations, it has identified the need to establish a more centralized form of control, as it can no longer maintain its traditionally decentralized approach. Furthermore, the 'short-termism' of the US stock market has made the corporation increasingly sensitive to short-term results when translated into US dollars. Thus, although still relying on a long-term strategy for growth, it is necessary for short-term results to be delivered. All this means that greater central control is necessary. Consequently, all subsidiaries and franchised firms are receiving much more control in the way of corporate standards and procedures. These are written by HO and are expected to be followed by all subsidiaries and franchised branches.

The Company Secretary of EL views these written procedures as basically good business practice and not to have caused any tensions or conflict. For example, there are numerous legal specifications, hygiene standards and corporate policies to follow.

One such policy is concerned with the involvement in the local community. As a result, EL and its employees are actively involved in community relations, whereby they raise funds such as the Charity Fund for medical needs and the Philanthropic Fund, which aids projects for the needy within Europe, and they also provide management techniques and training for local hospitals. As well as these written procedures and policies, EL, like any other subsidiary, must meet financial targets and levels of profit forecasts set by HO. Everything is measured against an agreed Business Plan which covers all aspects and is agreed upon with corporate management at the end of the previous year. This high degree of tight control may be the result of its franchise status. However EL does retain its autonomy to the extent that it can make its own decisions, on the basis of the Business Plan, concerning local elements of the business, for example product pricing in the domestic market and capital expenditure up to a certain level.

EL is also structured on a cross-functional matrix approach, sharing auxiliary service functions, such as information technology (IT), finance and personnel, with its sister companies located in Europe. In order to save duplication of costs and resources for the same market, EL and its European sisters specialize in different products and production technologies.

To What Extent Do These Differences Affect Business?

W–G's Managing Director's view is a fair representation of those of all other managers interviewed in the study. He believes the differences in culture pose no serious problems for the multinational business. This multicultural dimension, he argues, is beneficial to the company and to a certain extent differentiates it in Europe. Although the subsidiary is almost entirely Scottish in its composition of the workforce, it is heavily influenced by the

USA – for example, in training procedures and investment policies. The extent to which this produces beneficial or adverse affects for business depends entirely on the local managers in charge of the subsidiary. The USA will issue rules and regulations that apply to all units, but unless these are questioned, monitored and adapted to local conditions by local management they will not work. He therefore believes that there ought to be an on-going interpretation and adaptation of HO policies on the local level. This would not happen so easily if the local management were American; he believes that the Americans would not be fully familiar with the cultural factors involved and would thus lead to misunderstandings. He finds that although the Americans do have very good ideas, there do exist 'silly rules', which he would be reluctant to apply solely to conform with the US head office. The Managing Director of W–G concludes that

> to establish business in a foreign country requires that you must adapt to that culture in order to survive. However you must identify two or three key elements which differentiate you or identifies you as the host or inward investor, and make sure that they are instilled in the company. For W–G these were: top product quality, process control and, more recently, cost reduction. Technology was also a differentiating factor, which was brought over from the US initially. The rest of the time you have to fit in.

Furthermore, W–G's Managing Director believes that there are no significant cultural barriers encountered in bilateral communications between the USA and the UK, and that misunderstandings are just as likely to occur between Livingston (Scotland) and Boston as they are between Livingston and London.

The Company Secretary of EL believes the secret of working with the USA is actually getting them involved and working alongside each other. He further adds:

> To avoid problems, the key factor is *communication* and a recognition of the particular problems facing different markets. If the corporate centre, in this case the US head office, does not view everyone as 'Americans with strange accents', then it will prosper. Furthermore, in order to ensure a global organisation has a global perspective on its market, that being the 'world', non-US citizens should be placed into senior management posts (respondent's emphasis).

DISCUSSION AND CONCLUDING REMARKS

This chapter has investigated certain managerial and organizational aspects of three American subsidiaries operating in Scotland in an attempt to examine the implications of American and British cultures for such cross-border partnerships between the two nations. The study revealed that, notwithstanding similarities between the two cultures, significant differences do exist between the UK and the USA which have direct implications for the work environment. This has provided both the American and the British managers with many challenges in co-ordination, control and communication. It has also provided both sides with the opportunity to learn from each other and benefit in this way in the long term.

On the whole the study has confirmed that most of the cultural differences and their implications are visible and important for the companies investigated, and in some cases they have created a certain degree of tension and frustration. The British culture places a great emphasis on flexibility, reflected in many aspects of their life, from their famous unwritten constitution to bending the law when it does not suit them, to their common law legal system, to their shop-floor shift-work arrangements. This clashed visibly, within the confines of the companies studied, with the American culture, with its emphasis on formal rules and procedures. This is a culture characterized by, among others, a written constitution, clearly defined roles and functions, minutely spelled-out and legally enforced business contracts and a greater use of written formal rules; a culture which took up Weber's (1947) bureaucratic model and worked it into a model of professionalism. At the same time, paradoxically, the informality and high spiritedness of the American entrepreneurial culture caused frustrations among the British employees who wished to do their work at a pace which would allow them to ensure the work was done according to the rule book.

There were other aspects of the two cultures which have left their imprints on the companies investigated: class distinction and its reflection within the workplace in the form of hostile management–employee relations and a relatively strong trade union tradition in the UK, and a more blurred demarcation between management and rank and file, at least in terms of symbolism and outward signs, in the USA. These cultural differences and clashes, in any case, do not appear to have stood as significant barriers which could hinder cross-border business between the two countries, perhaps because of similarities and mutual understanding which exist between them rooted in close historical, social and political links.

None of the three companies has found great difficulty in overcoming the cultural differences identified. Furthermore, the study demonstrated that the American MNCs' preferred way of organizing and controlling their subsidiaries in Scotland was to delegate as much autonomy as possible to the local management.

It is also evident from these three cases that there are both convergent and divergent forces taking part in the shaping of organizations and their management. The divergent forces are clearly visible in the case of W–G, where significant culture changes have taken place during its operations in

Scotland. This firm was, from its very founding, an American-owned subsidiary. In its early years, the organization was successfully 'Americanized', with the powerful influence of having US expatriate managers controlling its operations. However, over the years W–G has learned that in order to survive they had to adapt to the local culture. This naturally resulted in the replacement of the Americans with UK nationals in the management team, and consequently the organization was transformed into more of a British firm. These findings clearly show that local environmental forces and the national culture of the host country, which are reflected in the general attitude, values, behaviour and expectations of the people employed within the firm, are responsible for the divergence the company took in organizing and managing its resources.

Each culture is very different in various aspects which are outlined in the study and, translated into the workplace behaviour, both work well within their own system. However, with the increasing globalizing trend of the business world, this means that cultures must interact with one another and work together. Although in this case study this inter-cultural process has not appeared to cause any major upsets, perhaps because of the common Anglo-grouping of the two cultures, it can naturally be a difficult and frustrating process. This is where the converging forces tend to take effect, aiming at minimizing these difficulties and controlling foreign operations. The natural desire for an international manager is to make his/her work easier by converging business practices across global operations. This is evident from the study where in all three cases there is an extensive amount of written rules and procedures from HO. With the increasing trend of globalization, this tendency may accelerate the converging forces.

Finally, it is also important to note that some of the clashes and tensions observed in the cases studied here could have in part been a reflection of the distinctive management styles and organizational ways of doing things specific to the individual companies. Moreover, these companies are subsidiaries of large multinational firms with a widespread geographical and production reach. As a result, the magnitude of complexity that they face in managing their internal organizational matters, such as co-ordination, integration, differentiation and control, brings with it its own imperatives. These, in turn, are bound to cause frictions, tensions and frustrations in their own right alongside those which might have their roots in national cultures of the parent companies and their Scottish subsidiaries.

6 Globalization of Technology and the Movement of Scientific Personnel in MNEs in Europe

Marina Papanastassiou, Robert Pearce and George Anastassopoulos

INTRODUCTION

In this chapter, we examine the movement of scientific personnel involved in Research and Development (R&D) within multinational enterprises (MNEs). Traditional theories on foreign direct investment (FDI) and the MNE view, in general, any transfer of any form of knowledge as a one-way centrifugal movement (Dunning, 1988). Thus knowledge is centrally created (within the headquarters of a limited number of home countries) and then is transferred to the periphery of MNE groups (i.e. subsidiaries) in order to assist in the realization of production and marketing plans of MNEs. Pioneering work by Ronstadt (1977, 1978) and Behrman and Fischer (1980) and some recent research has shown that this trend in MNEs is more or less obsolete (Papanastassiou and Pearce, 1995, 1996, 1997, 1998). Papanastassiou and Pearce have shown in previous work that MNEs have a globalized perspective on technology which is closely related to the different roles of MNE subsidiaries. Although MNEs try to internalize most of their creative resources through the development of internal linkages, many external linkages are also developed in order to make more efficient the creation and spread of these assets. In this chapter, we examine some aspects of the creation of internal linkages in the creation and emission of technology within MNE groups. Competitive demands and the so-called 'globalization of production' has urged a parallel trend in the globalization of R&D and technology (Dunning, 1994). MNE groups are not viewed as monolithic organizations but as complex networks where different parts assume different responsibilities. R&D and technology contribute to this complexity, which in turn affects the decentralization and networking of technology (Bartlett and Ghoshal, 1990). Adopting some of the well established terminology on the different roles of overseas R&D laboratories we discern the following: support laboratories (SLs), locally integrated laboratories (LILs) and internationally interdependent laboratories (IILs).

Another – and in many cases complementary – potential source of innovation can come from the host-country environment – i.e. from universities, other firms, research institutes, etc. Different views on the orientation and form of strategic positioning of R&D can determine different roles for overseas subsidiaries. In the case of centralization of R&D capacity subsidiaries are usually involved in the production of mature and standardized goods. This type of subsidiary is called a truncated miniature replica (TMR). Another type of subsidiary related to the centralization of R&D is the rationalized product subsidiary (RPS) which is involved in the production of intermediary goods. The final type of subsidiary is the world or regional product mandate (WPM/RPM) which is related to genuine decentralization of technology as it is involved in the production of new innovative products using its own R&D laboratory, usually an LIL.

In this chapter we will present some evidence on MNE operations in four European countries – Belgium, Greece, Portugal and the UK (Papanastassiou, 1995). Data on these subsidiaries were obtained through a postal questionnaire survey research conducted in 1993–4. The number of questionnaires sent out was 533. Out of the 145 responses received 99 were in the UK, 16 in Greece, 20 in Belgium and 10 in Portugal. The data are presented in the form of frequencies, which give us the differences among industries, home countries and host countries, and average response rates, which give us degree of importance.

RESULTS

In analyzing the movement of scientific personnel within MNE groups we accept that this movement will be from and towards the centre as an effective response to the pressures of globalization of production (Haug *et al.*, 1983; Pearce and Singh, 1992).

Movement and Roles of Scientific Personnel

Questions in the survey tried to capture the quantitative aspect of the movement of scientific personnel, in terms of percentages, and then to provide some qualitative elements with regard to what the personnel does. We would expect that following the tradition of a product cycle model (Vernon, 1966), foreign companies involved in FDI will 'export' their personnel in key positions at least for a certain amount of time. But as subsidiaries gain deeper roots in their host economies this commitment will be diminishing as well. According to our sample we would also expect that high-technology industries would require parent-company scientific personnel more often than medium-technology and low-technology industries, and also that subsidiaries in Other Europe (i.e. Greece, Belgium and Portugal)

would be more likely to make frequent use of such home-country personnel in scientific operations.

In investigating the roles of such home-country scientific personnel three
potential roles were identified: (a) managerial, (b) scientific and (c) a combination of both scientific and managerial duties. Participation in scientific
roles was more prevalent, with 46 replies, while managerial followed with
43 replies and participation in both roles with 40 replies. The findings, in
Table 6.1, show that, by sectoral grouping, medium- and low-technology
industries have little difference in the use of home-country personnel in
the scientific work of the laboratory, but both were somewhat below the
high-technology grouping. Using home-country personnel to organize the
laboratory's programme of work may be somewhat more prevalent in
medium- and low-technology than high-technology sectors. Participating in
both roles is somewhat more common in high-technology sectors. Perhaps

Table 6.1 Proportion of scientific personnel of subsidiary laboratories that come from
the home country of the MNE, per cent

	Home-country personnel in laboratory employment			
	0	*1–49*	*50 and over*	*Total*
Sector				
High-technology industries[a]	33.3	33.3	33.3	100.0
Medium-technology industries[b]	50.0	18.8	31.3	100.0
Low-technology industries[c]	60.0	10.0	30.0	100.0
Total	43.2	24.7	32.1	100.0
Home country				
USA	53.7	4.9	41.5	100.0
Japan	10.0	80.0	10.0	100.0
Europe[d]	31.0	34.5	27.6	100.0
Total	43.2	24.7	32.1	100.0
Host country				
UK	44.6	28.6	26.8	100.0
Other Europe[e]	40.0	16.0	44.0	100.0
Total	43.2	24.7	32.1	100.0

Notes:
a Covers: telecommunications, scientific instruments, electronics and electrical appli-
   ances, automobiles and pharmaceuticals.
b Covers: rubber, petroleum food and drink and industrial chemicals.
c Covers: building materials, mechanical engineering, metal manufacture and products
   and other manufacturing.
d Covers: subsidiaries of European MNEs in countries other than the home country.
e Covers: subsidiaries in Belgium, Greece and Portugal.

the nature of the roles in high-technology industries (more integrated within the group and with local science) makes it somewhat less desirable, less necessary or less feasible to separate the managerial and bench-research roles. On a home-country level US firms tend to employ home personnel more often or not at all in their overseas scientific operations, especially when focusing on the managerial role (Table 6.2).

Other results in Table 6.2 show that Japanese firms tend to have a continuous presence of home personnel abroad, and particularly in playing both roles. This may be associated with the fact that Japanese companies are relatively new so they may need parent supervision and, therefore, with the less deep overseas technological tradition of these subsidiaries. On a host-country level, the Other Europe group presents a stronger presence of home-country personnel than the UK (Table 6.1), with a stronger result in the 'over 50 per cent' category. In the Other Europe group, the key role of home-country personnel is to organize the laboratory's programme of work (Table 6.2), indicating that less actual pure scientific work needs to be done in the laboratories of these subsidiaries and more concern is placed on how to integrate these laboratories effectively with other local operations.

Three types of movement of host-country personnel were examined; (a) to the parent, (b) to another R&D laboratory of the MNE group and (c) to another host-country R&D facility (Haug *et al.*, 1983). For all industries host-country scientific personnel is moved to the parent quite extensively (Table 6.3), with pharmaceuticals, food and drink, petroleum and other manufacturing showing above-total average response. Movement to other MNE laboratories also appears as a strong choice, showing the networking of scientific linkages not only from and towards the parent but also from and towards the other parts of the 'periphery' of the MNE group. Thus peripheral R&D linkages are also important in the decentralization of R&D as they promote a more genuine version of technological internationalization. Pharmaceuticals and the food and drink sector tend to be more sensitive to this option. Though movements of personnel to host-country laboratories are rare they are again of above-average relevance in pharmaceuticals, food and drink and petroleum. This suggests that the intra-group linkages of these laboratories complement linking into the local science base. Our view of a fully global technological strategy would imply this course of action. Automobiles have above average local institution personnel links, though relatively few within the group, and mechanical engineering has a limited movement of personnel in general. European firms opt for the peripheral movement slightly more often than USA MNEs and clearly more than Japanese companies. The above-average movement of US laboratories' personnel to 'other MNE laboratories' could indicate a European strategy and consequently the treatment of Europe as a separate region with distinct demand and supply conditions.

Table 6.2 Roles of home-country scientific personnel in MNE subsidiary laboratories, per cent

Sector	Roles of home-country personnel								
	Mainly to organize the laboratory's programme of work			*Mainly to participate in the scientific work of the laboratory*			*To participate in both roles*		
	Less than 10	*10–49*	*50 and over*	*Less than 10*	*10–49*	*50 and over*	*Less than 10*	*10–49*	*50 and over*
High-technology industries[a]	69.6	13.0	17.4	45.8	12.5	41.7	52.2	13.0	34.8
Medium- and low-technology industries[b]	65.0	5.0	30.0	50.0	13.6	36.4	64.7	7.5	35.3
Total	67.4	9.3	23.3	47.8	13.0	39.1	57.5	7.5	35.0
Home country									
USA	52.6	15.8	31.6	36.8	15.8	47.4	58.8	5.9	35.3
Japan	88.9	11.1	11.1	88.9		11.1	44.4	11.1	44.4
Europe[c]	73.3	6.7	20.0	47.8	16.7	44.4	64.3	7.1	28.6
Host country									
UK	75.0	7.1	17.9	51.7	6.9	41.4	64.0	4.0	32.0
Other Europe[d]	53.3	13.3	33.3	41.2	23.5	35.3	46.7	13.3	40.0

Notes:
a See Table 6.1.
b See Table 6.1.
c Covers: subsidiaries of European MNEs in countries other than the home country.
d Covers: subsidiaries in Belgium, Greece and Portugal.

Table 6.3 Frequency of movement of host-country personnel to other scientific laboratories

	Average response[a]		
	Parent (i.e. home-country laboratories)	Other MNE group laboratories	Other host-country R&D facility
Industry			
Food and drink	2.12	2.00	1.29
Industrial and agricultural chemicals	1.83	1.47	1.21
Pharmaceuticals and consumer chemicals	2.21	2.07	1.33
Electronics and electrical appliances[b]	1.69	1.50	1.27
Mechanical engineering	1.57	1.33	1.00
Metal manufacture and products	1.75	1.75	1.25
Petroleum	2.00	2.00	1.33
Automobiles	1.60	1.44	1.33
Other manufacturing[c]	2.00	1.67	1.19
Home country			
USA	1.77	1.71	1.24
Japan	1.82	1.33	1.29
Europe[d]	2.03	1.76	1.28
Host country			
UK	1.76	1.56	1.22
Other Europe[e]	2.09	1.88	1.32
Total	1.86	1.66	12.50

Notes:

a Respondents were asked to evaluate movement of personnel to each type of facility as occurring frequently, occasionally or never. The average response was then calculated by allocating responses of frequently the value of 3, occasionally the value of 2 and never the value of 1.

b Includes computers and telecommunications.

c Includes building materials, instruments, rubber, miscellaneous.

d Covers: subsidiaries of European MNEs in countries other than the home country.

e Covers: subsidiaries in Belgium, Greece and Portugal.

The strong average response of European MNEs regarding their movement towards the parent suggests a centripetal strategy with less evident signs of a genuine decentralization strategy. Japanese firms also seem to depend technologically on the skills developed in central laboratories. On a host-country level it is obvious that the diversified technological dependence of laboratories located in the Other Europe group contrasted with the stronger technological position of R&D laboratories located in the UK.

The fact that the movement of scientific personnel towards host-country facilities is limited could indicate the internationalization of R&D and the 'elimination' of geographical boundaries, could enable firms to emphasize the transfer of their scientific personnel in their world-wide operations (Pearce and Singh, 1992).

Explaining the Intra-firm Movement of Scientific Personnel

The following four possibilities were examined as reasons behind the movement of host-country personnel; (a) training, (b) improvement of knowledge of existing MNE technology, (c) participation in the R&D programme in another MNE laboratory and (d) part of an exchange programme (Table 6.4). We could associate (a) with basic skill needs but also, in the long run, with less dynamic subsidiaries and with either strong centralized R&D creation or with the presence of other strong peripheral R&D centres. Option (c) could be strongly explained as a genuine part of R&D internationalization, where a final high-technology product is achieved as a group-level effort in which subsidiaries play substantial integrated roles supported by personnel movement. On the other hand choice (b) may suggest technological dependence of the subsidiaries in question. Finally, (d) may suggest the existence of adoption of initiatives developed outside the MNE group such as government intervention, etc.

The most prominent reason is found to be (b), with 38.5 per cent of the total replies. The fact that (c) is the second most important factor (32.2 per cent) indicates more clearly that subsidiaries are going through a creative transition. Training comes third with 23.1 per cent of all replies, indicating that once parents establish subsidiaries, and as subsidiaries assume more complicated roles than those in the past and as the infrastructure in the host-economies improves (e.g. education), they do not need to transfer personnel so extensively. The most distinctive results for the home country are for Japan, especially the very high value of the transfer of personnel for improvement on the knowledge of existing MNE-group technology. Taken with their low valuation of personnel transfer to participate in group R&D programmes, this suggests the Japanese subsidiary laboratories are still more locked into current technology, and less likely than US labs, in particular, to be supporting their subsidiaries' aim in creative transition. Subsidiaries in industries like food and drink, industrial chemicals, electronics and other manufacturing are clearly in a creative transition. Pharmaceuticals and automobiles seem to be also in a clear evolutionary process, while mechanical engineering and petroleum have a more traditional attitude towards transfer of personnel, with training retaining a strong position. European companies and those in Other Europe, weigh more significantly reason (d); this can perhaps be explained as partly owing to the European Union (EU) initiatives which support these companies and countries. Sub-

Table 6.4 Reasons for movement of host-country scientific personnel to other institutions, per cent

Industry	Reasons[a] (percentage)			
	A	B	C	D
Food and drink	21.4	42.9	35.7	
Industrial and agricultural chemicals	27.8	27.8	33.3	11.1
Pharmaceuticals and consumer chemicals	23.1	42.3	23.1	11.5
Electronics and electrical appliances[b]	17.9	39.3	35.7	7.1
Mechanical engineering	37.5	25.0	37.5	
Metal manufacture and products		50.0	50.0	
Petroleum	37.5	25.0	25.0	12.5
Automobiles	25.0	50.0	25.0	
Other manufacturing[c]	20.0	40.0	36.0	4.0
Home country				
USA	21.5	36.9	36.9	4.6
Japan	17.6	52.9	23.5	5.9
Europe[d]	27.6	36.2	27.6	8.6
Host country				
UK	19.8	39.5	38.3	2.5
Other Europe[e]	27.4	37.1	24.2	11.3
Total	23.1	38.5	32.2	6.3

Notes:
Reasons for movement of scientific personnel:
A Predominately to train them for the work in the host-country laboratory.
B To improve their knowledge of existing MNE technology.
C To participate in R&D programme in the other MNE group laboratories.
D Part of an exchange programme with other scientific organizations.

a Respondents were asked to tick the most relevant case.
b Includes computers and telecommunications.
c Includes building materials, instruments, rubber, miscellaneous.
d Covers: subsidiaries of European MNEs in countries other than the home country.
e Covers: subsidiaries in Belgium, Greece and Portugal.

sidiaries in the UK are more involved in group technology (either acquiring it (b), or helping especially to create it (c)) through personnel exchange than those in Other Europe. Subsidiaries in Other Europe have more need to transfer personnel for scientific training. This reflects the UK's stronger scientific background generally and also the more creative roles of subsidiaries in the UK.

Econometric Tests of the Movement of Scientific Personnel

The movement of scientific personnel was investigated in regression tests. Two parallel sets of regressions were run, one including the roles of laboratories among the independent variables and the second including the sources of technology used in subsidiaries' operations. The set of independent variables include industry and country dummies, those that indicate roles of laboratories – i.e. *ADAPT* (indicating an SL role), *DEVEL* (indicating an LIL role) and *GROUPRAD* (indicating an IIL role) – those that show sources of technology – i.e. *IMPTECH* (for imported technology), *HOSTTECH* (for technology created in the host country) and *SUBRAD* (for technology created in the subsidiary) – and finally a set of quantitative variables including *SALES* (representing the absolute size of a subsidiary in terms of the $ million value of its sales), *RELSIZE* (indicating the relative size of a subsidiary in the form of its share of total MNE-group sales), *EXPRAT* (the percentage of a subsidiary's production that is exported), *INTRAEXP* (the share of a subsidiary's exports that go to another part of its own MNE group) and finally *INTEREXP* (the share of a subsidiary's exports that comprise intermediate products).

As an econometric technique OLS is used, although the dependent variable was a qualitative one. In theory, the PROBIT estimation method is a more appropriate technique because it provides more accurate estimates of probability values which is useful for prediction purposes. However, as the basic reason for these econometric estimations was to test the degree of significance of the independent variables on the dependent and not to make predictions, the OLS method is preferred (Casson *et al.*, 1991). Preliminary calculations using PROBIT showed almost identical results to the OLS case.

The first dependent variable was movement of personnel to the parent laboratory. This is strongly positively related (Table 6.5) to situations where the R&D laboratory role is either SL involved in adaptation (*ADAPT*), or an IIL involved in pre-competitive research (*GROUPRAD*). In the first case the laboratory will probably seek the parent's expertise to increase familiarity with the product technology that needs to be adapted. In the second case the laboratory belongs more to a basic research network where obviously the parent laboratories are central, so that personnel movement is crucial to the effective integration of the network's research operations and concerns. The positive strong results on these two variables endorse the previous arguments.

The second dependent variable tested was movement of scientific personnel to other (i.e. non-parent) group laboratories. This test is very significant because it tells about the technological boundaries in MNE groups and shows the end of a dominance for the one-way parent subsidiary transfer, with movements around the periphery becoming very important and showing the existence of creative group networks in science. The positive sign on *RELSIZE* shows that laboratories from the relatively large subsidiaries are most involved in this type of 'peripheral movement', probably connecting with similar R&D laboratories in complementary programmes

Table 6.5 Regressions with movement of scientific personnel as dependent variables (only significant results are presented)

	Personnel moved to parent		Personnel moved to other group laboratory		Personnel moved to host-country institutions	
Intercept	0.7841 (1.42)	2.5252*** (4.31)	1.1309* (1.98)	1.9845*** (3.77)	0.2100 (0.35)	1.5582** (2.66)
Electronics and electrical engineering	−0.6852** (−2.44)	−0.7255** (−2.65)		−0.6095** (−2.51)		
Industrial and agricultural chemicals				−0.3484* (−1.72)		
Pharmaceuticals and consumer chemicals						
UK		−0.4117* (−1.92)		−0.4385** (−2.23)		
Japan						0.5531** (2.05)
SALES					0.005** (2.25)	
RELSIZE			0.0104* (1.73)			
EXPRAT			−0.0066** (−2.39)	−0.0067** (−2.47)		
INTRAEXP			0.0078*** (2.91)	0.0071*** (2.91)		
ADAPT	0.2805** (2.46)		0.3143*** (2.56)			
GROUPRAD	0.4187*** (4.06)		0.3107*** (2.98)		0.3066*** (2.77)	
HOSTTECH				0.1925** (2.07)		
SUBRAD				0.2121** (2.38)		
R^2	0.6040	0.3837	0.6203	0.5496	0.5071	0.2810
F	2.36**	1.46	2.61***	2.75***	1.39	0.80
n	52	68	53	66	48	62

Notes:
*** Significant at 1 per cent; ** significant at 5 per cent; * significant at 10 per cent.

and/or assisting the operations of weaker laboratories in the region. The presence of this type of movement is negatively related to the subsidiaries' degree of export orientation (*EXPRAT*) but positively related to the proportion of those exports which do occur that are traded intra-group (*INTRAEXP*).

The negative sign on *EXPRAT* suggests that rationalized product (RP) operations do not need to support their use of existing technology by movement of scientific personnel and that RPM/WPM subsidiaries do not need to transfer personnel to gain assistance for their efforts. Once this is taken into account, however, group interdependency does surface in the fact that intra-group exports are more likely to generate such movement than extra-group (positive sign on *INTRAEXP*). Against that background the positive sign on *ADAPT* is likely to imply support for the adaptation of product/processes to host-country (rather than export) markets.

The positive sign on *GROUPRAD* again (for the first dependent variable) shows high movement of personnel in labs playing a role in group research programmes. By source of technology used in subsidiaries, scientific personnel movement is strongest in these using host-country technology and their own R&D results. Thus the movement reflects the possession of knowledge already in the subsidiary and may therefore be motivated by the transfer of it to other subsidiaries, which may be technologically weaker or may possess complementary knowledge. These results would certainly suggest that movement of personnel 'to improve their knowledge of existing group technology' is more as a complement to their own creative efforts than an attempt to absorb it in a submissive (dependent) manner.

Finally the last regression investigates movement of personnel to host-country scientific institutions as a dependent variable. As this type of movement has been seen as relatively weaker, the regressions are less able to reveal strong factors behind it when it does occur. Once again labs involved in group-level (basic) research programmes (*GROUPRAD*) are most likely to do it, as are laboratories associated with large subsidiaries.

CONCLUSION

Overall the results support the view that technology creation and use in MNEs is now very much associated with integrated scientific networks supported by multi-directional personnel movement. MNEs use their internalized channels extensively in order to create and distribute technological inputs throughout their operations. In the case of transfer of the human capital input its roles vary according to the level and type of technological independence of the overseas subsidiary. Thus some of this personnel movement is associated with adaptation where this is necessary (i.e. *ADAPT* is significant for the first two dependent variables in the regressions, but not the third), suggesting some personnel movements may help to adapt for the local market technology from elsewhere in the group. There is also a clear suggestion that it often occurs from a position of creative strength. Thus personnel movement is not generally associated with the issue of imported technology (*IMPTECH* is always negative signed in the regressions), but more often positively associated with technological capability and ambition in the subsidiary (notably the persistent positive significance of *GROUPRAD* in the regressions).

These results, in turn, indicate the need to accept a new theoretical perspective regarding the creation and transmission of technology which contradicts the centralized view advocated in theoretical models such as the product cycle. To be more precise, theories of industrial organization in combination with strategic approaches to the MNE (as was outlined in this chapter) can provide a sound theoretical background in the understanding of the current and future issues involved in the globalization of production. Finally, following Dunning's investment development path theory (Dunning and Narula, 1996) it is evident that such movement of scientific personnel is associated with the ownership advantages of foreign firms which, in turn, provide a potential framework for the upgrading of the location advantages of host economies. If the desired goal of governments is to 'help' their countries to promote the development of *created assets* then one way of doing this is to encourage FDI that is associated with genuine technology creation.

Part Two

European Dimensions of Multinational Subsidiary Operations

7 Subsidiary Strategy and Regional Economic Impact: A Conceptual Framework

Louise Hurdley and Neil Hood

INTRODUCTION

The globalization of the world economy has stimulated extensive litera-ture on multinational enterprises (MNEs) since the early 1960s (Dunning, 1997). Researchers from several disciplines, including economics (Hymer, 1960/1976), politics (Servan-Schreiber, 1967) and management have been fascinated by the MNE phenomenon for several decades (Birkinshaw and Hood, 1998). More recently, this extensive MNE theoretical platform has generated a stream of research on MNE subsidiaries, much of which dates back to Garnier (1982). The work ranges from examining the headquarters–subsidiary relationship (Hedlund, 1981), through to the role of the subsidiary (White and Poynter, 1984), and subsidiary evolution (Egelhoff *et al.*, 1998). It is clear that foreign subsidiaries have a critical role to play in the success of the MNE (Birkinshaw and Hood, 1998), in terms of both selling the firm's products internationally and high value-added activities such as R&D. The study of MNE subsidiaries has thus emerged as a valid research topic in its own right.

One of the most frequent and persistently asked questions about MNE activity, both by ordinary people (*Economist*, 1993; Rapoport, 1993) and by policy makers is: 'Is its impact on economic welfare a good or bad thing?' (Dunning, 1993). This is often followed by: 'If it is good, how can it be made even better?' (Young *et al.*, 1994). The economic impact of foreign direct investment (FDI) on host countries is well documented (Koopman and Montias, 1971; Dunning, 1977; Porter, 1990) but less attention has been paid to the impact of MNE activity at the regional level. For the purpose of this chapter, it is useful to define a region in relation to regional economic policy. A system is presented in which there are three gradations of region; macro, micro and subordinate region. This study concentrates on the subordinate region that comprises districts within countries, such as the North East and the East Midlands in England. Young *et al.* (1994) summarize and synthe-size the different strands of literature relating to MNEs and regional eco-nomic development, with particular reference to the European Community

(EC). They conclude (1994: 669) that 'further work is needed to identify the comparative impacts of the wide range of subsidiaries typically operating in regions and countries across Europe'. Several categories are singled out as worthy of further investigation, including new entrants versus established subsidiary. This study takes a qualitative approach to investigate the impacts of new entrants in the UK, in order to progress our understanding of MNE subsidiaries and regional economic impact. This will provide a platform for comparative work with established subsidiaries as suggested by Young *et al.* (1994).

This chapter is part of a larger project that examines the subsidiary strategy and regional economic impact of Japanese automotive transplants in the UK. This particular sector was chosen for examination because of the scale of Japanese direct investment in the UK economy (with 247 Japanese manufacturers in the UK in 1997, which represents 30 per cent of the EU total, JETRO, 1998), and the importance of the automotive sector to regional, national and global economies (Womack *et al.*, 1990). In addition, Japanese direct investment in the UK is a relatively recent phenomenon (Dicken, 1988; Morris, 1988) and hence the subsidiaries can be classified as new entrants. The objectives of the study are twofold. First, to establish the type of subsidiary strategy (defined by determinants identified in the existing literature on subsidiary strategy) adopted by the Japanese-owned car manufacturing plants in the UK. Secondly, to examine the regional economic impact (using criteria set out in previous studies) of these affiliates. This will allow us to suggest recommendations for policy makers on attracting and developing appropriate FDI to maximize the positive economic impact of MNE subsidiaries at the regional level.

The next section outlines the theoretical context of the study by looking at the literature on the internationalization of business, MNE subsidiary strategy and the consequences of MNE activity. The conceptual framework is followed by the specific research questions. Attention is then turned towards the empirical work and there is a discussion on the preliminary findings. Finally, the chapter concludes with policy implications.

LITERATURE REVIEW

There are three stages to the literature review as shown in Figure 7.1. First, the literature on the *internationalization of business* was reviewed to provide a contextual background for Japanese direct investment in the UK, and more specifically in the automotive sector. Secondly, the work on MNE subsidiary and corporate strategy from the *international business strategy* literature was examined in order to develop a taxonomy to describe the roles of the three Japanese-owned automotive affiliates in the UK.

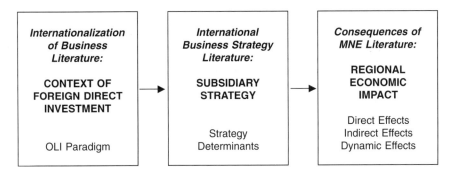

Figure 7.1 Stages of the literature review

Finally, attention was turned to the *consequences of MNE activity* to define how to measure the regional economic impact of the three transplants in the UK. This sets the conceptual context for this chapter and then defines the research questions.

The Internationalization of Business

There is a significant history of scholarly interest in MNE activity that provides the theoretical context of this study at the macro level. This is particularly important for the automotive sector since the majority of firms operate within a global context. Theorizing about MNE activity can be divided into three main periods: the early 1960s, the late 1970s and the 1990s. The work by Dunning (1958), Hymer (1960/1976) and Vernon (1966) exploring the economic implications of FDI was largely stimulated by the upsurge of outward investment by US corporations during the 1950s. This was complemented by literature on firm-specific issues (for example Knickerbocker, 1973; Vernon, 1974), and also by empirical studies on both the determinants and effects of FDI (see Caves, 1996 for a review of these). The late 1970s witnessed the emergence of the internalization theory (Buckley and Casson, 1976) and the eclectic paradigm (Dunning, 1977). These paradigms looked at the advantages possessed by firms and the way in which they are operationalized when companies choose to internalize the markets for their products rather than some other route (such as a contractual arrangement). This work was later supplemented by evolutionary theories of the firm that recognized the improvement of competitive advantage through innovation (Nelson and Winter, 1982). The 1990s saw an increase in the economic interdependence between countries and further developments in theory on MNE activity, specifically on asset-augmenting rather than asset-exploiting FDI (Teece *et al.*, 1997).

```
┌─────────────────────────────────────┐
│     Internationalization of Business │
│              Literature:             │
│                                      │
│       Firm-specific Advantages       │
│      Location-specific Advantages    │
│       Internalization Advantages     │
│                                      │
│             OLI Paradigm             │
│                                      │
│             CONTEXTUAL               │
│      BACKGROUND OF INVESTMENT        │
└─────────────────────────────────────┘
```

Figure 7.2   Explaining the contextual background of FDI

It can be seen that existing theoretical work approaches the subject from a number of different perspectives. However, the various research findings can be regarded as complementary rather than contradictory since the research is on different but related aspects. Indeed, it is Dunning's seminal work on the eclectic paradigm (1977) which tries to tie together much of the research under the headings of firm-specific (or ownership 'O'), location-specific ('L'), and internalization ('I') advantages. This is possible since the vast majority of work relates back, in some way or other, to Hymer's (1960/1976) work on market imperfections. More recently a reappraisal of existing theories of international production has shown that the dominant economic paradigms, first enunciated in the 1970s, are both robust and flexible enough to accommodate the contemporary world scenario (Dunning, 1997).

The basic proposition of the OLI paradigm is that the extent, ownership and pattern of MNE activity at any given moment of time depends upon the configuration of the competitive ('O'-specific) advantages of MNEs relative to those of non-MNEs, the competitive ('L')-specific attractions of one country or region relative to another, and the benefits to firms of linking these two sets of advantages by internalizing the market for the O-specific advantages – i.e. internalization (I) advantages. The eclectic paradigm will thus be adopted to explain the context of Japanese automotive investment in the UK. This is shown in Figure 7.2.

International Business Strategy

From this wealth of research into the underlying trends, patterns and processes of FDI, a stream of research on MNE subsidiaries has emerged which can be divided into three main schools of thought (Birkinshaw and Hood, 1998): headquarters–subsidiary relationships; subsidiary role; and subsidiary development. During the late 1970s and 1980s, researchers focused on different aspects of the HQ–subsidiary relationship (Brandt and Hulbert, 1976; Negandhi and Baliga, 1981). The underlying assumption was a dyadic relationship between the subsidiary and its HQ, and that the parent company retained decision making autonomy. As a more complex view of MNE activity emerged – transnationals, heterarchies and networks – research turned towards empirical work on the role of the subsidiary. The studies took slightly different approaches but generally suggested three or four types of subsidiary (White and Poynter, 1984; Bartlett and Ghoshal, 1986; Jarillo and Martinez, 1990; Taggart, 1997). Several authors, such as Bartlett and Ghoshal, assumed the subsidiary's role was 'assigned' by the parent company, while others (including White and Poynter, 1984) regarded the subsidiary as having more autonomy in determining its strategy. Developments in theory on MNE activity during the 1990s led to interest in the dynamic nature of the subsidiary – i.e. how and why do the activities of the subsidiary change over time? The premise is that capability accumulation generates enhanced status and scope of the subsidiary's activities (Birkinshaw and Hood, 1997).

The current literature on subsidiary and corporate strategy was examined in order to develop a taxonomy to describe the roles of the three Japanese-owned automotive affiliates in the UK. The corporate–subsidiary interface was surveyed before turning to existing frameworks for analyzing subsidiary strategy. This produced the criteria for investigating the strategic role of the affiliates.

The Corporate–Subsidiary Interface
There are two dominant models of international business strategy, both developed during the 1980s. Porter (1986) developed the *co-ordination–configuration* paradigm whilst Prahalad and Doz (1987) formed the *integration–responsiveness* framework. The co-ordination concept explains how the MNE arranges its value chain activities across different locations in order to strengthen its competitive position and maximize performance. The configuration concept assesses the extent to which the company's activities are concentrated in one location (high configuration), from which the MNE's international network is served, or how dispersed these activities are across a number of locations (low configuration). There has been a significant amount of empirical work carried out on the co-ordination–configuration concepts which confirms the model has an analytical and descriptive output for MNE strategy (for example, Ghoshal and Bartlett, 1988; Roth and Morrison, 1990; Taggart, 1997). This confirms the importance of co-ordination and configuration in determining subsidiary strategy and the two constructs will thus be applied in this study.

The other main area of work in international business strategy is based on the ideas of Prahalad and Doz (1987). The main thrust of the integration–responsiveness approach is that MNEs operating in global industries pursue and maintain competitive advantage by locating themselves along the two dimensions in a unique way to reflect the characteristics of the industry and the individual firm. These concepts have been validated by many researchers, including Ghoshal and Bartlett (1988), and Martinez and Jarillo (1991) Roth and Morrison (1990). It is a logical extension to use these constructs to explain subsidiary strategy. Consequently, both *integration* and *responsiveness* will be used in this project, in addition to *co-ordination* and *configuration*, to measure the corporate–subsidiary interface that ultimately determines subsidiary strategy.

Frameworks for Examining Subsidiary Strategy

A number of frameworks have been put forward to specifically address subsidiary strategy, including White and Poynter (1984); Bartlett and Ghoshal (1986); Jarillo and Martinez (1990); Taggart (1997). The main strands of these models are used to contribute to the development of a taxonomy of subsidiary roles to apply to the three Japanese-owned automotive affiliates in the UK.

First, White and Poynter examined the activities of foreign subsidiaries along three dimensions: *product scope, market scope* and *value-added scope*. Since this model has been supported by UK evidence (e.g. Young *et al.*, 1988), and it also provides assistance to local managers in developing subsidiary roles, these three concepts will be utilized here. Secondly, Bartlett and Ghoshal concentrated on the differential *strategic importance* of national markets in terms of the MNEs' overall objectives, and related this to the level of *competence* of the local affiliate in each case. This model is useful at a corporate level since it allows the MNE to organize its network to achieve global objectives. However, it provides the local manager with less assistance in increasing bargaining power with company headquarters than the model proposed by White and Poynter (1984). Consequently, these concepts will not be included in this taxonomy of subsidiary strategy. Thirdly, Jarillo and Martinez (1990) developed a framework based on the integration–responsiveness approach. It provides a reference point for local managers when they want to change the strategic position of their particular affiliate, and strengthens the case for including integration and responsiveness in this subsidiary strategy taxonomy. Finally, Taggart (1997) has brought together the findings of several authors to develop a co-ordination–configuration paradigm for subsidiary strategy. This provides further UK evidence that market scope, co-ordination and integration are important determinants of subsidiary strategy.

It is clear that the concepts of co-ordination, configuration, integration and responsiveness are core elements in determining subsidiary strategy and that all of the above frameworks use a combination of these factors. Market scope, product scope and value-added scope are also frequently highlighted as key determinants, and thus all of these constructs will be

```
┌─────────────────────────────────────┐
│                                     │
│    International Business Strategy   │
│            Literature:               │
│                                     │
│         Co-ordination                │
│         Configuration                │
│          Integration                 │
│        Responsiveness                │
│         Market Scope                 │
│         Product Scope                │
│       Value-added Scope              │
│            Autonomy                  │
│                                     │
│            Strategy                  │
│          Determinants                │
│                                     │
└─────────────────────────────────────┘
```

Figure 7.3   Establishing MNE subsidiary strategy

included in a taxonomy to describe subsidiary roles in this study. In addition, the issue of autonomy has been explored by a number of researchers, many with a slightly different focus such as market area decisions (Hedlund, 1981) and product range supplied (Egelhoff, 1988). However, the importance of establishing a degree of consultation between corporate HQ and the subsidiary in the decision making process is generally agreed. Hence, autonomy will also be used here.

In relation to this study, the relevant factors to be included in a taxonomy to describe the roles of the Japanese automotive affiliates in the UK are *co-ordination, configuration, integration, responsiveness, market scope, product scope, value-added scope* and *autonomy* (see Figure 7.3).

The Consequences of MNE Activity

Attention is now turned to the relationship between subsidiary strategy and regional economic impact. Much of the academic work on the consequences of MNE activity to date has concentrated on the economic (Hill and Munday, 1991; Morris and Imrie, 1993) and social (Hurdley and White, 1999) impact within specific countries. Nevertheless, increasing attention has been paid to the impact of MNEs at the regional level, the main areas of interest being the creation of clusters (Schimtz, 1992), industrial districts and local networks. Work by Young *et al.* (1994) summarizes and synthesizes different strands of literature from the area of MNEs and regional economic development, particularly in terms of generating dynamic comparative advantage. The conclusions were that the direct effects have been positive whereas the indirect effects such as spillover effects, especially regarding local sourcing, have been disappointing. Young *et al.* (1994) mention the role of government agencies and the significance of regional incentive policies in maximizing regional economic impact. This is supported by studies in which the view is that policies should be conducted at the lowest possible level, with regionally based and regionally controlled initiatives being vital.

The literature on the impact of MNEs at the regional level mentioned above suggests it is useful to divide economic indicators into three categories when assessing regional economic impact: direct effects, indirect effects and dynamic effects. The establishment of an MNE subsidiary has obvious *direct effects* on the local, and national, economy. The main areas of consideration are the effects on employment, output, R&D and the balance of payments. For instance, Dunning (1993) shows that most investments directly affect the level, growth, stability, quality and rewards of the labour force. Output is important because as an affiliate becomes established, and additional aspects of the value chain are developed, output will increase. Furthermore, as the parent company gains confidence in the performance of an overseas subsidiary, there is increased opportunity for further capital injections and expansion. Evidence shows that while overseas R&D is growing, the majority of activity is concentrated in the home countries of MNEs rather than in subsidiaries (Cheng and Bolton, 1993). Finally, governments are particularly interested in MNE subsidiary activity when considering the balance of payments and the structure of trade within a region.

When considering *indirect effects*, it is necessary to observe both the upstream linkages (the effects on suppliers) and downstream linkages (the effects on customers) involved. The literature identifies several types of linkages that MNEs may form with their suppliers, such as information, financial, procurement and technical assistance (for example, Lall, 1980). Downstream linkages between MNE affiliates and their business customers may affect the latter's competitiveness and innovatory capabilities (Dunning, 1993). This is particularly relevant to the automotive industry in terms of sales and after-sales servicing, maintenance and repair facilities. Arguably, the most researched spillover effect of MNE activity is the impact on rival firms and the competitive position of the industry (Dunning, 1993)

The academic debate on *dynamic factors* that encourage 'developmental' subsidiaries stresses the importance of the internal competencies of the affiliate, and the initiative of local management (Roth and Morrison, 1992). More specifically, research by Amin *et al.* (1994) features the efforts of indigenous managers and improvements in plant performance, while it is recognized that subsidiary mandates are earned through the entrepreneurial efforts of subsidiary management rather than given by parent-company management (Birkinshaw, 1996). Young *et al.* (1994) conclude that, at the

```
┌─────────────────────────────────────┐
│      Consequences of MNE Literature: │
│                                      │
│             Direct Effects           │
│            Indirect Effects          │
│            Dynamic Effects           │
│                                      │
│               Impact                 │
│             Determinants             │
│                                      │
│         REGIONAL ECONOMIC            │
│               IMPACT                 │
└─────────────────────────────────────┘
```

Figure 7.4   Establishing regional economic impact

European regional level, MNEs have not had a major influence on dynamic comparative advantage. They go on to suggest that local sourcing and technological innovation are possible ways of encouraging clusters.

In drawing together some of the main ideas presented above, it is appropriate to examine three types of economic impact indicators when assessing FDI at the subsidiary level: *direct*, *indirect* and *dynamic* (see Figure 7.4).

This completes the literature review and provides the basis for the conceptual framework for this study.

CONCEPTUAL FRAMEWORK

The conceptual framework, shown in Figure 7.5, has been developed to investigate the context of a particular FDI project, the subsidiary strategy adopted by the affiliate and the regional economic impact of the manufacturing plant. More specifically, it will be used in this study to examine the three Japanese-owned automotive transplants in the UK.

This conceptual framework generates three specific research questions:

1. What are the key determinants of the direct investment made by Nissan, Honda and Toyota in the UK?
   This is measured by using the ownership, location and internalization advantages from the OLI paradigm.
2. What type of subsidiary strategy has been adopted by each of the three Japanese-owned automotive manufacturing plants in the UK?
   This is measured by using the eight main determinants of subsidiary strategy outlined above – i.e. co-ordination, configuration, integration, responsiveness, market scope, product scope, value-added scope and autonomy.

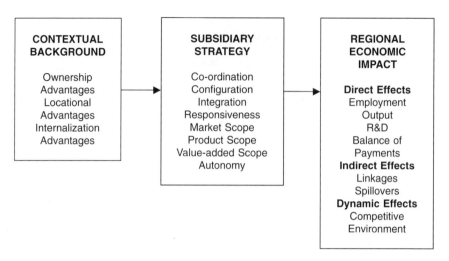

Figure 7.5   The conceptual framework

3. What has been the regional economic impact of each of the three Japanese-owned automotive manufacturing plants in the UK?

   This is measured by using the three categories of regional economic impact discussed previously – i.e. direct, indirect and dynamic effects.

By addressing these research questions, we will be able to offer insights into the relationship between the type of subsidiary strategy adopted and the regional economic impact of each of the three Japanese-owned automotive manufacturing plants in the UK. This will explore whether certain types of subsidiary strategy generate a more positive regional economic impact than other types. We will then be able to define the implications of these findings for policy makers. While the shortcomings of basing such conclusions upon three cases from a single industrial sectour are recognized, it is hoped this empirical work will improve our understanding of subsidiary strategy and regional economic impact.

METHODOLOGY

The first stage of the project was to review the extensive secondary data available on the three cases in order to define the context of the investment. This includes company annual reports, government and trade body publications and newspaper articles. Time and resource constraints enforced this approach and while the limitations of secondary data are recognized, every effort was made to cross-reference the information to improve reliability. In addition, the main findings were corroborated in the

Table 7.1   Measuring the context of FDI using the eclectic paradigm of international production

1	Ownership-specific Advantages (O)
E.g.	Intangible assets such as expertise or technology-based utilities; product innovations; production management; organization of work; organizational and marketing systems; advantages of common governance
2	Location-specific Advantages (L)
E.g.	Trade barriers; most types of labour; natural resources; proximity to final markets; conditions of transportation and communication; degree of government intervention; cultural distance
3	Internalization-specific Advantages (I)
E.g.	Ability to control supplies of inputs and their conditions of sale; ability to avoid costs of transaction and negotiation; buyer uncertainty about the nature and value of inputs

Source: Adapted from Dunning (1993), p. 81.

personal interviews explained below. This was deemed acceptable since research question 1 provides the contextual background, with the main value-added aspect of the project being in questions 2 and 3. The measures used are outlined in Table 7.1.

The second stage was to address the remaining research questions. Since research questions 2 and 3 were largely exploratory, a qualitative approach was most appropriate. The advantages of qualitative data are well documented and include local groundedness, richness and holism, collection over a sustained period and inherent flexibility (Miles and Huberman, 1994).

A semi-structured interview guide was selected as the data collection method since cross-case comparison requires some standardization of instruments so that findings can be laid side by side in the final analysis (Miles and Huberman, 1994: 35). In implementing the research design, the relevant government agency in each region was contacted first and the research topic was presented to them. All agreed to take part and facilitate access to the Original Equipment Manufacturers (OEMs) with their endorsement.

In total, 19 semi-structured, in-depth interviews were carried out with three sets of people. First, senior representatives from the government agencies were interviewed: Northern Development Company (NDC); West Country Development Agency (WCDA); and East Midlands Development Company (EMDC). An additional interview, suggested by the Chief Executive of NDC, took place with the Tyne and Wear Development Corporation. Secondly, three interviews were conducted with each OEM comprising the Managing Director/Senior Director, and representatives from both production and R&D. Finally, a sample of five component suppliers to the

OEMs was questioned to supplement the above data by providing additional perspectives on the indirect and dynamic effects on regional economic impact. This further validation from component suppliers was sought on these constructs since they are particularly difficult to measure.

The literature on subsidiary strategy and regional economic impact was used to develop the questions used in the interview guide. The measures developed are shown in Tables 7.2 and 7.3. A semi-structured rather than a structured questionnaire was selected owing to the exploratory nature of the study. Each interview lasted between one and two hours, providing sufficient time to explore the constructs without interviewees becoming impatient.

The interview transcripts were then analyzed by three concurrent flows of activity: data reduction, data display and conclusion drawing/verification

Table 7.2   Measuring subsidiary strategy determinants

Construct	Measurement
Co-ordination	Level of technological transfer between subsidiaries; linked marketing activities between subsidiaries; linked production requirements between subsidiaries; linked purchasing between subsidiaries
Configuration	Location of strategic skills and resources within the MNE; location of other skills and resources; location of R&D within the MNE; location of purchasing activity within the MNE
Integration	Manufacturing decisions linked to local or world-wide market areas; product and quality specification developed by HQ or subsidiary; extent to which subsidiary serves MNE customers world-wide; centralization and sharing of technology development within the internal network; dependence of subsidiary on linkages within the internal network; centralization of production planning
Local responsiveness	Homogeneity of customers and their needs; extent to which competitors and their strategies are easily identified; stability of technology and the level of manufacturing operations; life cycle of product line and manufacturing process; homogeneity of the executive group
Market scope	Measured on a scale from mainly UK to world-wide
Product scope	Measured on a scale of the proportion of the subsidiary's product line developed in-house
Value-added scope	Measured on a scale identifying complexity of subsidiary R&D capability from none to the generation of new technology for the corporate parent
Decision making autonomy	Market-area decisions; product range supplied; advertising and promotions; R&D; production; and manufacturing technology, measured on a four-point scale, with illustrative examples

Source: Adapted from Taggart (1998).

Table 7.3   Measuring regional economic impact

Direct effects	Measurement
Employment	Total employment, workforce mix, percentage of workforce previously unemployed/economically inactive, residence of employees and number of Japanese expatriates
Output	Number of unit produced per annum, turnover (£) and productivity
R&D	Nature, technology transfer between the subsidiary and other parts of the MNE, location of main group R&D relevant to the subsidiary, total R&D employment in the UK, proportion of new products and components designed in the UK, collaboration
Balance of payments	Proportion of exports, value of exports (£), destination of exports

Indirect effects	Measurement
Linkages	Suppliers and customers
Spillovers	Competitors, membership of employer or trade organizations, community initiatives

Dynamic effects	Measurement
Competitive environment	Indigenous resources and capabilities, market structure, indigenous demand characteristics, availability of support or related sectors, public image

Source: Extracted from Dunning (1993), Chapters 10–19.

(Miles and Huberman, 1994). Data reduction for each of the interviews used simple codes for each main variable, as well as viva voce quotations from the respondents. A combination of restrictive codes and more illustrative quotations was used to improve the efficiency of the analysis procedure whilst retaining the 'richness' required in an exploratory study. This reduced data was then displayed in a matrix for each individual interview, and then grouped to form one matrix for each of the three companies. This enabled within-case analysis..The comparison of the final three matrices facilitated cross-case analysis.

PRELIMINARY FINDINGS

Contextual Background

The eclectic paradigm of ownership-specific, location-specific and internalization advantages was used to explain the main determinants of Japanese automotive investment in the UK. The Japanese OEMs had two main *ownership advantages* over their competitors: production management in the form of lean production and the ability of the parent company to develop productive and co-operative inter-firm relationships with their suppliers. This is consistent with the findings of Womack *et al.* (1990) when they examined the Japanese OEMs in the USA. When looking at the *location advantages*, both the home country and the host country should be considered. Since the 1950s, the Japanese government has played a crucial role in influencing the ability of Japanese automotive firms to generate competitive advantages relative to their competitors and to locate their value-added activities outside the home country. During the 1980s, the Japanese auto firms decided to establish European manufacturing facilities to gain access to the increasingly protected European market place. Each company chose a UK green field site since the general political, social and economic environment created by the British government generated an 'investment climate' favoured by the parent companies when calculating the risk factor involved in locating in different countries. It was interesting to note that several interviewees mentioned the importance of Prime Minister Thatcher in the decision to locate in the UK. In relation to *internalization advantages*, the Japanese automotive OEMs selected FDI in order to guarantee quality control, ensure the successful transfer of the Japanese management philosophy and work styles, and to overcome the problems associated with licensing agreements. The requirements of establishing manufacturing facilities in each of the Triad markets (Asia, North America and Europe) in order to become more responsive to local consumer tastes was also present in each of the firm's stated corporate objectives. For example, 'localized vehicle production is an important way in which Toyota makes a contribution to different countries, by providing mutually beneficial long-term relationships with local companies and a commitment to the employment of local labour'.

Subsidiary Strategy

The three Japanese OEMs adopted different modes of entry into the UK automotive industry but the results indicated that each of the subsidiaries was now moving towards a similar strategic role. Honda formed an on-going relationship with the UK through its alliance with Rover that began in 1979 as a technical collaboration and later evolved into a cross-shareholding (subsequently terminated in 1994). Nissan decided to ship kits for one model to the UK for assembly in 1986 but gradually built up relationships with European suppliers to reach a local content figure of 80 per cent in 1990 (with two-thirds of the suppliers being located in the UK). Toyota, on the other hand, began production in 1993 with a local content of 60 per cent and reached 80 per cent the following year. Despite the differing modes of entry, each of the subsidiary plants evolved to fulfil an increasingly important strategic role within their global networks as self-contained European production networks have grown up. The findings relating to the eight determinants of subsidiary strategy are discussed below.

- *Co-ordination* was found to be high at the European level but low with respect to the global corporate network. Each of the OEMs had set up a European headquarters (EHQ) in order to minimize the effort required by the parent company in communicating with each of the European national markets. In two of the cases, pan-European sales/marketing, pricing and production decisions were made by the EHQ with little consultation with the individual subsidiaries. For instance, initially Toyota (GB) had a direct relationship with Tokyo for operational issues, pricing and marketing support on a daily basis. The creation of Toyota Motor and Manufacturing Europe (TMME) has resulted in many of those decisions now being made in Brussels with little liaison with Japan. This supports such work that concludes that regional headquarters (RHQ) do not indicate a strong desire to seek consensus with national units and to share power with them. Hence, co-ordination with the rest of the global enterprise was controlled by the RHQ and the subsidiary had little or no control over this. However, one of the OEMs had located their EHQ in the UK and there was some evidence to suggest a higher degree of consultation with local managers, particularly on the model/sales mix and pricing issues. This concurs with the findings of Hyakuya (1994) who concluded that the location of the EHQ was important in determining the level of local involvement.
- A low degree of *configuration* was observed in each of the three cases. Despite the fact that each of the OEMs operated from numerous sites across the world, the strategic skills and resources remained firmly in Japan. For instance, the Finance Directors for two of the three UK subsidiaries were of Japanese nationality at the time of interview. One manager said 'The FD is Japanese and probably always will be'. Interestingly, the company financial data was predominantly prepared and circulated in Japanese. The main financial dialogue was with Tokyo, rather than the EHQ, with little involvement or input from the local UK subsidiary managers. In addition, all interviewees stated that responsibility for the long-term strategy of the subsidiary was in Japan. For example, the Nissan parent company HQ in Tokyo decides on the five-year business plans, and beyond, for each of its subsidiary operations.
- The levels of *integration* of the subsidiaries showed a similar pattern to that of co-ordination owing to the influence of the EHQ. The manufacturing decisions were linked to European, rather than global, markets. However, the quality and productivity measures adopted were those used by plants throughout the corporate networks, and the global HQ made comparisons between the different manufacturing sites. Indeed, it was

stated that the achievement of the Nissan subsidiary reaching quality and productivity equal to that in Japan was critical to the decision to invest in building a second model in Britain.

- *Responsiveness* in two of the subsidiaries was low when production commenced but had increased as local R&D operations developed and the parent-company management were convinced of the need to adapt to local market tastes and preferences. Several interviewees suggested that Japan was happy to let the subsidiaries become more responsive after the efficiency of the plants in producing the standard company products had been demonstrated. Responsiveness for one subsidiary was initially higher than in the other two owing to its strategic partnership with a British OEM, which increased the Japanese MNE's understanding of the European customer tastes.
- *Market scope* was largely European for all of the subsidiaries. This was not surprising since one of the main reasons for establishing a UK manufacturing facility was to serve the, increasingly protected, European market place. There were a couple of examples of the subsidiary exporting some components back to Japan for home country assembly. However, this constituted a minor part of the overall output and it was not anticipated that this would grow significantly in the future (largely owing to the OEM shareholding in many of the component suppliers in Japan).
- There were several examples of *product scope* increasing as the local R&D operations became more established. Nevertheless, there was no indication from the interviewees that decisions on the range of products produced would be devolved from the EHQ in the future, hence limiting the subsidiary's control over this aspect.
- A high degree of *value-added scope* was observed at each of the manufacturing subsidiaries. For instance, 'total capital investment at the manufacturing site now stands well over £1 billion and the facility comprises a press, body and paint shops, final assembly, casting, engine machining and assembly, and plastic injection moulding'. Conversely, the same interviewee commented that 'the body design of vehicles is still concentrated in Japan and it is unlikely that this will change in the future'.
- The subsidiaries exhibited very limited decision-making *autonomy* within certain key functions, namely finance, design and development and business strategy. However, local managers had control over human resource issues (with the exception of Board appointments) and some input into marketing issues (although the final decision remained largely with the EHQ). This is consistent with previous work that analyzes the locus of decision making autonomy in different functional areas (Huang, 1999). It is interesting to note that Hofstede (1980) found that Japanese MNEs maintained a higher degree of control over their subsidiaries than MNEs of other nationalities.

Regional Economic Impact

When assessing the regional economic impact of the affiliates, there was evidence of direct, indirect and dynamic effects, but to varying degrees (note that all figures were current to 1998). Regarding *direct effects*, there were significant positive effects on employment, output and the balance of payments. For instance, Nissan had 4300 employees, Honda 3000, while Toyota employed 2500 people across two manufacturing sites in the UK. The majority of these jobs were full-time, semi-skilled or skilled, filled by predominantly male employees, and involved good benefits. In terms of output, Nissan produced 280000 vehicles, Honda 110000 and Toyota 220000. The majority of vehicles at each subsidiary were assembled for export and hence had a positive effect on the balance of payments. For instance, 75 per cent of the Carina E model assembled at Toyota's Burnaston plant was sold to 16 European countries, while the engine plant also exported to Turkey and Japan. The direct effects of the three subsidiaries were also reflected in the balance of trade figures. For instance, NMM (UK) spent about $2.4 million in 1998 to expand its plant in order to supply Primera parts for knock-down assembly by Nissan South Africa. Nissan South Africa aimed to sell about 5000 Primeras per year. It was the first time that a Nissan plant outside Japan had shipped knock-down parts for local production at a Nissan plant in a third country. Finally, the evidence on R&D facilities showed that they ranged from purely adapting parent-company technology to developing new products for the European market place. However, the overall control and focus of R&D for each company remained firmly in Japan, while mainland European countries also played a role. For example, Nissan European Technology Centres at Cranfield and Sunderland had some responsibility for the planning, design, development and testing of vehicles produced in Europe, but the European technological and engineering research took place in Brussels. Furthermore, the European design centre for the styling of vehicles was based in Germany. There was no doubt, though, among interviewees that 'the fundamental research is still carried out in Japan'.

The main *indirect effect* of the Japanese affiliates appeared to be via the automotive components industry. For instance, many component suppliers had adopted teamworking practices at the insistence of the Japanese automotive OEMs in order to address quality issues, and reported positive improvements. Furthermore, the adoption of new techniques to develop a lean supply chain had affected the way suppliers did business with non-Japanese OEMs in Europe. Thus, the linkage between the Japanese automotive subsidiaries and their component suppliers had had a positive spillover effect on their OEM automotive competitors. There were many illustrations of this and most industry commentators have agreed that the Japanese have rejuvenated the UK automotive components industry by their demonstration effect on suppliers. The fact that each of the affiliates had a particularly high local content was also important in generating the magnitude of this positive effect. Further positive indirect effects were evident through involvement in research and development programmes for the UK automotive industry. Two of the affiliates, for instance, were involved in joint research programmes with several universities, funded jointly by the Japanese OEM and the Engineering and Physical Science Research Council. One of the programmes focused on improving the engineering interchange between the subsidiaries and their component suppliers, while the other was on creating new ways of providing customer satisfaction during the car delivery process. The output from these research projects was disseminated throughout the UK automotive sector as opposed to purely benefiting the Japanese OEMs.

Finally, there was limited evidence to support a positive impact through *dynamic effects* on the regional economy. For instance, when considering policy makers, the Northern Development Company was formed as a result of the success in creating a 'one-stop shop' to attract Nissan to the North East. Furthermore, the success of the Nissan manufacturing plant had created a high media profile for the North East which had been capitalized upon in attracting further FDI. Indeed, Nissan representatives had themselves helped in negotiations with prospective investors by explaining the benefits of setting up facilities in the region.

POLICY IMPLICATIONS AND CONCLUSIONS

It was clear that the national economic, social and political environment was particularly important in the original decision by the Japanese OEMs to locate in the UK. The mention of the 'Thatcher factor' indicated the influence of personal relationships in such FDI negotiations and the significance of the ambassadorial role in nurturing international investment. This is obviously implemented largely by the national UK government but the regional organizations can influence and lobby policy to achieve these ends. It was clear that despite different modes of entry, each of the subsidiaries was moving towards a similar role within their global corporate networks, and that there were few marked differences between them when measuring subsidiary strategy. The interview evidence suggests that subsidiaries that are highly integrated with the rest of the global network have a greater potential to positively affect regional economic impact.

The overall findings on regional economic impact supported previous work in that the direct effects had been positive and the dynamic effects very limited. However, this study provided new empirical evidence to show that indirect effects, through linkages and spillovers, can be extensive. The main influence on regional economic impact was through the demonstration effect on UK automotive component suppliers. It should also be noted that this effect is not just confined to the region containing the subsidiary plant, so there is also a positive effect on national competitiveness. Furthermore, the positive impact achieved through high local content was significant, and it should be noted that this was supported by legislation (which was largely determined at the European and national rather than the regional level).

Announcements about future investments by the OEMs raise questions about other issues than subsidiary strategy in determining regional economic impact. For instance, the Honda parent company announced that it would open a second plant in Swindon at the end of 2000, creating a further 1000 jobs. The influence of the EHQ being located in the UK and the longer-term relationships with local component suppliers and the UK economy as a whole (owing to the previous strategic partnership with Rover) must be considered. Conversely, the Japanese HQ decided to locate a second Toyota plant in Valenciennes, France. The influence of a EHQ outside the UK and the shorter-term relationships with UK component suppliers may have been influential. The fact that the UK government has chosen to defer entry to the single European currency has also been highlighted as a possible influence on this investment decision. In light of the continuous investment at Nissan's Sunderland plant, the influence of the 'one-stop shop' government agency model adopted in the North East could also be investigated to establish whether this type of model helps to maximize the positive regional economic impact of Japanese affiliates. All of these issues clearly raise new questions and suggest areas of future research for those working in this area.

8 Differentiating MNC Strategy at Subsidiary Level

James H. Taggart

INTRODUCTION

The role that headquarters defines for the subsidiary is one of a number of guidelines established by corporate executives within which most subsidiary management teams continue to evolve – explicitly or informally – a strategy to influence the development of the affiliate. This philosophy appears to underlie many approaches to subsidiary research (for example, White and Poynter, 1984; Bartlett and Ghoshal, 1986; Jarillo and Martinez, 1990; Taggart, 1998). While the models produced by these writers are sound and helpful, none seems to give sufficient emphasis to the nature of the relationship at the headquarters/affiliate interface. The potential strategic input of subsidiary managers is also underplayed.

One study (Taggart, 1997) has sought to contrapose two of the strategic dimensions that run through many analyses of affiliate behaviour. These are the level of autonomy possessed by the subsidiary and the nature of its relationship with headquarters. The strongly behavioural aspects of this approach are in some contrast to the operations emphasis of the four models identified above. The purpose of this chapter is to subject Taggart's autonomy–procedural justice (A–PJ) model to empirical evaluation. It will also assess critically the subsidiary strategy classifications of the model and interpret the findings from the perspective of subsidiary managers and others. The chapter is organized as follows: the next section gives the conceptual background to the A–PJ model, followed by a description of the methodology used for this study. The results are set out, discussed and interpreted in terms of implications for subsidiary managers, headquarters and local policy makers. Finally the conclusions are given, together with some thoughts on how this model may be developed further.

BACKGROUND

Autonomy

In an early study of subsidiaries of European multinational companies (MNCs) operating in the USA, Picard (1980) identified two common types of reporting structures. Where the subsidiary chief executive reported directly to the MNC president, hierarchical factors tended to lower the subsidiary's degree of autonomy. However, operational flexibility could be maintained if the relationship between the two executives was good. Where the chief executive reported only to the local board (which would include representatives of the parent), subsidiary autonomy was higher. In this case, the hierarchy was not able to impose control from parent to subsidiary, but symbiosis between the two could be maintained by personal contact and good interpersonal relationships between subsidiary and headquarters' management. This result was confirmed by Garnier's (1982) study of MNC affiliates in Mexico. He found a strong correlation between affiliate autonomy and the number of parent-company representatives on the subsidiary's board. Although he does not discuss this finding in depth, it seems clear from his consideration of organization factors that having a mix of parent and subsidiary executives at board level will have implications for the level of informal contact and the nature of relationships between headquarters and subsidiary. Hedlund's (1981) study of autonomy in subsidiaries of Swedish MNCs demonstrated a high level of decision making and control at affiliate level, and certainly significantly higher than in comparable samples of US and Japanese subsidiaries. Headquarters influence in this 'mother–daughter' structure was maintained by very personal contacts with the subsidiary, informal and variable management style and absence of respect for organizational hierarchies. The nature of the HQ–affiliate relationship seemed to be unaffected by ownership (wholly-owned or joint venture (JV)) and by the cultural distance of subsidiary from headquarters.

Stopford and Wells' (1972) comprehensive review of issues facing MNCs identified the tight linkage between the exercise of control and autonomy on the one hand, and the creation of a sense of shared values and co-operation between headquarters and subsidiaries. Jaeger (1983) noted that centralized MNCs were accordingly required to spend significantly on the use of expatriates and extensive training programmes to maintain active co-operation at subsidiary level. Though he does not extend this discussion, it may be reasonably inferred that giving more autonomy to subsidiaries will avoid these heavy costs. However, personal interaction at the HQ–affiliate interface will still be a necessary lubricant. In a study of innovation at subsidiary level, Ghoshal and Bartlett (1988) suggested that the degree of creation is correlated with affiliate autonomy and the intensity of head-quarters–subsidiary communication. While these results were not wholly conclusive, the implication again is that the cost of autonomy may be mitigated by effective corporate–affiliate relationships, leading to an efficient use of the corporation's innovative resources.

Turning specifically to the question of global subsidiary mandates, Roth and Morrison (1992) indicate that even though the affiliate may have a dominant role with respect to its product mandate, it nevertheless remains part of an interdependent network. This interdependence is critical to the implementation of an effective global strategy by the MNC. Thus, the relative product and R&D independence of the affiliate should be offset by a proactive corporate vocation to encourage ownership of a common mission, depoliticization of managerial decision making, managerial entrepreneurship and desensitization of management dissent. The question of management style was also taken up in a rather complex study of Japanese subsidiaries in Italy (Gnan and Songini, 1995). Management style was assessed along two dimensions: hierarchy, which corresponded with central control from headquarters; and involvement, which was linked to higher levels of flexibility and autonomy at subsidiary level. The key finding, of interest here, is that involvement was heavily influenced by cross-functional mechanisms, based on shared values and good personal relationship across the HQ–subsidiary interface. Both of these factors are commonly used in cultural control systems, as defined and interpreted by Prahalad and Doz (1987).

Procedural Justice

Bartlett's (1981) study of organizational evolution within five health care MNCs identified a corporate goal 'to construct an organizational climate in which flexible, constructive and co-operative interaction between managers with different perspectives was institutionalized'. This would allow, for example, corporate and subsidiary managers to negotiate an appropriate balance of views in issues where both were involved. In turn, this called for underappreciation of the MNCs' broad objectives and the willingness to adapt, co-operate and compromise. Managers at all levels had to broaden perspectives, communicate more effectively throughout the international network, strive for co-operation and flexibility and create a supportive value system. With such an organizational climate, corporate managers were able to devolve much more decision making to subsidiary level, particularly where specific local expertise existed. In these cases, subsidiary managers came to dominate operational, and often strategic, decisions. This perspective is supported by Hassard and Sharifi (1989), who observe that the strategic decision making process will be improved (and shared at multiple organization levels) where a strong and supportive corporate culture is first created and put in place. The trust developed by the latter allows the former to be decentralized.

Kashani (1990) is even more specific on the sequence of activity. His study of nine MNCs, involving seventeen global marketing programmes, indicated that an extensive programme of headquarters facilitation to build understanding and trust was required before subsidiaries became involved in major marketing decisions. Where facilitation was weak or absent, global marketing programmes failed to develop the expected competitive advantage. De Meyer (1993) made much the same point about international R&D, though he observes that the role of a supportive corporate culture may be secondary to operational and technical characteristics of parent and subsidiary.

In a series of three papers, Kim and Mauborgne (1991, 1993a, 1993b) defined the concepts of procedural justice in MNCs as relating to subsidiary managers' perspective of how fairly their units have been treated in the annual strategy making process. 'Procedural justice' is firmly linked to commitment, trust and social harmony within the MNC; it is also correlated with perceptions of decision outcome fairness (Kim and Mauborgne, 1991). They suggest that procedural justice will be most highly valued by powerful and resource-rich subsidiaries that are central to MNC global strategy. Empirical results indicate that, compared to the multidomestic end of the industry spectrum, subsidiaries that experience procedural justice are more likely to comply with corporate strategic decisions. They are also better able to balance the conflicting demands of global efficiency and local responsiveness (Kim and Mauborgne, 1993a, 1993b). As global integration is negatively, and local responsiveness positively, associated with the level of subsidiary autonomy (Prahalad and Doz, 1987), interactions between the latter and procedural justice are implied. However, Kim and Mauborgne do not make any explicit evaluation of this issue.

A–PJ Model

The foregoing discussion has indicated that research on autonomy often links level of decentralized decision making with social aspects of managing the corporate–subsidiary interface. Also, researchers in these social processes (particularly procedural justice) have noted implicit or explicit links with the level of subsidiary autonomy. The proposal of a two-dimensional model displaying the interactions of autonomy and procedural justice (Taggart, 1997) gives four interpretations of subsidiary strategy (see Figure 8.1). *Vassal* subsidiaries have low levels of both autonomy and procedural justice (low A–low PJ). This is an unattractive role and may often be characterized by suspicion and dissent between headquarters and subsidiary, coupled with an impression of powerlessness at the latter level. The *collaborator* subsidiary (low A–high PJ) has little self-determination but the relationship with corporate management is generally positive. The adaptable nature of this type makes it a functional and propitious member of a tightly integrated global network. The *partner* affiliate (high A–high PJ) yields the ideal posture from the perspective of subsidiary managers; it is likely to be viewed by headquarters as proactive and capable, and may well be a centre of excellence (Surlemont, 1996). A much less attractive strategy space is occupied by the *militant* subsidiary (high A–low PJ), which may

Procedural Justice

Low   *High*

	Low	*High*
High	*Militant*	*Partner*
Autonomy	*Vassal*	*Collaborator*
Low		

Figure 8.1   The autonomy–procedural justice framework

often be an unwilling acquisition or a *partner* whose network relationship
have sourced. It is as uncomfortable a locus as the *collaborator* is
comfortable. These alternatives in the overall strategy space are well
supported in the original study, and are also clearly differentiated across
a limited number of other operating and strategic variables (Taggart,
1997). However, that study was wholly exploratory in nature, and it seems
appropriate to subject the A–PJ model to a somewhat wider empirical
validation.

RESEARCH QUESTIONS

The original A–PJ model (Taggart, 1997) was justified across a range of
seven strategic dimensions – integration, responsiveness, co-ordination,
configuration, market scope, product scope and value-added scope. All
but responsiveness and market scope were found to differentiate strongly
across the four classifications of subsidiary, and the interpretation of those
results allowed some helpful characterization of the different types of affiliate. In addition, the A–PJ framework is incrementally validated by such
configurational analysis (Miller and Friesen, 1984). The purpose of this
chapter is to provide a further test of the model, and additional validation
across alternative strategic dimensions. This exploratory approach will also
yield enhanced interpretation and description of the four subsidiary types.

Porter (1980) highlighted the critical effect of competitive dynamics within the industry in the way a firm organizes itself to maintain competitive advantage. This echoes aspects of earlier economic analysis of firm competitiveness (Coase, 1937; Williamson, 1975; Teece, 1981). Porter explained competitiveness at industry level as the resultant of five forces. Other writers have identified more specific variables that have an impact at firm level (Galbraith and Schendel, 1983; Dess and Davis, 1984; Robinson and Pearce, 1988). Along with internationalization, competitive positioning helps to determine the fit between business strategy and industry environment, and is therefore linked to performance (Morrison, 1990: 135). Thus, we have the first research question of this study:

RQ1: Are aspects of industry competitive dynamics at subsidiary level differentiated by the A–PJ framework in some systematic way?

Hamel and Prahalad (1985) identified differences in competitive methods as an important differentiator between domestic firms and Japanese subsidiaries in the USA, this echoing many of Levitt's (1983) observations about international competition. More specifically, Douglas and Craig (1983) evaluated the relationship between performance in international markets and a number of marketing mix variables, though pressures for standardization and differentiation must also be assessed carefully to achieve optional results (Bartlett and Ghoshal, 1986). The importance of other aspects of competitive methods has also been recognized – for example, in technology (Franko, 1989), manufacturing (Ferdows *et al.*, 1986; De Meyer *et al.*, 1989) and services (Voss *et al.*, 1997). To these considerations of international competitive methods, Kogut (1985a, 1985b) has added two further perspectives. First, a competitive advantage transferred to a subsidiary must be actively developed by recipient if it is to be sustainable. Second, industry and locational factours must be carefully balanced against subsidiary-specific components to maintain sustainability. Competitive methods are clearly not only important in themselves, but also operate within broader configurations of constituents in determining subsidiary strategy. Thus we have the second research question of this study:

RQ2: Are competitive methods at subsidiary level differentiated by the A–PJ framework in some systematic way?

METHODOLOGY

Sample

A pre-tested postal questionnaire was designed and sent to the CEOs of 300 randomly selected MNC manufacturing subsidiaries located in Scotland

Table 8.1 Characteristics of respondents' subsidiaries (Mean values)

	Scotland (92 respondents)	Ireland (120 respondents)
Age (years)	13.5	13.1
No. employed	410	210
Sales (£ million)	135.3	43.4
Exports (per cent)	47.4	80.8

Source: Postal survey (1996).

and a further 350 located in Ireland. After a follow-up mailing, responses were received from 212 subsidiaries (32.6 per cent), 92 from Scotland and 120 from Ireland (30.7 and 34.3 per cent, respectively).

The covering letter that accompanied the research instrument requested that, if the CEO was not in a position to respond, then the instrument should be passed to another executive who was involved in the annual strategy making round with corporate management. In the event, CEOs completed 45 (21.2 per cent) of the questionnaires, other directors 97 (45.8 per cent) and other managers 70 (33.0 per cent). Completion of one-third of responses by non-directors may introduce an element of measurement error (despite the plea in the covering letter), owing to the high strategic content of the research instrument. A summary of basic characteristics of respondent subsidiaries is shown in Table 8.1.

Measures

Procedural justice was measured with five standard measures (Kim and Mauborgne, 1991; Taggart, 1997), and measurement followed the rigorous procedures identified by these authors. However, Kim and Mauborgne used individual perspectives while the present research asked respondents to assess the subsidiary top management team's perceptions of procedural justice (see the Appendix, p. 120). After pre-test these measures were included unchanged in the final instrument. Correlations between them are high ($p < 0.01$) and the Cronbach alpha is 0.83, a satisfactory level for validating research. The measures for procedural justice were accepted as valid and reliable.

Seven measures of subsidiary autonomy were used (see the Appendix), drawn from Gates and Egelhoff (1986) and Taggart (1997). Some minor alterations were made after the pre-test. Correlations between these measures are all high ($p < 0.001$) and the Cronbach alpha is 0.89, a satisfactory level for validating research. The measures for procedural justice were accepted as valid and reliable.

Measures of competitive dynamics and competitive methods were drawn from a research instrument developed by Morrison (1990) in a study of US international firms. Twenty of these measures were selected, adapted, tested and included in the final research instrument. They were measured on a seven-point Likert scale. For competitive dynamics the scale was: 1 = not at all characteristic, 7 = fully characteristic. For competitive methods, the scale was: 1 = not at all important, 7 = very important. The questions and acronyms for these variables are set out in the Appendix.

Data Analysis

Data from the postal survey were analyzed in four stages. First, factor analysis was used to confirm the mutual orthogonality of the seven-variable autonomy and the five-variable procedural justice dimensions. Both groups of variables loaded uniquely and significantly on their respective dimensions. Second, as correlations within the dimensions and the Cronbach alphas were satisfactory, the two groups of variables were aggregated and averaged (Ghoshal and Bartlett, 1988). These two new variables were used as input for both hierarchical and non-hierarchical cluster analysis, as the combination gives a more robust classification (Dess and Davis, 1984; Johnson, 1995).

Third, analysis of variance assessed whether the clusters of subsidiaries so identified showed significant differences across the two groupings of strategic variables described above (competitive dynamics and competitive methods). Finally, with respect to the two research questions addressed by this paper, a *post hoc* method was used to test the significance of differences between the clusters. The appropriate tool was Duncan's multiple range test (Roth and Morrison, 1990), owing to the exploratory nature of this research. This procedure determined whether systematic variation across clusters of subsidiaries as postulated in RQ1 and RQ2.

RESULTS

Factor analysis confirmed that the dimensions of the model (autonomy, procedural justice) are orthogonal and that the variables load significantly and uniquely on their respective dimensions. When the eight measures of competitive dynamics and twelve measures of competitive methods were added to factor analysis, an eight-factor solution was obtained. Two of these were autonomy and procedural justice, with the variables loading significantly and uniquely on to either of two model dimensions. Thus, the competitive dynamics and competitive methods do not seem to be functionally related to the model dimensions, and the original two-factor solution seems robust.

Cluster analysis identified a stable four-group solution with between-groups variance accounting for 73.0 per cent of the total. This solution falls within the acceptable range of four to seven groups, using the method suggested by Roth and Morrison (1990), and appears to be robust. Table 8.2 shows the means of autonomy and procedural justice for this solution. The F-test is given for interest and should not be interpreted in the usual way, as the clustering technique ensured that the groups of companies are significantly separated along the two axes.

Four cross-tabulations were carried out across the clusters to ensure that structural factors were not unduly affecting the cluster formation. No significant effect was found for subsidiary location (Scotland, Ireland), home country of parents (USA, Europe, Japan, other), or job title of respondent (chief executive, other director, other manager). A marginal industry effect did emerge (chi-square = 12.98, df = 6, p = 0.05). Engineering firms (mechanical electrical, instrument, electronic, vehicle) firms were distributed as expected; chemicals firms had a few more *vassals* and a few less *militants* than expected, while for 'other' manufacturers, this position was reversed. Thus, the cluster solution appears highly robust, except for this minor industry effect, but it should be borne in mind when interpreting other results below.

An initial analysis of variance across the four clusters showed that there was no systematic variation of subsidiary type with age (F = 0.77, p = 0.51), employment level (F = 0.84, p = 0.47), or sales level (F = 0.43, p = 0.74). Analysis of variance using the eight competitive dynamics was then carried out, and the results are shown in Table 8.3. The design shows clear separation of the clusters (Rao's R = 2.19, p < 0.001), and there are a number of significant differences between the types of subsidiary. *Collaborators* show higher values than *militants* on a number of variables. Customer needs and purchasing practices are standardized world-wide to a greater extent for *collaborators*. They use more concentrated distribution channels, and their international activities are more restrained by governments. *Vassals* use more concentrated distribution channels than *militants*, they face substantially less product awareness in their international markets and less intense competition at home. *Vassals* also use more concentrated distribution channels than *partners*, together with much more standardized product technology; however, product awareness is significantly greater for *partners*. Finally, this type of subsidiary is less restrained by governments in its international activities than *collaborators*.

Table 8.4 shows the analysis of variance for the twelve competitive methods variables and the design again shows significant separation of the clusters (Rao's R = 1.85, p = 0.002). Compared to *militants*, *vassals* have less control over overheads, use less R&D, are less innovative in marketing techniques and are less concerned to monitor marketing opportunities. They use less advertising, and are less likely to take advantage of computer

Table 8.2 Cluster analysis: means of four-cluster solution

Variable	Cluster 1: vassal subsidiaries ($n = 39$)	Cluster 2: collaborator subsidiaries ($n = 70$)	Cluster 3: militant subsidiaries ($n = 52$)	Cluster 4: partner subsidiaries ($n = 51$)	F-statistic[c]
Autonomy:[a]					
Decisions about markets supplied	1.49	2.11	3.98	3.49	80.99
Decisions about product range	1.95	2.29	4.12	3.57	82.75
Decisions about advertising and promotion	2.51	2.41	4.60	4.12	58.91
Decisions about R&D	1.87	2.16	4.04	3.69	61.12
Decisions about production	2.08	2.36	4.31	4.06	44.13
Decisions about product pricing	1.77	1.94	3.62	3.20	34.47
Decisions about product design	3.64	3.16	4.65	4.41	30.96
Procedural justice:[b]					
Communication with HQ	2.05	4.41	3.10	5.84	78.46
Challenging HQ views	1.97	4.26	3.00	5.75	69.94
HQ has local knowledge	3.28	5.17	4.42	5.94	39.58
HQ accounts for decisions	2.79	5.66	3.90	6.08	58.31
HQ makes consistent decisions	3.33	5.16	3.88	6.00	44.11

Notes:
a For autonomy, higher scores signify more autonomy.
b For procedural justice, higher scores signify more procedural justice.
c All F-statistics are significant at $p < 0.001$.

Table 8.3   Means of competitive dynamics variables[a]

Variable	Cluster 1: vassal subsidiaries: (n = 39)	Cluster 2: collaborator subsidiaries: (n = 70)	Cluster 3: militant subsidiaries: (n = 52)	Cluster 4: partner subsidiaries: (n = 51)	F-statistic	p-value	Difference between Clusters[b]
NEED	3.67	3.79	3.02	3.25	2.16	0.09	2 > 3
PURCH	3.13	3.39	2.67	3.10	2.19	0.09	2 > 3
DOM	3.44	4.26	4.48	3.75	2.27	0.08	3 > 1
INT	5.28	5.76	5.58	5.69	1.28	0.28	
DIST	4.33	4.13	3.40	3.71	3.48	0.02	1 > 3,4;
PROD	4.38	5.21	4.67	5.00	3.31	0.02	2 > 3
ACT	3.26	3.79	2.73	3.00	3.88	0.01	1 < 3,4
TECH	4.82	4.51	4.42	4.10	1.51	0.21	2 > 3,4
							1 > 4

Notes:
a Higher scores signify higher levels of emphasis for all variables.
b Results of Duncan's multiple-range tests ($p = 0.05$).

integrated manufacturing (CIM) and CAPM. Compared to *partners*, *vassals* are also less likely to be involved in R&D, innovative marketing, market monitoring, CIM and CAPM. They are less likely to emphasize speciality products, probably have a poorer industry reputation and put less stress on developing a highly skilled sales force. *Partners* are distinguished from *militants* by higher customer service and greater emphasis on quality products, but by less stress on the use of advertising. They are separated from *collaborators* by more constant monitoring of market opportunities, more emphasis on speciality products and skilled sales forces and by a higher reputation in the industry. *Collaborators*, in turn, are segregated from *militants* by less control of overheads, and from *vassals* by more emphasis on R&D expertise, greater use of CIM and CAPM.

To summarize this rather complex analysis of competitive dynamics and competitive methods, *vassals* are significantly separated from *collaborators* by three variables, from *militants* by ten, and from *partners* by eleven. *Collaborators* are distinguished from *militants* and *partners* by five variables each. *Militants* are separated from *partners* by three variables. This scenario of extensive systematic variation across the typology of the A–PJ model gives a clear and positive response to both RQ1 and RQ2. However, the nature of the competitive dynamics and competitive measures variables allows further interpretation, and the characteristics of the four types of subsidiaries will be further explored in the next section.

DISCUSSION

Two observations can be drawn from the foregoing analysis. First, it is clear that the autonomy and procedural justice dimensions give a good internal

Table 8.4 Means of competitive methods variables[a]

Variable	Cluster 1: vassal subsidiaries: (n = 39)	Cluster 2: collaborator subsidiaries: (n = 70)	Cluster 3: militant subsidiaries: (n = 52)	Cluster 4: partner subsidiaries: (n = 51)	F-statistic	p-value	Difference between clusters[b]
CONT	5.95	5.96	5.38	5.78	2.63	0.05	3 < 1,2
CUST	5.95	5.93	5.81	6.39	2.32	0.08	4 > 3
RD	3.64	4.14	4.37	4.90	3.24	0.02	1 < 2,3,4
MARK	3.46	3.99	4.65	4.55	4.55	0.00	1 < 3,4
MON	4.51	4.83	5.31	5.53	4.14	0.01	1 < 3,4; 2 < 4
ADV	3.08	3.26	3.75	3.06	1.83	0.14	1 < 3,4; 3 > 4
SPEC	4.15	4.41	4.10	5.27	4.04	0.01	4 > 1,2,3
REP	5.74	5.79	5.96	6.33	2.75	0.04	4 > 1,2
NIC	4.51	4.50	4.29	5.02	1.50	0.22	
AGT	3.87	4.21	4.60	5.04	3.23	0.02	4 > 1,2
CIM	3.13	4.01	4.17	4.33	3.30	0.02	1 < 2,3,4
CAPM	3.44	4.17	4.35	4.29	2.04	0.11	1 < 2,3,4

Notes:
a Higher scores signify higher levels of emphasis for all variables.
b Results of Duncan's multiple-range tests ($p = 0.05$).

resolution of four distinct groups of subsidiaries that conform to the typol-ogy developed by Taggart (1997). While not an obvious result, it is not wholly unexpected that such a solution should emerge from two well defined dimensions that have been demonstrated as orthogonal. The second observation is, perhaps, more consequential; the four groups of subsidiaries are also clearly and significantly separated by the 20 strategic variables used in the analysis. Since these were shown earlier to be independent, individ-ually and collectively, from the measures of autonomy and procedural justice, then the typology appears to be capturing some real and important aspects of subsidiary strategy. As this research project set out to validate the basis of the A–PJ model, these observations together with the specific responses to RQ1 and RQ2 give a satisfactory results. However, it is imme-diately relevant to enquire further into the nature of each type of subsidiary. This is now done with respect to the characteristics set out in Tables 8.3 and 8.4. In addition, the following discussion also draws on ten post-test inter-views with subsidiaries in both Scotland and Ireland.

The *Vassal* Subsidiary

This type operates in a most uncomfortable strategy locus (low A–low PJ, see Figure 8.1); subsidiary managers would hardly find this position attrac-tive, nor would host governments welcome a large proportion of such af-filiates. Of all four types, *vassals* are most clearly characterized by their use of concentrated international channels of distribution, and they are most likely to operate within standardized product technology. On the other hand, they have to contend with a much lower level of international product awareness and put relatively little emphasis on developing innovative mar-keting techniques. They are least likely to monitor market opportunities and are less concerned with sales force skills. Reputation within the indus-try is not highly valued by them, and they put significantly less weight on advanced operations tools like CIM and CAPM. These factors appear to be characteristic of the type of subsidiary that serves a tightly defined role for headquarters, following central dictates without overt argument, and with little obvious evidence of advanced management skills or aggressive management initiatives at local level.

This profile was well illustrated by an Irish subsidiary in a specialized sectour of the textiles industry. Following a fairly settled history up to the mid-1980s, the firm has been through a number of changes of ownership, and now has a UK-based parent. Until recently, it was the principal manu-facturing centre for Europe and, effectively, the MNC's European head-quarters. A new production plant with advanced technology and substantial R&D has been built in England, and the Irish subsidiary has been conse-quentially downgraded in both manufacturing and strategic contribution. It has lost its regional HQ status, and relationships with HQ have deteriorated rapidly. The plant director observed that the group CEO visited his plant once a month, occupied his office for a day and made a number of operational decisions without reference to him. This was not a happy subsidiary to visit.

The *Collaborator*

This type (low A–high PJ) is a more comfortable fit with headquarters and other elements of its international network. Compared to other subsidiary types, they appear to work with the most intensive levels of international competition, their international activities are most restrained by governments and they put heavy emphasis on cost control. In some ways, this profile is perhaps characteristic of firms in global industries, though the question of government regulations may be more closely linked to the *collaborator's* lack of autonomy.

Another of the Irish subsidiaries interviewed was a large manufacturing plant within a highly internationalized healthcare MNC. It had been established in Ireland for over 20 years, employed 900, its current sales level is approximately £100 million per annum, of which 98 per cent is exported. The MNC operates with a tightly integrated network and, owing to the sensitive nature of its business, the affiliate appreciates that its operational environment must conform to corporation-side standards. Overall strategy is also tightly controlled by headquarters and local management recognizes this as a constraint on their activities. Nevertheless, their creativity and proactivity is given an outlet in areas like internal and external benchmarking, aspects of new and adapted product design and in-subsidiary human resource development. The affiliate management team regards the apparent high level of procedural justice as a direct trade-off for lack of local decision making. Both headquarters and subsidiary executives put a consistently high investment into building and maintaining good relationships, specially in those areas where key decisions must be made on a corporation-wide basis. Despite the centralized nature of the MNC, the sense of local ownership in this subsidiary is pervasive. While the legal position of headquarters and shareholders is clearly recognized and willingly accepted, the social responsibility of the subsidiary management team towards the local community is an ever-present factor.

The *Militant* Subsidiary

With low levels of procedural justice and extensive local autonomy, this subsidiary type has been characterized above as a difficult fit within an MNC's international network. Indeed, it is not easy to understand at arm's length why headquarters is prepared to tolerate a situation of this nature. The *militant* strategy locus is characterized by intense domestic competition, where a premium is placed on developing innovative marketing techniques and extensive use of advertising, and where CIM is particularly intensively utilized. Customer needs and international purchasing practices demonstrate little standardization, world-wide distribution channels are relatively diffuse and there is little government regulation of international activities. Control of overheads is not a key factor, there is little emphasis on speciality products and niche markets are regarded as unimportant.

In order to indicate that such an unusual combination of characteristics may still be contained proactively within an MNC's network, reference is made to a post-test interview carried out with a defence industry subsidiary in Scotland of a major US military supplies manufacturer. The affiliate has been in place for some 30 years and, unlike its parent, it has diversified substantially away from its core defence-related business. Over the years, local management has used an uninterrupted stream of good operating results to bargain decision making away from headquarters. In the last few years, the development of corporation-wide information technology systems has put pressure on the level of local autonomy, and this has led directly to a more aggressive relationship at the HQ–subsidiary interface. The subsidiary CEO is aware of the opportunity cost of this situation and is determined to improve the quality of relationships with corporate managers. He is, however, adamant that extensive local autonomy is crucial to continued profitability. The situation was encapsulated by the tone of the CEO's anticipation of a coming visit of the parent board of directors to his plant; he sounded as though he was expecting extraterrestrial beings.

The *Partner*

High levels of autonomy and procedural justice make this an attractive strategy type from the perspectives of both local managers and host governments. It may be reasonably speculated that corporate managers are also relaxed about *partner* affiliates. They may be further characterized by the highest levels of emphasis on customer service, the need for local R&D and constant monitoring of market opportunities. They develop speciality products, and prize a good reputation within the industry. They develop premium products for market niches, use highly skilled sales forces and utilize CIM. Coupled with their view that standardized technologies are unimportant to their businesses, this profile suggests that *partners* have many of the attributes of Prahalad and Doz's (1987) multifocal strategy, as well as Bartlett and Ghoshal's (1986) strategic leader.

The type is well represented by the Scottish subsidiary of a Scandinavian mechanical engineering MNC. Originally acquired about ten years ago, the parent introduced new investment in facilities, leading-edge technologies and access to world markets in exchange for revised working practices. The subsequent development of this partnership between headquarters and subsidiary has led to strong operating performance, confidence in the future among the subsidiary management team and excellent if robust relationships across the HQ–subsidiary interface. In tandem with this process, corporate managers have gradually relaxed their control over affiliate activities and the balance of decision making responsibility has now swung decidedly in the subsidiary's direction. Despite the relatively mellow working environment, the subsidiary CEO is clear that continued *partner* status is entirely dependent on maintaining the international competitive edge that his business has developed.

SYNTHESIS

This work is largely supportive of the original A–PJ model, but goes much further in describing and evaluating the strategic and operating characteristics of the four subsidiary types. Two observations may be made here. First, the conceptual types *vassal*, *collaborator*, *militant* and *partner* can be identified as holistic configurations of attributes among a sample of MNC subsidiaries. Second, they are broadly recognized as such in discussion with the post-test interview firms. Unlike the dimensions corresponding to integration, co-ordination, configuration and strategic importance of local market (where the author has found a substantial degree of misunderstanding among MNC subsidiary managers), autonomy and procedural justice are quickly recognized and comprehended in post-test interviews.

The four *vassal* CEOs interviewed agreed and substantiated their location in the low A–low PJ strategy space and accepted that this was a poor positioning. They described a number of tactical and operational moves that were being planned and/or utilized to re-position their firms. They were, however, distinctly uneasy about the use of the term '*vassal*'. This last point also applies to the four *militant* CEOs, though again they accepted and corroborated the underlying characteristics. Broadly, however, re-positioning of *militants* requires some degree of concession by headquarters. Failing this, *militant* CEOs seemed quite prepared to defend their position – and, in particular, their level of autonomy. The situation with *collaborators* and *partners* was, perhaps, more straightforward. The former were happy with their positioning and had no desire to move, even to the high A–high PJ sector. *Partner* CEOs regarded their strategic location as the end of much focused activity to establish an acceptable and proactive relationship with corporate managers. There was evidence of a substantial determination to defend and develop this positioning.

CONCLUSIONS

This chapter set out to evaluate the A–PJ model and to provide a degree of empirical validation using a range of strategic variables measured in a sample of manufacturing MNC subsidiaries located in Scotland and Ireland. The model strategy types (*vassal, collaborator, militant, partner*) emerged as clearly differentiated groups of affiliates, and the separation of strategic variables across these types enabled them to be characterized in more detail than previously. The post-test interviews added a degree of descriptive richness and indicated that subsidiary managers recognize the impact of the model dimensions and consequent strategy types.

There are three broad implications that emerge from this work. First, there are clear indications that subsidiary managers who are suitably motivated may strategically reposition their subsidiaries over time through a combination of maintaining competitive edge and negotiating with headquarters. Second, corporate managers may be able to pick up earlier warning signals of declining subsidiary performance by becoming more sensitive to the interplay of autonomy, procedural justice and HQ requirements for network responsiveness. Third, host governments and their regional economic development agencies may be able to use the A–PJ perspective to identify opportunities (especially where formal inward investor after-care programmes are being implemented) to increase the local embeddedness of their populations of foreign subsidiaries.

Two further arenas of enquiry are also suggested by the results reported here. First, the suggestion of an industry effect on subsidiary strategy type emerged here as a by-product of the research. This may prompt further detailed investigation, especially among the sunrise industries that are so keenly sought by host governments. Second, though no country-of-origin effect was found, it should be recognized that both autonomy and procedural justice may well be – at least in part – culture-bound concepts. A dedicated research project based on formalized measures of cultural values and perceptions may give different A–PJ outcomes to those reported above.

APPENDIX: POSTAL QUESTIONNAIRE ABSTRACT
(AUTONOMY AND PROCEDURAL JUSTICE)

The following categories of decision-making have been identified:

1. Decided mainly by the parent company or regional headquarters *without* consulting with or seeking the advice of this subsidiary.
2. Decided mainly by the parent company or regional headquarters *after* consulting with or seeking the advice of this subsidiary.
3. Decided jointly with *equal weight* being given to the views of subsidiary and HQ.

4. Decided mainly by this subsidiary *after* consulting with or seeking the advice of the parent company or regional headquarters.
5. Decided mainly by this subsidiary *without* consulting with or seeking the advice of the parent company or regional headquarters.

Referring to the above, please indicate below which category (i.e. 1,2,3,4 or 5 above) best describes the decision-making authority that this subsidiary has in terms of the eight functional areas listed on the left-hand side of the table. Please mark 1,2,3,4 or 5 against each function as appropriate.

Market area supplied by subsidiary	
Product range supplied by subsidiary	
Pricing of subsidiary's products	
Design of subsidiary's products	
Advertising and promotion of subsidiary's products	
R & D at subsidiary	
Production operations at subsidiary	

Procedural justice refers to how the HQ strategy-making process for its subsidiary units are judged to be fair by subsidiary top management. In the following 5 questions, please circle the appropriate number to indicate your perception between either end of the scales in terms of how you feel the top management team views each of these aspects.

Effective two-way communication exists between this subsidiary and corporate or regional HQ during the process of formulating the parent company's strategy.

> *This does not apply at all* **1 2 3 4 5 6 7** *This applies fully*

This subsidiary has adequate and legitimate opportunity to challenge the strategic views of corporate or regional HQ during the process of formulating the parent company's strategy.

> *This does not apply at all* **1 2 3 4 5 6 7** *This applies fully*

Corporate or regional HQ is knowledgeable of the local situation of this subsidiary.

> *This does not apply at all* **1 2 3 4 5 6 7** *This applies fully*

This subsidiary is provided with an account of the final strategic decisions of corporate or regional headquarters.

> *This does not apply at all* **1 2 3 4 5 6 7** *This applies fully*

Corporate or regional HQ is fairly consistent in making decisions across all subsidiary units within this multinational corporation.

> *This does not apply at all* **1 2 3 4 5 6 7** *This applies fully*

Competitive Dynamics

An important part of understanding international competition is to understand the competitive dynamics within your industry. Considering only the principal sector of the industry within which your business competes, indicate how characteristic each of the following statements are in describing your industry. Please circle the appropriate number against each question.

	Not at all characteristic						*Fully characteristic*
1. Customer needs are standardized world-wide	1	2	3	4	5	6	7
2. Standardized purchasing practices exist world-wide	1	2	3	4	5	6	7
3. Domestic competition is intense	1	2	3	4	5	6	7
4. International competition is intense	1	2	3	4	5	6	7
5. Distribution channels highly concentrated world-wide	1	2	3	4	5	6	7
6. Product awareness exists world-wide	1	2	3	4	5	6	7
7. International activities are restrained by governments	1	2	3	4	5	6	7
8. Standardized product technology exists world-wide	1	2	3	4	5	6	7

Competitive Methods

23. Listed below are various competitive methods that might be important to competing in your industry. Indicate how important each item is to the current strategy of your subsidiary. Please circle the appropriate number against each question.

	Not at all important						*Very important*
1. Tightly control overheads	1	2	3	4	5	6	7
2. Emphasize customer service/service quality	1	2	3	4	5	6	7
3. Develop engineering and R&D expertise	1	2	3	4	5	6	7
4. Develop innovative marketing techniques	1	2	3	4	5	6	7
5. Monitor market opportunities constantly	1	2	3	4	5	6	7
6. Emphasize advertising	1	2	3	4	5	6	7
7. Emphasize specialty products	1	2	3	4	5	6	7
8. Build reputation in industry	1	2	3	4	5	6	7
9. Produce high priced products for market niches	1	2	3	4	5	6	7
10. Utilize highly skilled sales force/agents	1	2	3	4	5	6	7
11. Utilize computer integrated manufacturing (CIM)	1	2	3	4	5	6	7
12. Utilize computer aided production management (CAPM)	1	2	3	4	5	6	7

9 European Integration and Structural Change in the Multinational: Evidence from Foreign Subsidiaries Operating in Portugal

Ana Teresa Tavares and Robert Pearce

INTRODUCTION

Economic integration and corporate integration by multinational enterprises (MNEs) represent two of the most paramount shaping factors in the contemporary world economic system. In spite of their overwhelming relevance in today's economic reality, there are considerable *lacunae* in the literature concerning eventual links between these two phenomena, already pointed out by Dunning and Robson (1988) and Robson (1993). Hence, opportunities exist to explore this theoretical and analytical gap.

One way of looking at this particular question is by hypothesizing that forming or acceding to an economically integrated space will lead to strategic reactions by economic agents, notably multinational firms. This will occur probably owing to an enhanced scope (and imperative) for rationalization of activities in order to achieve increased intra-area efficiency.

Notwithstanding, the impact of economic integration on multinational activities is far from linear. Indeed, it may lead to dichotomous pressures: on the one hand towards centralization, especially in industries where economies of scale are pervasive (the lifting of trade barriers facilitating exports from the centralized headquarters to the distinct markets in the bloc), and on the other hand it may be conducive to decentralization (*a priori* in line with comparative advantage), as freedom of trade allows for increased opportunities to reap the benefits from corporate internalization.

The chapter will be divided into four main parts. First, a brief explanation concerning the approach and basic concepts used will be provided. The next section will discuss theoretically how accession to an economically integrated area may impact and benefit a 'peripheral' and relatively small economy (in the context of that area). It will conceptualize a two-stage process in terms of industrial restructuring motivated at least partially by economic integration. The next section will explicitly refer to the Portuguese case and present quantitative and qualitative evidence that may

123

help to document, in this particular example, how the hypothesized process of structural change has been partly induced (directly and/or indirectly) by European integration. Finally, some conclusions and suggestions for future research will be derived.

Background

The motivation for the present study stems from the considerable neglect to which the interface between processes of economic integration and corporate integration has been subjected (Dunning and Robson, 1988; Robson, 1993). It may pay dividends to bridge this gap. First of all, economic and corporate integration processes share, in the abstract, certain features. They can be seen as having the same underlying *raison d'être*, based on the assumption that the integrated governance of units permits the avoidance of unnecessary costs, simultaneously generating synergistic benefits (Tavares and Pearce, 1998a). The concept of transaction costs (Coase, 1937; Williamson, 1975; Buckley and Casson, 1976) is relevant in this context.

Both economic and corporate integration represent dynamic evolutionary processes, and involve differentiated networks that are marked by a considerable degree of intra-systemic heterogeneity. It is exactly this aspect of heterogeneity that will be explored here, in order to link the two phenomena under scrutiny. First of all, the MNE is conceptualized as a system composed of distinct types of subsidiaries. In this vein, a typology of subsidiary roles (or strategies, given that the subsidiary might be more than a recipient of a centrally attributed role) is instrumental in order to illustrate how economic integration may lead to endogenous changes in the MNE, notably through evolution in the nature of the activities and intra-group profile of its subsidiaries.

The typology used here is a tripartite and parsimonious version of the well known 'scope typology', being invoked in pioneering work developed by White and Poynter (1984), D'Cruz (1986) and Pearce (1992). The three main types of subsidiaries considered are:

- *Truncated miniature replicas (TMRs)*, defined by a narrow market scope (the host-country market), wide product scope (as they replicate the parent's product range) and usually rather limited value-added/functional scope, though they may have freedom to adapt the product range to local demand; quite obviously, TMRs are typical of a trade-constrained environment, and are rendered inefficient when trade openness occurs.
- *Rationalized product subsidiaries (RPSs)*, which are subsidiaries with a narrow product range and a broad market scope, as they are specialized in the supply of a part of the product range (or components) to export markets; their functional scope tends to be even more restricted than TMRs, as they tend to obey rather stoically centrally emanated directives.

- *Product mandates*, characterized by the ability to develop, produce and eventually market-specific product(s) for a certain market area. This subsidiary type is undoubtedly the one with superior value-added scope *vis-à-vis* the above-mentioned two categories. It may be envisaged also as the type with more potential in terms of developing a creative interaction or 'positive dialectic' with the host economy. There are three sub-types encapsulated in this category: world product mandates (WPMs), regional product mandates (RPMs), and sub-regional product mandates (SRPMs), when they develop products for the world, regional (in terms of a group of countries) or sub-regional (smaller group of countries within a region) markets, respectively (see also chapter 6 in this volume).

Directly linked with this consideration of differentiated subsidiary roles is the principle that there are quite distinct motivations underlying international production. In this chapter, the typology proposed by Dunning (1993) is adopted, contemplating four main motivations for a MNE to develop international productive activities, notably resource-seeking, market-seeking, efficiency-seeking and strategic asset-seeking. The last three categories will be emphasized in later sections, and in the case of Portugal particular support is found for the market-seeking and for the efficiency-seeking hypothesis (which is consistent with the results advanced by Buckley and Castro, 1998).

Last but by no means least, it must be emphasized that the consideration of distinct subsidiary roles and investment motivations is conceptualized in a dynamic fashion, allowing for distinct evolutionary paths in subsidiary development (Birkinshaw and Hood, 1997) and for a pluralistic approach in terms of underlying reasons for investment, based in the coexistence of such different motivations, even in the same MNE.

Empirical evidence on p. 134 will support the ideas presented above. Furthermore, these issues will be related to the potential contribution of multinational subsidiaries to the host country, which naturally differs according to the very nature of activities and linkages developed by the MNE in that host economy.

THEORETICAL CONSIDERATIONS ON HOW A PERIPHERAL ECONOMY MIGHT BENEFIT FROM ACCESSION TO AN ECONOMICALLY INTEGRATED SPACE

Accession and Industrial Restructuring: A Two-stage Approach

A peripheral economy entering an economically integrated scheme should perceive the benefits and objectives as involving essentially two distinct phases. The first phase involves a period of quite fundamental transition and industrial restructuring, in order to establish the country's initial status as a specialized economy that has a basis for competition in the wider integrated area. The second phase then seeks to build on the initial position by operationalizing and/or engineering new localized sources of competitiveness, which may emerge as viable only once the industrial sector is decisively oriented to the new economically integrated environment.

The first stage can be represented as basically involving a fundamental reorientation of the country's strategy for industrialization, from import substitution to export orientation. Pre-economic integration, we may hypothesize a predominantly local market-focused industrial sector producing quite a wide range of goods, the precise composition of which reflects mainly the structure of local demand and the structure of protection (Tavares and Pearce, 1998a). Thus this industrial structure is unlikely to decisively reflect static comparative advantage (the protection structure may be partly set to support industries that are out of line with it) and the technologies used may reflect (and rarely transcend) the standardized norms in the industries.

The restructuring process (reorientation to the post-economic integration environment) will narrow the industrial structure around those sectors that are best able to activate sources of static comparative advantage to meet the demands of the wider economically integrated area. Those industries that were most dependent on protection and/or out of line with static comparative advantage are most likely to be run down. Industries that previously met particularly idiosyncratic elements of local demand may survive as 'eccentric' niche sectors, or may generalize into specialist suppliers of these 'local-culture goods' to the whole integrated space. The most decisively expanding sectors will be in principle those that embody genuine sources of comparative advantage. In eclectic framework terminology (Dunning, 1977), the essence of the process is a change of location advantages – that is, from the negative location advantages of trade restraint to the positive location advantage of cost effective local inputs.

The adoption of a *regional* strategy as the *modus operandi* of MNEs in the area emerges to replace a *multidomestic* approach (Porter, 1986), when the economically integrated scheme becomes operative. Rationalized product subsidiaries (RPSs) are most likely to be activated in the peripheral economy, either as *de novo* investments or through the metamorphosis of truncated miniature replicas (TMRs).

Intra-group diffusion of knowledge may mean (possibly, though not necessarily) that these RPSs can achieve 'first-phase' objectives for the host country more effectively than might indigenous firms, whose pre-integration competitive horizons had been unable to transcend the local market. The MNEs (given that they tend to have access to a more systemic perspective than local firms) can discern fairly directly how they can use

local inputs to produce goods that will be competitive throughout the economically integrated area (or as competitive as the MNEs' competencies
– ownership advantages – allow), for instance to detect and operationalize
an intrinsic source of comparative advantage. MNEs may very well provide
stronger ownership advantages in the form of product/process technology
and region-wide market knowledge and already extant market access
(distribution networks). Hence intra-group knowledge transfers and effective planning procedures in MNEs may assist host countries (through
the localized RPSs) to speed up the phase-one restructuring (compared
to that available through reformulation of indigenous industry). With
limited government ability to plan the restructuring of indigenous industry
(partly owing to limited knowledge of needs in the wider integrated space)
the emergence of a local industrial sector that is internationally competitive, around current sources of comparative advantage, will depend on the
new market forces of the economically integrated area. These forces
may be less than fully effective and could, perhaps, work detrimentally to
peripheral economies, in particular, in terms of biases against full realization
of competitiveness (eventually because their sources of location advantage
– for example, low-cost labour – may provide severe challenges to the
most disadvantaged sectors of core economies and present unwelcome
stresses to their internal adjustment mechanisms). Hence, perhaps, the
implementation of corporate integration within the economically integrated space by MNEs may speed up, and even better approach the optimal
efficiency of, the industrial adjustment process in peripheral or 'non-core'
economies.

Welfare Implications and Created Comparative Advantage

The first stage should provide a one-off set of efficiency improvements: for
the integrated bloc as a whole, for individual countries (though the inter-
country distribution of the overall benefit may be contentious) and for
MNEs that can now access the benefits of corporate integration through
the implementation of a regional strategy. At the end of this evolutionary
process the peripheral economy should have an improvement in national
welfare that derives, *inter alia*, from an improved efficiency in its industrial
sector which reflects a greater activation of its sources of static comparative advantage, all of which, in turn, reflect the country securing its *share* in
the region-wide benefits of market-stimulated improvements in resource
allocation. The MNE has benefited because it can distribute its current firm-
level source of competitiveness (its ownership advantage) more widely but
discriminatingly, such that it works with location advantages that best com-
plements it and therefore greatly improves efficiency of production (and
thus pan-regional profitability). Once these adjustment benefits have been
worked through and been fully realized both the peripheral economy and

the MNE will begin to articulate the different aims of phase two. This is very much the desirable scenario, in which a shared developmental vision is developed by both the MNE and host-country institutions. Nonetheless, reality has shown that this 'synergistic partnership' is often not developed. In this vein, industrial policy might have a role to play (Tavares and Pearce, 1998b).

If phase one ultimately involved moves toward the optimized use of sources of competitiveness that essentially remained unchanged in the process (through the removal of inefficiencies, distortions and myopic (bounded rationality) perspectives reflecting poor diffusion of knowledge in the pre-integration area), the defining aim of phase two is generation of new (or vastly revitalized) sources of competitiveness.

Once the industrial sector of a peripheral economy has established a competitive position in the supply of certain goods to the markets of the wider economically integrated region it could (with some awareness of retaining efficiency in its current production operations) take something of a free ride on greater dynamism and growth in core areas, in terms of securing some enhancement of its own development and income improvement. Hence if its products are ones the supply of which other countries in the region are unlikely to wish to accede (from an even more peripheral or 'low-level' status) and if growth in core countries does generate more demand for these goods, then real incomes in these industries may grow somewhat (albeit in a very passive way, and also one that could be vulnerable to lower-cost competition from outside the region if external trade barriers on these goods are low enough) merely as a 'trickle-down' of extra demand from more positive growth processes elsewhere. The more logical ambition would be to pursue the derivation of new sources of competitiveness, perhaps by application of local knowledge to the industrial sector (through both local firms and MNEs).

Beyond the fact that upward pressure on real wages that is not matched by higher productivity is always a source of some degree of vulnerability (even given the benign scenario above), a peripheral economy will look for ways to move up the ladder of comparative advantage positively rather than, in effect, relying on core-country dynamism to lift the whole ladder (and thus provide some income gains to those countries in the lower range). This aim can be manifested in creating, and/or operationalizing commercially, new types of comparative advantage. The broad potentials have logically taken the form of investment in human capital (education and training) and in knowledge (scientific research activated in commercial development). During an import-substitution era indigenous firms facing a small and poor local market, in a protected environment and with little access to foreign markets (and no creative stimulus from needs in these markets) have little incentive to seek knowledge-activating innovations that could provide higher value-added industry. Accession of the peripheral economy to the wider integrated area provides the market scope and competitive stimulus that should inculcate in local firms the desire to become part of a national system of innovation (Lundvall, 1992) that generates new knowledge and activates it commercially. In effect, this process moves towards derivation of *created* comparative advantage, which provides a basis for aggressive industrialization (movement into new industries, fundamental regeneration of existing ones) that aims to move the economy qualitatively towards the core.

These forces also affect MNE operations as the peripheral economy moves into stage two. Here it may be that MNE scope (as a differentiated network, Bartlett and Ghoshal, 1989; Forsgren and Johanson, 1992) provides greater sources of vulnerability to the peripheral economy, but also greater positive potentials and opportunities. The upward pressure on labour costs of an RPS that are likely to emerge in phase two (if phase one has been successful and constitutes a basis for international competitiveness) raise a real possibility of closure and movement of production elsewhere (the RPS' ownership advantage is a very standardized and easily transferable technology – i.e. it has a considerable public good component). However if the RPS provides the MNE with a generally favourable view of the peripheral economy as a location within the integrated space it might support investigation of transformation into a RPM (or at least into a SRPM), if effective sources of localized creative inputs appear to be emerging. Supportive intra-group knowledge (parts of relevant technology, market ideas, market access) may mean that a RPM subsidiary of a MNE can contribute to engineering comparative advantage in the peripheral economy.

This may include spillovers to local input suppliers, a local science base (e.g. universities) and so forth. Overall, the process means that RPMs create locally (and seek to internalize intra-group) new ownership advantages from knowledge elements of location advantages (thus somehow diluting the distinction between the two types of advantages). This localized facet of its ownership advantage also embeds the subsidiary in the peripheral economy to a quite substantial degree and should generate a shared dimension of creative dynamism.

Basic Strategy Set Available to a MNE After Economic Integration

Figure 9.1 illustrates diagrammatically, and in a deliberately simplified manner, the main strategic options available to a MNE subsidiary when trade barriers are lifted as a consequence of economic integration. It is clear that the MNE must abandon the former 'truncated' approach and effect specialization if it wants to remain competitive in the context of trade fluidity. The MNE will then have, in the present analysis, three main restructuring paths, as shown in Figure 9.1.

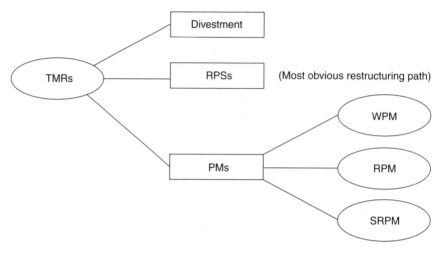

Figure 9.1   Evidence based on MNEs' subsidiaries operating in Portugal

The Surge in FDI and MNE Activities in the Years Following Accession

Both quantitative and qualitative changes seem to have occurred concerning FDI and MNEs' activities in Portugal since accession to the EU in 1986. The qualitative aspects have been considerably neglected, and it is hoped to shed some light on these issues later in the chapter.

Quantitatively, in terms of FDI flows (see Figure 9.2), it suffices to state that they multiplied by a factor of 20 during the period 1987–91 (after what Simões, 1992, called a 'wait-and-see' period in 1986) to understand that suddenly the attractiveness of Portugal as an investment location was boosted. This fact is probably due not only to accession *per se* but also due to the Single Market Programme imperatives (again consistent with Buckley and Castro's, 1998, findings) and to other indirect effects of integration associated with a greater awareness of the country as a potential investment recipient.

In quantitative terms it is also important to remark that divestment grew considerably during the period, although divestment figures should be regarded with caution as there are several problems with them in the Portuguese case. The investigation of divestment far transcends the aims of this chapter, in fact it would justify a study of its own, though it is relevant to emphasize here the parallel increase in FDI inflows and divestment. This may also relate to the subsidiary restructuring perspective developed on p. 125. Thus divestment may mean closure of TMRs and inflows would usually correspond to the set up of RPSs.

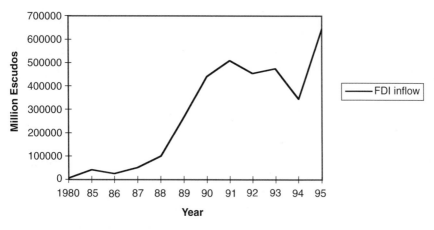

Figure 9.2   FDI inflow in Portugal, 1980–95

Source: Banco de Portugal (Portuguese Central Bank).

Table 9.1   FDI inflows in Portugal, by investing country, 1986–95, per cent

	1986	1987	1988	1989	1990	1991	1992	1993	1994	1995
OECD	96.1	93.0	92.8	83.9	87.6	85.3	86.2	95.1	87.5	94.2
EC	*76.3*	*65.8*	*69.1*	*69.1*	*70.8*	*68.4*	*76.6*	*75.3*	*73.8*	*79.8*
USA	8.6	14.3	11.7	1.3	3.1	7.9	3.7	11.1	4.4	2.1
Japan	0.7	2.2	0.8	0.5	2.2	1.0	0.4	1.3	0.8	0.3
Other	10.5	10.7	11.2	12.9	11.5	7.0	5.5	7.4	8.6	11.9
Rest of the world	*3.9*	*7.0*	*7.2*	*16.1*	*12.4*	*14.7*	*13.8*	*4.9*	*2.5*	*5.8*
Total	*100.0*	*100.0*	*100.0*	*100.0*	*100.0*	*100.0*	*100.0*	*100.0*	*100.0*	*100.0*

Source: Banco de Portugal (Portuguese Central Bank).

Importance of EU FDI in Terms of Share of Total Inward FDI in Portugal

An analysis of the disaggregation of FDI inflows shows the overwhelming importance of EU countries as investors in Portugal. During the period under scrutiny, the share of EU investment represented between two-thirds and four-fifths of total inward FDI in the economy (see Table 9.1). It is worth noting that before accession this investment hardly constituted half of total inflows. However, it should be said that these figures are overstated as often FDI by non-EU MNEs is effected through their EU headquarters. Despite this qualification, the growth observed in the EU investors' share constitutes an example of the surge in intra-EU FDI motivated by the announcement of the completion of the Single Market Programme (Molle and Morsink, 1991; Clegg, 1996). As already mentioned, it is presumed that the sudden increase in FDI in Portugal was both due to accession and to the Single Market prospects, in particular to relocation of facilities in consequence of rationalization and corporate restructuring in the pursuit for efficiency.

Evidence on Changes Post-accession and on the Nature of MNE Activities in Portugal

This analysis is based on a survey conducted among the 500 biggest multinational subsidiaries operating in Portugal. At the time of writing, 89 responses had been received, constituting an 18 per cent response rate. From these, it was deliberately chosen not to consider 13 responses, owing to doubts concerning the appropriateness of these firms to the sample (for instance, when doubts existed about the presence of an articulated European strategy).

One of the first concerns to understand the reality and evolution of MNEs' subsidiaries in Portugal was to identify the motivations underlying their establishment in the country. The results obtained fairly reflected our *a priori* expectations. The main motivation emphasized by the managers of these subsidiaries was the relatively lower costs of production, which was deemed quite important across all industries and home countries of the MNEs. The second most important reason for choosing Portugal as an investment destination was to improve competitiveness in the EU market (for a detailed description of all the motivations mentioned in the research instrument and quantification in terms of relative importance see Tavares and Pearce, 1998c; the same source also has data validating all the issues mentioned in this section). The main aspect to stress here is the explicit support for the efficiency-seeking hypothesis, and also for the market-seeking motivation (here the relevant market being the EU). This conclusion was also reached in the study by Buckley and Castro (1998). From our data the pan-European outlook of non-EU MNEs (Asian, the USA) is especially worthy of reference, whereas EU MNEs tend to be in relative terms more local-market focused (which is in line with previous studies undertaken by Hood and Young, 1988; Slewaegen, 1988; Pearce and Papanastassiou, 1997). This finding also relates to the markets supplied by foreign MNEs' subsidiaries operating in Portugal. Three time periods were considered in the survey: before 1986 (EU accession), now (1998) and in 10 years' time, to allow for perception of dynamic changes (though the forecasts relating to the third period need to be regarded with caution). Non-EU markets were quite unimportant. The host country, Spain and other EU countries' markets (except Portugal and Spain) had a pervasive importance. In dynamic terms this relevance was decreasing for the first and increasing for the two last markets.

Concerning export propensity, the evidence was overwhelming: exports as a share of production represented over 90 per cent for 44.6 per cent of the subsidiaries surveyed. Portugal emerged quite pervasively as an export platform, which is consistent with the efficiency-seeking hypothesis (owing to low input costs) and also brings out the issue of eventual dependence and vulnerability. In fact, many subsidiaries were exporting their whole production to their parent, this embodying evidence of a highly hierarchical structure and dependence on the groups' central headquarters' decisions and directives (which is a stylized fact when most subsidiaries are RPSs).

This conclusion is confirmed by the high intra-group trade (assessed by the ratio of intra-group exports to total exports) pattern of these subsidiaries (41.3 per cent responded that this ratio was higher than 80 per cent).

Subsidiary Roles and their Development with Accession to the EU

The main findings concerning this fundamental aspect of the investigation are synthesized in Table 9.2. Three moments in time were used to allow for subsidiary development (Birkinshaw and Hood, 1997). A persistent decline in TMRs is particularly manifest in the data. RPSs constitute the most frequent subsidiary type, with an increase in importance following accession of Portugal to the EU. Not surprisingly, the least common subsidiary type is the product mandate (PM), though it is anticipated that its relevance will possibly tend to increase in the future (a word of caution applies here, concerning the accuracy of expectations on the part of the respondents).

Basically, a rationalization process is immanent in the data, with Portugal serving in many cases as an export platform.

Potential Contribution of MNE Subsidiaries to the Host Economy and Scope for Embeddedness

Although the chapter cannot take into account fully the complexity of this extremely important topic, it is usually thought that this contribution will depend on the extent and nature of linkages developed with local economic agents (suppliers, customers, local scientific bodies, among others). The quantity and quality of such linkages is usually related to the fashionable label of 'embeddedness' (Granovetter, 1985).

Several aspects surveyed may be linked to this issue. The subsidiaries were, for instance, asked about the proportion of inputs imported from the MNE group. More than half (54.4 per cent) responded that they imported between 10 and 40 per cent of their inputs from their group. This may mean that there is a considerable scope for using indigenous suppli-

Table 9.2 Evaluation of the relative importance of distinct subsidiary roles/strategies, by home country and industry, 1986, 1998 and 2008

Roles of subsidiaries[a] (average response[b])

	A			B			C		
	Before 1986	Now	10 years' time	Before 1986	Now	10 years' time	Before 1986	Now	10 years' time
By home country									
EU	2.50	1.78	1.64	2.14	2.75	2.67	1.71	1.81	2.15
Other Europe	1.00	1.88	1.63	3.50	2.80	2.78	1.00	1.63	2.00
Japan and South Korea	1.00	1.29	1.33	2.50	3.00	3.17	2.50	1.43	1.50
USA	1.75	1.50	1.20	3.00	3.17	3.60	1.00	1.33	1.60
Total	2.14	1.71	1.57	2.45	2.82	2.81	1.60	1.70	2.01
By industry									
Automobiles and transportation equipment	3.67	1.40	1.00	1.67	3.80	3.75	1.33	1.60	1.50
Car components	1.00	1.45	1.50	4.00	2.75	2.91	2.50	2.09	1.90
Chemicals and plastics	1.60	2.45	1.78	2.00	1.64	2.22	2.40	1.64	2.00
Electronics and electrical appliances	2.63	1.25	1.25	2.13	3.31	2.92	1.25	1.42	2.08
Metal manufacture and products	2.50	2.33	2.60	2.50	2.75	3.00	1.50	1.50	1.67
Textile, clothing and footwear	1.50	1.30	1.56	3.29	3.23	2.92	1.17	1.50	2.10
Other manufacturing	1.75	1.91	1.56	2.40	2.62	2.58	1.75	2.00	2.30
Total	2.14	1.71	1.57	2.45	2.82	2.81	1.60	1.70	2.02

Roles (or strategies) of subsidiaries:

A TMR – the Portuguese subsidiary produces some of the parent's already existing product lines (or related product lines) for the Portuguese market.

B RPS – the Portuguese subsidiary produces a certain set of component parts or existing final products for a multicountry or global market.

C PM – the Portuguese subsidiary has autonomy and creative resources to *develop*, produce and market a restricted product range (totally innovative products) for multicountry (regional or global) markets.

Notes:

a Respondents were asked to evaluate each role/strategy as (1) our only role/strategy, (2) our main role/strategy, (3) a secondary role/strategy and (4) not a part of our role/strategy.

b The average response (AR) was calculated by allocating 'only role' a value of 4, 'main role' a value of 3, 'secondary role' a value of 2 and finally 'not a part of our role' a coefficient of 1.

Source: Data compiled by Ana Teresa Tavares.

Table 9.3 Percentage of purchases bought from local (Portuguese) suppliers at present

0–40	40.1–80	80.1–100	N/A	Total
46	12	15	3	76

Note: *N/A*: not available.

ers. In a specific section concerning linkages to the local economy, and in particular concerning suppliers, 66 out of 76 firms used independent indigenous firms as sources of supply. In terms of percentage of total purchases bought from Portuguese firms, the distribution of frequencies in Table 9.3 is applicable.

Thus, more often than not, the subsidiaries surveyed buy a relatively small part of their total supplies from local firms. It should be emphasized that this amount is highly industry-specific. In dynamic terms, 13 firms stated that before EU accession this proportion of local supplies was even more reduced, whereas the majority of subsidiaries considered that it did not change with economic integration. When asked about prospects of evolution in the utilization of indigenous suppliers (in the next ten years), eight of the firms anticipated that they would buy less than now, whereas 30 subsidiaries expected to purchase more from local firms.

A further aspect surveyed related to the motivations underlying local sourcing. In this context, the most pervasive incentive to use local suppliers was because it was cheaper (mentioned by 44 firms). The second most frequent motive (considered by 39 subsidiaries) was the possibility of working creatively with local suppliers. The latter might induce some optimism on the potential for positive linkages, though it implies an effort on both the part of indigenous industry to upgrade their competitiveness and capabilities and on the part of government policies, if the potential of MNEs to contribute to regional/host-country development through linkages is to be fully realized (further development of this issue can be found in Tavares and Pearce, 1998c).

Other Indicators of the Impact of Accession to the EU for FDI and MNE Activities Carried Out in Portugal

One pervasive observation is that 40 out of the 76 subsidiaries considered chose to set up their subsidiaries after accession, which directly or indirectly may constitute evidence that there was an impact in terms of Portugal's attractiveness as a recipient of foreign investment. Indeed, when asked directly about that, more than half (56 per cent) of the subsidiaries acknowledged the relevance of accession to the EU and the prospect of the Single Market (reinforcing what has been already said) for the nature and scope of the activities undertaken in Portugal. In terms of their assessment of their positioning in terms of the MNE group, 37 per cent envisaged their position as relatively stable, 28 per cent thought they were enhancing the strength of their position and 17 per cent considered that they had scope for upgrading their role in the group's context. Only 9 per cent felt in a position of vulnerability. Regarding the latter, the most frequent cause for vulnerability expressed was fear of a relative loss of attractiveness of Portugal's location advantages *vis-à-vis* their Central and Eastern European counterparts. Finally, it could be inferred that MNEs still see national, EU/regional and global factors as separate influences on their activities. When asked which of the three factors was the most important, the majority (67 per cent) considered global issues, followed by EU/regional aspects (23 per cent) and, lastly, by national idiosyncrasies. Nonetheless, seeing these three forces as alternatives is in our perspective rather myopic and might have led to a certain under-estimation of regional factors (more emphasized throughout the questionnaire). Complementarity between these forces appears a viable assumption, as well as the existence of a global–regional nexus in terms of MNEs' strategies.

CONCLUDING REMARKS AND INDICATIONS FOR FUTURE RESEARCH

The present investigation presents selected empirical evidence on the nature and evolution of the activities of multinational subsidiaries operating in Portugal. In particular, and using this small economy as an archetype, it tries to identify eventual processes of structural change in foreign MNEs developing their productive activities in this host country. In this vein, the chapter documents certain patterns deemed relevant for the understanding of the impact of economic integration on the evolution of subsidiaries' activities, notably concerning dynamic changes in their roles, export propensity, markets supplied by them and linkages with the host-economy environment (through the analysis of an original and new database).

The theme here analysed is complex and multifaceted, thereby allowing for several possible theoretical and empirical developments. The next step of this research will consist of econometric testing of the postulated impact of economic integration on corporate restructuring. A cross-country study would also be extremely relevant to compare this impact on subsidiaries located in distinct 'peripheral' and also eventually certain 'core' countries, in the EU context. The consideration of the issue of the differentiated contribution of distinct subsidiary types to host-economy development may be also worth pursuing, probably trying to derive implications for industrial policy at distinct levels (regional, national and supranational), thus bringing the question of subsidiarity also under scrutiny.

10 How Local Managers Influence Strategy in MNCs

James H. Taggart and Michael Sanderson

INTRODUCTION

In the arena of international business the multinational corporation (MNC) operates in a turbulent and quickly changing environment. As a consequence, the relationship between corporate headquarters (HQ) and an individual subsidiary is of paramount importance in assisting an MNC successfully to harness its resources and satisfy strategic objectives. This requires a holistic approach, ideally involving full co-operation between corporate HQ and the respective subsidiary managers under its control. This, however, is complicated by acquisitions and mergers – for example, a subsidiary may find itself hostile to a new owner and therefore experience problems in the direction of its affairs.

This type of turbulent scenario is becoming more commonplace as multinationals compete in a fierce global market place, anxious to remain ahead of rivals and maintain competitive advantage (Porter, 1986). The ideal of a subsidiary classified as a 'profit centre' brings certain pressures, in that each plant within the MNC's portfolio has to adopt an appropriate strategy or role to ensure that overall organizational goals are achieved.

With reference to the subsidiary itself, much debate surrounds the actual effectiveness of the business unit structure. As Keuning (1998) observes:

> However, the business unit structure is not without its problems. It keeps top management at a distance from operations and discourages it from intervening, even though it holds the final responsibility.

The distinction noted here is that while a subsidiary may consciously develop its own strategy, it is in the interests of the corporate HQ that it is evolved via negotiation or consultation between the parent and affiliate. It is therefore imperative that the communication and decision making processes that occur between corporate HQ and an individual affiliate are effective.

Academics and practitioners are keenly aware of the importance of corporate strategy, but the practical aspects of subsidiary strategy represent a somewhat neglected area. Decentralization and devolved decision making capability are of concern to managers, yet scant attention has been paid to how these factors impact on the subsidiary itself. One aspect of subsidiary strategy identifies the ability of local managers (within parameters set by corporate HQ) to influence development of the affiliate via a deliberate course of action over a specific time period. The subsidiary can therefore adapt and evolve its role within the MNC. This form of subsidiary strategy may therefore act as a vehicle for local managers to influence corporate strategy and hence actively shape the future direction of the MNC. This process may, in turn, enhance the status of the particular subsidiary within the MNC's portfolio.

Currently a number models are available to assess this phenomenon, and since the early 1980s they have contributed to the evolution of a distinct research area. These models examine different aspects and propose a variety of criteria for the development of subsidiary strategy. This chapter evaluates the impact of two major variables which have an effect on subsidiary strategy: the degree of autonomy possessed by a subsidiary and the level of procedural justice as perceived by subsidiary management in relation to the MNC's strategy processes.

The approach here draws on an interaction framework (Taggart, 1996), called the autonomy–procedural justice (A–PJ) model (see also chapter 8 in this volume). The literature review attempts to situate this model within the population of subsidiary strategy frameworks that have been evolved. The A–PJ model is then evaluated via two case studies from the electronics industry, which seek to evaluate the influences that act on proactive subsidiaries. A key aspect of this chapter embraces the ability of subsidiary managers to negotiate with the corporate HQ and so influence the development of the affiliate, with the aim of strengthening the bargaining power that they possess within the MNC.

It should be borne in mind that foreign-owned MNCs have traditionally located in the UK, not only to access its domestic market of 60 mn, but also to access the wider EU market of 350 mn. In the current political situation in which the UK is outside the euro-zone, UK-based MNC subsidiaries may be at increased risk of rationalization, group HQs may decide to relocate within the Single Currency zone. The benefits to the corporate centre include an end to operating in a climate of political uncertainty, reduced exchange risk, less need to hedge and buy currency forward, closer proximity to the larger EU market and location in a world-currency zone.

Thus the importance to the subsidiary of its relationship with HQ is critical at this time. Unless the subsidiary has a strong position within the group, it may be vulnerable to environmental turbulence. In this chapter we consider how local managers may influence strategy within the MNC while maintaining and strengthening their subsidiary's situation in the group structure. We also assess the implications for UK-based foreign-owned firms exporting into the EU.

SUBSIDIARY STRATEGY – A REVIEW OF THE LITERATURE

Formal research into subsidiary strategy can be traced back to the work of Hedlund (1981), who identified the relationship between subsidiary autonomy, and corporate HQ informality. Hedlund's study concluded that the level of independence enjoyed by the subsidiary was seen to be directly linked to the level of informality between the HQ and subsidiary. White and Poynter (1984) proposed the first coherent model of subsidiary strategy. Their typology identifies five subsidiary strategies within MNCs; strategic independent, product specialist, rationalized manufacturer, miniature replica and marketing satellite. This research advocated that subsidiary managers could actively develop the subsidiary role and hence its importance within the MNC's portfolio, though this could not be seen as a short-term process. White and Poynter's model is based on three strategic dimensions: market scope, product scope and value-added scope.

A further model developed by Bartlett and Ghoshal (1986), defines four states of subsidiary strategy: strategic leader, contributor, implementer and finally black hole. This framework may be of more benefit to corporate managers in assessing the contribution made to the MNC by each affiliate. It fails to provide an analytical framework to determine how local managers may actively influence their roles within the MNC, particularly with respect to negotiation and enhanced bargaining power with corporate HQ. The focus of this model, therefore, may be regarded as 'top-down'.

Jarillo and Martinez (1990) revert to the 'bottom-up' approach with a subsidiary model developed from Prahalad and Doz's integration–responsiveness framework (1987). Their investigation of Spanish subsidiaries considered the strategic influences of integration and localization, and recognized that autonomy is a critical facet. They identified three types of subsidiary strategy: autonomous (low integration – high localization), receptive (high integration – low localization), and active (high integration and localization). Again, local managers may use this framework to evaluate and adjust the affiliate's strategic posture over time. However, it fails to identify or discuss the low integration – low localization strategy space. This limitation is addressed by Taggart (1997), who distinguishes a fourth classification – the quiescent subsidiary. This contribution offers more scope for subsidiary managers to evaluate current strategy and future action in consolidating the affiliate's position within the MNC.

All of the above models suffer from the same weakness – they have a common preoccupation with a mechanistic view of subsidiary strategy. Behavioural aspects, that will normally have a significant impact on the development and implementation of strategy, are virtually ignored. Taggart's A–PJ framework (1996) draws attention to this previously de-emphasized influence affecting the relationship between corporate headquarters and subsidiary. This framework is now examined in some depth.

AUTONOMY AND PROCEDURAL JUSTICE

Previous research on autonomy in MNCs can be traced back to Picard (1980), who studied subsidiaries of European multinationals located in the USA. The crux of this research hinged on the identification of differing reporting structures, which was related to the level of local autonomy. When a subsidiary chief executive reported directly to the MNC president, affiliate autonomy was lower. However, if the chief executive reported to the local board, subsidiary autonomy levels were found to be higher.

The matter is more complex, as informal interpersonal relationships may have a bearing on the autonomy enjoyed by a subsidiary. If a relationship between a subsidiary chief executive and HQ management is positively forged, with sound communication channels established, greater flexibility may well show up in the decision making process. The importance of this was expressed by Hedlund (1981), who noted a strong pattern of decision making and control at subsidiary level associated with good relations and contact with HQ, and a lack of an authoritarian culture.

The extent of co-operation exhibited between corporate HQ and affiliate may be influenced by management style (McGregor, 1960). Gnan and Songini (1995) researched this aspect within Japanese subsidiaries located in Italy. Their methodology focused on two dimensions: hierarchy (the control exerted from HQ), and involvement (which linked the flexibility demonstrated at corporate HQ with the level of autonomy at the affiliate level). They established that involvement was influenced by shared values and positive personal relationships existing between HQ and the subsidiary. Hence organizational culture may be considered as a contributing behavioural factor in the assessment of the HQ – subsidiary interface in MNCs (see, for example, Huczynski and Buchanan, 1997).

The antecedents of the procedural justice dimension are also well established. Bartlett (1981) considered the concept of organizational evolution in MNCs, and identified the importance of involvement between corporate HQ and subsidiary managers. A supportive organizational climate would enable the delegation of decision making and empower subsidiary management to make decisions which reflect local circumstances. Later, Hassard and Sharifi (1989) observed that a supportive corporate culture, if integrated throughout the organization, aids the facilitation of trust, and in turn benefits decision making processes at all levels. Thus it may be possible to differentiate between organizations that exhibit higher levels of trust towards the decision making capability of subsidiary managers, compared to those that impose a central will upon subsidiary management.

Extensive research on the precisely defined procedural justice concept in MNCs was carried out by Kim and Mauborgne (1991, 1993a, 1993b). This tackled the question of management perception in relation to how fairly subsidiary units had been treated as a result of the annual corporate plan

being developed and implemented. The concept of procedural justice dove-
tails with issues of harmony and trust, and importantly the perception of
fairness of strategic decisions taken as viewed by subsidiary management
is a cornerstone of the procedural justice dimension. Thus this behavioural,
and in many ways intangible, facet is a vital dimension in the A–PJ model
of subsidiary strategy.

It may be observed that previous research on autonomy suggests an interaction between organizational behaviour issues and the degree of decentralized decision making permitted at affiliate level. This is the basis of the
A–PJ framework.

THE A–PJ MODEL

The interactions between autonomy and procedural justice give rise to four
alternative strategy situations for the affiliate. Where low levels of both
autonomy and procedural justice exist, we find the *vassal* subsidiary. A combination of high autonomy with low procedural justice identifies a *militant*
subsidiary. Conversely, low autonomy and high procedural justice describes
the *collaborator* subsidiary. A final classification emerges where both high
levels of autonomy and procedural justice are found, resulting in the *partner*
subsidiary (see Figure 10.1 and Chapter 8 in this volume).

The weakest blend of dimensions is in the *vassal* position, where relations between corporate HQ and affiliate may be depicted as poor. A lack

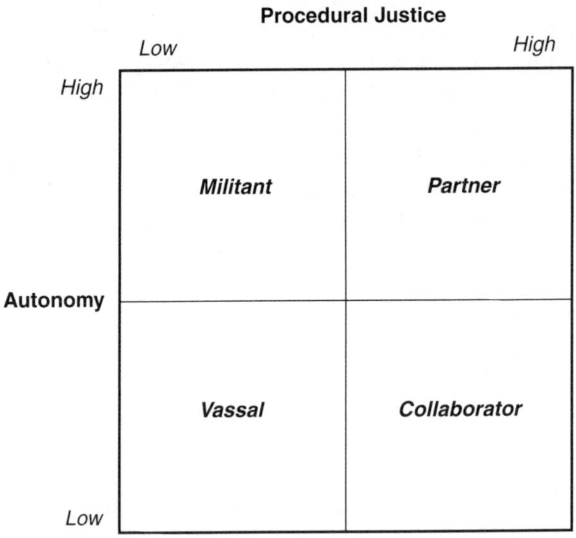

Figure 10.1 The autonomy–procedural justice framework

of trust coupled with a feeling of alienation and emasculation at the subsidiary are common scenarios for those in this position. The *militant* subsidiary often arises from an unwanted acquisition (by those acquired). The parent company may find difficulty in controlling and directing the affiliate; thus, historical high autonomy may be retained and communication across the HQ–affiliate interface is often minimal. The *collaborator* type enjoys a positive relationship with HQ, making it well integrated within the MNC network. It is however heavily directed by higher-level management who dictate decisions which are expected to be accepted and adopted without question. The final strategy may be seen as ideal, in that headquarters view the *partner* affiliate as a key asset with expertise in its particular niche. Often, this type may be considered a centre of excellence; subsidiary managers enjoy a strong appreciation and backing for their professionalism and capability. The *partner* situation is thus characterized by good relations with HQ, and a high level of latitude in the decision-making process.

An accurate assessment of the current state of a subsidiary in the A–PJ framework allows its managers to identify strategic problem areas and suggests ways of resolving them. The model may also be useful in helping subsidiary managers to evolve their subsidiary in a positive way, and to determine alternative methods of increasing its individual value within the MNC network. It may also act as a catalyst in determining the future direction of a subsidiary's contribution towards the MNC's overall objectives.

In the following part of the chapter, the A–PJ model is used to examine two case study firms that were interviewed in depth during the early part of 1998. Both are examples of the process of change in subsidiary strategy over time, and both highlight the need for corporate managers to be aware of this type of dynamic, so that affiliates may make the greatest possible contribution to the achievement of MNC objectives.

RESEARCH METHODOLOGY

The methodology involved in-depth interviews with top subsidiary managers of two electronics organizations in a case study approach. Three members of senior management from each subsidiary were interviewed separately, giving a total of six interviews. Both of the electronics plants had experienced major operational changes in previous years, and so an insight could be gained of subsidiary strategy change within this turbulent interval. As well as establishing the current position, the interviews were also aimed at establishing future strategy development and evolution.

A semi-structured questionnaire was devised, with questions formulated and expressed using a Likert (1961) scale as a gauge of management perceptions on the issues raised. This type of approach has been used extensively in the measurement of behavioural issues.

The questionnaire was divided into two sections. The first involved perceptions of procedural justice and local autonomy on the part of respondents covering 'five years ago', the current position, and 'five years from now'. The second section of the questionnaire contained more open-ended questions designed to assess the nature and source of both internal and external changes, and these were related to the responses from the first section.

RESULTS

Case Study 1: Huber–Avex Inc.

The Huber Corporation is an American multinational, with a portfolio of interests ranging across energy, minerals, chemicals, electronics and wood products. Each is run as a separate division under the Huber Corporation headquarters. The electronics division is known as Avex Inc.; divisional headquarters are in Alabama, USA; the subsidiaries are spread world-wide – in the USA (California and Tennessee), Mexico, Singapore, Sweden and Scotland.

Our research focused on the Scottish subsidiary. This green field site, that dates from the late 1980s, was intended to service the European market. Its core business involved manufacturing of printed circuits and computer products, and it initially served the needs of multinational clients within Scotland's Silicon Glen. This particular subsidiary had recently experienced a major restructuring.

The Scottish subsidiary had been a regional HQ (since 1995) for operations outside the USA, and the subsidiaries in Singapore and Sweden reported to it. In its role as a regional headquarters towards both subsidiaries under its remit, Avex Scotland generally took a very positive line. However, its relationship with divisional HQ in Alabama was not good. Over the years, the Scottish plant had become very autonomous in its role of regional HQ. Divisional HQ had limited knowledge of the local situation, whereas Avex Scotland had little input into the overall group strategy. Despite its regional HQ function, this subsidiary has little involvement in R&D, advertising and promotion and product design. These factors may have acted as an overall limitation on the practical level of autonomy enjoyed by the subsidiary, which was recognized to be high in all other areas.

Our analysis suggested that, historically, Avex Scotland has been a *militant* subsidiary (see Figure 10.2), but the situation is now changing. A restructuring has led to enhanced integration of the global network of sub-

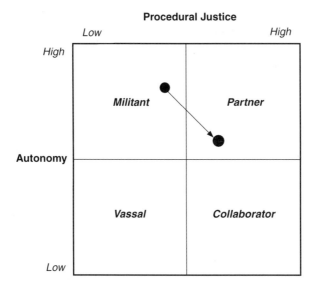

Figure 10.2   A–PJ: Avex Scotland

sidiaries, with the sister subsidiaries in Singapore and Sweden becoming autonomous in their own right. An executive was seconded from divisional HQ to head the subsidiary management team in Scotland. This dramatically improved communication links between them, and further integrated the Scottish affiliate within the MNC's network. The restructuring has resulted in a positive outcome. A reduction of autonomy (and friction) coupled with closer links with divisional headquarters has led to a classification shift. Avex Scotland's new *partner* strategy may well be a much improved situation (see Figure 10.2).

Case Study 2: Fuji Electric Co. – Fuji Electric (Scotland)

Fuji Scotland is a subsidiary of the Japanese-owned multinational Fuji, which manufactures consumer and industrial electronics. This affiliate has been operating in the West of Scotland since 1991; it is responsible for manufacturing power transistor modules, with a strong emphasis on quality. After manufacture, products are supplied to sister companies within the Fuji organization, where they are added to more complex assemblies.

At the outset, Scottish autonomy was very low, with particular reference to product design and marketing. Several reasons for this were identified. Principally, corporate HQ saw its place as dictating the large majority of decisions to Fuji Scotland, and the notion of bargaining between the parties to shift the decision making focus was unfamiliar. In addition, the subsidiary was very dependent on HQ for knowledge in respect of key strategy areas

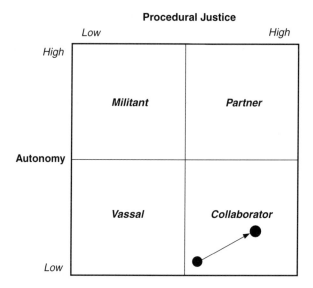

Figure 10.3   A–PJ: Fuji Scotland

like R&D, pricing, quality and product range. Without access to this knowledge, decentralization moves were not practical. However, in compensation, procedural justice levels were considered to be high. In particular, very good channels of communication had been established, and the relationships were described as cordial. This scenario was enhanced by the development of mechanisms such a briefing groups and frequent inter-plant visits to discuss common problems.

Over the past five years, the level of affiliate autonomy has been increased, though from a very low base, and local managers believe that substantially more movement on this front will be necessary if the subsidiary is to enhance its position within the group. Such movement will, of course, materially change the affiliate's position in the A–PJ framework. Movements to date are illustrated in Figure 10.3, where it can be seen that autonomy increases have not been sufficient to change Fuji Scotland's strategy classification from its initial *collaborator* position.

DISCUSSION

Researching aspects of MNC organizational characteristics can be problematic. Marginson *et al.* (1988) underlined the difficulties: 'Our findings point to the complex nature of the relationships between head offices, divisions and establishments.'

Our research approach has been bottom-up, focusing particularly on the activities and perspectives of subsidiary managers as they are affected by responses at the HQ – affiliate interface. Thus, there is a designed behavioural dimension to our investigation. Consideration of the two case studies leads directly to the key question of this chapter: to what extent does the A–PJ framework help in analyzing and interpreting such subsidiary situations? Would subsidiary managers find the framework helpful in navigating towards more advantageous strategy spaces?

In the Avex scenario, we saw movement in Figure 10.2 that charted the rapid development of subsidiary strategy in a relatively short space of time, under the impetus of changing circumstances within the group. Having been deprived of the autonomy it had enjoyed as a divisional HQ as a result of restructuring, the effect was ameliorated by closer integration with corporate HQ. However, despite the reduction, it should be noted that levels of autonomy still remain relatively high.

The nature of previous autonomy levels at Avex Scotland may be judged from an observation made by one senior manager: 'Actually, in a lot of instances, HQ would tell us to do a lot of things, and we would not really do them.'

This viewpoint is perhaps understandable for any subsidiary who may feel that HQ does not fully appreciate the full extent of what they face at local level, and a feeling of frustration may ensue. It is suggestive of the problems that may be encountered if little emphasis is placed upon the importance of the HQ – affiliate relationship.

Initially high levels of autonomy coupled with low levels of procedural justice (as evidenced by the quote above) are problematic for the subsidiary, placing it in the unfavourable '*militant*' category. This particular category may, in many cases, apply to subsidiaries that are viewed as profit centres. The perceived autonomy is beneficial, but a low perception of procedural justice implies unsatisfactory communication between parent and affiliate, with HQ oblivious to some of the practices taking place at locally.

However, the benefit of the A–PJ model lies in the ability of subsidiary managers to evaluate their framework position, and positively adapt the subsidiary response to ensure a more favourable outcome. It can therefore be possible to reassess the relationship which currently exists, and seek to move the orientation towards a more positive strategy space. Initially, this outcome will benefit the subsidiary, but the group as a whole should be enriched thereafter. In a climate of rationalization, perceived poor performers may find themselves redundant in the long-term aspirations of the MNC's strategic plan.

In our case study example, an identification of a serious communication problem had resulted in a change of approach by subsidiary managers, who consciously formulated a plan to target and eliminate the identified weakness. This involved improving communication levels generally, facilitation of greater personal interaction with HQ managers and greater integration of the subsidiary and its interests within the organization network. Autonomy is still high, but strategic decisions are now subject to discussion and negotiation between HQ and affiliate.

This shift in attitude and relationship between HQ and subsidiary is summed up by the sentiment:

> There is no hesitation now in picking up the phone and saying to someone in the States – 'Do you know anything about this?' – whereas before we'd sit here in the dark and not really know what to do.

We would argue, then, that the A–PJ framework may be used proactively to identify such organizational behaviour weaknesses between corporate HQ and the subsidiary. This, in turn, may evoke a deliberate strategy to improve the balance of autonomy and procedural justice, with the aim of increasing affiliate and network effectiveness. At Avex Scotland, this approach is summarized in the subsidiary motto of 'think global, act local'.

In the second case example, we noted that the classification of Fuji Scotland had remained unchanged despite some improvement in the levels of autonomy experienced by the affiliate in a five-year period. Interviews with senior managers strongly suggested that low autonomy led to frustration and a conspicuous lack of organizational flexibility. Further improvement may well be reliant on measuring more accurately the autonomy perceptions of local managers and comparing with those of corporate executives (Marginson *et al.*, 1988).

Clearly, the good communication channels previously established with corporate HQ must be maintained, and augmented autonomy will be required to enable a movement from '*collaborator*' to '*partner*'. As well as improving the subsidiary's strategy position, this move would help to remove or attenuate the strong feelings of powerlessness at Avex Scotland. Discussion and negotiation with corporate executives may smooth the way by developing increased subsidiary involvement in decisions that have an affiliate-specific element. There may also have to be increased willingness at HQ to tolerate, and even encourage, debate about future directions and decisions.

IMPLICATIONS

Although models of subsidiary strategy have previously addressed the influence of strategic dimensions affecting the corporate HQ – affiliate interface, the behavioural aspects until now had been largely ignored. The findings highlighted by the two case studies indicate that subsidiary management perceptions are assessable and useful. They also suggest the real possibility of evolving an appropriate strategy at subsidiary level that is sensitive to the needs of local managers and overall MNC objectives. The autonomy and procedural justice dimensions are clearly of strategic importance, and offer substantial scope for subsidiary managers to align strategy effectively with corporate requirements. Management style and organization culture may also be influential determinants in successful subsidiary development, and their impact on the dynamic of the parent – affiliate interface should not be underestimated.

The A–PJ model adds to the debate on what strategic variables have the greatest impact on development of a subsidiary in a turbulent business environment. Whether this model will prove to be an adequate framework for deeper behavioural insights will depend on further research. At the very least, it offers the multinational subsidiary an opportunity to evaluate management perceptions and categorize them in a meaningful and practical way.

As the Single Currency develops, and as the euro-zone becomes more defined and distinct, there will be an increasing need for international firms on the periphery of Europe to develop and implement strategies that suit rapidly changing conditions. This kind of influence may, initially, be more important for the Avex subsidiary than for Fuji Scotland, as the latter is entirely a within-network supplier. Avex, on the other hand, stands to gain substantially from its improved levels of procedural justice and higher level of integration with the parent network. Despite its 'divorce' from the Swedish subsidiary, the strategic moves outlined above may well put it in a better position to manage the competitive pressures that will follow non-membership of the euro-zone. Overall, peripheral subsidiaries may well be among the most vulnerable to parent rationalization moves as the competitive effect of the euro-zone becomes apparent. Scotland's exclusion – via the UK's non-membership – carries obvious dangers.

In this kind of adverse environment, the type of manifest 'survivalist' strategies followed by MNC subsidiaries located in Ireland may become role models for their peers in Scotland (Taggart and Taggart, 1997). Research has shown that Irish affiliate executives have at their disposal a wide range of tactics and policies for dealing with a threatening parent, ranging from management buy-out, through persuasion, negotiation, moral blackmail and other intensely interpersonal means, to the use of political pressure (blatant as well as overt), forming pressure groups with other network affiliates and developing substantial R&D 'skunk-works'. The overall aim is obvious: if rationalization is necessary, the Irish affiliate will not be the next to go. In all of this activity, Irish affiliate members make tangible use of all aspects of procedural justice, and make assumptions about the level of local autonomy available to them that would often surprise corporate executives.

CONCLUSION

Despite recent growth, the domain of subsidiary strategy research is still very much in its infancy. The development and refinement of adequate models enabling appropriate analyses of complex arrays continues apace, as it must in a turbulent international business environment where competition is fierce and stability is rare. This turbulence often acts as a trigger to rationalization and concentration of activities. It also affects the nature of behavioural relationships which, in turn, impact on the parent and subsidiary strategic reactions. If shareholder expectations are to be satisfied, then these relationships must be controlled and co-ordinated effectively.

The A–PJ framework identifies a credible set of four distinct variations of subsidiary strategy, formed from interactions of autonomy and procedural justice dimensions. Its main value may well be the ease of applicability of the model. It is not overly complex, and a profile of a subsidiary should be fairly unambiguous. Our case study approach largely supports the A–PJ model in terms of a descriptive aid. However, while the prognostication from this research is positive, its value as a dynamic method of ensuring proactive subsidiary development requires further testing. Indeed, to do this, it may be necessary to follow the fortunes of a subsidiary over a longer time scale.

Perhaps the ultimate test of the validity of this framework is in the feasibility of a repositioning of a subsidiary currently occupying an unfavourable strategy space in the A–PJ framework. As subsidiary strategy involves the formulation of a deliberate course of action to invoke change and improve a current situation, further case study examples will be necessary to improve our understanding of a whole range of circumstances beyond those considered in the two case examples.

Overall, the contribution of the A–PJ model is stimulating in that it offers a perspective on behavioural factors which may well impact substantially on subsidiary performance. These factors are likely to be subject to change over a period of time, and so an awareness of influences in the form of communication processes and decision making capabilities is surely to the advantage of subsidiary managers as they strive to optimize achievement.

11 Inter-Alliance Rivalry: Theory and an Application to the Global Telecommunications Industry

Geert Duysters, Rebecca Guidice,
Bert M. Sadowski and Ash Vasudevan

INTRODUCTION

The rapid proliferation of alliances has not only ushered in a new era of co-operation among companies big and small, but also ushered in a new era of competition between alliances. In the telecommunications industry, the linking up of a number of smaller companies such as the Swiss, the Dutch and the Swedish public telephone operators (PTOs) in Unisource in the early 1990s took place in parallel with the creation of strategic alliances between much larger companies such as France Telekom and Deutsche Telekom. These co-operative agreements have increasingly become an integral part and a cornerstone of the competitive strategies of companies. Even more, they are increasingly considered as being more important in achieving business objectives than other forms of international expansion in telecommunications (Molony, 1999). As in other industries, 'competition through co-operation' has become the mainstay of a firm's attempt to gain business advantages. The virtual explosion of co-operative agreements on a world-wide basis has led to a new form of competition: group versus group rather than company versus company (Gomes-Casseres, 1994).

Collaborative rent-seeking behaviour in alliances (Lado *et al.*, 1997) has developed into a competitive necessity for companies that is no longer disputed. However, the determinants for this behaviour have largely been unexplored. It is now commonplace to observe that alliance groups are competing against each other. In telecommunications, the re-establishment of Concert, as a joint venture between British Telecom and American Telephone & Telegraph (AT&T) in 1998 can be seen as a response to the expansion of Global One in international network-based services. The creation of Global One in 1996, in turn, based on a transformation of the European venture of France Telekom and Deutsche Telekom called Atlas and the involvement of US Sprint, was a reaction to an earlier participation of AT&T in the European Unisource venture. From this discussion, some more general questions emerge: To what extent is the establishment of strategic alliances by focal players in an industry inducing alliance rivalry? What are the conditions that trigger the likelihood of a response from other focal players? What are the determinants fostering increased alliance rivalry between a group of firms?

From a managerial perspective it is important to recognize that merely focusing on intra-alliance dynamics (such as partner selection, structure, governance, unilateral commitments, trust, opportunism) offers only a partial slice of reality that confronts the use of alliances in building competitive advantage (Lado *et al.*, 1997). Equally important to recognize is that an alliance is more likely to compete against another alliance. Building and sustaining collaborative advantage requires therefore not just a thorough understanding of the internal alliance process, but also an understanding of the external competitive implications of alliances. It is crucial to acknowledge that the rapid growth of co-operative agreements among firms for pre-competitive and post-competitive purposes has made it difficult to consider initiating alliance actions as just independent firm-level behaviour of companies (the focus of competitive analysis). For instance, research has demonstrated that the increasing use of alliances has been related to innovation (Hagedoorn 1993; Powell, *et al.*, 1996) to the penetration of new markets (Contractor and Lorange, 1988), to an speeding up of market entry (Kotabe *et al.*, 1996) and to the acquisition of knowledge (Kogut, 1988; Nohria and Garcia-Pont, 1991). A conceptual framework integrating collaborative and competitive behaviour that can guide future research and managerial practice is, however, currently lacking.

This research is a step in that direction. By looking at the dynamic interplay between competition and co-operation, the objective of the chapter is to construct elements of a process theory on alliance-based competition that seeks to identify the conditions under which alliance formation elicits or averts an alliance-competitive response. The importance of exploring this issue gets to the heart of what makes an alliance effective from a competitive point of view. In this context, 'alliance-competition' is defined as competition between a group of alliances operating in similar markets, offering competing products and services, and targeting similar customers. 'Inter-alliance rivalry' is characterized as the degree of alliance-competitive tension between alliances resulting in collaborative but rivalrous rent-seeking behaviours between alliances to gain competitive advantage.

By laying the foundation for this unexplored yet critical field of inquiry, this chapter reviews, first, the theoretical literature on alliance competition and inter-alliance rivalry. In defining the assumptions and limitations of the model, it then develops a conceptual model that specifically investigates the interaction between an alliance action and the alliance response it induces. Drawing from a rich stream of empirical research, the chapter then examines particular market and firm-specific characteristics that are likely to influence alliance competition and inter-alliance rivalry. In this part of the chapter, formal propositions are advanced that explain the relationship between alliance formation and the likelihood of alliance response. We then summarize the results of the theoretical discussion and draw some recommendations for managers engaged in alliance activity and for further research in the area.

Owing to their recent formation, strategic alliances in the telecommunications service industry represent an ideal case for illustrating the issues of alliance competition and inter-alliance rivalry (Antonelli, 1995) (For an overview on major companies and strategic alliances in the telecommunication service industry see Appendixes 1 and 2, pp. 166–7.)

TOWARDS A PREDICTIVE THEORY OF ALLIANCE-COMPETITIVE ANALYSIS AND INTER-ALLIANCE RIVALRY

Theoretical Background

In the literature on competitive analysis and strategic alliances, new forms of alliance-based competition and inter-alliance rivalry have received scant attention. While research on competitive analysis has largely focused on the moves and counter-moves from a single focal firm's perspective, the literature on strategic alliances has mainly focused on issues related to *intra-alliance* dynamics such as trust, dependence, governance, structuring and management. Issues related to *inter-alliance* dynamics have largely been neglected. Research undertaken by Gomes-Casseres (1996) and by Doz and Hamel (1998) has been among the first exploring the increasing frequency of collaboration as a reflection of a fundamental shift from traditional forms of competition (firm versus firm) to new forms (group versus group). These studies have provided a basis for investigating the underlying principles of and antecedents of alliance competition.

Conventionally, research on alliance activity has mainly focused on the question as to why and when alliances are formed (Powell and Brantley, 1992; Kogut and Zander, 1993). More recently, some studies have advanced our understanding of 'with whom' firms are likely to form alliances (Gulati, 1995). In dealing with the competitive implications of alliances, research has typically focused on the performance/financial benefits of alliance formation (Berg *et al.*, 1982; Hagedoorn, 1993) or examined the implications of trust, opportunism, partner rivalry-and sustained co-operation as a means of achieving competitive benefits (Hill, 1990; Gulati, 1995). Using a transaction cost or a social network perspective, researchers have started to explore the relationship between governance mechanisms and the evolution of trust and its implications for realizing benefits of co-operation (Gulati, 1995). In examining the relationship between competition and co-operation, however, research (with the exception of the strategic behaviour approach) has largely focused upon the internal characteristics of the alliance. There it has been argued that it is important to acknowledge the mixed-motive nature (competition plus co-operation) of alliances and its implications for dependence, trust, and mutual benefit (Singh and Mitchell, 1996). Although this approach has considerably advanced our understanding of the internal processes of alliance dynamics, it falls short in characterizing the external competitive implications of alliances.

The objective of the chapter is to extend research in this area by examining the external competitive implications of alliance formation that might bridge the tension between competition and co-operation. By looking at the market context, we develop an integrative framework of mechanisms driving alliance-based competition. In this context, the chapter defines 'inter-alliance dynamics' as the external competitive tension between alliances that in turn affects the intent of creating, building and sustaining of advantages relative to other alliances competing for similar competitive gains such as same markets, same products, or same customers. Based on this focus the analysis shifts to the analysis of particular actions (alliance formation) that induce a reaction (alliance response) under certain competitive contingencies.

Assumptions Guiding the Model

In order to derive a means of exploring the competitive dynamics of co-operative ventures, alliances are viewed as competitive actions initiated by firms in order to attract new customers or to retain or better serve their current customers. This motivation certainly underlay the growth of strategic alliances in the telecommunications industry, where their establishment was primarily related to the international expansion of large customers (Monlouis, 1998). Therefore this seems a valid assumption regardless of whether the alliance was formed for the purpose of improving efficiency, improving competitive position against rivals, or learning from partners (Kogut, 1988): the means are geared toward the end objective of securing a short-term or long-term competitive edge.[1]

It is, furthermore, assumed that an initial business condition causes two or more organizations to explore the possibility of forming a co-operative alliance. In telecommunications, such initial condition has been the liberalization of European telecommunication markets in the late 1980s and 1990s. As a response, a majority of European PTOs developed an interest in establishing network-coverage alliances with each other and to expanding into the US market. This interest became evident in intensive search processes for partnering firms and concerns among major companies of being left out in alliance formation (Graack, 1996).

In concentrating on the trade-off between competition *vis-à-vis* co-operation, the alliance dynamics of focal firms within for-profit strategic alliances[2] are examined. This assumes that there are competitive dynamics only between focal firm *A* and focal firm *B*, but that focal firm *A* and focal firm *B* do not form an alliance with each other. Therefore, ideally some companies stay in the centre of gravity in the alliance 'circus', competing effectively with their alliances with each other in international markets.[3]

Furthermore, the focus of examination is on *intended alliances*, those resulting from the purposive actions of firms (Kogut, 1991) that can be either reactive to a variation induced by an action within an environment, or proactive, forestalling unpredictable behaviour by other organizations (Bresser and Harl, 1986). Competition is therefore an objective phenomenon largely influenced by the rational behaviour of firms interested in initiating and responding to alliance formations. The actions (alliance formations) and responses (alliance formations) are manifestations of collaborative rent-seeking behaviour among firms.

As shown in Figure 11.1, the model posits that particular market characteristics (competitive uncertainty, number of value-generating partners, technological intensity, industry growth, competitive proximity and market concentration) play a central role in determining the likelihood of a competitive alliance response to an alliance action (formation). Given the asymmetrical nature of firm strategy, structure and performance and the resulting heterogeneity it spawns in the market, it will be argued that firm-specific attributes (alliance experience, firm strategy, firm size and alliance type) will moderate the relationship between context and likelihood of alliance response.

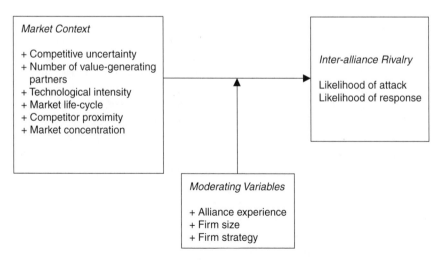

Figure 11.1   An integrated framework of alliance-competitive analysis and inter-alliance rivalry

Some Hypotheses on Alliance Competition and Inter-alliance Rivalry

Market Context
Past research has documented the role of the specific industry and market characteristics in shaping the frequency and pattern of inter-firm alliance agreements (Porter and Fuller, 1986; Auster, 1992; Hagedoorn, 1993; Harrigan, 1988). In the ensuing discussion, we examine the impact of a particular set of variables – representing a general consensus in the literature (Auster, 1992; Hagedoorn, 1993; Grandori and Soda, 1995) – on the relationship between the operating environment and inter-firm alliance formation: competitive uncertainty, the number of value-generating partners, technological intensity, market concentration, industry growth and competitive interconnectedness.

Competitive Uncertainty
The interdependence or interconnectedness between existing competitors results in competitive uncertainty (Burgers *et al.*, 1993; Chen, 1996). It reflects the extent to which the fates of the competing firms are tied to each other. In other words, competitive uncertainty results from a firm's inability to predict the effect of a competitive action on the market position of its competitive rivals. Consider the following example: British Telecommunications (BT) obtained in June 1993 20 per cent of the shares of MCI, an acquisition that was valued by market analysts at that time at \$4.3 bn. The alliance provided MCI with an European base and BT with an American one. However, the alliance was certainly a response to AT&T's international expansion in its Worldsource alliance in May 1993 (Oh, 1996).

In this context, it is argued that any change in market position might thus influence the likelihood of a response from rivals (Hay and Morris, 1979; Chen, 1996). Past research has argued that because a firm cannot predict whether there will be a response or what the response will be, the firm may enter into alliances to reduce the number of competitors (Pennings, 1981; Contractor and Lorange, 1988; Kogut, 1988). In the context of blurring industry boundaries and the rising incidence of inter-industry competitors, research has documented the emergence of an inter-industry competitive uncertainty (Ela and Irwin, 1983; Dussuage *et al.*, 1992; Kotabe *et al.*, 1996). Because firms have limited influence over the sources of uncertainty in the environment, alliances serve as proactive mechanisms or options (Kogut, 1991) to respond to such uncertainty.[4] Finally, Bresser and Harl (1986) have argued that collective strategies serve to minimize the decision making uncertainty because the 'couplings provided by a market mechanism (which links the fates of business firms) have been weakened for a subset of organizations which now co-operate' (Bresser and

Harl, 1986: 411). Based on the above discussion, we make the following argument:

P1: The greater the competitive uncertainty, the greater the likelihood that firm *B* will form an alliance in response to firm *A*'s alliance formation.

Number of Value-generating Partners
It is well acknowledged that scarce resources play a significant role in shaping and influencing competition in the market (Porter, 1986; Prahalad and Hamel, 1990; Hamel and Prahalad, 1994; Chen, 1996). Problems occur when resources are scarce or widely dispersed and when the survival of firms depends upon the frequent occurrence of complementary resource exchanges between firms. The ability to extract maximum rents from the resource exchanges is often conditioned by the firm's ability to find a partner with complementary resources (Dyer and Singh, 1998). As the rate of alliance formation accelerates, the number of available firms will decrease, all other things being equal. If the incentive is to find the *right* partner and if many good partner firms are available (within the industry, among suppliers or distributors, or in related industries), a firm will have a limited incentive to rush into an alliance. Although firms that enter the alliance race first have the largest number of firms from which to choose partners, they have been observed to form alliances with short notice and minimal planning (Gomes-Casseres, 1994), often in conditions of market and technological uncertainty.

If the number of desirable partners decreases, however, a firm would have little incentive to wait and see which firms its competitors choose as partners. For instance, to avoid isolation in their international expansion strategies, Deutsche Telekom and France Telecom began in December 1993 heavily to invest in their alliance activities in response to newly created international alliances between British Telecom and MCI (at that time called Concert) and between Japan KDD, AT&T and Singapore Telecom (called Worldsource) (Graack, 1996). As in the example, the firm would respond quickly in an attempt to gain a strategic advantage or to offset the competitor's advantage. This also would undermine the initial advantage of an earlier alliance action. First-movers are able to capitalize on the most attractive partners from the available, yet scarce, pool of potential members (Grant and Baden-Fuller, 1995; Gomes-Casseres, 1996). Latecomers in this context face the tangible risk of not being able to find partners with complementary resources to create rents (Dyer and Singh, 1998). Moreover, a lesser number of value-generating partners available in the market may cause fewer in-kind responses to be elicited from competitors.[5] In other words, the scarcity of partners raises barriers to response by foreclosing on any additional opportunities for sharing knowledge, risk, technology, and so on by locking in attractive partners.

P2: The fewer the number of value-generating partners available in the market, the greater the likelihood that firm B will form an alliance in response to firm A's alliance formation.

Technological Intensity
Past research has widely documented that alliances are utilized to gain access to technology-related competencies and resources. They also mitigate the risk of commercializing complex, untested, technologically intensive products (Teece, 1986; Contractor and Lorange, 1988; Hagedoorn, 1993; Singh, 1995; Doz and Hamel, 1998). In Internet-related technology and services, access to competencies has been considered as crucial to telecommunications companies. As a result, a number of alliances have been established between established telecommunications companies and suppliers of these technologies and services. In February 2000, Deutsche Telekom announced that it had formed an alliance with Cisco, the Internet equipment manufacturer, to develop Internet technology and services. In November 1999, Cisco became engaged in an alliance with US Sprint that offered Internet access solutions. In September 1999, AT&T started a venture with Cisco to develop and implement Internet-based networks (*CommunicationsWeek International*, 1999).

These kind of alliances represent actions or reactions initiated by firms to changing technological conditions (Auster, 1992; Singh, 1995). A consensus among researchers evaluating the prevalence of alliances under such circumstances is that as an option, alliances represent the best means of coping with daunting technological challenges (Hagedoorn, 1993) and establishing possible conditions for enhancing competitive advantage. Research has extensively documented the impact of technological intensity of the industry in shaping the frequency and pattern of inter-firm alliances (Badaracco, 1991; Auster, 1992; Hagedoorn, 1993; Kotabe *et al.*, 1996). Therefore, it can be postulated that technological intensity has been a powerful motivator for firms to quickly respond to their competitors' alliance formation (Kotabe *et al.*, 1996).

P3: The greater the technological intensity of the industry, the greater the likelihood that firm B will form an alliance in response to firm A's alliance formation.

Market Life Cycle
A great deal of research has investigated the evolution of markets (e.g. Porter, 1980; Whetten, 1981; Miller and Friesen, 1984; Harrigan, 1985; Auster, 1992). Though labels may vary, the literature identifies four common stages of market development: birth, growth, maturity and decline. Within a market, each stage reveals different technological, environmental and competitive conditions (Auster, 1992). It has been argued, both theoreti-

cally and empirically, that the evolution of technology market and structure does influence the frequency and pattern of agreements linked to a firm (Auster, 1992; Cainarca *et al.*, 1992; Harrigan, 1988). More specifically, research has shown that the introduction stage of a market (Auster, 1992) and technology (Cainarca *et al.*, 1992) – which is typically characterized by extreme uncertainty and a need for adaptive efficiency – is associated with a high frequency of R&D agreements. As firms are competing for ideas, product concepts and technology choices (Prahalad, 1995) in this stage, R&D agreements enable firms to compete as well as maintain their flexibility. In the emerging market of home-banking services, Deutsche Telekom in 1997 established a strategic alliance between its Internet division, T-online, and Microsoft to develop home banking services and to market Microsoft's Internet and Intranet products. This also was a response to the earlier established joint venture with Bertelsmann/America Online (*CommunicationsWeek International*, 1997).

As the market evolves to the early development stage, the focus of agreements shifts from exploratory R&D efforts to joint development agreements following the partial resolution of uncertainty. As the market stabilizes and becomes placid, factors such as incremental innovations, economies of scale and scope become more critical, and agreements that enable participants to draw on critical resources to exert more control and stabilize their respective competitive positions become more popular (Hrebiniak and Joyce, 1985; Auster, 1992; Beekun and Ginn, 1993). In the final stage it seems inconceivable that firms would form alliances. The declining stage is commonly an outcome of major technological shifts, social and demographic changes, or regulatory changes that make current products and processes obsolete (Harrigan, 1988; Porter, 1980). Under such circumstances, agreements involving divestments or defensive collusion (Cainarca *et al.*, 1992) will be more of the norm. According to Auster (1992), any form of activity that might take place will involve limited technological linkages in an attempt to revitalize the market or to delay the death of the industry.

Following this line of reasoning, we argue that the propensity toward alliance-based competition is greatest in the growth stage – where the incentive is high to gain rapid access to specialized assets that complement a firm's innovations and speed up the potential for commercial success – and in the maturity stage – where strategies aimed at oligopolistic rents are likely to elicit a competitive response. The propensity toward alliance-based competition is lowest in the introduction stage (owing to uncertainty regarding technology, product, market and end-users) and in the declining stage.

P4: The likelihood that firm *B* will form an alliance in response to firm *A*'s alliance formation is related to the stage of market life cycle. More specifically, the response likelihood is greatest in growth and maturing stages, and lowest in introduction and declining stages.

Competitor Proximity

Research on competitive analysis has argued that the competitive proximity of firms serves as a useful window to assess the consequences of competitive attacks and counterattacks on the focal firm (Barnett, 1993; Chen, 1996). Following Chen (1996), we define 'competitive proximity' as the combined degree of market commonality and resource similarity among competitors. Assessing market commonality requires that a firm analyzes not only the number of markets in which it competes but also how many of these markets interconnect with a competitor's markets (Barnett, 1993; Chen, 1996; Gimeno and Woo, 1996). Competitors that overlap in a number of strategically important markets may be seen as direct rivals, each of whom has a greater likelihood of responding in kind to the competitor's alliance action in an attempt to nullify the effect of the alliance on the firm's competitive position. MasterCard's strategic alliance with Excite was a direct and similar response to an earlier strategic alliance between Visa and Yahoo (*Alliance Analyst*, 15 September 1998).

Resource commonality is defined as the degree to which competitors possess similar types and amounts of strategic and resource endowments (Chen, 1996) such as technological know-how, experience and internal assets. Given this definition, firms with analogous resources are likely to display similar strategic behaviour, capabilities and competitive strengths and weaknesses (Chen, 1996). Thus, a firm is more likely to retaliate to any alliance action by its competitors when the alliance is likely to impact its resource profile. Thus, given the components of competitive proximity, market commonality and resource similarity, we suggest that competitive proximity will be an influential indicator of a firm's propensity to react to a rival's alliance action.

P5: The greater the competitive proximity, the greater the likelihood that firm *B* will form an alliance in response to firm *A*'s alliance formation.

Market Concentration

The structural characteristics of the competitive environment influence the behaviour of firms (Pfeffer and Salancik, 1978). Previous research has shown that strategic alliances are most likely to be formed in an environment characterized by moderate concentration (Pfeffer, 1972; Pfeffer and Nowak, 1976; Rajagopalan and Yong, 1995). In highly concentrated markets, such as monopolistic or collusive markets, in contrast, a firm has the market power necessary to obtain resources independently in order to sustain and enhance its competitive advantage. Consequently, no incentive exists to either initiate an alliance or respond to a competitor's action. Moreover, an alliance with a dominant firm is likely to be met with great antitrust opposition, thereby further reducing the incentive to form an alliance.

The increase in alliance activity in the transition from a monopoly to a more competitive environment was clearly observable in telecommunications. With the liberalization of European telecommunications' markets in the later 1980s and 1990s, a major incentive for European PTOs to compensate for the erosion of dominant positions in their respective home markets was to expand internationally by establishing international co-operative ventures (Graak, 1996).

In a less concentrated market, or a market leaning toward pure competition, in contrast, a firm is highly dependent on scarce external resources and is limited in its ability to secure them. This lack of market power diminishes the attractiveness of the alliance with a firm in such a market as it will probably not lead to a reduction in competition. Moreover, if one accepts the opportunistic nature of firms, there again exists no incentive for an alliance action or response. In contrast to excessive or minimal market concentration, in a moderately concentrated market such as an oligopolistic market, a firm has comparable market power in relation to its competitors. An alliance action or reaction in this instance may be beneficial if it capitalizes on both internally developed assets and access to external resources. Thus, a competitor's alliance action will probably be seen as a threat requiring an immediate response if the firm is to maintain its competitive position.

P6: In a moderately concentrated market there is a greater likelihood that firm *B* will form an alliance in response to firm *A*'s alliance.

ORGANIZATIONAL-LEVEL MODERATING VARIABLES

So far, we have implied that within a population of firms we are likely to observe similar competitive engagements and responses, with the aforementioned contingencies. In other words, given a particular context (e.g. greater competitive proximity) all firms will display similar strategic behaviour (e.g. more likely to respond). Consequently, within the population, this implies a deterministic rather than voluntaristic orientation toward the competitive and general environment. However, resource-based theory suggests that even within a population, firms are often heterogeneous, possessing different resource profiles, competencies and capabilities that influence the propensity for competitive engagement and response (Chen, 1996). Following this line of research, we propose that a few differences at the individual firm level will moderate the relationship between an alliance action and a subsequent response.

Alliance Experience

The sheer numbers of alliances that have been formed over the past decade suggest that firms are gaining experience in alliance formation. However, experience alone does not build any collaborative know-how and is not enough to ensure a competitive advantage or to guarantee success with future alliances (Simonin, 1997). Following proponents of organizational learning (e.g. Kogut, 1988; Hamel, 1991; Inkpen and Crossan, 1995), we argue that it is quality and not quantity of alliance experience that is crucial. Firms must acquire and internalize know-how from alliance experiences, if they desire to derive the maximum tangible and intangible value from their alliance relationships.[6]

Further support for our argument can be found in the resource-based theory literature. This theory suggests that a sustained competitive advantage requires that assets be valuable, rare, imperfectly imitable and non-substitutable (e.g. Barney, 1986; Reed and DeFillippi, 1990). Research has suggested that alliance know-how meets this criteria to a greater extent than does alliance experience. For example, it is often easier to imitate a competitor's experience than it is to imitate a competitor's causally ambiguous and idiosyncratic skills and abilities (Simonin, 1997). In the telecommunications industry, it seems that after a period of fast established alliances, which were also quickly dissolved, more continuity is expected to dominate the previously turbulent alliance landscape (Molony, 1999). For example, AT&T, until 1999 a member of the Unisource alliance, announced in 1998 the creation of a strategic alliance (Concert) with a European competitor of the other Unisource partnering firms: British Telecom. Telefonica of Spain's journey through the alliance 'jungle' started in 1993 with Unisource. After leaving Unisource in 1997 to join Concert, the company ended up in striking in 1998 an alliance deal with Worldcom-MCI 1998. However, some companies seems to have accumulated sufficient alliance experience to continue their current international partnerships (Molony, 1999).

Following this line of thought, we argue that alliance experience will moderate the intensity of alliance competitive engagement and response. Firms that not only have alliance experience but also have internalized lessons learned from their alliances will be less apt to respond quickly to a competitor's alliance action. These firms know what alliances entail, and thus are not in a rush to respond. Because they have developed a multitude of skills and capabilities, they are better able to assess the situation and determine whether a response would be beneficial. In fact, analysis may reveal that the firm is quite capable of successfully competing alone.

P7: The greater the collaborative know-how that firm B has acquired from its alliance experiences, the lower the likelihood that firm B will respond quickly to firm A's alliance formation by forming an alliance of its own.

Firm Size

Firm size has often been referred to as a critical moderating variable in organizational theory (Kimberly, 1976), thereby influencing the types of strategies that are needed to compete effectively (Chen and Hambrick, 1995). Therefore we argue that relatively smaller and larger organizations are less likely to respond to a competitor's alliance action. Smaller organizations often lack the necessary slack resources (Smith *et al.*, 1991) or capability to pursue an alliance or might not be influential enough to secure partners with which to form an alliance agreement (Gomes-Casseres, 1996). In addition, smaller firms often focus on market niches, thus reducing the type of strategic capabilities that they can obtain from alliances (Burgers *et al.*, 1993). Large firms, in turn, though more likely to possess the necessary slack resources, are often structurally complex and bureaucratic as well as inhibited by structural inertia (Hannah and Freeman, 1989), all of which limits their ability to respond.

Even before liberalization between 1990 and 1995, international alliance activities in European telecommunications were mainly undertaken by the top four players in the industry (Deutsche Telekom, France Telecom, Telefonica of Spain and Dutch Telecom) responding to international expansion strategies of their US American counterparts and their European competitors (Graak, 1996).

In contrast, medium-sized firms face considerable competition, for a strategic action is likely to disrupt the firm's market share to some extent. Because these firms are neither large nor small, they do not possess the same advantages as a small firm (i.e. focus strategy) or as a large firm (i.e. greater market power). Further, though they cannot capitalize on the advantages, they will probably be exposed to similar disadvantages, such as fewer slack resources, increased complexity and slower information processing. Thus, we argue that a medium-sized firm is more likely to respond to a competitor's alliance formation.

P8: If firm *B* is of medium size, the greater the likelihood that it forms an alliance in response firm *A*'s alliance formation.

Firm Strategy

In examining the relationship between usage of co-operative linkages in relation to the external environment, Beekun and Ginn (1993) argue that firms will adjust their co-operative linkages to better align themselves with a changing environment. However, they also suggest that various strategies will have different focuses that, in turn, will affect which environmental factors they attend to. For instance, the *prospector* in Miles and Snow (1978) typology is said to have an external focus, proactively scanning the environment for opportunities and threats relative to the *analszer*, *defender* and *reactor*. Characteristics such as this suggest that the prospector might be more responsive to a competitor's alliance formation than perhaps a defender would be who is often characterized as taking a passive attitude toward external events (Beekun and Ginn, 1993) and having an internal focus.

A firm's strategic profile will also influence or be influenced by its choice of reference point (Fiegenbaum *et al.*, 1996). This argument is also consistent with the case of BT joining together with AT&T in Concert as an offensive response to the establishment of a rival high-technology alliance between MCI-WorldCom in 1998 (*CommunicationsWeek International*, 1998). In addition, a firm's choice of reference point will affect which environmental factors the firm emphasizes. Specifically, a firm with a focus on targets internal to the organization (e.g. production efficiency or quality improvement) might not attend to many environmental changes; and if it does, it will perceive those changes differently than a firm with an external reference point (e.g. competitors' actions). It may be suggested that the firm with an external focus will more likely perceive the competitor's move as an important event that requires a response.

P9: The likelihood of firm *B* forming an alliance in response to firm *A*'s alliance formation will be influenced by its choice of strategy and strategic profile. More specifically, firm *B* is likely to form an alliance in response to firm *A*'s alliance action if its strategic behaviour is more externally focused than internally focused.

DISCUSSION AND CONCLUSIONS

It has been argued that a new form of competition is emerging – alliance versus alliance – in an effort to create, build and sustain competitive advantage. In building a theoretical context to gain a better understanding of the antecedent conditions of alliance-based competition, the chapter has recognized that co-operation among firms has been a strategy enabling firms to influence not only their respective competitive positions as members of an alliance but also the competitive position of their 'competitive alliance others' in an attempt to generate sustained competitive advantage. Such a perspective is hemmed in by the principles of the competitive paradigm and its applications for conducting a 'co-operative' competitive analysis. As global competition continues to intensify and the wave of alliances continues to proliferate, a more thorough understanding of a rapidly emerging mode of competition – namely, alliance-based competition – seems warranted.

Until recently, international expansion of telecommunications service companies has been erratic and alliance failures have been rather frequent. Predictions about the reasons for the establishment (and the termination) of particular alliances have therefore been difficult to undertake. Increasingly, it seems, however, that the analysis of alliance activity examined through the lens of competitive analysis and co-operative strategies will add to the understanding of the establishment of alliances in telecommunications.

The most obvious and major research implication stems from the theoretical development of the alliance-based competition concept using the action – response dichotomy of competitive analysis. By bridging the literature on alliances and the literature on competitive analysis, the chapter conceptualizes competition as between alliances and examines the resulting competitive relationship as one that involves a competitive move (alliance action) and a competitive countermove (alliance response). From this basis, progress can be made toward empirically-based research on not only the explanatory power of this model but also on the use of alliances as competitive weapons to establish and sustain advantages such as better cost structures, improved quality, improved margins, better speed in manufacturing and distribution, deepening core competencies and enlarging market for products both within and across industries, to name only a few. It would be reasonable to assume, in this age of alliance-based competition, that the potential to sustain an alliance-based advantage would be a function of the *competitive strength* of the alliance (including but not limited to factors such as financial and competitive strength of partners, competitive positions of partners and combined alliance experience of partners), the *competitive elements* of the alliance (for instance, the combined degree of strategic and tactical elements in the alliance) and the *competitive impact* of the alliance (such as the number and intensity of competitive responses, barriers to imitation, etc.). In this regard, the mutual forbearance hypothesis needs to be revisited. While multipoint competition involving a two single firms A and B may have very different implications for mutual forbearance than two alliances, say $A1$ and $B2$, where the very notion that a combined entity is better than a single entity may cause strategic and tactical behaviours reducing the degree of mutual forbearance and intensifying multipoint competition.

The variables offered are by no means meant to be exhaustive. Rather, the aim was to propose a framework for conceptualizing alliance competition and inter-alliance rivalry and to begin the process of integrating research in strategic alliances and competitive analysis. The intention of the chapter was that as research progresses, the general model presented above will give rise to a more detailed and developed theory of alliance-based collective competition. In other words, additional inquiry should enrich this theory and add to its usefulness.

Appendix 1   Major Companies in the Telecommunications Service Industry, Ranked According to Capital Value, November 1999

Ranking	Company	Value 30/09/99 $ million	Total revenue $ million	Employees
1	NTT	195786	91387	138150
2	NTT DoCoMo	188881	29290	9342
3	Vodafone AirTouch[a]	146973	13064	24000
4	AT&T	139012	53223	150000
5	MCI Worldcom	134630	17678	77000
6	Deutsche Telekom	124023	38043	186000
7	AOL	115310	4777	12100
8	Bell Atlantic	104578	31566	140000
9	SBC Communications	100455	28777	129850
10	BT	98507	27920	124700
11	France Telecom	89920	26251	169099
12	BellSouth	84842	23123	88450
13	GTE	75406	25473	120000
14	Ameritech	73384	17154	70525
15	Telstra	66689	11880	52840
16	Mannesmann[a]	62282	20305	116247
17	Telefonica	51206	18605	103662
18	Telecom Italia	45671	25008	123966
19	Sprint FON	42384	16017	55900
20	MediaOne	41434	2882	16000
21	TIM	39951	6569	8893
22	China Telecom	36341	3182	12530
23	Sprint PCS	32012	1225	9000
24	Bell Canada	31971	18683	58000
25	NTT Data	31615	6670	10334
26	US West	28796	12378	54483
27	Singapore Telecom	28589	2876	NA
28	Hong Kong Telecom	26602	4171	13643
29	Cable & Wireless	26543	13083	50671
30	Orange	23563	1997	6144
31	Swisscom	22560	6971	21946
32	Cox Communications	22023	1717	9785
33	Nextel Communications	21278	1847	9700
34	Sonera	20916	1728	9068
35	Qwest	20694	2243	NA
36	Global Crossing	20358	424	148
37	Alltel	19828	5194	21504
38	Korea Telecom	19274	7748	56887
39	Telefonos de Mexico	18329	8348	63944
40	Level 3 Communications	17748	392	2100

Note:
a Mannesmann and Vodafone AirTouch merged in February 2000.
Source: *CommunicationsWeek International* (15 November 1999).

Appendix 2   Major Global Strategic Alliances in the Telecommunication Service Industry, 1999

Name of alliance	Current focal firm(s)	Established	Remarks
Concert	BT AT&T (*1998)	1993	Exit of focal firm MCI (1998)
Global One	Deutsche Telekom France Telecom Sprint	1996	
Unisource	Dutch PTO Swiss PTO (*1993) Swedish PTO	1992	Exit of focal firms: Telefonica (1997) AT&T (1999) Partners will divest interest (2000)
MCI–WorldCom	WorldCom MCI Telefonica (*1998)	1998	
Worldpartners	AT&T KDD of Japan SingTel Unisource	1993 (as Worldsource)	
Cable & Wireless	Cable & Wireless Regional joint ventures with different local companies	Since 1860	

Note: * 6.
Source: *CommunicationsWeek International*, Company Reports.

Notes

1. A discussion of the full range of relationships between the focal firm and its various stakeholders, such as those subsumed under other relationships (as informed by network theory), exceeds the scope of this chapter.
2. The focus in this chapter is on for-profit strategic alliances. The study excludes non-profit organizations because their motive for forming alliances often has more to do with enhancing the quality of their services than with combating competitive rivalry.
3. While this condition does not necessarily concur with reality (competitors co-operate in certain areas and compete in other areas), we believe that it is sufficient enough and does not impede the central purpose of developing arguments about the dynamic interplay between an alliance and alliance response.
4. See Doz and Hamel (1998) for a description of such alliance races.
5. Doz and Hamel (1998) argue that getting the 'first-order challenge' (combining specialized technologies) and the 'second order challenge' (integrating complex technologies into new products/services) right the first time enables the first mover to greatly eliminate any second-order solutions in competing for the future. This in turn requires forging partnerships with the right value-generating partners.
6. Companies such as Federal Express, Oracle, and Hewlett-Packard have in-house databases that systematically document, track and monitor their alliance relationships from the idea conception stage to eventual termination.

Part Three

Emerging European Markets

12 Typology of Business Networks in Eastern Europe: Comparative Case Studies

Emanuela Todeva

INTRODUCTION

The debates on privatization and company restructuring in Central and Eastern Europe (CEE) have been almost entirely dominated by the argument that privatization is the only means for enterprise restructuring. Our secondary analysis of a number of published case studies aims to highlight a new dimension of the transition process, and to introduce the argument for the structural dependencies and barriers for change, usually underestimated in the academic literature. We analyze the factors reported in the cases that determine the company performance, and particularly those related to government policies, industrial linkages and managerial strategies for survival in a turbulent environment.

The concept of 'business network' is used in this chapter to describe the *regular and repetitive transactions that an enterprise maintains with its suppliers and buyers within the value chain* (see also Porter, 1991). The term 'network' includes the *complexity of relations between companies, based on past contractual arrangements and present business links*. The information on these linkages is rarely reported in the published cases. However, through a secondary analysis of the available information we highlight some of the main enterprise linkages with buyers, suppliers and government agencies, and their transformation under the new market conditions.

BUSINESS NETWORK STUDIES IN TRANSITION ECONOMIES

The literature on business networks suggests that firms establish long-term contractual relationships in order to reduce transaction risk (Meyer, 1998), to increase resource commitments in profitable assets, to establish positions in new business networks (Johanson and Mattson, 1988) and to increase its control within the value chain (Todeva, 2000). Meyer (1998) argues that the assumptions of the neoclassical market model hold only for some markets, such as those of raw materials, natural resources and agricultural goods. In

171

industries where industrial marketing, customized supplies and sales and business-to-business relations predominate, market transactions are not a viable option for businesses, owing to high search costs, information costs (Casson and Cox, 1997), contract monitoring costs (Jarillo, 1988) and potential costs of contract enforcement in cases of unreliable partners. Businesses attempt to reduce these costs and to enhance their uncertainty management competencies through establishing relationships with governments, through influence on law and regulation and through the use of allies and co-operative relations (Clarke and Varma, 1999).

The establishment of interdependent network relations by firms is explained by the resource-dependence theory (Van de Ven, 1976; Pfeffer, 1987) and, more recently, by the information cost theory (Casson and Cox, 1997). According to Davis *et al.* (1996), the enabling conditions for establishment of business networks include trust relationships, domain consensus, information sharing and sharing of the gains from the exchange. The authors argue that without these conditions, even well developed business networks would collapse from the attempts for opportunistic behaviour. In their framework, the authors distinguish between networks for resource supply, for marketing of outputs, for access to information and for access to capital (Davis *et al.*, 1996). Defined in this way, business networks may be viewed as investments in intangible market assets (Mattson, 1987).

On the other hand, business networks represent a vast complexity of situations, when 'competitors in one market co-operate in another, and are suppliers and customers to each other in a third' (Johanson and Mattson, 1988). Therefore, the buyer–supplier relationships cannot adequately represent the interdependencies of firms within their value chain. Important 'partners' could be also various external stakeholders and governments (Davis *et al.*, 1996; Holm *et al.*, 1997). In the context of the former centrally planned economies, the link with the government and the firm's dependencies on government decisions are particularly evident.

STRUCTURAL DEPENDENCIES AND BARRIERS TO TRANSITION REFORMS

Most of the firms in the region were designed by the planning authorities in each country with high asset specificity, in order to serve a particular range of clients. The development of their business networks was driven by the output target (as fixed by the central plan, and required as a major input for another state firm). These material and product dependencies were coupled with locational distortions where firms were located to serve social purposes of employment and regional development targets. Investments in manufacturing capabilities were located by the central planners according to social objectives rather than to increase efficiency within the value chain.

Often proximity to resources and markets would play a secondary role in investment decisions, assuming that the centralized distribution of resources was a sufficient mechanism for the functioning of the firm.

One of the barriers to restructuring is that, by design, firms were closely tied up in buyer and supplier asset specificity. With the liberalization reforms and the subsequent increase of macroeconomic instability and business risk, firms' strategic responses were driven by their existing linkages. The privatization itself, unless it involved a foreign partner, did not adequately facilitate the operational breaking of the former business networks.

In our analysis of the published case studies, we review different means used by firms to extend their choice of suppliers and buyers, and to increase their control over their value chain. Using Porter's (1991) framework for analysis of competitive advantage, we look at the way firms evaluate and respond to the power of suppliers and customers, and the way they protect themselves from substitutes and other rival products or services. However, the cases show that most of the strategic responses of firms involve strong links with government agencies, and strong dependencies on government macroeconomic policies (Davis *et al.*, 1996).

SOURCES OF BUSINESS RISK AND RISK MANAGEMENT IN TRANSITION ECONOMIES

The intense transition reforms in CEE created macroeconomic instability that raised the risk of business operations throughout the whole region. The instability of the business environment exposed enterprises to multiple risks, such as market risks, financial risks and resource management risks (Ritchie and Marshal, 1993). The *market risks* that firms faced were determined mainly by the changes in demand, by the increased variations in consumer tastes and confidence, by the decline in individuals' purchasing power and by the changes in government regulations. A major market shock to firms was the breaking of the COMECON trading block – including the member countries Bulgaria, CSFR (Czechoslovak Federal Republic), GDR (German Democratic Republic), Poland, Hungary, the former USSR and Romania, the associated members Mongolia, Cuba, Vietnam and Yugoslavia as observer – where most of the regional foreign trade occurred.

The *financial risks* were determined by the instability of exchange rates (driven by high inflation); by the increased taxation; by the level of bad debt accumulated by the firms; and by the withdrawal of state subsidies and reliefs. The weak financial system in the region (Meyer, 1998) was not capable of supporting firms for their transition costs, associated with changes in the firms' product range and market orientation.

The *resource management risks* were induced by the unavailability of raw materials, qualified labour and advanced technology. The disrupted communications and trade relations owing to the collapse of the COMECON trading block led to multiple resource management risks. Suppliers from COMECON countries were usually obstructed by difficulties in intergovernmental negotiations of payments between member countries.

If we look at the transition policies in CEE from a risk-management perspective, the liberalization of trade and prices dramatically increased market risk. The liberalization of prices is seen by managers in our cases as one of the major factors that led to massive increase of inter-enterprise debt, accumulated from non-receivables between buyers and suppliers. The monetarization of the economy increased the financial problems and difficulties in obtaining credits, and blocked the payments between firms.

All these risks varied across industries and across countries, and this determined the different speed of the decline and recovery of different transition economies.

The analysis of the business environment in CEE economies suggested our underlying hypothesis that the *adjustment behaviour of firms during the transition is predetermined by government decisions, by the macroeconomic conditions in the country, by the position that each firm occupies in a particular industry and its control over the value chain*. For analytical purposes seven new categories were developed to allow comparability between the cases and the companies from different countries.

We interpret the effect of the macroeconomic environment as related to *dependencies on government decisions*. The information available on the industrial structure, relevant to each particular case, is interpreted as dependencies on *intra-industry, inter-industry and inter-firm linkages*. Reported personal and professional linkages that affect business decisions are interpreted as *personal, professional and political networks*. Information on firms' structure, organization and capabilities is extracted from the published cases under the categories of *intra-firm dependencies*, and *accumulated resources and capabilities/access to markets*. In addition, the specific market conditions are described under the category *uncertainty of resources*. The strategic response of each particular company is described under the category *strategic behaviour, adaptation and repositioning*.

All these categories are indicative, and they serve mainly the purpose of providing a comparable framework for interpretation of the published cases. Our secondary analysis provides a profile for each company, with emphasis on firms' dependencies and responses to the business risks.

TYPOLOGY OF BUSINESS NETWORKS

The case studies used in this chapter originate from a number of publications (Estrin, 1995; Hirschhausen and Hui, 1995; Johnson *et al.*, 1996). The cases of firms from Bulgaria and Romania stem from unpublished research reports (Estrin *et al.*, 1997), used in this paper with the permission of the authors.

Our comparative analysis of the cases identified two main criteria that determine the type of strategic response of the firms: (a) structural dependency of the firm; and (b) market dependency. According to these criteria we divided all cases into the following groups: (a) business networks based on *transformed dependencies*, comprising firms established under the old system of central planning; (b) *newly established business networks*, evolved from new business start-ups or the appropriation of business operations by new legal entities such as joint ventures (JVs), or acquisitions; and (c) firms that *failed to transform their network relationships*. In addition, the cases are divided into two sub-groups referring to national business networks and international business networks, according to their main market and access to foreign partner. The grouping of *international business networks* includes firms engaged in economic transactions with foreign partners, and refers to the modes of foreign market entry of international firms by Young *et al.* (1989). If firms report only repetitive transactions with partners within the home market, their business networks are treated as *national*.

The first group of cases (Table 12.1) represents firms with a long history that have successfully *transformed their dependencies* within the business network of suppliers, buyers and other contract agencies. The assumption is that the withdrawal of the state and the collapse of the central plan has required firms to replace the old mechanisms of allocation of resources. In doing so, firms have repositioned themselves within the value chain.

Table 12.1 Business networks based on transformed dependencies

National business networks	
	1 Lithuania – Industrial holding company (electronics)
	2 Hungary – Hungartextile holding (textile/cloth)
International business networks through:	
Shared ownership	3 Latvia – PAF (minibus assembling)
Industrial cross-border co-operation	4 Czech Republic PSP – Heavy Engineering (iron processing machinery)
Licensing and exporting	5 Czech Republic – Spolana (chemicals)
Exporting	6 Romania – Clujana Trading Company (leather and leather substitute shoes)
Sub-contracting and exporting	7 Czech Republic – Motorpal (auto parts, fuel injection)
Equity joint venture	8 Slovak Republic – CS-07 (food processing/ chocolates and sweets)
Joint venture and sub-contracting	9 Poland – Szczecin shipyard (shipbuilding)

Transformed Business Networks

Lithuania – Industrial Holding Company (Electronics)
(Hirschhausen and Hui, 1995)

Dependence on government decisions
  Most Investment Funds in Lithuania were established in 1992 with no
  regulatory framework on the composition of assets and no competition
  control; Creation of multiple funds by the same people; In 1992, the professional group of managers in the electronics established the EBSW
  Investment Fund.

Inter-industry dependencies
  In 1992 EBSW Investment Fund bought 40 per cent of the shares of TV-
  2, 30 per cent of TV-1; In addition managers acquired directly another 25
  per cent of TV-2 shares and 30 per cent of TV-1 shares; 5 per cent of the
  Investment Funds in Lithuania hold 52 per cent of the invested vouch-
  ers in the electronic sector; each investment fund controls a commercial
  bank, one or more insurance companies, a distribution network and
  trade firms; in this way, an investment fund with the smallest possible
  amount of capital have become the majority owner of a large network of
  enterprises.

The Lithuanian case of a holding company in the electronics industry
demonstrates how a highly centralized and capital-intensive business
network from the past has transformed itself into a private holding
company with effective control over the entire industrial sector of
Lithuanian electronics.
  The authors of the case argue that the inconsistency of government policies related to privatization issues, has allowed a highly organized professional network of 'managers' within the electronics sector to take control
of the majority of vertically integrated assets. The mechanism of consolidating the former network has been facilitated by the privatization programme of the Lithuanian government.
  The case does not provide sufficient information whether this transformation of ownership has led to changes in efficiency, or even in profitability. However, this case demonstrates that the restructuring of the electronics
industry in Lithuania is not a market-led transformation. A professional
network of managers have reinforced previously existing inter-industry
linkages and dependencies on suppliers and markets. They have used the
dependencies on centralized government subsidies and the regulatory
reforms in Lithuania as a vehicle for achieving their private aims.
  It is also evident from the case that the new business formation is lobbying the government to conclude new commercial agreements with the

CIS countries, in order to facilitate access to Russian markets for the private holding company.

Hungary – Hungartextile Holding (Textile/Cloth) (Estrin *et al.*, 1995)

Dependence on government decisions
The 1988 Act on Economic Associations transformed the former Economic Associations into holdings with independent subsidiaries; The intention of creating the holdings was to create asset management structures, which will perform many administrative functions, including those of the subsidiaries.

Intra-firm dependencies
It was established as a holding in June 1989; In 1991 the subsidiaries became loss-makers themselves; from March 1992, it was supervised by the government through State Property Agency; the holding lost all of its production, but kept part of its predecessor's purchasing and sales functions; there is cross-ownership between subsidiaries, and the holding controls between 80–98 per cent of the shares in each subsidiary.

The company controls 30 per cent of the total output of the Hungarian textile/cloth industry. This case shows, in contrast with the Lithuanian electronics company, that the actual ambitions of the managers are not to run the holding company, but to use it as a legal entity that bears the liabilities of the loss-making firms. The expectations are that these loss-making firms will be closed by the government to clear the bad debts.

The devolution of administrative control in Hungary has changed the ownership status of the members of Hungartextile Holding. However, the case does not suggest a major change in the supplier and buyer networks of the main firm. The change of ownership and the formation of the holding company has not led to a diversification of products, or to access to new markets. On the contrary, the case shows that in spite of the significant changes in the structure of ownership and control, the loss of COMECON markets (43 per cent of their output in 1991) has made all of the subsidiaries of the holding into loss-making firms.

The high level of technology (60–70 per cent of Western standard) has created overcapacity, which poses additional questions for a rationalization of the business. The changes in ownership have not altered the dependency of the firm on government decisions and on the structure of the textile/cloth industry and the intra-firm linkages between the subsidiaries. This case is also an example of the fact that the interests linked to the privatization are focused on the high value-added business functions, such as sales, procurement and resource management.

Latvia – PAF (Minibus Assembling) (Hirschhausen and Hui, 1995)

Accumulated resources and capabilities/access to markets
The company was a supplier of minibuses to the entire Soviet Union; until 1992 it was the only producer in the Former Soviet Republics (FSR) of 12-seat passenger and ambulance vans; 93 per cent of its production is distributed in the FSR.

Inter-industry dependence
The company PAF is a centre of a large network of ten major and 100 minor suppliers of materials and components; 10 per cent of the suppliers are from Latvia, and 80 per cent from the FSR and the most strategic one is GAZ; at least three of its major Russian suppliers have decided to start minibus production themselves (GAZ, Bratsk, Uliyanov).

This is a case of internationalization of the business network through *shared cross-border ownership* in the sector of minibus assembling. The Latvian company has in the past been heavily dependent on Russian suppliers and the Russian market. This forced the company management and the Latvian government to initiate in 1995 a cross-ownership deal with the Russian company GAZ – their strategic supplier.

The case shows that the main factor driving the successful transition of the firm is its access to the Russian market, rather than the change of ownership. The change of ownership in this case is motivated by the attempt to tie up GAZ, who is the main supplier of parts and a potential competitor. This is a defensive strategy by PAF, which has high specificity of its assets and aims to protect its position in a business network that is located in Russia. The internationalization of ownership, and the reinforcement of the former dependencies within the production chain has helped the company to maintain its position on the Russian market.

Czech Republic – PSP Heavy Engineering (Iron Processing Machinery) (Estrin *et al.*, 1995)

Dependence on government decisions
In the past the company was supported by government orders through a state foreign trade firm, which sub-contracted work for a large multi-governmental investment project in Ukraine and Russia through an Investment Engineering Group; the state provided long-term, low-interest, government guaranteed bank loans; the state foreign trade firm used to bear all risks; in 1988, the Investment Engineering Group split into several parts, and the Principal Contractor Unit became a division in PSP; in 1993 the outgoing Czechoslovak government agreed to stop its

investment in Ukraine, to pay the loan collateral and the interest payments in yearly instalments for ten years and to pay PSP lost profits; the government transferred ownership of the assets to all major suppliers to the project and one potential buyer of the products expected from the Ukrainian venture.

Accumulated resources/access to markets
Most of its overdue receivables were recovered, and the irretrievable ones were sold to the government; the company used the unclear relationships on the multigovernmental investment project in Ukraine as a secure market, utilizing the cheap government loan, and completing its part in the international investment project; its technological equipment for coal power stations, cement and ceramic industries is sold mainly to privatized construction companies; the firm plans to grow in a niche market of environmental technology, using preferential government loans.

PSP is a very good example of how an influential management team in this sector, and an appropriately selected Board of Directors and Supervisory Board, have succeeded in lobbying the Czech government for a number of favourable decisions. These government actions have enabled the firm to transform its international business network, based on *industrial cross-border co-operation* involving the governments of the Czech Republic and Ukraine.

The case shows that the firm has survived through 'extracting' financial resources from the Czech government in a variety of ways, rather than through repositioning itself on the market. These include the clearance of the bad debts of the firm and preferential loans. The case shows also how through its political network the company has turned its dependency on the Ukrainian market, and the inter-government negotiations of cross-ownership, into an advantage, by sheltering itself from the shocks of inflation and the unfavourable exchange rates.

Czech Republic – Spolana (Chemicals) (Estrin *et al.*, 1995)

Accumulation of resources and capabilities/access to markets
Size was 10 000 employees in 1992, after 17 per cent reduction of the labour force; highly diversified production in industrial chemistry, man-made fibres, plastics, agrochemistry, gastrochemistry and synthetic hormones for the medicine.

Dependence on government decisions
Cancellation of debt in 1991 by the government; Dependent on cheap crude oil from Russia and a range of imports.

Strategic response

 Significant proportion of their products are made under the licence of foreign firms; has an R&D co-operation agreement with the University for Chemical Technology in Prague; 55 per cent of its exports are to Germany and the Benelux countries; the loss of domestic markets was compensated by rapid growth in exports; credits obtained were secured by immovable assets exceeding 1.3 times the credit.

The main form of internationalization for Spolana is *licensing* and *exporting*. This case demonstrates the point that without a major transformation of ownership, or changes in its relationship with suppliers, the company has survived through increased exports to Western markets, and through the internationalization of its business network of clients and licensors. The successful restructuring of the firm was supported by the government with the cancellation of firm's debt in 1991, which enabled it to obtain fresh credits.

Romania – Clujana Trading Company (Leather and Leather Substitute Shoes) (Estrin *et al.*, 1997)

Inter-industry dependence

 High degree of vertical production integration – the company has the capacity to ensure all necessary inputs and semiproducts for its own use, and also for other shoe producers.

Strategic behaviour

 Decrease of production for sales on domestic market from 63.7 per cent (in 1991) to 50.5 per cent (in 1994) and a forecast of further decrease to 33 per cent (1998); increased production for foreign markets from 36 per cent (in 1991) to 49.5 per cent (in 1994) and was forecast to be 67 per cent (1998); planning retechnologization of the factories with the support from the State Ownership Fund.

This is an example of a successful linkage between the production firm Clujana and financial institutions – the State Property Fund and the Private Property Fund called IV Muntenia. The Romanian company is an example of a firm that has expanded its national business network, and has simultaneously increased its international business relations through exports. The link with the two new Ownership Funds within its national business network has enabled it to secure financial resources, and to get access to foreign markets as they manage its *exporting* activities and the overall internationalization. It could be argued that the major change for the company is the shift of control – from ministerial control to control by the two ownership funds, who also facilitate its access to markets.

Czech Republic – Motorpal (Auto Parts, Fuel Injection)
(Estrin *et al.*, 1995)

Accumulated resources
  The company comprises seven plants in six towns and 3800 employees.

Uncertainty of resources
  The collapse of COMECON and the decline in the domestic market led
  to a 60 per cent cut in orders; delayed payments by clients caused secondary indebtedness and shortage of cash.

Dependence on government decisions
  In 1990 Motorpal became a joint stock company; the two major changes
  that affected trade were the 1990 currency devaluation through changes
  in exchange rates, and the 1991 price liberalization; as part of the macroeconomic stabilization wages were frozen for the first half of 1991 and
  remained regulated until the end of 1992, which led to social unrest in
  the firm; the government cancelled part of the debts of the firm and the
  debt of many of its suppliers and customers, but the banks applied this
  credit to the interest, not to the loans of the firms.

Intra-industry dependence
  Active participation in R&D with engine producers.

Strategic behaviour
  In 1991–2 two new products were produced for the West European
  market, which is a proof of good technical skills; Motorpal is exploring
  new markets in Middle East, North Africa, India, Indonesia and
  China.

The Czech company Motorpal operates in the automotive industry, producing auto parts and fuel injection units. In comparison with the other
cases, it is one of the largest firms and one of the most experienced in
conducting international business operations. However, survival has been
determined not so much by managerial competencies in restructuring and
adjustment, but by their almost monopolistic position in the sector, by their
technical expertise and know-how, by their intensive capitalization by the
former socialist governments and their business ties with the car manufacturer Skoda, through which they have gained access to new business
partners in Germany.
    In spite of the fact that the managers do not report specific business link-
ages, it is evident that in addition to the reputation of a former COMECON
market leader, the company has benefited from sub-contracting to Skoda's
acquirers, Volkswagen. It is clear in this case that the main revenue of the

company at present comes from their *exporting and sub-contracting* activities.

Slovak Republic – CS-07 (Food Processing/Chocolates and Sweets) (Estrin *et al.*, 1995)

Dependence on government decisions

The legal system provides weak penalties for not fulfilling a contract; the Ministry of Agriculture and Grocery had no power to manage the firm with exception of appointing the General Director and evaluating the economic results annually; in 1992 the firm became a Joint-Stock Company, administered by the Fund of National Property who appoints the Board of Directors (a General Director and four Vice-Directors) and a Supervisory Board.

Intra-industry dependence

In the past, 80 per cent of production was purchased by wholesale organizations; their collapse led to increase of inventories; the firm now access the local market only through small businesses.

Uncertainty of resources

Above 70 per cent of exports were to COMECON markets; the collapse of the system for integrative sales in 1990 led to discoordination of production and sales.

Strategic behaviour

It has agreed a sale of 32 per cent of the shares to the Swiss firm (Jacobs–Suchard), to increase to 66 per cent through future investment; at present it sub-contracts to a German company against delivery of technology and ingredients; obsolete products and packaging were replaced by purchase of packaging materials from Austria, Germany and Italy; most recent strategies include diversification of production and discontinuity of some product lines; there is a planned full merger with Jacobs–Suchard, a build-up of new distribution channels through new domestic and foreign partners, acquisition of technology and expansion into the former COMECON markets.

The Slovak company 'CS-07' has agreed an *equity joint venture* with Jacobs–Suchard, after 27 per cent of the labour force was sacked. The interest of the foreign company was instigated primarily by the presence of their international competitors (Nestlé and BSN/France) in the Czech Republic. This shows that the expansion of international business networks in CEE should be considered more as driven by the wider global competitive environment than by competitive advantages within the region, such as new business opportunities that derive from the regulatory reforms in each country, or enterprise competitiveness.

Poland – Szczecin Shipyard (Shipbuilding) (Johnson *et al.*, 1996)

Dependence on government decisions
The firm was administered in the past by the Industrial Shipbuilding Union, directly accountable to the Ministry of Industry; governments used to locate clients and negotiate with customers through the state trade company 'Centromor', for a 2 per cent commission of a ship's selling price; the government provided all finance for a new ship construction, which included subsidies for unprofitable projects (often up to 50 per cent of the total construction cost); the new managing director secured the co-operation of the Polish Development Bank (PDB), a government bank designed to assist in large-scale enterprise restructuring; in 1991 the yard and the PDB created a joint venture 'Container Ship', with 50 per cent ownership each; the PDB operated as a guarantee for fleet owners' prepayments and to provide working capital.

Accumulation of resources and capabilities/access to markets
Major customers in the past were Eastern Bloc countries, particularly FSR; the trading company paid the yard in domestic currency upon completion of a project; in 1988 it signed a contract for four container ships for German ship owners, the first one being delivered in 1991; in 1992 it signed contracts with German fleet owners for another 13 container ships worth \$300 mn; total contracted ships for 1992 were 48, or 40 per cent of the international market for medium size containers.

Strategic behaviour
By 1991 the company had \$150 mn debt because of expensive bank loans and Soviet insolvency; it was forced to delay payments to over 1500 suppliers and a number of commercial banks; it created a new marketing office in 1989 to pursue clients and to identify a niche world market; the labour force was reduced from a peak of 13 000 (in the 1970s) to 6000 (in 1991); in 1992 the production value was \$182 mn and required 5000 workers; it aimed to narrow its product focus and to develop a niche market – for container ships, particularly in the medium class; it closed two out of six slipways and a number of other departments comprising 1500 workers which were transferred to the main production line; it reduced product cycle time for a single ship from 2–4 years to 11 months; remuneration was changed from piece rate payment per task to hourly wages adjusted by qualification category; it reversed the compensation hierarchy and put highly qualified workers on top; no overtime work was permitted; the new average salary was twice the national

average; it eliminated many of the employee amenities; it developed competitive advantage by focusing production, and increased productivity by reducing the production cycle, by the implementation of a performance-enhancing compensation scheme, by the shedding of non-productive assets and by reducing the number of employees directly involved in ship assembly.

This is an exemplary case of internationalization of an old business network, built on a joint venture (JV) with a government-owned bank. The success of the Szczecin shipyard, at the time of the case study, is due not only to the strategic restructuring efforts of its management team, but also to the business relationships it established with the PDB. This new access to financial resources reduced the dependency of the firm on externally secured bank loans.

However, the most important elements of the business network are the *contracts with German ship owners*, that provide the firm with an access to important new customers and secure revenue. These contracts could also be attributed to former personal and professional contacts and business links, as well as the expertize of their Chief Executive in negotiations.

Newly Established Business Networks

Under the category of *newly established business networks* (Table 12.2) we have grouped firms that have appeared on the market as new business start-ups, or new legal entities, that do not bear directly the liabilities of former state enterprises.

Czech Republic – Tipa (Footwear Industry) (Estrin *et al.*, 1995)

Accumulation of resources and capabilities/access to market
   Size was 600 employees in ten industrial sectors; accumulation of different technologies and contacts which allowed diversification; managers rely on their own information of the market opportunities and their avail-

Table 12.2   Newly established business networks

National business networks	
	1 Czech Republic – Tipa (footwear industry)
International Business Networks through:	
Contractual joint venture	2 Hungary – Elegant Charm (textile/garments)
Acquisition	3 Hungary – Interchokolade KFT (food processing) Chocolate

able skills; managers maintain a rich network of contacts and connections which facilitates business operations such as: finding sources of inputs, leasing offices and work spaces and identifying high-profit market niches and take-over opportunities.

Personal, professional and political networks
The group of the nine founders of the business are former executives from nearby state and co-operative farms established in trade, travel, information, production and agriculture; they knew each other for many years from High School.

Dependence on government decisions
To offset the burden of taxes the firm received subsidies in 1991.

Strategic behaviour
It is constructing a plant for wood processing with second-hand machinery from a bankrupt Swiss co-operative; all investments have been made using loans, or leasing service; planning JVs with German and Italian partners, and a JV with a Russian partner to facilitate barter deals; exporting labour to Germany; Planning to expand into a milk processing with an investment in a plant; planning an acquisition of a packaging plant and establishment of a regional savings bank; planning to expand in Slovakia by acquiring some businesses – looking for businesses with a high profit margin; registered two Investment Funds at privatization and trained the managers; operating within the regional boundaries.

Tipa began as a small business start-up in the retail sector with a regional focus of operations. The company has grown rapidly through an intense diversification, and has achieved high profit margins in all activities as identified by their well informed managerial team. It is unclear why the company has been classified by its managers as operating in the footwear sector, as it is actually involved in businesses in ten different industrial sectors, including agricultural production, travel services, construction (also export of labour in construction), agricultural machinery sales, foreign trade, shoe production, frozen food and ice-cream production and sale, a bakery for bread production, general retail and wholesale, a real estate agency services and telecommunications and security services. As some of the facilities were acquired from former state firms, the link with the government has been strong.

At the centre of this business network stands a group of nine former executives from local state and co-operative farms who have known each other for many years. It seems that the business has grown around the personal ties that each individual has maintained from the past.

Hungary – Elegant Charm (Textile/Garments) (Estrin *et al.*, 1995)

Intra-firm dependencies

The company was established in 1990 as a spin-off from the main Group of ten plants; some of these plants had obsolete technology and become financially a drain on the Group; initially the largest shareholder was the main group – with a 48.9 per cent share, equivalent to the machinery and equipment arbitrarily overpriced; the second shareholder was OTP Bank with 25.5 per cent and three smaller private firms (a small trading house, an agricultural co-operative and a small private firm) with 25.6 per cent combined; later on, the equity stakes of the three smaller firms were sold to a single private firm; it produces leather clothing, which is capital-intensive and takes a lot of the firm's profit for refinancing routine short-term credits; there is a deep gap between production and marketing capabilities, and a lack of co-ordination between the two; there is a lack of marketing department and as a result the company is losing 4–5 per cent from the final sale price as it is dealing through trading houses; the present Director General had been the former head of Trade and Co-operation Department at the old Group.

Uncertainty of resources

The company is undercapitalized owing to its small collateral, necessary for credits; the domestic market for finished products has shrunk owing to a fall in household consumption; the Group utilized only a small part of the capacity of the company and this created the need to find new markets outside the orbit of the Group; there was uncertainty of ownership – some of the small shareholders were liquidated, others sold their shares and the Group was also in liquidation.

Intra-industry dependence

There is a large number of firms on the domestic market which compete with imports rather than between themselves; the intensity of competition is caused by the narrow specialization of producers and their direct access to the retail market; the retail firms actually design the value chain by selecting the network of suppliers of final products.

Strategic behaviour

The firm has a co-operation agreement with Levi Strauss for jeans; there is a signed agreement between the main Group and Elegant Charm that the company cannot enter into business relations with the Group's suppliers and partners for five years; there is aggressive sub-contracting to utilize up to 108 per cent of capacity; they are gradually creating an independent design department, which made up to 15 per cent of the sales;

they are gradually closing down several loss-making product lines, such as leather clothing and fur products, these capacities were converted to textile-sewing; the management would like to acquire the shares owned by the Group after the Group's liquidation, at a price of 75 per cent of their value, offering to take 50 per cent of them and the other 50 per cent to be offered to the workers; the management has also started negotiations to acquire the shares from OTP Bank; it is planning a take-over of one of the plants of the Group, or to purchase the facilities rented at present.

The case shows a company, established as a spin-off of a major industrial group of ten plants, which has managed to survive through a co-operative agreement with Levi Strauss. This is an example of an international business network that demonstrates both the efforts of CEE firms to internationalize and the interests of Western partners to expand eastwards in this highly labour-intensive industrial sector. The internationalization of the company is achieved through the *contractual joint venture* with Levi Strauss and through *exporting*. However, the company itself has no marketing or sales department, and this demonstrates its dependency not only on the international partner, but also on the trading houses that operate as intermediaries in its business dealings.

Hungary – Interchokolade KFT (Food Processing/Chocolate)
(Estrin *et al.*, 1995)

Dependence on government decisions
Nationalized in 1947, integrated into an industrial trust in 1963 and decentralized in 1981, when it was forced to merge with a sugar factory; this led to depletion of company's reserves owing to the world sugar crisis and depressed prices in the sugar industry; taxes on profits were not paid in 1991 owing to extremely high taxes on wages introduced with the new income tax system in 1988; received export subsidies until 1990 and experienced a significant decline in export performance afterwards; the Swiss partner 'Globalfood' became an almost exclusive owner in 1992.

Intra-industry dependence
The Hungarian confectionery industry was highly competitive after 1987, with four state enterprises, 37 bakery firms owned by municipalities and 30 co-operatives; by 1991 the industry was dominated by three firms which were ranked 19, 32 and 98 on the Hungarian industry list of the top 200 firms; exogenous factors have quite a strong impact, because price fluctuations on the sugar market are large and this affects profits.

Uncertainty of resources
  Total increase of costs between 1988 and 1991 – 77 per cent, including
  138 per cent wage costs, 142 per cent fixed costs, 43 per cent materials
  and 62 per cent energy; rapid increase of wages without significant
  layoffs; tenfold increase of bank debt (1988–91) owing to higher interest
  rates, inflation and delayed payments; irredeemability of most receivables, which doubled between 1990 and 1991 and increased more than
  ten times after 1988.

The Hungarian company has been gradually acquired by the Swiss multinational company 'Globalfood'. This *acquisition* obviously brings international expertise and market opportunities for one of the four largest
Hungarian manufacturers in this sector. However, in this case it is suggested
that by joining the international business network of Globalfood subsidiaries, Interchokolade KFT has lost autonomy, and has become a dependent division which provides manufacturing facilities and access to the
Hungarian market for the Swiss multinational firm.

Firms That Failed to Transform Their Business Networks

For a number of state firms the output markets went through a dramatic
drop in demand, or rapid increase in foreign competition. The two cases in
this category explain the reasons why firms were unable to restructure and
to transform their dependencies on narrow output markets.

Poland – Pafawag (Engineering/Railway Rolling Stock)
(Estrin *et al.*, 1995)

Accumulation of resources and capabilities/access to market
  Size was 2184 employees in 1991; decrease of employment with 30 per
  cent between 1988 and 1992; the largest firm in the rolling stock industry, the largest producer of electric locomotives and the sole Polish manufacturer of multipartite electric sets; previously exported to USSR, China,
  India, Iraq, Bulgaria, Hungary, Yugoslavia, Czechoslovakia, Morocco and
  Syria; holds a large portfolio of social assets – a large housing district,
  medical clinic, vocational and technical secondary schools, a cultural
  centre, sports clubs, holiday resorts and canteens; it had began to diversify production beyond the typical industry profile; did not carry any
  burden of long-term credits.

Uncertainty of resources
  Lack of financial resources to replace obsolete machines and in this way
  to reduce production costs.

Dependence on government decisions

Rapidly shrinking subsidies for the Polish State Railways; the drop of domestic demand occurred relatively late (in 1991–2), but was much sharper than in other industries and unevenly spread among the various product groups; frequent changes of national economic conceptions and economic restructuring programmes (partly owing to unstable governments) made it impossible for the firm to develop and implement a consistent strategy; the Ministry of Privatization approved a plan for privatization, including establishing a JV with a foreign partner and with foreign capital to restructure the production and upgrade the products to Western standards.

Intra-industry dependence

The industry consists of ten enterprizes that produce railway rolling stock for the Polish Railways, for the city transport, for internal industrial transport and for export; some firms exported about 70 per cent of their output to COMECON countries; technical and organizational backwardness led to the inability to launch competitively priced modern products; there is large underutilized and obsolete production capacity; there is demand, but the main customers are railway companies that rely on government subsidies, and therefore are unable to place new orders; difficulty in separating various elements of the technology lines, and lack of potential buyers for them.

Strategic behaviour

Pafawag did not use long-term credits after the increase of interest rates in 1990; however, the interest on short-term credits to finance its working capital amounted to 10 per cent of total costs; the firm was able to find alternative suppliers who offered either cheaper products, or more favourable terms of payment; the firm increased production of items unconnected with the rolling stock market; however, the potential was limited, because of other firms from the same industry who could offer lower prices for the same items and services; the firm attempted to lower costs of materials, energy and transport, but because of the interdependence of technological lines the firm was unable to sell unnecessary assets; part of the social assets were leased; the number of employees in marketing and accounting was increased; there was increased financial and marketing autonomy of particular departments; one department for casting was liquidated in 1992.

The Polish firm Pafawag is an engineering company, manufacturing railway rolling stock. In the beginning of the reforms in Poland they were able to acquire high profits owing to their monopoly position on the market. However, their rapid decline after 1990 suggests unavoidable bankruptcy.

The main factors that have driven the firm to that position are the collapse of the home market and the inability of the Polish government, their main customer, to invest in the renovation of the railway rolling stock.

Hungary – Radion (Electronics/Radio and Electrical Works)
(Estrin *et al.*, 1995)

Accumulation of resources and capabilities/access to market
Size was 1776 employees in 1991, which has decreased by 46 per cent since 1988; the R&D expenditure in 1990 was 64 per cent of the 1988 level, which meant that the firm has given up its ambitions to remain competitive; the firm has sales channels to the FSR.

Uncertainty of resources
The growth of material costs and inventories exploded in 1991, and this weakened the financial basis of the firm; there was a dramatic increase in corporate debt linked to the former defence industry and closure of all military outlets; lack of funds and unavailablity of credit; under-capitalization, accompanied by a rapidly increasing technology gap; serious market and sales problems.

Dependence on government decisions
Liberalization of imports flooded the market with competitive products; there was a slump in economic activity by 25–30 per cent and a consequent decline in living standards led to a shrinking of domestic sales by 50 per cent (between 1988 and 1991); in 1991 the firm was forced to declare bankruptcy; no real co-operation could be expected from the domestic banks who are not able to judge the crisis management perspectives of heavily indebted manufacturing firms; there is a need for debt relief programmes and/or injections of funds for technological renewal and temporary protection of the domestic market; the abolition of the import-licensing system was not accompanied by the imposition of any significant tariffs on imports, and the sudden liberalization of imports did not leave time for the domestic manufacturers to adjust; there was strict bankruptcy and liquidation legislation.

The Hungarian firm Radion, a radio and electrical works, is a case where a bankruptcy declared in 1991 has still not led to a closure. It seems that the firm has been unable to reposition itself on the market. According to the authors of this case, the managers of Radion were aware that in this capital-intensive industry, competitive advantage derives from rapid technological changes, quick adjustment strategies and rapid product design and renovation. However, under the pressure of the business environment, they were

not able to apply this knowledge, and had to restructure the firm successfully in order to raise its competitiveness.

DISCUSSION AND CONCLUSIONS

As a result of our comparative analysis, we have developed a classification
of the case studies that includes three main groups: transformed business
networks, newly established business networks and firms that failed to
transform their business networks. In our conceptual framework for the
analysis of the adjustment behaviour of firms we use a number of theoretical arguments. First, is the role of the central plan in the design of value
chains. Second, is the role of the transition macroeconomic environment
and its effect on firm performance. Third, is the effect of the withdrawal of
the state on firm's strategies (Todeva, 2000). The functioning of the central
plan during the socialist period established structural links between firms
that have forced them into vertically and horizontally integrated production systems. These interlinked enterprises remained dependent on government decisions throughout the transition period, and the uncertainty of
the new market conditions increased business risk and risk-management
strategies.

   The research on CEE identifies a list of contradictory objectives that
companies had to pursue in relation to enterprise restructuring: (1) managers had to develop new business functions (particularly marketing and
sales) and therefore bringing in new staff, while simultaneously they had to
reduce the labour force; (2) managers had to reduce costs, while at the same
time they had to diversify into new products and markets, requiring additional investment; (3) they had to increase internal financial accountability
within the firm under a dramatic decline in available working capital, which
forced them to use alternative and 'risky' methods of payment, and to go
into arrears in payments and receivables; (4) they also had to reduce the
labour force, while some of the methods for privatization suggested a strong
interest in keeping it intact.

   If we add to this picture the time and resource constraints that managers
from the region experienced, one could understand why managerial decisions were not always adequate to the complexity of the situation. The
dependency on past experience and networks was also reinforced by
the need to secure scarce and expensive resources, and to engage in some
contracts that would ensure the survival of the firm.

   The cases included in this analysis aim to demonstrate the wide variety
of business networks and co-operative relations that have evolved during
the transition period in CEE. Some of the cases show that firms have con-
solidated former dependencies, designed by the central planning system.

However, the variety of responses by firms indicates the ability of the managers to find new niche markets for survival and new opportunities for internationalization.

The firms included in our analysis show that, in spite of the general similarities at industry level, CEE companies are not homogeneous by history and current business strategy. The differences in transformation of structural linkages, formerly established by the central plan, is seen as being driven mainly by forces external to the enterprise. These external factors derive from the instability of the business environment in the region, from the collapse of the COMECON market and the depression of the home market in each country and from the structural dependencies within the economy owing to mis-allocation of resources by the central plan.

The companies that have transformed their former dependencies and business networks show their ability to control the external environment primarily through lobbying governments (PSP Heavy Engineering), and through influencing the regulatory framework for privatization (Lithuanian Industrial Holding) For most of the companies in this group, the transition policies have not affected their dominant position in their industries, in spite of the collapse of the market demand (Spolana, Motorpal). Their strategic response overall has been to consolidate their position in the value system (PAF, Hungartextile Holding). The former industrial linkages of the firms, and the personal and professional relationships maintained by their chief executives, have determined both the positive and the negative outcomes of their adjustment.

The companies with established new business networks demonstrate blurred firms' boundaries (Tipa), examples of increased dependency on the national and foreign trade firms, or on international partners in JVs and acquisitions (Interchokolade, Elegant Charm).

The lack of a marketing function by the former socialist enterprises has been one of the most evident reasons for the managers' failure to adapt to the drop in demand. Most of the cases show that an access to new markets facilitates company restructuring. This suggests that the discussions on value chains and downstream links and the extent to which companies control the elements of the entire value system are critical in explaining many of the difficulties in enterprise restructuring experienced in the CEE countries.

13 Exporting, Entry Modes and Transition: A Case Comparison Between Russia and China

Trevor Buck, Igor Filatotchev, Peter Nolan and Mike Wright

INTRODUCTION

In the 1990s, the International Business literature featured an avalanche of articles addressing the joint venture (JV) activities of multinational enterprises (MNEs), often in the context of former Communist economies in the process of economic reform. In 1999, this culminated in a whole issue of the *Journal of World Business* (34(1)) being devoted entirely to foreign JVs in China.

Generally, however, these papers have been concerned with the short-term, with cross-sectional enterprise-level case studies or large data-sets covering fairly short periods of time. (Exceptions include the presentation of two longitudinal cases by Hoon-Halbauer, 1994, for the period 1984–9, one of which is extended here.) Besides its generally static or short-term orientation, this literature has been mostly concerned with the important subject of the *operating* performance and problems of JVs. This chapter, however, concentrates on a major *strategic* decision in Russia and China by the foreign investor and host company: the choice of entry mode as a response to long-term national influences, not just short-term, enterprise-level factors (Whitley, 1992), and the long-term implications of entry-mode choices.

This long-term focus on foreign trade and direct investment (FDI) is chosen in the light of the need for transition economies to compete on global product markets, including survival in the face of competition from imports (Rodrik, 1996), and of the crucial role of inward FDI (and embodied technical progress) in economic development (van Marrewijk, 1999). Although Russia and China both possess abundant resources including materials and cheap labour, their manufactured products before economic transition did not generally exhibit levels of design and quality which were competitive by world standards, and the achievement of competitiveness could not depend solely on indigenous supplies of capital and know-how (Sachs and Wu, 1994: 111).

Data on inward FDI in the 1990s into Russia and China give important insights into their respective reform processes: while FDI into Russia has been significant and moderately successful in a relatively small number of projects, (49 cases are surveyed in McCarthy and Puffer, 1997), Russia's aggregate inflow of foreign capital has been negligible compared with China's. Despite her extensive natural resources in the form of oil, gas, timber, minerals and metals, Russia attracted only $3900 mn in FDI during the period 1989–95 (equivalent to $1.10 *per capita* in 1995), with only half of this relatively small sum in the form of JVs. Over the same period, China received $121 700 mn ($18.20 *per capita*), virtually all in JVs (IBRD, 1996a: 64; UNCTAD, 1997: 348–50). In 1996, however, it should be noted that the value of Chinese inward FDI fell by a quarter in one year and by another 30 per cent in 1997, with JVs in 1997 representing only around half of this total (*China Statistical Yearbooks*, 1997, 1998).

One arguable consequence of these contrasting FDI inflows during a vital period for both countries, and the restructuring of manufacturing production that they facilitate, is that China has proved able to produce manufactured goods to world standards, with 81 per cent of her exports coming from the manufacturing sector (data from the World Bank), though long-term competitiveness requires continued capital inflows and technical progress. On the other hand, on world markets, Russia has generally failed to make the transition from primary extractive supplier to industrial producer, continuing to export raw materials in return for manufactured imports, with manufactured goods comprising only 8 per cent of total exports (EBRD, 1997: 65).

As its main research question therefore, this chapter investigates, informed by two carefully chosen cases, the extent to which this long-term outcome at the national level can be explained by contrasting patterns of national culture, economic and political ideology and by the contrasting paths of Chinese–Russian economic reform. After a comparative account of the conditions for foreign trade and investment in Russia and China, there follows an evaluation of theories at the levels of the organization and of the business environment that seem potentially useful in this context, a report on two matched case studies intended to inform practitioners and to suggest theoretical developments rather than to prove or disprove a particular theory and finally some conclusions.

FOREIGN TRADE AND INVESTMENT IN TRANSITION: RUSSIA AND CHINA

There are many similarities between Russia and China as economies in transition from Communism (Nolan, 1995: 135–50). These include massive geographical scale, cheap labour, large potential markets to attract foreigners and generous endowments of natural resources. In addition, both countries adopted somewhat similar economic and political ideologies during their Stalinist–Maoist periods, with a common emphasis on Party control, heavy industry, large industrial enterprises and heavy bureaucratic and tariff protection against manufactured imports. There, however, the similarities end: China's revolution in 1949 was much later than Russia's, with implications for the training of cadres; levels of urbanization and education were much lower in China; and Russia did not inherit China's tradition of small-firm entrepreneurship (Nolan, 1995: 119).

The biggest differences, however, are in national culture and, relatedly, in the regulation of foreign trade and investment. The measurement of national culture is controversial, with researchers distributed along a continuum from enthusiastic advocates (e.g. Shane, 1994; Naumov, 1996) to skeptical dissenters (e.g. Ralston *et al.*, 1997: 82), with some in between (Kogut and Singh, 1988: 422). A balanced view would seem to be that, notwithstanding measurement difficulties, there are widely acknowledged cultural differences between Russia and China that have interacted with the pattern and pace of economic reforms, the regulation of foreign trade and entry modes, and the subsequent performance of foreign ventures.

Russia

For example, Russia is identified with high levels of group orientation as opposed to individualism, coupled with low tolerance of power-distance relations (Naumov, 1996). During the 1970s and 1980s, this meant that officials in regional and local authorities, enterprise managers and employees gradually accumulated decentralized control over their factories. Furthermore, democratization after 1991 essentially extended a blocking veto from these parties to economic reforms (Nolan, 1995: 301). Thus, despite Russia's membership of the International Monetary Fund (IMF) after 1992 and the influence of US creditors, economic reforms that were intended as 'shock therapy' did not produce liquid, US-style capital markets (Blasi *et al.*, 1997: 149; Estrin and Wright, 1999). Rather, the central privatization programme of 1992–4 produced a pattern of insider ownership and control of industry that essentially reinforced the existing blocking veto of managers and employees on all plans to restructure enterprises (Buck *et al.*, 1998). There was a deep distrust of foreign investors in Russian industrial firms, where they were seen as speculators and asset-strippers, and an anxiety to find 'friendly' outsiders who would not threaten existing employment levels (Filatotchev *et al.*, 2000).

In other words, national institutions and culture interact with corporate governance at an enterprise level to determine the resistance felt by potential foreign investors to their offers of finance. Despite the legality of JVs with foreigners, continued tariff barriers and the interaction of culture with reform policies essentially produced an environment that was hostile to foreign industrial investors unless they participated fully in all the assets and liabilities of large privatized firms, yet did not threaten dominant insider control (Blasi *et al.*, 1997: 150–5). This impasse was worsened by the weak enforcement of the property rights of minority shareholders in Russian firms (Filatotchev *et al.*, 2000), and amounted to an informal regulation that prevented foreign investors from 'cherry-picking' the best Russian assets and abandoning the unappealling 'rump' of privatized firms. It effectively demanded high-commitment forms of foreign entry without high control, an option that lacked appeal for potential foreign investors without extremely high levels of expected return.

Thus, it is argued that Russian culture has spawned a business environment with insider groups within enterprises holding the balance of control. They are intolerant of distant power (especially foreign investors) but uncertain property rights for shareholders and a weak, democratic central government have also contributed to high levels of country risk. In 1995 foreign investors perceived Russia's country risk to be the highest in the world, at 90 out of a maximum 100. To give some idea of the severity of these perceived risks, Venezuela was perceived to be nearest to Russia, with a country risk score of 74 (Economist Intelligence Unit, *Economist*, 6 January 1996: 100).

China

The main plank of Russian economic reform has clearly been 'shock therapy' which includes industrial privatization, a policy option so far generally resisted in China, where 'gradualism' has been the rule, without allowing any challenge from opponents (Nolan, 1995: 230). Although sharing Russia's strong group orientation, as opposed to the West's individualism (Ralston *et al.*, 1997: 185), China differs significantly in relation to the tolerance of power distance. Indeed, there is consensus among researchers concerning China's high tolerance of power distance, high conformity (Shane, 1994: 630), low self-direction (Ralston *et al.*, 1997: 195), strong bureaucratic control (Shane, 1994: 630) reinforced by an absence of political freedom and a continuing Maoist ideology of Party control (Hoon-Halbauer, 1994: 91), and *guanxi*, or the influence of contacts (Hoon-Halbauer, 1994: 87) which reinforces conformity. Whitley (1992: 218–38) confirms China's weakly developed legal system but well developed authority relations.

This environment has provided a shield around foreign traders and investors, since the ownership rights of foreigners are protected. In the fourth quarter of 1995, country risks in China were estimated to be quite low at 46, between Greece and South Africa. Anxious to protect Party control and group orientation from foreign influence however, the Chinese government has over the years applied ceilings on foreign levels of commitment in local ventures. Foreign involvement in the late 1970s was at first limited to 35 per cent of any venture, then raised in 1985 to 49 per cent, and since 1988 majority foreign ownership of JVs has been allowed (Tan, 1997: 226), though still subject to State approval. In this way, and through a privatization process stalled in its early stages, the State has 'held back' foreign levels of commitment in China. Significantly, local 'fiefdoms' comprising SOE managers and State representatives (Boisot and Child, 1988) effectively protected the JV stakes of foreigners, and obedient, conforming SOE employees, confronted by local fiefdoms, were unable to prevent the 'cherry-picking' of SOE physical and human assets, syphoned-off into JVs. Indeed JVs have often been involuntary, with obedient SOEs being centrally coerced into ventures with particular partners without regard to contingencies and entry modes.

With the need for foreign capital and know-how representing the central challenge to transition economies, it seems pertinent to try to make sense of the national-level FDI inflows and the business environment at a national and enterprise level (Whitley, 1992), through some theoretical lens.

ORGANIZATIONAL AND INSTITUTIONAL THEORIES OF FOREIGN INVESTMENT

Theories of foreign trade and investment that can potentially contribute to an understanding of entry modes in transitional economies such as Russia and China can be grouped under the headings of *organizational theories* (Internalization theory, Eclectic theory, Internationalization I-model and Internationalization U-model) which apply to the enterprise or micro-level, and *institutional theory*, which is concerned with the national or macro-economy. Before considering these theories, however, it should be noted that any analysis of foreign trade and investment in transition economies (e.g. Russia and China) involves a two-sided (dyadic) situation. On the one side, enterprises in transitional economies, with their own institutions and national culture, are at the pre-exporting or exporting stages of development, which could one day progress to a contemplation of outward investment. On the other side, MNEs from countries with their contrasted national institutions and cultures, well advanced into the exporting stage, are now contemplating their entry mode in a transitional economy. In the review of cases in Russia and China that follows, therefore, the two-sided nature of organizational and institutional theories in this context should be remembered. Though all these theories assume that foreign and host-country firms seek the entry mode offering the highest expected risk-adjusted return on investment (Agarwal and Ramaswami, 1992: 3), each theory has a different purpose and nature that needs to be explained in order to judge their relevance to the task at hand.

Internalization theory has been described as 'the TC [transaction cost] theory of the multinational corporation' (Madhok, 1997: 40), and is concerned with a MNE's static locational advantages and internalization advantages (Buckley, 1988) in the determination of optimal entry mode and location (Johanson and Vahlne, 1990: 16), where internalization advantages include the uncertainties associated with foreign trade and investment. Controversially for Internalization theorists, Dunning (1988) added ownership advantages to the list of independent variables in his Eclectic theory. Interestingly for what is to follow, high contract uncertainty (high risks) is predicted to lead to high-commitment forms of entry mode, as firms try to protect themselves from local opportunism in foreign locations with direct investments. This apparently contradicts other predictions and has been the cause of empirical confusion, as noted below. For the purposes of this chapter, however, it should be noted that both Internalization and Eclectic theory are static, optimizing theories applied mainly to cross-section databases and cases. Their application here is therefore limited.

Much the same can be said about the (Innovation-based) I-models of Internationalization theory (Andersen, 1993). These theories see a firm's internationalization as amounting to an innovation decision (Andersen, 1993: 212), but again, their application here is limited because they are concerned with small and medium-sized firms (SMEs) (Andersen, 1993: 221) and seem inapplicable, on the one hand, to large Russian privatized firms and Chinese State-owned firms and, on the other, to large Western MNEs.

Upon reflection, however, large Russian and Chinese firms have a lot in common with the small firms studied by early Internalization theory and I-models. Traditionally, these firms have had neither the opportunity nor the incentive to promote exports of their own products, and any actual exporting activity was conducted by State trading monopolies on their behalf (Zloch-Christy, 1998). This means that early international business studies such as Wiedersheim-Paul *et al.* (1978) and work before 1982 reviewed by Andersen (1993: 213) takes on a fresh relevance, at least for firms in transitional economies, since this work analyzes pre-exporting stages of internationalization, where managers (a) are not interested in exporting, then (b) are willing to fulfil unsolicited export orders, and finally (c) actively explore the feasibility of exporting. Actual exporting then follows, at first on an experimental basis.

Besides I-models, U-models, or Uppsala models, of internationalization have greater potential, in relation to MNEs and to firms in transitional economies, though firms here are mainly in the pre-exporting stage. They are knowledge-based theories that rely on the notion that foreigners first concentrate their efforts on countries with the lowest 'psychic distance' from their home base, where this concept includes cultural, developmental and language distance. As they increase their knowledge of locations that are perceived to be distant, their entry modes incrementally involve higher levels of commitment and control (Andersen, 1993: 211; Björkman and Forsgren, 1997). This amounts to the prediction that lower risks mean less market-like and more hierarchical forms of entry, which apparently contradicts Internalization theory (see pp. 197–8 above). The distinction (Anderson and Gatignon, 1986: 7) between environmental (external or country) risk and contractual (or internal) risk should be noted, however, and only higher contractual risks associated with controlling agents to a particular transaction, as opposed to uncontrollable macro risks, require more commitment. Cultural differences are seen as effectively increasing country risks.

Where country risks are high, MNEs are hypothesized to prefer low-commitment, market-based entry modes (Hill *et al.*, 1990: 122) such as exporting though a local agent or licensed production, or hybrids like JVs. However, desired entry mode choices may be deliberately suppressed by government actions. For example, even where country risks are high, governments may insist that foreign investors 'leapfrog' (Petersen and Pedersen, 1997: 126) to high-commitment entry modes – or, alternatively, governments may give approval only to low-levels of foreign commitment, even where country risks are perceived to be low, thus holding back higher levels of commitment. The question of 'fit' between local contingent factors and actual entry modes now arises as an important consideration if the long-term efficiency of entry modes is an important consideration (Anderson and Gatignon, 1986: 3).

Since large MNEs have easier access to the 'exit' option from a proposed transaction than their local SOE partners, regulations may introduce a lack of 'fit' between local contingencies and allowed modes, and foreign FDI may cease to be a zero-sum game for host governments (Peng, 1999). For example, governments demanding high levels of foreign commitment in high-risk environments may experience reduced FDI inflows while, elsewhere, restrictions on commitment levels when risks are low may achieve high levels of FDI inflows, but may lead later to the costs of low commitment – e.g. low levels of innovation.

In addition, there may be subtle interactions between government regulation, culture, institutions and enterprise governance. For example, managers and employees with a tradition of enterprise control may persuade the government to adopt a privatization programme that conveys enterprise control to insiders, thus resulting in a corporate governance regime that effectively blocks outsiders.

It should not be surprising, therefore, to note that, while Internationalization theory does offer some insights for this study, it has produced contradictory results. For example, Shane (1994: 632) surveys contradictory findings in relation to the estimated impact of risks on entry modes, already alluded to above. In addition it has been found in practice in long-term studies that its predictions have been upset (Shane, 1994: 632; Brouthers, *et al.*, 1998) by governmental interference in the form of FDI regulation, by the tendencies for certain industries to use particular entry modes and by cultural differences that have persisted rather than converged (Ralston *et al.*, 1997). This does not mean that these theories are refuted, merely that their mechanisms can be obstructed in practice.

This phenomenon of State interference with entry-mode decisions brings us to Institutional theories, and Shane (1994) offers a model of potential value for this chapter, though the timing of his study necessarily meant the exclusion of all transition economies. Using panel data for US licensing agreements (i.e. market-like entry) and wholly-owned subsidiaries (i.e. high-commitment entry) across all industries in 1977 and 1982, he controlled for industry and FDI regulations to test his predictions concerning the tendency for foreign perceptions of power distance and integration (reflecting solidarity and trust measures) to influence companies' entry-mode choices. Despite quite small samples, he found that, after controls, measured cultural differences had a significant impact on entry modes.

The next section therefore considers two matched cases that cast light on Shane's (1994) approach, which implicitly combines the impact on entry-mode choice of risks from U-models of Internationalization and of variables representing FDI regulation, etc. from Institutional theory. The purpose of these case presentations is to investigate the applicability of Shane's approach to economies in transition and to make judgements concerning the value of further case collection and theory development.

CASE STUDIES IN RUSSIA AND CHINA

Entry-mode theories have typically been tested using quantitative evidence from large samples (Kogut and Singh, 1988; Agarwal and Ramaswami, 1992; Woodcock *et al.*, 1994; Brouthers *et al.*, 1998), but such a methodology is ruled out for many transitional economies where published industrial and enterprise-level data are extremely problematical, and may even amount to a 'virtual economy' (Gaddy and Ickes, 1998), hiding the true state of affairs. Case studies offer an alternative, but they can inform only theoretical development rather than test theories. Even with cases, access in transitional economies may be limited to 'showpiece' ventures, though these can still be quite revealing.

In this chapter, two matched cases were carefully chosen within the same industry, thus avoiding the issue of industry controls in entry-mode choice (Shane, 1994: 633). Indeed, the similarities between the cases extended beyond a common industry. To control for the effects of different initial firm size, resource endowments, technologies and products and industrial concentration and to focus on differential country risks, different cultures, paths to economic reform and FDI regulation, the authors took advantage of a unique period of Sino–Soviet relations which began with China's isolation from the West after the end of the Korean War in 1950. In this period, China accepted extensive economic aid from the USSR and many industrial projects in China were direct clones of existing Russian factories.

Most of these cloned plants are in the north of China, still inaccessible to researchers, so it was decided to study the Gorky Automobile Plant (GAZ) in Nizhny Novgorod (NN, formerly Gorky), and its Chinese clone, the Beijing United Automobile and Motorcycle Manufacturing (BUAMM) Company, which is part of the Beijing Automobile Manufacturing Group (BAG). BUAMM was visited by two of the authors in July 1995 and the Beijing Jeep Company (BJC), a JV formed by BUAMM and Chrysler Inc., was visited twice by one author for a week in December 1994 and again in July 1995. From 1996 to 1999, one author continued to monitor the case through eight meetings in Beijing with our research partners at the Economic System Reform Institute (ESRI) a think-tank of the State Council. GAZ was visited by another author in October 1995. From 1996 to 1999, further material on GAZ was collected from analysts and brokers on the Russian capital market, together with telephone interviews with relevant parties.

Semi-structured interviews at GAZ and BUAMM were designed to build longitudinal cases relevant to the main research question of this chapter (see p. 194 above). They were conducted by the research team directly in English, Mandarin and Russian, and no interpreters were necessary, despite sometimes being present. The semi-secret nature of each of the firms visited precluded some of the usual methodological precautions in regard to case study collection (Eisenhardt, 1989). For example, Gorky was the place of exile for academician Sakharov and a closed military city to foreigners until 1991, and in China a high proportion of the target company's output in 1995 was still military. Thus, tape-recordings and the collection of exhaustive data on many 'precise and measurable constructs' (Eisenhardt, 1991: 62) was out of the question. Nevertheless, some triangulation was achieved. In the case of GAZ, interviews were conducted over three days with three senior managers and two shopfloor employees, with four representatives of the NN Regional Administration – which was in dispute at the time with GAZ over a number of issues – and with the Chairman of the NN State Property Committee which supervised GAZ's privatization and remains a GAZ shareholder. In Moscow, as mentioned above, GAZ annual reports and confidential company profiles of GAZ were collected from four independent sets of analysts, from 1995 to 1999.

In Beijing, interviews initially took ten days and were conducted at the national level with a member of the ESRI, with the Beijing Municipal

Economic Commission, the BAG Holding Company, with the BUAMM
'rump' State plant, with native and American managers at BJC, and with
the Bei Nei engine plant in Beijing, one of BUAMM's main suppliers (of
Russian-designed engines).

The case comparisons are now presented. Although they are matched in
terms of industrial classification, initial size, technology and resource
endowments, it should be noted that each company in Russia and China
was subject to very different regimes of economic reform, corporate governance and attitudes towards foreign investors.

GAZ

GAZ was founded in 1930 with the support of the Ford Motor Company
and the then-friendly US government, and its first product was a version of
the Ford 'A' truck in 1932. Later, it developed independently into a fully
integrated vehicles complex, making its first Volga car in 1956 plus a range
of medium and small trucks and Jeeps. Upon privatization in 1993, GAZ
had its main assembly lines in NN covering 450 hectares and nine suppliers of components in surrounding towns. By 1995, GAZ had virtually
abandoned medium and large trucks (401 500 produced in 1993), concentrating on Gazelle small trucks (73 000 in 1995) and had increased the
annual production of Volga cars from 108 000 in 1993 to 157 000 in 1995.
Although the original Volga design does not approach world standards of
build quality or design, it is sturdy, sells cheaply at well under half the price
of Western imports of the same size and offers cheap parts and good after-
sales service.

In terms of Western corporate governance, GAZ is probably Russia's
most progressive manufacturing firm, being one of only four manufacturing companies in December 1999 that were not directly linked with the
resource-extraction sectors, yet appeared in the *Moscow Times*-50 index of
companies with tradable shares. In addition GAZ enjoys most-favoured
status with the Russian government, making it less reliant on foreign
capital. In this sense, the choice of GAZ as a case gives a very favourable
impression of economic reform and prospects in the rest of Russian
manufacturing.

Although listed in the Russian Trading System, it was found by the
authors in 1998 that 20 per cent of GAZ's voting shares were in the hands
of outsiders, with fewer than half that number (i.e. 10 per cent of the total)
being freely tradable: managers openly retained 13 per cent and other
employees the remaining 67 per cent. One half of outsiders' shares (i.e. 10
per cent) were strictly non-tradable, held by Avtobank on behalf of the
EBRD as part of a relatively small ($25 mn) JV with Hayden Paints which
they helped to finance. With 10 per cent of GAZ shares in free float, it
is relatively easy for foreign investors to obtain a toehold stake in the

company, but until recently, they could consider only a stake in the whole company, including substantial liabilities (see below).

Even when outsiders have been able to acquire shares, however, obstructive registration procedures give outsiders, as minority shareholders, insecure property rights over shares acquired (EBRD, 1997: 95), and make them reluctant to make deeper commitments. One financial institution in Moscow that had successfully accumulated a significant proportion of GAZ shares was able to nominate a director to the GAZ Board. When this director was interviewed by two of the authors in Moscow, he disclosed that he was a virtual observer at Board meetings and powerless to influence strategy. GAZ directors also admitted to one of the authors in a separate interview that employees could sell shares only to a small private company owned by the GAZ President himself.

GAZ itself is one of the largest corporate hierarchies in the world, with low productivity, despite massive scale economies in vehicle manufacture. With a mixed output of 267000 vehicles in 1995 and 86000 direct employees GAZ, however, produced around only three vehicles per employee. This compares with the authors' calculation (based on *Fortune*, 7 August 1995: F29) that the world's leading 26 vehicle manufacturers in that year produced on average 20 vehicles per employee.

Faced with such combinations of low productivity levels and high country risks, foreign investors generally decided, until recently, not to attempt any substantial investments in GAZ. Besides low productivity and high risks, analysts in Moscow, acting on behalf of potential Western investors, cite GAZ's social liabilities as the most important barrier to foreign investment. These liabilities include subsidized company housing for 106000 employees and their dependants in over 1000 tower blocks of apartments, and childcare, healthcare, etc. Until recently, incumbent GAZ managers, other employees and their political supporters, with majority stakes in the company and control of the Board, were unwilling to allow outsiders to 'cherry pick' the most productive assets in a JV with GAZ, without assuming responsibility for the overall level of GAZ wages and employment, and for the social liabilities and non-performing assets of the integrated company as an entity.

Most of the large motor-vehicle manufacturers in the world are reported by Moscow analysts to have considered acquiring stakes in GAZ without any significant commitment resulting. Minor JVs have been concluded with CZ of the Czech republic for diesel turbo-injection systems, with Steyr of Austria for a diesel engine, with Rand-Ingersoll for 'guaranteed moments' pneumatic instruments and with Hayden Inc. for new paint equipment. These ventures have been of a very market-like, low-commitment variety however, and in the case of Hayden, the deal needed a loan of $25 mn from the EBRD to make it feasible. There has been no implemented JV involving foreign producers for vehicle assembly itself, GAZ's core operation.

To some extent, however, GAZ has been able to restructure using domestic funds, without recourse to foreigners, as Russia's most favoured manufacturing company. Its product range was transformed during the period 1990–5, away from large and medium trucks towards the light Gazelle range. Although the old Volga continues to be produced and sold in large numbers, a new Volga (model GAZ-3111) has been developed and was planned for launch early in 2000 after four years of postponements. Its retail price, however, seems likely to be $14 000, about three times that of the old Volga. The 1998 ruble collapse, however, enhanced its prospects in relation to imported vehicles.

It seems that GAZ's Russian-financed restructuring programme was facilitated through political contacts rather than serious market appraisal. Neither the Gazelle range nor the new Volga has achieved significant export sales and the new Volga has enjoyed the benefit of government decrees forcing government agencies at all levels to favour it in preference to imported models. As with Russian manufacturing in general, GAZ has so far been unable to achieve combinations of price, product design and build quality demanded by world markets, even for Russia's most favoured manufacturer.

Some recent developments within the GAZ case should, however, be noted as being of potential significance for Russia's inward FDI in the longer term. There are now tentative signs from GAZ that the economic crisis of 1998 has reduced the hostility of managers and employees in former SOEs to foreigners in JVs, as they became aware of GAZ's precarious position in Russia and globally. For example, the company in 1998 secured a $65 mn loan from the EBRD to finance a new JV with Hayden Inc. for a new Gazelle paint shop and GAZ 'signed a memorandum' for a massive $1450 mn JV with Fiat to assemble Fiat Palio, Siena and Marea models at NN in renovated diesel and paint plants, from Italian-made kits. This proposed JV, 'Nizhegorod Motors', was to be owned 40 per cent each by GAZ and Fiat and 20 per cent by EBRD.

The willingness of GAZ incumbents to accept such a proposal is no doubt a result of the mid-1998 economic crisis in Russia, and the desperate situation for many SOE employees in unrestructured enterprizes. The irony is, however, that this more welcoming response to foreign capital arose at the very moment when the same crisis has caused a dramatic collapse in domestic consumer demand, with loan defaults increasing Russia's already high country risks, thus deterring all except the least committed forms of foreign trade and investment. Subsequently, in mid-1999 Fiat postponed their JV with GAZ indefinitely, and the Finance Director of GAZ complained that EBRD was more concerned with repayments on previous loans than with fresh advances. Negotiations with GAZ to build component plants for GAZ-built Fiats were also postponed. In 1999, foreigners ironically now received a warmer welcome in GAZ, and probably in the rest of Russian manufacturing, even in JVs, just at the moment when the Russian market became less attractive to foreigners. Indeed, enterprise incumbents have changed their stance for the same reason.

Beijing Jeep (BJC)

BUAMM and its BJC alliance with a US producer has always been a show-piece foreign JV, and easy access has prompted a plethora of Western studies (Mann, 1989; Aiello, 1991; Hoon-Halbauer, 1994; Harwit, 1995; Tan, 1997; Warner, 1997; Peng, 1999). Nevertheless, it is suggested that the down-turn in its prospects makes a longitudinal study invaluable, although even the first report (Mann, 1989, reprinted 1997) was given the sub-title 'The Short, Unhappy Romance of American Business in China'.

The plants that eventually made up BUAMM within the BAG holding company after 1973 were built around 1956, modelled on GAZ and aided by the USSR. They began by producing variants of GAZ trucks, the GAZ 69 Jeep and the Volga, but Sino–Soviet relations soured around 1959, and GAZ withdrew its co-operation. Truck production levels at BUAMM are still a military secret, but in 1994 it produced 50 000 conventional Chinese Jeeps, 30 000 tricycle vans, 52 000 light trucks in a JV with Isuzu and 46 000 Jeep Cherokees and other Jeeps in a JV with Chrysler discussed below. Indicative of the sprawling, inscrutable and unmeasurable nature of Chinese economic reforms, BUAMM in 1995 employed 9600 directly with about 4000 in the Chrysler JV, but large multiples of these numbers were employed in 139 linked township and village enterprise (TVE) enterprises all over China supplying components and materials. In addition, 96 BJC service centres operate throughout China, and Aiello (1991: 60) reports that just one of these centres employed 700–800 workers in 1990.

Despite being originally cloned on GAZ, the matched Chinese case study BUAMM is by now quite different. The extent of its production of medium and light trucks is a military secret, and little can be known about its network of relational suppliers scattered among every Chinese province except Tibet, but in light trucks and other vehicles it is clear that the group has undergone extensive restructuring under China's gradualist economic reforms. In addition to a substantial JV with Isuzu for the production of light trucks and the Chrysler JV at BJC, discussed below, the unprofitable BUAMM 'rump' of the original State enterprise had tripled its annual output of Chinese-designed Jeeps to 50 000 p.a. in 1994 compared with 1983. While maintaining its 1994 output of tricycle vans at 30 000, BAG added 52 000 light trucks (in the Isuzu JV), and within BJC, 25 000 Cherokee Jeeps and 21 000 Chinese Jeeps.

Concentrating on the 1984 JV with the American Motor Co (AMC, taken over by Chrysler in 1987), the BJC was formed at a time when the government imposed a 35 per cent maximum stake for foreigners in minority JVs.

For a 31 per cent stake – increased to 42 per cent by 1992 after the State raised the limit to 49 per cent in 1985 (Harwit 1995: 79) – AMC contributed equipment for a Jeep Cherokee assembly-line, technical drawings and $8 mn in cash. Although these assets were supplied with only an intermediate level of commitment by AMC, who could relatively easily and cheaply exit the JV, AMC felt quite sure that its property rights were strongly protected by local 'fiefdoms'.

For the remaining 69 per cent stake (later 58 per cent), BUAMM provided its southern Beijing factory, some equipment and the contacts necessary to secure building permission and import licences, etc. BUAMM also supplied a labour force, comprising 40 per cent of its youngest, best workers. This clearly amounted to the characteristic 'cherry-picking' of JVs. SOE employees were powerless to block this, with local fiefdoms and a culture of obedience and conformity, unlike their Russian counterparts.

Compared with GAZ, the biggest contrast was provided by the way in which BJC was developed quite separately in southern Beijing, away from BUAMM, left as a 'rump' SOE in northern Beijing, with all its liabilities and underperforming assets. BUAMM selectively contributed 78 per cent of its prime assets to the JV and its best workers, who were now paid around double the wages of those who remained with BUAMM. In recognition of BUAMM's social provisions, AMC agreed to pay $1 mn p.a. to the SOE parent, but it can be seen that BJC was able to achieve substantial amounts of re-equipment and output restructuring, largely unencumbered by the liabilities and financial deficits of the parent SOE.

It was clear to the authors, however, that BJC was seen by the Chinese central government from the start as a 'flagship' JV (Harwit, 1995: 74, p89) and that the State had coerce BAG to agree to the selective integration comprising the BJC JV in the first place. 'Forced' JVs are a significant feature of China (Beamish 1993: 29) and Eastern Europe (Brouthers and Bamossy, 1997: 289) and can hardly be expected to yield the same level of trust between JV partners that genuine, two-sided co-operation can achieve. It also emphasizes that the State can be a significant contingency factor for inward FDI decisions.

Since the BJC venture has already survived more than fifteen years, it would appear to have been a limited success, in the light of Hoon-Halbauer's (1994: 7) report of 50 per cent failure rates and a dissatisfaction rate among foreign JV executives in China of 61 per cent. It seems clear, however, that not only did the State to some extent coerce BUAMM into agreeing to the JV in the first place, it has also sustained the venture – e.g. in 1986 when, after BJC had been closed down for two months, the State allowed BJC to survive by providing access to hard currency (Harwit, 1995: 75). To a large extent, BJC is a bureaucratic operation on the Chinese side, somewhat insulated from market forces, and this is quite typical of China (Osland and Cavusgil, 1996: 108).

Levels of trust between BJC's partners has been low. Led to believe that BJC would eventually assemble 40 000 Cherokees p.a. (with an increasing local content) and would make a Chinese Jeep only as a short-term expedient, according to Aiello (1991: 48), BUAMM was also promised (1) a new Jeep model, but AMC discovered that its existing designs were unsuitable for the Chinese market, and a new model would cost $700 mn to develop, (2) a BJC technical centre in China for R&D work, and (3) an international sales network for Cherokee exports. In 1997, however, only 25 000 Cherokees had been assembled, from US-made kits, and production of the old Chinese model still continued at 21 000 p.a. Tan (1997: 217) claims that BUAMM was a victim of a blatant 'bait-and-switch' sales technique which kept US factories in work but provided no significantly new models. The takeover of AMC by Chrysler in 1987 also damaged relations between the JV partners, and the company's subsequent merger with Daimler–Benz in 1998 is also likely to disrupt trust.

Thus, while BJC has produced Jeep Cherokees which were for a short time globally competitive in terms of build quality and production cost, the absence of significantly new models now threatens the venture's survival on product markets. Promized exports beyond S.E. Asia and Russia have not materialized. Year-on-year Jeep Cherokee sales to April 1999 fell by 41 per cent, and an ostensibly 'new' all-terrain vehicle (model BJ2020R), still based on the old Cherokee design, must face a number of negative developments besides the sluggishness of the local market: new, direct competition is expected from production in Shenyeng of a new Chevrolet Blazer, which GM feels confident to be able to price at a level 10 per cent above the dated Cherokee. Possible WTO entry by China in 2001 would reduce tariffs on imported cars from 80 per cent–100 per cent to only 25 per cent.

It can be argued that BJC's weak competitive position in 1999 has been caused principally by Chrysler's low level of commitment to the venture. This was originally demanded by a Chinese government which now bemoans the lack of technical progress within BJC: indeed, some of the technical changes made to the Cherokee have been designed to reduce Chrysler's costs rather than to improve product design features. With its low level of US-partner commitment, there is a danger that BJC may fall victim of the 'assembly plant' syndrome for products aimed at the Chinese market. In 1999, largely as a result of the 1998 collapse in Asia, which also prompted Russia's latest crisis, the Chinese government offered new foreign investors higher levels of ownership and control. For existing ventures like BJC, the government demanded greater levels of output, more technological inputs from Western partners and more local sourcing: developments that might have occurred spontaneously with higher levels of foreign commitment in the first place.

Discussion of the Two Cases

An earlier account of the BJC and VW longitudinal Chinese cases by Hoon-Halbauer (1994) presented 31 pages of verbatim interviews. The cases here were necessarily presented more briefly in an attempt to inform theoretical development, policy makers and practitioners.

From GAZ's perspective, with negligible exports and quite guarded moves to involve foreign investors with the know-how to produce products of the design and build quality needed to export on world markets, the company, although one of the most advanced and fortunate Russian industrial firms, has yet to show evidence that it has embarked even on the very first stage of the pre-exporting process, whereby management are seriously committed to exporting. From the perspective of MNEs contemplating investment in GAZ as an alternative to direct exporting to the Russian market, there seems to have arisen a situation whereby national culture, enterprise governance and State regulation have interacted to deter all low-commitment forms of entry by foreign investors, who have responded with negligible FDI flows in the face of country-risk assessments that themselves depend upon cultural, governmental and legal factors. Rather, to the extent that foreigners have entered the Russian automobile market, they have opted for direct sales. The further downturn of the Russian economy after 1998, however, changed the relative bargaining positions of enterprise incumbents *vis-à-vis* foreign investors. Low-commitment foreign entry now seems to be demanded, or at least tolerated, by enterprise managers and other employees at the very moment when foreign investors are less prepared than ever to provide the supply of funds.

The Chinese BJC case provides an interesting variation on this theme. With BJC, US investors faced quite low country risks, largely as a result of the characteristics of Chinese culture and institutions, and took every opportunity to increase their commitment levels as State regulations on foreign ownership were relaxed. The holding back of foreign commitment is, however, consistent with low levels of technical progress in a Chinese factory, treated by the US partner as an assembly plant to cater for local product demands rather than for exports. As a result, the Chinese JV is in a state of crisis, with an outmoded vehicle range. As with Russia, the deteriorating economic situation since 1998 prompted further relaxations of regulations on inward FDI, this time in the opposite direction, permitting higher rather than lower levels of foreign commitment, just when foreign investors are willing to supply only quite low levels of FDI.

These observations have implications for theory development and testing as well as for practitioners.

CONCLUSIONS

In relation to the development and testing of theory, three conclusions can be supported.

First, *a synthesis of Internationalization and Institutional theories* is promising in relation to transition economies: Internationalization theories recognize the dynamic nature of the process of, on the one hand, foreign market entry by MNEs, and on the other, the exporting strategies of local firms in transitional economies. Institutional theories recognize the importance the dyadic interaction of national and macroeconomic variables, and also the interaction of national culture and government in the evolution of corporate governance regimes at enterprise level. In particular, insider control of firms in Russia has been accompanied by weak protection of the minority shareholder rights of outsiders. Together, these factors have major implications for attitudes towards foreign investors.

Crucially in transition economies, national and macro variables may be neither stable nor conducive to entry. The cases suggest that in transition economies where minority ownership rights are not protected as in Russia, FDI will be reduced, and market-like entry (or no entry at all) may be preferred until such time that these institutional conditions are changed. In cases where minority ownership rights are protected, as in China, FDI will initially be greater. However, where States impede increases in foreign level of commitment beyond the JV, foreign investors are likely to become frustrated and further development – e.g. the integration of businesses, in technological terms – may fail to occur. Therefore, further theoretical development is needed to consider the juxtaposition between institutional barriers to entry and the stages approach of Internationalization theories.

From the perspective of MNEs, the Russian case made it clear that, certainly for transition economies, the range of factors to be analyzed must be extended to embrace the MNE that chooses the no-inward-FDI strategic outcome. Although most recent studies in International Business have concentrated on the entry modes of large MNEs and the markets–hierarchies spectrum from exports to subsidiaries, in considering transition economies there needs to be a greater understanding of the drivers of the entry–no entry decision as a precursor to the analysis of entry mode. Evidence from the Russian case also indicates a need to analyze more carefully the high-commitment entry modes in transition economies. Focus solely on local subsidiaries obscures potentially important differences between green field developments and local acquisitions. In transitional economies, for example, difficulties in making acquisitions because of hostile insiders may mean that foreign investors seek alternative entry modes. Acquisitions of minority stakes as a prelude to full acquisition may be problematical because of the difficulties created by insiders in relation to obtaining corporate informa-

tion and board representation (Wright *et al.*, 1998). Against this background, green field developments may hold attractions in principle, but may
also be subject to regulatory constraints or uncertainties. Similarly, market-
like entry must distinguish direct exporting from licensing and franchising.
Furthermore, the cases emphasize that JVs must be included as a hybrid
entry mode, perhaps sub-divided into different types according to ownership and control proportions.

From the perspective of the Russian firm, theory must also accommodate
the firm that chooses not to export, nor to accept foreign partners with
the know-how to facilitate exporting. This pre-exporting stage is a not a
new suggestion since the International Business literature has long been
concerned with pre-exporting activity, but usually in a small-firm context
(Wiedersheim-Paul *et al.*, 1978). A key aspect of transition is the development of enterprises that can compete on world markets. With negligible
exports at present and quite guarded moves to involve foreign investors
GAZ, although one of the most advanced and fortunate Russian industrial
firms, has yet to show evidence that it has embarked even on the very first
stage of the pre-exporting process as a precursor to further stages, whereby
management at least give a serious commitment to exporting. This is
seen as the logical outcome of a privatization process that gave enterprise
control to incumbent managers and other employees. The recent internationalization literature, by focusing on the MNE considering foreign entry,
appears to have neglected the position of local firms as potential recipients
of foreign investments. In the context of economic transition, there needs
to be further theoretical consideration of the development of export potential among local firms.

Second, any subsequent tests of modified theories demand *suitable data*.
Measures of cultural differences are already available and measures of institutional factors can be constructed for FDI regulation and other State controls. Some modifications are suggested, however, particularly to the range
of future testing, in terms of time periods, country coverage and the variety
of independent variables employed. Following Gaddy and Ickes (1998)
there are serious doubts about the quality of official data from Russia,
and Chinese data probably include an element of wishful thinking also.
However, Shane's (1994) exploitation of US Department of Commerce
FDI data could be replicated, or destination data from another developed
country could be used. In any case, it is probably wise to supplement new
databases with further cases from a variety of industries and transition
economies.

Third, any tests must confront the problem of *interaction between dependent variables* – e.g. culture and FDI regulation, or levels of industrial crisis
and cultural attitudes.

In addition to these three proposed theoretical developments, practitioners may be interested in the attitudinal shifts since 1998 that seem to

have occurred in relation to Russian and Chinese FDI regulations and, inter-relatedly, in culture and the attitudes of enterprise incumbents to foreign investors. Policy makers are powerless to influence cultural change, other than in the very long term, but the two cases also suggest tentatively that governments may even lack power in relation to FDI regulation, since foreign investors have no shortage of potential investment locations offering attractive combinations of expected return and country risks. Besides culture, however, country risks are determined by factors over which governments do have some influence – e.g. political stability, property rights protection and enforcement (particularly for minority shareholders), currency stability, as well as direct controls over inward FDI and the repatriation of profits. Changes in these elements of country risk may be more successful in attracting inward FDI than direct controls over entry modes in an environment of unchanged or increased country risks. In this context, the protection of minority rights in Russia is a live policy issue. Existing laws require enforcement, particularly in relation to greater transparency in information provision, in order to promote the participation of all shareholders in enterprise strategic decisions (OECD, 1999). In Russia, the recently enacted law on the protection of shareholders' rights, providing for fines and sanctions in cases of violation, is a step in the right direction to reduce foreign investors' perceptions of country risks.

14 Obstacles to Inbound FDI: The Case of Russia

Grahame Fallon and Alan Jones

INTRODUCTION

The fall of the Former Soviet Union (FSU) in 1991 marked the formal end of communism in Russia, and resulted in the emergence of an independent Russian Federation, which has sought to move gradually towards a modern capitalist economy by means of a programme of market-led reform. The *de facto* transformation of the Russian economy has, however, been in progress for over a decade, beginning with Michael Gorbachev's attempts to reform socialism from within by means of the twin programmes of '*glasnost*' and '*perestroika.*' Given the length of time which has now passed since these early attempts at economic reform, it now seems an appropriate time to take stock of the contribution which foreign direct investment (FDI) can make in theory, and is making in practice, to the processes of economic transition and transformation in modern Russia.

FDI is vital to Russia's continued economic transformation and development (Puffer *et al.*, 1998), having the potential to make domestic production more efficient; promote innovation and/or improvement in products, processes or organizational structures; re-allocate Russia's national resources to fit better with Russia's comparative advantage; help the country to capture new foreign markets; and to help it to adjust to demand and supply conditions in the global market (Dunning, 1994). FDI can also provide a 'package of attributes' which are of specific value in promoting 'market-oriented institution formation and behaviour' in transition economies such as Russia (EBRD, 1998). It can contribute directly to capital (Borensztein *et al.*, 1995); it can stimulate faster progress in restructuring enterprises, so helping to boost their productivity and export performance (Hunya, 1997); and it can also provide technological and organizational benefits for domestic suppliers and competitors (EBRD, 1998).

Despite the advantages which it can bring, Russia has to date experienced a relatively modest inflow of FDI from foreign-based TNCs. Notwithstanding an abundant natural resource endowment, a clear economic strength in science and technology, and high average levels of education, Russia has proved unable to match the FDI inflows attracted by leading transitional economies in Central and Eastern Europe (CEE).

This chapter seeks to explain the reasons for Russia's limited success in attracting inbound FDI, in terms of a set of environmental features, which include the country's unique political and economic history and culture; its distinctive taxation and legal framework; the prevailing problems of oligarchy, crime and corruption; and the nature of Russian privatization and its current management style. These issues are considered within the overarching contexts of Russia's political history, current problems of economic transformation, and distinctive brand of capitalist development to date, and on the country's development as a post-communist, market-based economy.

The chapter begins by considering Russia's relative failure to date in terms of the volume of inbound FDI investment which has been attracted. The chapter then considers the potential advantages of inbound FDI for host-nation economic performance and transition, and goes on to review the types of inbound FDI which Russia might seek to attract, and the resultant benefits which might accrue to an FDI host country. The importance of country-specific influences on the location of inbound FDI is then examined. The main body of the chapter then goes on to explore the political and economic obstacles to inbound FDI in Russia, and concludes by exploring the implications of this poor FDI record, in terms of the constraints which it imposes on the economic transition, transformation and development of modern Russia.

FOREIGN DIRECT INVESTMENT

Russia's Relative Failure to Date

Despite an abundant natural resource endowment, clear economic strength in science and technology, and high average levels of education, Russia has proved unable to match the FDI inflows attracted by leading CEE transition economies. FDI entering Russia more than doubled from US$1.7bn in 1996, to US$3.75bn in 1997, following advances in the country's privatization programme (EBRD, 1998). In cumulative terms, however, foreign investment in Russia remains modest. Between 1989 and 1998, the cumulative inflows of FDI into Russia stood at only US$9.2bn, a figure equivalent to little more than half that achieved by Hungary (US$16.9bn), and only-three quarters of that recorded by Poland (US$12.4bn) (EBRD, 1998), (see Table 14.1).

Expressed in *per capita* terms, Russia's poor performance in attracting inbound FDI is revealed in even starker form. Russia was ranked only fourteenth out of the 25 CEE and FSU states in 1997 on the basis of her FDI

Table 14.1 FDI in Russia 1989–98 (net inflows of equity capital recorded in the balance of payments)

	FDI inflows (1996) (US$ mn)	FDI inflows (1997) (US$ mn)	FDI inflows per capita (1997) (US$)	Cumulative FDI inflows (1989–98) (US$ mn)	Cumulative FDI inflows per capita (1989–97) (US$)
Russia	1700	3752	25	9201	63
Hungary	1986	2100	207	16903	1667
Poland	2741	3044	79	12442	321
Czech Republic	1388	1275	124	8473	823
FSU[a] and CEECs[b] overall	12439	17101	43	74471	187

Notes:
a FSU, excluding the Baltic states.
b CEE and Baltic States.
Source: Adapted from EBRD (1998) p. 81.

per capita (US$25). This position constituted an improvement on performance over the previous decade. Between 1989 and 1997, Russia attracted a cumulative inflow of FDI *per capita* equivalent to only US$63; this figure contrasts with an inflow of US$1667 *per capita* in the case of Hungary; and US$823 *per capita* in the case of the Czech Republic. Overall, Russia's performance in attracting inbound FDI ranked twentieth out of the 25 countries in the region in terms of FDI *per capita* (EBRD, 1998).

The FDI that arrives in Russia is also heavily concentrated in relatively few regions. This concentration testifies to foreign investors' continuing anxieties over the progress of economic transition in Russia as a whole, as well as to the territorial differentiation of investment conditions between the countries' regions. Large regions with a developed market infrastructure, high *per capita* incomes and abundant resources attract the largest shares of inbound FDI. According to Russian government sources (Institute for the Economy in Transition, 1998), five economic regions, comprising approximately 49 per cent of the Russian population, attracted 90 per cent of total inbound FDI in 1997. Moscow, St Petersburg and Nizhny Novgorod received approximately 75 per cent of total FDI entering Russia in 1996 (Jego, 1997). In the same year, FDI in Moscow accounted for 66 per cent of total foreign investments in Russia, and had almost ten times the national average share in FDI (Bylov and Sutherland, 1998). Moscow's share of inbound FDI had fallen to under 60 per cent by 1997, but approxi-

Table 14.2 Investment in Russia as a percentage of the previous year's expenditure, 1992–5

Investment	1992	1993	1994	1995	Average
New investment in productive fixed capital	−44	−19	−33	−17	−28
Share of investment expenditure on equipment	25	24	20	19	N/A
Total	−30	−12	−26	−13	−20

Note: N/A = Not available.
Source: Adapted from Plakin (1997).

mately 70 per cent of all foreign investments continued to accrue steadily to the Moscow, St Petersburg and Moscow *Oblast* regions (Institute for the Economy in Transition, 1999).

While the overall volume of inbound FDI into Russia is relatively small, and investment is heavily concentrated in a small number of regions, many of those investment projects which do take place are also unusually small for the organizations that are operating them; for example General Motors' investment in the production of the Chevrolet Blazer in Tatarstan is a quarter share of US$250mn with the local Tartar government and the Russian government providing the rest of the investment. For an organization with a turnover equivalent to US$170bn this seems little more than a tentative commitment, but is characteristic of current inflows of FDI into the Russian economy as a whole.

The low level of FDI which flows into Russia is matched by difficulties in domestic investment in the productive sector. Table 14.2 (adapted from Plakin, 1997) shows the shrinkage in domestic investment in Russia during the period from 1992 to 1995. Total investment fell by an average of 20 per cent p.a. and new investment by 28 per cent over this period and since then, as may be seen from Table 14.2, it has been declining at a slower but significant rate (9.6 per cent p.a.).

The failure of domestic investment and FDI are not unrelated, since the market conditions prevailing in Russia have not been favourable for either. The FDI inflow of US$1.7bn received in 1996 was offset by a massive US$22.9bn outflow from the economy to accounts abroad, or hoarded as foreign exchange (Robinson, 1997). Thus a shortage of domestic investment reflects that of FDI, transmitting the clear message that since 1991 the position for investment has changed little and the creation of a market economy is being indefinitely delayed.

Although Russia remains a political and economic giant, at least in CEEC and FSU terms, the country is clearly not punching its weight in terms either of domestic investment or inbound FDI. The following section of the chapter explores the potential advantages which Russia could enjoy from higher volumes of inbound FDI, and to consider country-specific influences on the location of such FDI. It then goes on to consider a range of possible explanations for Russia's poor record in attracting FDI to date, together with the resultant implications for her economic well-being and transition.

Potential Advantages of Inbound FDI for Economic Performance and Transition

The failure to attract greater inflows of FDI is isolating Russia from major potential economic benefits. Dunning (1994) argues that the economic competitiveness of countries can be advanced by five main means: by making domestic production more efficient; by innovation and/or improvement in products, processes or organizational structures; by reallocating resources to fit better with a country's comparative advantage; by capturing new foreign markets; and by adjusting quickly to demand and supply conditions in the global market.

FDI can facilitate this process as follows: it can provide resources not attainable domestically; it can provide market knowledge required to mould production to the demands of the international market; it can improve domestic supply conditions through its demands upon local suppliers; it may provide a stimulus to market-oriented R&D and a source of technology transfer in products and processes; it may extend the market of domestic suppliers; it may provide a source of new and effective management practice; it may provide an effective alternative to domestic entrepreneurship, management and work culture; it may foster economies of agglomeration; and it may provide a bridge to alliances and to the wider global economy (Dunning, 1994). In the specific context of the Russian economy, the benefits of FDI are also seen in the fact that foreign investors will be more dynamic than local state and private enterprise – restructuring more quickly, operating more capital intensively, providing more training and operating with higher labour productivity (EBRD, 1998).

Within the specific context of former communist economies such as Russia, inbound FDI has the ability to contribute to the success of transition and to economic performance in three main ways. First, FDI can contribute directly to capital accumulation, helping to address shortages which arize owing to low domestic savings and limited financial intermediation (Borensztein *et al.*, 1995). Secondly, it can stimulate faster progress in restructuring enterprises, so helping to boost their productivity and export performance (Hunya, 1997). Thirdly, it can provide technological and organizational benefits for domestic suppliers and competitors. FDI can, in general terms, provide a 'package of attributes' that can contribute to 'market-oriented institution formation and behaviour' in transition economies (EBRD, 1998). The presence of FDI can lead to a positive 'spillover' effect for local firms, through the stimulus of greater competition, and by means of both backward and forward linkages (Hunya, 1997; Mayhew and Oriowski, 1998). Local suppliers can have higher standards of product quality and supply reliability forced upon them, while higher standards may also spread to other suppliers through demonstration effects (EBRD, 1998; Matouschek and Venables, 1998).

Types of Inbound FDI and Host-country Benefits

Foreign corporations' motives for FDI exercise a major influence on the benefits which accrue to host economies. Dunning (1994) argues that corporations engaging in FDI are seeking specific and identifiable advantages; they will expect to benefit from some or all of the following: natural resources – physical and human (resource-seeking FDI); access to markets – local or adjacent (market-seeking FDI); product or Process rationalization/specialization – across or along the value chain (efficiency-seeking FDI); the acquisition or linkage into foreign assets including technology, organizational efficiency or markets (strategic asset-seeking FDI).

Most flows of FDI in the 1980s and 1990s have taken place within the Triad, and have been of the efficiency- or asset-seeking kind. In contrast, inbound FDI from developed to developing countries and economies in transition (such as Russia) during this period has been motivated primarily by the search for natural resources or market access:

> Many [such] countries are being drawn into the hinterland of globalising firms from developed countries as, in their bid to remain competitive, these firms are continually seeking new markets and cheaper, better quality and more stable sources of supply. (Dunning, 1994)

There is some evidence of 'strategic asset-seeking' in the aerospace sector. For example, Lockheed Martin have been involved in a joint venture with the state-owned Khrunichev centre using Russian rocket production technology (specifically the Proton Rocket) to launch telecommunications and other satellites for commercial purposes. A further example is provided by Dasa's (Daimler Benz aerospace division) investment in the Rokot project which is converting SS19 Ballistic missiles into low-orbit launchers for commercial purposes (also with the Khrunichev centre) (Ostrovsky, 1997). However, strategic asset-seeking FDI remains untypical in modern Russia. Resource- and market-seeking FDI are pre-eminent, being particularly common in sectors such as the food industry, automobile assembly and oil and gas production. The oil sector has been a central focus of foreign investment activity, but also serves to illustrate the difficulties of undertaking FDI in Russia (p. 219 below).

Resource- and market-seeking FDI can lead to a range of benefits for host countries such as Russia. It can help them to: 'restructure their economic activities in line with dynamic comparative advantages'; it can also help in 'reducing the costs of structural adjustment'; and by 'fostering more demanding purchasing standards by firms and consumers'. It can thus contribute to the speed and effectiveness of their economic transition and development, by 'raising the productivity of their resources and capabilities, improving quality standards and stimulating economic growth' (Dunning, 1994).

Country-specific Influences on the Location of Inbound FDI

Competition among developing and transition countries including Russia to attract footloose inbound FDI is becoming increasingly intense, as governments vie with one another to exploit the resultant domestic economic and social benefits. Host-government attitudes towards inbound FDI have softened in many countries during the past 25 years, following the realization of its potential for enhancing the competitiveness of national resources and capabilities. Many governments have reviewed and reshaped their economic strategies in order to attract FDI, abandoning restrictions on FDI inflows and introducing sound macroeconomic policies and privatization, the privatization of state-owned industries, deregulation, liberalization and anti-monopoly policies as a means to this end. Direct intervention in markets has also been reduced in many countries, leading to the removal of subsidies, tariff- and non-tariff barriers (NTBs) to trade and price controls. There has also been a widespread reform of national legal, financial and commercial infrastructures.

Some countries achieve greater success in attracting inbound FDI than others, owing to their 'historical' and 'geographical' circumstances. Dunning (1993, 1994) suggests that the geography of inbound FDI is affected by a range of generic country characteristics. Some of these impact chiefly on direct production costs and benefits, including: the spatial distribution of natural resources, created assets and markets; and input prices, quality and productivity and investment incentives and disincentives. Others impact chiefly on market-seeking FDI, including: inter-country differences in political ideologies, culture, language, business, customs and the ethos of competitiveness; national economic systems and host-government policies; the organizational and institutional framework for resource allocation; societal and infrastructural provisions (commercial, legal, scientific, technological, educational, transport and communications); cross-border transport and communications costs; and the presence or absence of artificial barriers to trade (such as import controls) (Dunning, 1993, 1994).

Progress in development or transition exerts a major influence on potential host-countries' ability to attract inbound FDI; broadly speaking, FDI can be seen to be attracted by long-term economic opportunities in recipient countries. Although Russia's economic potential is great, her ability to attract inbound FDI has been restricted by her mixed successes to date in unlocking this potential through market-oriented reforms (EBRD 1998, and see p. 220 below). Successful economic reform is the key to FDI for transition economies such as Russia, since it opens opportunities for profitable investment, while it also reduces risks, so encouraging potential investors to take advantage of these opportunities.

Transition economies' willingness and ability to attract FDI inflows should not be judged merely in terms of their macroeconomic stability and their introduction of non-discriminatory regimes for dealing with inward investors. 'Effective markets' and 'sound financial institutions' constitute vital pieces in the inward investment jigsaw (EBRD, 1998). The creation of an investment climate conducive to FDI also depends on host-governments' ability to create a range of favourable environmental conditions, including supportive political and economic conditions; the ability to exercize corporate governance without arbitrary bureaucratic interference; the existence of a transparent and fair taxation and legal environment; the minimization of crime and corruption – or, at least, of their effects upon inward investors; and the existence of helpful government economic objectives and policies, including a privatization regime conducive to FDI. The presence or absence of each of these conditions is examined in the following sections of the chapter, in order to help explain modern Russia's indifferent record to date in attracting inbound FDI.

OBSTACLES TO FDI IN RUSSIA

Political and Economic Obstacles

The failure to attract greater inflows of FDI is isolating Russia from major potential economic benefits. An increase in the volume of inbound FDI, linked to a release of the domestic potential for investment, could lead to a very positive effect on economic growth, by enabling Russia to upgrade its competitiveness and comparative advantage. The tentative nature of many current investments is characteristic of Russia's current difficulties in attracting FDI, however, reflecting a mismatch between the expectations of organizations that provide, or would provide, FDI and the perceptions of the Russian recipients. It also reflects poorer opportunities for FDI, particularly because of a failure of the privatization process to open up appropriate opportunities. In contrast to the experience elsewhere in the former communist bloc, the nature of privatization has been an obstacle to the development of FDI, preserving pre-competitive forms of management and operation (Hughes and Helinska-Hughes, 1998).

The breadth of Russia's relative failure to attract FDI reflects a domestic misunderstanding of its potential contribution to economic transition and growth, and also the extent of obstacles to FDI. The obstacles to FDI operate on a number of levels in the economy and society, and reflect tensions between the acceptance of the market economy, the expectations of change, the experience of change and the persistence of the values and practices of the old order. At a practical level, foreign investors when asked about the difficulties of investing in Russia listed the following: a confiscatory tax regime – more than 150 taxes are applied with particular vigour to foreign investors; the difficulty of enforcing commercial contracts and property rights in the courts; crime and corruption, which add to the costs and complexities of doing business; the hostility of local Soviet-era bureaucrats, whose poor understanding of how a market economy works can derail deals agreed at the federal level; the special trading privileges granted to importers with close contacts in the Kremli (Thornhill, 1996c).

This is not an exhaustive list, though it contains the central practical elements of the difficulties experienced by Western businessmen in Russia and, of course, reflects the concerns those who have already made the effort to operate there. They are each examples of the obstacles to FDI but in some respects neglect the linkages and the framework which emerge from the manner in which transition is taking place in Russia, and the contradictory nature of the communism from which the new market capitalism is emerging. The obstacles to FDI in Russia can be categorized as follows:

Obstacles Based on Political History
Those obstacles that emerge from the political history of the Soviet Union are represented by both the broad political resistance to capitalism, or the defence of the old order in post-communist Russia. These derive from an idealistic perception of the values of communism set against the experience of reform, but also include the less idealistic aspect of communism in which the *'nomenklatura'* has sought to create a quasi-capitalist oligarchy to replace the communist oligarchy that obtained previously.

Problems of Transformation
Problems of transformation relate to the mismatch of institutions, law and the taxation system to the requirements of a capitalist economy, or result from the slow or inappropriate response to the needs of change.

'Faux' Capitalism
Alongside this, and resulting from it, is the particular form of capitalism that is emerging from the processes of reform, in particular the outcome of the process of privatization, and the management styles are emerging with them, which are not conducive to FDI (Yavlinksy, 1998).

The ability of FDI to improve the efficiency of domestic production, to stimulate improvements in products, processes or organizational structures, and to promote the reallocation of resources would appear to be of particular potential value in the Russian context, enabling domestic producers to function in ways that are more consistent with the expectations of capitalism in the West. The predicament in which Russia finds itself, and of which its failure to attract FDI is but one symptom, appears to be and has been treated as an essentially economic problem. But those elements that create the biggest obstacle to FDI are not only economic in character, they are imprinted with the specifically Russian context, in which the political and economic culture conspire with history to thwart much of the purpose and acceptability of Western-style modernization in modern, post-communist Russia.

Political and Economic Culture

The political and economic culture of modern Russia has evolved out of communism, and even the rapidly imported market capitalism, characterized by the Gaidar and subsequent reforms has increasingly to take account of that inheritance. Foreign investors' complaints against 'the hostility of local Soviet-era bureaucrats, whose poor understanding of how a market economy works can derail deals agreed at the federal level', constitutes a recognition that the institutional culture either cannot or will not grasp the purposes of Western capitalism and adopt them without examining them through a lens that has in some way been distorted by the experience of communism (Thornhill, 1996a).

The common experience of the bureaucracy and government in contemporary Russia is that of communism, thus capitalist ideas have had to be learned or acquired. This does not mean there is no conception of capitalism, but for many it is the capitalism with which Russian socialism competed, and which was perceived to be morally and often economically inferior. The strength and persistence of the organizational forms of Soviet Russia in the context of economic transformation reflects the strength of the message of communism and its forms. Moreover, contemporary Russia is separated from other nations that have experienced communism because Russia was the powerhouse of the communist system, and the fountainhead to which other communist countries looked for guidance; as the leading communist nation, Soviet Russia was an immense, self-confident, occasionally arrogant, superpower. Reform and transformation in broad terms may be seen as a rejection of communism, but the experience of communism in Russia is longer and deeper than anywhere else in the former communist bloc. It should not be surprising then, that whatever the enthusiasm of the reformers for capitalism, the institutions and culture of communism have persisted in modern Russia.

The reform process, which started in earnest in 1992, had four main aspects (Kuznetsov, 1994). First, it set itself the task of liberalizing all prices in the context of a tight monetary and budget policy; secondly, it sought to give total freedom to all forms of business activities; thirdly, it aimed to incorporate a social policy to offset the impact of the creation of the free market; fourthly, it attempted to create a process of privatization and remove the monopolies of state enterprises. This version of 'shock therapy' reform, the objective of which is to see a rapid conversion of the command economy to a free market on the basis of the above measures, has been only incompletely and imperfectly carried through. Attempts at monetary reform, for example, were initially jeopardized by the inflexibilities of the industrial sector, the effects of which have been described by Kuznetsov (1994):

> The policy of macroeconomic austerity in Russia was aimed, primarily at arresting inflation, but it was also expected to produce an adjustment reaction on the part of the state owned enterprise. The interrelation between the dynamics of monetary aggregates and enterprise responses in terms of production and employment policy in the market economy is thoroughly explained in the economic literature. In Russia, however, the programme of macroeconomic stringencies was applied to a non capitalist economy in the absence of competitive markets for factors of production and ready products, a comprehensive banking system, and a mature tax system. Objectively this made the success of the reforms as well as the possibility of an adequate response at the micro-level more problematic. Inter-enterprise arrears and the persistence of over employment have become probably the two most discussed phenomena symptomatic of the defeat of the reforms at the micro level.

These initial failures have since given way to a *de facto* gradualism of approach that reflects the interaction of the existing social and economic institutions with the political process. The creation of democracy in Russia qualified the ability of the state to push through the reform process, setting up a confrontation between the reformers and the gradualists – those that resist the process altogether or those, like the oligarchs discussed below, for whom the reform is opportunistic.

According to Johnson (1994), this outcome can be seen as an inevitable consequence of the 'shock therapy' itself, since its social consequences undermined the government that implemented it, while the approach did not permit sufficient time for institutions and organizations to adapt. Moreover, Johnson argues that the social impact of 'shock therapy' may contribute to the legitimization of those 'conservative' forces nostalgic for the certainties of communism:

As convoluted as the Soviet command economic system was, the Soviet people understood how it worked. They devised entire networks devoted to gaining access to scarce goods which, while time consuming allowed them to get much of what they needed at known prices. This is no longer the case. Faced with all these rapid, uncomfortable, changes it comes as no surprise that people strenuously object to the results and demand a return to the old system.

Whatever the impact of reform to date, the failure to attract FDI reflects the creation of a 'faux' capitalism in which some of the elements of the process of reform have themselves been obstructive in the creation of appropriate conditions for growth, and those aspects of reform that might be effective in creating conditions in which the domestic investment and FDI might be effectively combined have been neglected or opposed (see, for example, Yavlinksy, 1998).

Russia's attempts at 'shock therapy' reform have in this respect failed to take full account of all of those elements that constitute Western market capitalism – it is not just a mechanism, but requires institutional arrangements, fiscal and legal frameworks and a broadly approving culture and ethics that enable it to function with acceptable levels of risk. These elements did not spring up fully formed in the West but are the outcome of an historic process. The global market economy which, with all its uncertainties, has been enabled by a slow process of institutional and intellectual change, is a recent phenomenon, supported by a slowly derived acceptance of the value of free trade and FDI. In this form it is younger than the communism that it is seeking to supplant, and it should not be surprising that the institutional framework which it is seeking to replace does not simply evaporate.

With respect to FDI itself, there is a cultural inheritance in Russia that regards foreign investment with suspicion; most Russians are familiar with the history of the post-revolutionary civil war and the role played by Western capitalist interests in seeking the demise of the embryonic revolutionary state. Western participation in investment, particularly in the area of natural resources, is often regarded with hostility or seen as 'colonization' not only by Communist Party members of the Duma but also by state officials (Watson, 1996). There is also genuine doubt and resentment in these areas of the role of foreign as against domestic capital, particularly in the oil and gas industries where domestic producers and exploiters of oil see themselves as equally capable of delivering to domestic and foreign markets, but also of conserving the national heritage of natural resources. The position which Russia occupies with respect to FDI can be considered to be akin to that of some developing countries in the 1960s and 1970s, since the former's acceptance of FDI is more wary, and depends very specifically on the balance between the perceived advantages and the perceived costs of FDI. The perceived advantages include those listed above, while the perceived costs include the possibility that 'the monopoly power of TNCs would enable those companies to extract unacceptably high shares of the value added of their affiliates' (Dunning, 1994).

While it is difficult to establish evidence for a disposition against FDI as such, in Russia there is some anecdotal evidence of a wide misunderstanding of the relationships that obtain within market capitalism and the mutuality that is expected alongside the competition. The *Financial Times* (1994) reported the views of a long-time investor thus:

> Mr Haluk Gercek, in charge of the Moscow office of Enka, the Turkish construction company which has been able to bring its own funds and bank finance to Russian projects, believes the main problem is psychological. After 70 years of communism, Mr Gercek finds that many Russians have only a faint grasp of such concepts as private property, venture capital and investment. You can't fix this with laws and regulations. It is a matter of long-term acceptance of property rights and private ownership. People think they are doing you a favour if they offer you investment opportunities without offering security for your capital.

Taxation and Legal Framework

Many of the features that constrain the development of an encouraging environment for FDI reflect the enforced gradualism of economic reform in modern Russia. The process of transformation requires institutional change to create a taxation and legal framework in which domestic and foreign investment might flourish. However, progress towards creating such a framework has been slow in Russia to date, owing perhaps to two main reasons: first, the relatively short period which has elapsed since the fall of communism, following the 70 + years under which the previous framework had been developed; and secondly, owing to the traditional preoccupation of the Russian state with its own affairs rather than with business promotion.

Russia's taxation system presents a variety of obstacles to FDI, many of which have been listed by Alexander Chmelyev of Baker and Mackenzie (1998) in advice to investors issued on behalf of the American Chamber of Commerce in Moscow. The major problems for foreign investors in this context include: frequent changes to the tax system; stiff penalties for underpayments of tax, which can easily exceed the actual tax liability by a factor of two or three; the ease with which corrupt tax inspectors are able to manipulate these penalties; the presence of too many taxes levied at both the federal and local levels; and the confusion caused by presidential decrees which modify existing laws or append taxes onto them. This multitude of taxes not only makes compliance difficult, but also makes it challenging for TNCs to keep abreast of changes and amendments.

Russian tax rules also currently restrict many deductions that are true economic costs of doing business and that many Western businesses would expect to be normal deductible business expenses, including restrictions on interest expenses, advertising and business trips. The effective rate of taxation levied on foreign companies operating in Russia is therefore extremely high. A French company lawyer working in Moscow reported in *Le Monde* estimated the effective rate of taxation between 50 per cent and 80 per cent on foreign companies operating in Russia, and pointed out that there was a requirement to report accounts three times a year, and that the accounts of the company could be seized by the tax police on the slightest pretext and without recourse to appeal (Jego, 1997).

The operation of foreign investment projects in modern Russia has also been dogged with difficulties that arise from property law and from the operation of law associated with ownership of shares and the rights associated with them. Problems have also been encountered with the malfunctioning of legal and bureaucratic processes in the industrial sector. For example, Assi Domain, the Swedish paper group, felt compelled to withdraw its support for loans by the Karelian Segezhabumprom paper mill in which it had bought a 57 per cent stake at the cost of US$45 million, the difficulties arising from disputes over taxation which ended an attempt by the Karelian Regional government to declare Assi Domain's share ownership illegal (Burt, 1998). IBM had to close an assembly plant that could not compete with its own machines being imported duty-free by a favoured importer (Thornhill, 1997). Both Radisson and Marriot, the American hotel companies, have had difficulty establishing who owns the hotels which they manage in Moscow and the status of their holding in joint venture (JV) arrangements (Boulton, 1994).

TNCs' difficulties are made more complicated by the absence of legal mechanisms through which the companies might seek to establish their rights, and the persistence of crony relations from Communist times which impact upon the legal system. Thornhill (1996b) reports that:

Many Russian company directors, who are often former Communist party members with good contacts in Moscow ministries, still view outside investors with hostility. There are few legal mechanisms for enforcing shareholder rights. The investment bank Mr Jordan heads, Renaissance Capital, has recently been in confrontation with the Soviet-era managers of the Novolipetsk Metallurgical Kombinat after the bank acquired a 24 per cent stake in the metals plant and pressed for more financial information to be disclosed and auditors to be appointed.

The problems of the oil industry typify the fiscal and legal problems encountered in Russia by inward investors from the West during the period of political and economic transformation (Watson, 1996). Obstacles to inbound FDI have been encountered in terms of establishing ownership rights to the natural oil resources of Russia and also with the means for licensing their exploitation, including liability for safety, environmental and conservation issues. Difficulties have also arizen for Western TNCs over taxation, export rights and the role of interest groups. FDI in the oil sector has as a result been severely restricted, and, until recently, most projects undertaken by Western oil companies have been relatively small in scale, while major projects have been held in abeyance pending resolution of these problems.

More generally, the difficulties created for FDI by the Russian taxation and legal systems reflect the tensions within the country's political and economic process noted above. A *de facto* gradualism has emerged in the context of an initially rapid reform, whilst the 'faux' capitalism that has been created has few of the ordered processes in taxation and legal terms that a foreign investor might expect. The resultant problems for FDI have been exacerbated by a failure of the state apparatus to develop the financial relationships with citizens and business organizations that would be expected in a more mature capitalist economy. The Russian government has found it difficult to collect all of its tax revenue despite its tax police, although a major source of difficulty is the covert tax arrangements made with many larger domestic companies in Russia. Thornhill (1996b) reports that:

> The tax authorities estimate 60 per cent of tax arrears are owed by just 1000 large companies. Because of their political lobbying power, many of these enterprises regularly receive government forgiveness for the accumulated debt and much of the private sector goes unrecorded. That makes foreign companies and joint ventures, which tend to have more transparent financial accounts and are more obliging in paying taxes, an attractive target for the tax man.

Oligarchy, Crime and Corruption

FDI inflows into Russia are impeded by the growth of the oligarchy, crime and corruption. The political development of modern Russia has been likened to western European feudalism in the middle ages (Shlapentokh, 1996). As in feudal society, the power of institutions in modern Russia is arbitrary while many operate in some narrow private interest. Shlapentokh describes a state in which public authority is co-opted to private use, this extends across Russian society and manifests itself in corruption and crime at all levels but also in the concept of 'krysha' or 'roof.' At one end of the spectrum this concept demonstrates itself in the 'protection' afforded to street vendors and booth owners by criminals, or by the police in exchange for payment. At the other, it refers to 'sponsorship,' meaning the power or favours available to those employed by the state or in political power that derives from the authority of their office. President Yeltsin, for example, was accused of conferring special rights to import goods on political cronies and personal friends. Former prime minister Chernomyrdin, previously chairman of the large gas monopoly Gazprom, has also been said to have provided 'krysha' to his former organization, by allowing its survival despite earlier government plans for its break up as part of a general deregulation of Russia's oil and gas industries. (Shlapentokh, 1996).

Thornhill (1996a) argues that:

The transformation of the economy promoted by Russia's economic reformers remains only half-complete. The rapid attempt to stitch together the body of a capitalist economy has created some Frankenstein-like economic organizations, which still lurk in the shadows of the state economy and shun the competitive glare of the free market. Companies such as Gazprom, the giant gas monopoly which accounts for about 8 per cent of Russia's GDP, has ostensibly been privatized but in practice remain accountable neither to the state nor to shareholders. The company, which retains close links with Mr Victor Chernomyrdin . . . , appears to enjoy big tax advantages but discloses little information to private shareholders.

The rise of the so-called 'oligarchy' has become an additional, problematic feature of the modern Russian economy. The importance of the oligarchy in Russia today is reflected in its ability to exercise state power on its own behalf. The oligarchs' relationship to the state and influence over the dispositions of state property, as well as their power over the media and individual economic power, places them in a strong position to decide the conditions in which the processes of change will take place. In the presidential election in June 1996, Yeltsin relied heavily upon the financial backing and media power of a group of seven businessmen who claimed to control about 50 per cent of the Russian economy. They were regarded as oligarchs by both the Communist and the reformist opposition and, though claiming to be reformers, were seen to be hostile to deregulation and to foreign access to Russian opportunities. As major beneficiaries of the privatization process, they were perceived to have benefited from special arrangements to acquire important Russian assets at knock-down prices (Naudet, 1998). In return for their support in 1996, Yeltsin rewarded two of the oligarchs with government posts, although both were later dismissed as part of a belated attempt on the part of the President to restart reforms from a more conventionally liberal base.

Some reformist Russian politicians (for example, Chubais) have defended the oligarchs on the grounds that they offer the best prospects for the future of Russian capitalism as they will inevitably seek to secure legitimacy as the best source of security for their gains (Freeland *et al.*, 1997). However, the growth of the oligarchy is not necessarily conducive to the attraction of inbound FDI into Russia. The oligarchy represents an obstacle to the establishment of the rule of law in Russia because so much of its interests are framed within a more questionable style of operation, which fits well into the Communist continuum, and into the kind of corruption that surrounded Brezhnev and the *nomenklatura* of his period in high office (Service, 1998). When the oligarchs had a major influence on the 1996 Yeltsin government, for example, this was used to thwart taxation reforms, while moves towards further privatization at this time did little more than further concentrate ownership in their hands. Some TNCs do participate and co-operate with the oligarchs in connection with FDI in Russia. Such relationships may, however, be fraught with difficulties, since outsiders may be drawn into compromising themselves through illegal activities or tax evasion.

Corruption and criminality are ubiquitous in modern Russia, thus creating further barriers for TNCs to overcome. Corruption, by definition, is an opportunity available only to those in authority, and the suspicion that corruption takes place at the highest levels of Russian politics and society is not reassuring for those seeking to achieve competitive advantage through inbound FDI. The existence of widespread criminal and corrupt practice are important deterrents to FDI, especially where they relate directly to business or to competition. Companies are frequently denied legal redress against those which harm their interests, while widespread corruption frustrates the mechanisms for achieving a market economy in modern Russia.

The issue of lawlessness goes beyond this, extending into relations between the states and the federal centre, with powerful regional governors and senior politicians engaged in corrupt processes that create regional oligarchy. In Primorskii Krai, for example the governor, Evgenii Nazdratenko, set up a company including 213 local bosses of the 36 main enterprizes in a region called PAKT. Through its links to regional government it controlled export licences and the distribution of local quotas, while it also acquired shares in local privatized companies at knock-down prices in non-public auctions. It has also been accused of major embezzlement from the regional budget, while its companies and members have been accused of large-scale tax evasion.

The growth of the regional oligarchy can be seen in part as a problem resulting from the persistence of relationships from the pre-reform era. Such relationships apply at both the national and the regional level, reflecting not only the lawlessness of the economy but also its fundamental weakness. It remains to be seen whether the organizations formed in such a context will evolve into more conventional forms. However, at a number of levels the way in which capitalism is being established both legally and illegally underlines the distance between Western and Russian capitalism, and the difficulties faced by foreign investors in contemporary Russia.

Privatization and Management Style

In contrast to the experience of other former Communist countries, the nature of privatization in Russia has been an obstacle to the development of FDI, preserving pre-competitive forms of management and operation. (Hughes and Helinska-Hughes, 1998). Privatization should be the key to economic change within an economy in the process of transformation. The microeconomic response to price and trade liberalization is seen as central to the transmission mechanism of the process of transformation from a command to a market economy. It should also offer specific opportunities to the foreign investor to participate in FDI by taking control of, or sharing control of, and investing in existing production. In these circumstances the opportunities for effective JVs in which technology transfer, and the other benefits of FDI listed above, can occur, should be favourable.

However, in the case of Russia, the levels of foreign participation through share ownership in former Russian state-owned enterprises (SOEs) remain low, owing in part to a natural aversion to a risky market, but also to the particular outcome of Russian privatization. Kuznetzov and Kuznetzova (1996) have traced the changes in the structure of ownership of Russian organizations between 1991 and 1995, the main features of which are: the dominance of insider shareholders, both managerial and non-managerial; a slow growth in the shareholding of small shareholders from outside of the organizations; the relatively small growth of large outsider shareholders; and the failure of market infrastructure and dynamics to redistribute shares in ways that might enforce organizational change from the outside. The dominance of insiders has led to the creation of a 'nomenklatura management' that nurtures many aspects of the Communist system (Kuznetzov and Kuznetzova, 1998). The features that persist are those that reflect the routines of pre-privatization Russian organizations, not least because up to actual privatization, under the Gorbachev reforms, managers and directors were able to 'assume many of the rights of ownership even before the Russian privatization programme began' (McFaul, 1996).

Because of the principal method of privatization which allowed managers and workers to buy up to 51 per cent of the shares of an enterprise, it is not surprising that the strongest influence upon privatization has been internal to the organization. The distance between ownership and control that characterizes capitalist economies and the discipline that this implies is not typical of the Russian economy. The pattern of ownership and also the underdeveloped capital market favour the manager, while the threat of take-over or divestment is not available as a discipline to managers. Since the dominant ownership is a collective of the managers and the employees in most cases, the objectives of this group tend to prevail, these objectives tending to be control and job security, respectively (McFaul, 1996). In these circumstances the pre-existing conditions are able to persist and the pursuit of profit is subject to the pursuit of other objectives.

Privatization in Russia is said to have produced three main types of business organization, including those which preserve or reproduce aspects of the old order, those that serve the short-run interests of new managers and those that embrace capitalism (Baglione and Clark, 1997). Successful organizations have emerged which have survived and developed new attitudes to the demands of the market. However, many organizations survive with a large element of the traditional ideology and hierarchy unchanged, depending upon privileged access to state demand, or special rights like export licences (negotiated through time-honoured routes of patronage deriving from pre-existing relationships). Many organizations which remain have also been pillaged by their own management and burdened with debt and lack of investment, with their workforces intact and underemployed, holding on to the social wage that their employment gives them.

These circumstances create major difficulties for potential foreign investors in modern Russia. Even if it were easy to acquire the ownership of companies, they still face the danger of inheriting a large social wage and substantial corporate debts. Associated with that is the need to participate in an economy whose business practice is based substantially upon responding to the needs of, and within the limits of, the demand of the state, even after privatization. In addition, the expectations of management and the traditional context in which they operate might make it difficult to acquire the degree of information about the enterprise or the co-operation that might be required for effective joint ventures or mergers.

CONCLUSIONS

Modern Russia has, to date, been relatively unsuccessful in attracting footloose inbound FDI, as compared with fellow transitional CEE economies. These findings suggest that the scale and the net benefits derived from inbound FDI into Russia have both been constrained by infrastructural factors and government policies, constraining Russia's ability to achieve rapid economic transition, transformation and development along Hungarian, Polish or Czech lines.

The obstacles to FDI in contemporary Russia operate at a number of levels in the economy. At the macroeconomic level, though a degree of price stability has been achieved, Russia's political masters cannot guarantee a wider stability for long-term returns on investment even if the infrastructure for that investment were to exist. The Russian government has so far failed to implement those institutional changes that might in the longer term guarantee an inflow of FDI. The promised changes in the legal and taxation framework that would encourage FDI have not been forthcoming and this reflects the fragmentation of the Russian structure of authority.

The failure to achieve the framework necessary for the creation of a truly competitive economy remains the central obstacle to FDI in modern Russia. Essentially, Russia is not yet a market economy, although it has a privatized political and social structure which contributes to the uncertainty of the economic environment. At the microeconomic level the persistence of a culture that derives from experience under communism presents very great difficulties for investors in terms of the autonomy of enterprise managers, workers' expectations of a social wage and expectations about economic performance. The political and economic context in which FDI would have to be applied is still broadly mistrustful or actively hostile to FDI. Those aspects of the market economy that have been implemented have often appeared in forms (as in the context of privatization) that maintain the management structures of pre-reform industry, or in ways that address the needs of industrial and commercial oligarchies which are hostile to foreign competition. Foreign investors' expectations with respect to FDI cannot be met in the short term within the Russian economy, since investors require a level of economic certainty which does not exist in Russia today. Russia has also failed to compete effectively with other states to attract footloose inbound FDI, owing largely to her wariness about the expectations and likely conduct of 'potentially exploitative' foreign investors. Taking all of these factors into account, it should not perhaps be surprising that Russia is still so low down the list of recipients of FDI in the FSU and CEE. Measures should be taken to rectify this situation, when politically possible, if the resultant constraints on Russia's economic transition, transformation and development are to be reduced.

15 Control and Performance of EU–China Joint Ventures: The Perspective of Chinese Managers

Xiaming Liu, Yuguang Yang and Yingqi Wei[1]

INTRODUCTION

Since its opening to the outside world in late 1978, China has experienced a rapid increase in foreign direct investment (FDI) inflows. While wholly-owned subsidiaries (WOSs) have gradually become popular in recent years, equity joint ventures (JVs) as a whole are still the dominant form of FDI in the People's Republic of China (state statistical Bureau, *China Statistical Yearbook*, 1998). JVs can be preferred over WOSs under certain conditions (Beamish and Banks, 1987), and JVs will be chosen if the benefits of sharing equity (such as access to technology, markets and country-specific knowledge) exceed the costs (free riding by partners) (Hennart, 1991). In particular, international JVs (IJVs) offer foreign firms a strategic means to gain access to China's domestic market, reduce costs, acquire legitimacy, learn about the Chinese environment and gain power against their competitors (Osland and Cavusgil, 1996).

With rapid growth of IJVs in China, control and performance of these ventures have received great attention. Beamish (1993) derives various characteristics of IJVs in China both from the existing literature and his own new sample. Osland (1994) compares performance criteria used by partners in eight US–China JVs. Based on personal interviews Osland and Cavusgil (1996) discuss the determinants of performance of US–China IJVs. Yan and Gray (1994) conduct a comparative case study of four US–China JVs and discuss the interactions among the bargaining power of potential partners, the structure of management control and JV performance. Using a large secondary data set, Hu and Chen (1996) investigate the determinants of the performance of Sino–foreign JVs. Following a survey of American general managers in 34 US–China JVs, Ding (1997) identifies some factors affecting JV performance. By personal interviews with foreign managers from 11 different countries in 73 equity JVs in China, Vanhonacker and Pan (1997) show the difficulties that the foreign managers have in their operations in China. Based on a cross-sectional secondary data set for 129 foreign-invested firms in Jiangsu Province in China, Luo (1997)

232

identifies a number of business and investment strategy variables and their interactions that have significant bearing on performance. By surveying 67 US–China IJVs, Lin and Germain (1998) examine the impact of cultural similarity, relative power and age of IJVs on performance.

Though there is a reasonably extensive literature on IJVs in China, most studies focus on US–China JVs and the rest typically do not distinguish the origin of foreign investors nor foreign partners from different countries or regions. Relatively little research has been carried out on control and performance of EU–China JVs. Furthermore, with very few exceptions, many researchers tend to obtain and report the views provided by foreign partners only (Davidson, 1987; Shenkar, 1990; Teagarden and Von Glinow, 1990; US–China Business Council, 1990; Ding, 1997; Vanhonacker and Pan, 1997). Some studies such as Lin and Germain (1998) mix together the views of foreign and Chinese managers. Although the results from these studies are very useful to both researchers and businessmen who are interested in the control and performance issues of IJVs, the Chinese managers' perspective is largely neglected or blurred.

The distinctive approach of this chapter is to focus on the Chinese managers' perspective on control and performance. We draw on transaction cost economics and resource-dependence theory to form hypotheses regarding the determinants of and relationship between control and performance. These hypotheses are tested using a sample of Chinese managers in 51 EU–China JVs. A test for endogeneity for control and performance is carried out to examine whether there is a bi-directional relationship between control and performance.

The results from this study demonstrate that equity share and local knowledge significantly affect overall management control. Common strategic objectives, cultural similarity, Chinese government support and mutual trust have significant impacts on the performance of EU–China JVs. The results are compared with other studies on IJV in China. The managerial implications and limitations of this study are also discussed.

LITERATURE REVIEW AND HYPOTHESES FORMATION

Hypotheses Regarding Control

Equity Share and Control
Transaction cost economics argues that, because of the transaction costs of doing business in imperfect markets, it is more efficient for a firm to use internal structure rather than market intermediaries to serve a foreign market (Buckley and Casson, 1976; Dunning, 1981; Rugman, 1981; Teece, 1981, 1983; Caves, 1982; Hennart, 1982; Beamish and Banks, 1987). The failure of markets in intangible assets such as 'know-how' resources will

lead to the internal use of these assets. Transaction cost economics in its early form focuses on the use of WOSs as the main solution to the problem of transaction costs. This implies that the ownership stake is regarded as the key element in control (Stopford and Wells, 1972). Since equity position often determines the composition of the board of directors which appoints high-level executives, overall management control is positively determined by equity share (Mjoen and Tallamn, 1997). Thus, the traditional transaction cost theory suggests the following hypothesis:

H1a: Equity share is positively associated with overall management control in an IJV.

Other Critical Resources and Control
Resource-dependence theory suggests that control is determined by the possession of critical resources (Pfeffer and Salancik, 1978; Pfeffer, 1981; Blodgett 1991b; Mjoen and Tallman, 1997). Blodgett (1991a, 1991b) discusses five factors that constitute power in an IJV: government suasion, technology, local knowledge/market skills, control of intra-system transfer and financial capital provided for the venture. Yan and Gray (1994) group technology, management expertise, global support, local knowledge, distribution, procurement and equity share into 'resource-based components' of bargaining power which affect the structure of management control.

For the purpose of this study, we focus on the impact of three types of critical resources: technology level, managerial expertise and local knowledge. In broad terms, these three categories can cover many important critical resources identified in the literature. Based on resource-dependence theory, the following hypotheses are developed:

H1b: Technology level is positively related to overall control.
H1c: Management expertise is positively related to overall control.
H1d: Chinese partners' possession of local knowledge is negatively related to foreign partners' overall control.

Hypotheses Regarding Performance

FDI Size and Performance
Resource-dependence theory is concerned not only with control, but also performance. It suggests that strategic resources generate competitive advantage and superior performance (Pfeffer and Salancik, 1978; Barney, 1991; Chi, 1994). Not only is FDI a source of financial capital, it also contains a package of important strategic resources: technology, managerial and marketing skills. This can be critical to an IJV's success. A higher level of FDI means more financial capital available to the IJV, and perhaps more strategic resources contributed by the foreign partners. Thus,

H2a: The level of FDI is positively related to IJV performance.

Objective Compatibility and Performance
Unlike a WOS, an IJV is a special type of international alliance and each party has its own strategic objectives. To realize its aims each party has an incentive to engage in self-seeking pre-emptive behaviour. This is because each partner finds it 'advantageous to maximise his own gains at the expense of the venture' (Hennart, 1991). If there are significant conflicts in strategic objectives, problems arising from opportunism and bounded rationality cannot be handled efficiently within the IJV. To ensure the success of the IJV, there is a need for each party to find commonality in their goals and compromise with each other on differences. The efficiency of the IJV hinges on the convergence of the goals of parties to the agreement (Hennart, 1991). Thus,

H2b: The commonality and compatibility of objectives are positively related to performance.

Cultural Similarity and Performance
Following transaction cost economics, cultural similarity helps improve efficiency of an IJV. Differences in national cultures of JV partners could lead to differences in goals (Geringer and Hebert, 1991), and in approaches to co-ordination, operating methods and strategy implementation (Geringer, 1988). Killing (1983) regards the development of an effective and cohesive management team as one of the preconditions for JV success. The smaller the socio–cultural gap, the easier it is to establish the required cohesion.

In addition, cultural similarity ensures better communications and mutual understanding between JV partners. This enables JV partners to pool and share more effectively the information on host-country markets, infrastructure and government regulations from local partners and technology and managerial skills from foreign partners. Thus, foreign investors can economize on the information requirements of foreign investments and operations (Caves, 1982; Beamish, 1984; Rugman, 1985). Therefore, the following hypothesis is developed:

H2c: Cultural similarity is positively associated with performance.

Government Support and Performance
One unique characteristic of IJVs in China is their close connections with government partners (Beamish, 1993). The overwhelming majority of Chinese partners are state-owned enterprises (SOEs). Because of the Chinese heritage of centralized planning, the Chinese government still plays an important role in IJVs in China (Pearson, 1991). Government support to IJVs in China covers various aspects, including the guarantee of contin-

uous supplies of electricity and necessary raw materials at state-plan prices, lower-than-normal tax rates and reductions in the number and extent of government regulations. Relevant government officials' actions in the IJV's interest are regarded as an important success factor in China (Osland, 1994; Osland and Cavusgil, 1996). The above discussion leads to the following hypothesis:

H2d: Government support is positively related to performance.

Competition and Performance
Basic microeconomics indicates that a firm's performance is affected not only by internal factors but also by its external environment. Market conditions are considered to be an important external factor influencing JV success or otherwise (Littler and Leverick, 1995). Kogut (1988) observes a negative relationship between market concentration and IJV performance. Kogut (1989) and Luo (1995) show that growth of an IJV's market place has no significant impact upon IJV performance. Osland and Cavusgil (1996) find that US–China JVs enjoy above-average profits when operating in markets that are protected from outside competition by the Chinese government. Competition from companies that would export similar products into China would eliminate existing profit margins. Thus, our next hypothesis is:

H2e: Competition is negatively related to performance.

Technology and Managerial Skill Transfer and Performance
Existing research finds that Chinese government officials tend to use economic development criteria to assess the performance of IJVs (Hendryx, 1986; Campbell, 1989; Baird *et al.*, 1990; Ding, 1997). Technological and managerial skill transfers enable an IJV to enhance its competitive capability and achieve satisfactory performance. As a result, we have the following hypothesis:

H2f: Technology and managerial skill transfers are positively related to performance.

Trust and Performance
The essence of voluntary interfirm co-operation lies in 'co-ordination effected through mutual forbearance' (Buckley and Casson, 1988). However, forbearance becomes possible only when there is reciprocal behaviour (Oye, 1986) and mutual trust (Thorelli, 1986). Trust is one of the core concepts for IJV management studies (Parkhe, 1993). Without trust, transaction costs tend to be high because more monitoring and safeguards against opportunistic behaviour are needed (Park and Ungson, 1997). If an

IJV is established and operated based on mutual trust and commitment to long-term commercial success, opportunistic behaviour is unlikely to emerge (Beamish and Banks, 1987). Thus, an IJV can be an efficient form of organization. In view of the above discussion, it is hypothesized:

H2g: Mutual trust is positively related to performance.

Relationship between Control and Performance

Extant research on the relationship between control and performance is inconclusive. Killing (1983), Lecraw (1993) and Park and Ungson (1997) find that dominant control by one partner results in higher performance than shared control, because the latter is often associated with managerial conflicts (Gomes-Casseres, 1989). Beamish (1984) and Yan and Gray (1994) reach a different conclusion, because management control exercised by foreign and local partners can be differentiated and complementary.

As noted by Robson and Katsikeas (1998), whether foreign or local partner control produces better performance is uncertain. Studies to date demonstrate that foreign partner control lowers (Beamish 1984; Lyles and Baird, 1994) and raises (Lee and Beamish, 1995; Osland, 1994) IJV performance. Furthermore, there is a lack of consensus on the direction of the control–performance relationship. While a number of studies confirm one directional path from control to performance (e.g. Killing, 1983; Lecraw, 1993; Mjoen and Tallman, 1997), Reynolds (1984) and Kogut (1988) find no significant relationship between control and performance, and Yan and Gray (1994) identify a bi-directional relationship. In Yan and Gray's study, the bargaining power of JV partners affects the structure of management control which in turn affects performance, and the JV performance will alter the balance of the partners' bargaining power and hence the structure of control. Thus, there can be the following hypothesis:

H3: Control and performance are inter-related.

The hypothesized relationships discussed in this section can be summarized in the conceptual framework shown in Figure 15.1.

MODELS, DATA AND METHODS

Based on our analytical framework, the following models for control and performance are specified:

$$CONTROL = \alpha_0 + \alpha_1 EQSHARE + \alpha_2 TECHLV + \alpha_3 MANLV + \alpha_4 KNOWD + \alpha PERFORMANCE \qquad (15.1)$$

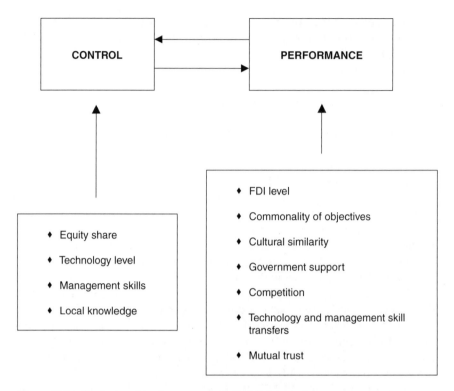

Figure 15.1   Control and performance analytical framework

$$PERFORMANCE = \beta_0 + \beta_1 INVEST + \beta_2 COMOBJ + \beta_3 CULTD$$
$$+ \beta_4\ SUPPT + \beta_5 COMPE + \beta_6 TECHTS$$
$$+ \beta_7 TRUST + \beta CONTROL \qquad (15.2)$$

Equation (15.1) states that foreign partner control (*CONTROL*) is determined by the foreign partners' equity share (*EQSHARE*), technology level (*TECHLV*), management level (*MANLV*), the Chinese partners' local knowledge (*KNOWD*) and IJV performance (*PERFORMANCE*). Similarly, (15.2) shows that IJV performance (*PERFORMANCE*) is influenced by the level of FDI (*INVEST*), commonality of strategic objectives (*COMOBJ*), cultural similarity (*CULTD*), government support (*SUPPT*), competition (*COMPE*), technology and managerial skill transfer (*TECHTS*), mutual trust (*TRUST*) and foreign partner control (*CONTROL*).

Since there can be a bi-directional or uni-directional relationship between control and performance, we follow Geroski (1982) and test for endogeneity of performance (control) in the statistical model of control (performance) to determine whether a simultaneous system should be estimated. If there exists a one-way relationship, the estimation of equations for control ((15.1)) and performance ((15.2)) collectively will lead to biased results. In other words, the following equations will be implemented individually:

$$CONTROL = \alpha_0 + \alpha_1 EQSHARE + \alpha_2 TECHLV + \alpha_3 MANLV$$
$$+ \alpha_4 KNOWD \qquad (15.1')$$

$$PERFORMANCE = \beta_0 + \beta_1 INVEST + \beta_2 COMOBJ + \beta_3 CULTD$$
$$+ \beta_4 SUPPT + \beta_5 COMPE + \beta_6 TECHTS$$
$$+ \beta_7 TRUST \qquad (15.2')$$

The test procedure for endogeneity is as follows: first, we estimate (15.3) below and obtain the residual named R. Second, we estimate (15.1') including R as one of the explanatory variables. If the coefficient of R, denoted as λ, is statistically different from zero, then performance is a determinant of control. Using a similar procedure, we can check whether control is a determinant of performance. If λs from both tests are not statistically significant, there is no need for a simultaneous (or structural) equation system, and (15.1') and (15.2') should be estimated individually:

$$PERFORMANCE = \gamma_0 + \gamma_1 EQSHARE + \gamma_2 TECHLV + \gamma_3 MANLV$$
$$+ \gamma_4 KNOWD + \gamma_5 INVEST + \gamma_6 COMOBJ$$
$$+ \gamma_7 CULTD + \gamma_8 SUPPT + \gamma_9 COMPE$$
$$+ \gamma_{10} TECHTS + \gamma_{11} TRUST \qquad (15.3)$$

The existence of heteroscedasticity is often encountered when using cross-sectional data, so we also carry out a White-test for heteroscedasticity to avoid possible misleading results.

There are three distinct IJV effectiveness measurement systems: simple outcome-based financial indicators, stability-based appraisal and multi-dimensional performance measurement (Robson and Katsikeas, 1998). The multi-dimensional system is customarily based on respondents' perceptual judgements. Satisfaction is of the most frequently employed subjective performance measures (Osland, 1994). Adopting the multi-dimensional performance system, we obtain the perceptual judgements on both performance and control from personal interviews with Chinese managers in 51 EU–China EJVs during August and November 1998. These managers were first asked to give their views on the extent to which they agreed to a set of standardized statements. As regards control, the statements include the degrees of superiority of foreign partner's technology and management skills, the role of local knowledge on the Chinese part, and the extent of the foreign partners' overall management control of the IJV. For performance, the statements cover the commonality of JV objectives of both foreign and

Chinese partners, cultural similarity, support from the Chinese authorities, competition in industries, technology and managerial skill transfers from foreign partners, mutual trust and the overall level of satisfaction with IJV performance.

Their assessments were recorded on a percentage scale, with 0 per cent equalling 'totally disagreed or dissatisfied' and 100 per cent meaning '100 per cent agreed or satisfied'. In addition to these perceptual measures, some objective measures such as FDI amount and equity share of the IJV were checked with the managers.

To control costs, 80 per cent of the EU–China IJVs interviewed were located in the metropolitan city of Shanghai and the neighbouring city of Kunshan, Jiangsu Province. For the purpose of comparison, the remaining ventures in the sample were from the metropolitan cities of Beijing, Tianjin and two cities in inland areas (mainly in Xi'an, Shaanxi Province). The list of EU–China IJVs was obtained from the Administrative Bureaux for Industry and Commerce of the corresponding cities. The original target list consisted of over 100 EU–China manufacturing IJVs with a minimum of two years of operating history. A covering letter was sent and follow-up telephone calls were made to explain the purpose of the research to the Chinese general (deputy) managers in the targeted ventures. Fifty-one of the targeted ventures agreed to participate in the survey. The respondents included general (deputy) managers, financial directors or functional managers from the Chinese side. The average length of the interview was about 1.5 hours.

Foreign partners in the 51 IJVs were from 11 different countries in the EU, and the average total FDI of these ventures was US$5.86 million. Table 15.1 provides the country of origin of the foreign partners, the industrial and regional distributions of the ventures and the distribution of the level of FDI.

The percentage scale was originally designed to allow the respondents to have a wide range of choice on degrees of agreement or satisfaction. However, an examination of the dependent variables indicates that the observed values for control and especially for performance seem to have a discrete jump at zero. Thus, OLS regression may lead to biased results because the residuals would not satisfy the condition $E(u_t) = 0$. Since the control and performance variables in the sample seem to be close to limited dependent variables, Tobit models (or censored regressions) are employed and the results are compared with those from the OLS estimations.

DISCUSSION AND COMPARISON OF RESULTS

Table 15.2 reports the means, standard deviations and correlations for all variables. The high correlations of trust with common strategic objectives, cultural similarity and government support will be discussed shortly.

Table 15.1 Basic characteristics of the sample

A		B	
Country of origin of Country	*Foreign partners* No. of JVs	*Sectoral distribution* Industrial sectors	No. of JVs
Belgium	2	Building materials	2
Finland	1	Chemicals	4
France	8	Electronics and communications	9
Germany	15	Food processing	3
Italy	3	Garments and other fibre	8
Luxembourg	1	products	
Netherlands	3	Leather, fur and down products	3
Spain	1	Machinery	16
Sweden	5	Medical and pharmaceutical	2
Switzerland	2	products	
UK	10	Metal products	1
		Plastics	2
Total	51	Rubber	1
		Total	51

C		D		
Regional distribution Regions	No. of JVs	*Distribution of FDI* Total amount	No. of JVs	Percentage
Shanghai	32	Below US$1 million	17	33
Kunshan	8	US$1–5 million	20	39
Beijing	2	US$5–15 million	8	16
Tianjin	2	US$15–30 million	4	8
Inland Cities	7	Above US$30 million	2	4
Total	51	*Total*	51	100

The endogeneity test indicates that λ is not statistically different from zero even at the 10 per cent level. This suggests that the formulation of a simultaneous equation system of (15.1) and (15.2) is not appropriate. Similarly, we also find that control is not a determinant of performance. Therefore, the estimations of respective single equations for control and performance are justified. In addition, the small values of the White statistics (8.08 and 11.86) indicate non-existence of heteroscedasticity in the observations for (15.1) and (15.2), respectively.

The results of OLS and Tobit regressions for (15.1) and (15.2) are presented in Table 15.3. From Columns (Ia) and (Ib), though there are some differences in the magnitudes of the coefficients on the same explanatory variables in the OLS and Tobit regressions for control, the levels of significance of these coefficients remain the same. This suggests that the bias in the OLS estimation may not be substantial.

Table 15.2 Descriptive statistics and correlations

	Mean	Maximum	Minimum	s.d.^{a}	Correlation	EQUSH	TECHL	MANL	KNOW	INVEST	COMO	CULTD	SUPPT	COMPE	TECHT	TRUST
CONTROL	0.3088	1.0000	0.0000	0.2525												
EQSHARE	0.4955	0.9500	0.1600	0.1872	EQUSH	1.0000										
TECHLV	0.6216	1.0000	0.0000	0.3133	TECHLV	0.0868	1.0000									
MANLV	0.4892	1.0000	0.0000	0.2219	MANLV	0.1858	0.4919	1.0000								
KNOWD	0.8873	1.0000	0.0000	0.1841	KNOWD	0.1140	0.1141	-0.0083	1.0000							
PERFORMANCE	0.7598	1.0000	0.0000	0.2149												
INVEST	0.5855	5.0000	0.0080	1.1150	INVEST					1.0000						
COMOBJ	0.7892	1.0000	0.0000	0.1917	COMO					0.1283	1.0000					
CULTD	0.6676	1.0000	0.0000	0.3021	CULTD					0.0324	0.3004	1.0000				
SUPPT	0.9000	1.0000	0.5000	0.1170	SUPPT					0.0339	0.2140	0.2800	1.0000			
COMPE	0.8637	1.0000	0.0000	0.2298	COMPE					0.1934	-0.0556	0.0620	0.0204	1.0000		
TECHTS	0.5402	1.0000	0.0000	0.2917	TECHTS					0.1042	0.3012	0.1642	0.1669	-0.1583	1.0000	
TRUST	0.8069	1.0000	0.0000	0.2186	TRUST					0.0920	0.5722	0.5257	0.4142	-0.0636	0.2998	1.0000

Note: a s.d. denotes standard deviation.

Table 15.3 Regression results for control and performance[a]

	Control			Performance			
Variables	OLS (Ia)	Tobit (Ib)	Variables	OLS (IIa)	Tobit (IIb)	Tobit (III)	
C	0.5992 (0.1760)***[b,c]	0.5458 (0.2067)***	C	-0.2458 (0.1949)	-0.2951 (0.1888)	-.01747 (0.2018)	
EQSHAR	0.4632 (0.1693)***	0.5652 (0.2024)***	INVEST	0.0241 (1.99E-05)	0.0242 (1.89E-05)	0.0266 (2.13E-05)	
TECHLV	0.0573 (0.1145)	0.1228 (0.1387)	OBJCON	0.3504 (0.1387)**	0.3752 (0.1333)***		
MANLV	0.0323 (0.1630)	0.0667 (0.1941)	CULTD	0.1893 (0.0842)**	0.1930 (0.0802)**		
KNOWD	-0.6440 (0.1708)***	-0.7445 (0.2003)***	SUPPT	0.7459 (0.2023)***	0.7674 (0.1956)***	0.7838 (0.2192)***	
			COMPE	-0.1257 (0.0975)	-0.1280 (0.0928)	-0.1055 (0.1039)	
			TECHTS	0.0366 (0.0749)	0.0403 (0.0756)	0.0783 (0.0842)	
			TRUST	0.0075 (0.1419)	0.0143 (0.1356)	0.3222 (0.1213)***	
Sigma		0.2523 (0.0296)***	Sigma		0.1441 (0.0147)***	0.1624 (0.0166)***	
R^2	0.3099	0.2944	R^2	0.5732	0.5706	0.4581	
Log likelihood	7.7857	-11.7327	Log likelihood	28.2585	22.8061	16.6564	

Notes:

a Number of observations = 51.

b Standard errors are in parentheses.

c *** and ** indicate that the coefficient is significantly different from zero at the 1 per cent and 5 per cent levels, respectively.

The results from the control regression in columns (Ia) and (Ib) show that the coefficient on equity share has the expected sign and is highly statistically significant. Both foreign investors' technology level and management level have the expected sign, but are not statistically significant. Finally, the coefficient on Chinese partners' possession of local knowledge has the expected negative sign and is highly significant.

From columns (IIa) and (IIb), we also find that the magnitudes of the coefficients on various explanatory variables from both performance regressions are quite close. In addition, all significant explanatory variables in the OLS regression remain statistically significant in the Tobit regression, although the level of significance of the common objective variable has risen from 5 per cent in the regression to 1 per cent in the Tobit regression. This suggests that the bias from OLS is moderate. The value of R^2 from the Tobit regression of (15.2) is 0.57. It is a reasonably good fit for a cross-sectional data set.

The results from the performance regressions show that all explanatory variables have the expected signs. While the common objective, cultural similarity and government support variables are statistically significant, the investment (FDI), competition, technology and management skill transfer and trust variables are not. Considering that trust is highly correlated with common objectives, cultural similarity and government support (see Table 15.2), it is possible that the insignificance of the trust variable is caused by the problem of multicollinerality among these variables. As indicated in column (III) of Table 15.3, after removing the common objective and cultural similarity variables, the trust variable is highly statistically significant.

The above results can be compared with extant studies on IJVs in China. In the case of control, the evidence from this study supports hypotheses **H1a** and **H1d**. The finding on **H1a** seems different from that of Yan and Gray (1994). In their study, while all four JVs are equally owned, two of them show an unbalanced, one-parent-dominant pattern of control. They conclude that the ownership split is consistent with only one dimension of control, Board membership, but not equivalent to management control. Our results show that equity share is *a* direct and significant determinant of control. We feel that the relationship between equity share and control needs to be assessed in a systematic way since control is simultaneously influenced by a number of factors. The fact that two equally owned JVs show an unbalanced control pattern does not necessarily mean that equity share is not *a* direct determinant.

Columns of (IIa) and (IIb) of Table 15.3 present the results on performance. **H2a** is not supported. This is contrary to the finding by Hu and Chen (1996). Our result suggests that perceived satisfaction of Chinese partners on performance is not significantly associated with the total amount of FDI, FDI may be seen as more a source of capital than a package of strategic resources.

H2b and **H2c** are supported by the evidence, a finding consistent with transaction cost economics. The finding for **H2b** coincides with that of Yan and Gray (1994), where common strategic objectives reduce distrust and lead to higher performance. Our result for **H2c** is consistent with that of Lin and Germain (1998), who argue that cultural similarity between partners is a critical antecedent for IJV success. Hu and Chen (1996) also find that cultural similarity significantly affects performance. However, their study uses country of origin as a surrogate for socio–cultural distance and finds that US investors enjoy a greater than average amount of success as compared with the other country categories (Hong Kong, Japan, Europe and others). There may be a problem with their measurement. Since the socio–cultural distance of mainland China with Hong Kong is certainly smaller than that with the USA, we should expect Hong Kong–China JVs to perform better than US–China JVs, rather than the other way round.

The positive relationship between government support and performance (**H2d**) is also confirmed. This is in agreement with Osland (1994) and Osland and Cavusgil (1996), but not with Luo (1995) and Hu and Chen (1996) who conclude that economic location-based advantages provided by the Chinese government yield no discernible benefit.

H2e is similar to one of Osland and Cavusgil's (1996) hypotheses that US managers are more satisfied when operating in market structures that are protected from competition. Our test result reveals a correctly signed but insignificant relationship between competition and performance.

H2f is not supported either. Interestingly, this result is consistent with Osland's (1994) finding that, on the Chinese JV managers' list of the most important performance criteria, there is no place for technology transfer. Chinese JV managers may have different assessment criteria than their parent companies or government officials. The latter group focuses on economic development criteria such as technology transfer, while the former is more interested in venture outcomes such as profit and product quality. Indeed, it is the possession and active utilization of superior technology and management skills by the venture that determine the competitiveness of an IJV. The issues as to which partner possesses the expertise our whether the expertise is transferred from one partner to the other may not be directly linked to venture outcomes.

From column (III) of Table 15.3, the significant impact of trust on performance is confirmed. It is interesting to note that the role of trust in our study is somewhat different from that in Yan and Gray (1994). While our systematic econometric study shows a direct relationship between mutual trust and performance, their comparative case study reveals that mutual trust together with common goals acts as the moderator adjusting the relationship between parent control and performance. The findings from both studies may be complementary to each other.

Finally, our test for endogeneity (**H3**) suggests that there is no interactive relationship between control and performance. This is inconsistent with the results from the following studies on IJVs in China: Ding (1997) finds that dominant managerial control exercised by foreign partners has a positive impact on JV performance; Hu and Chen (1996) suggest that the level of foreign control is related to Sino–foreign JV performance; and Yan and Gray (1994) indicate that control and performance interact with each other.

SUMMARY AND CONCLUSIONS

This study is concerned with the issues of control and performance in 51 EU–China JVs. Unique features of the study include its focus on EU–China JVs and the Chinese managers' perspective. The evidence indicates that overall control by foreign partners is positively associated with their equity shares but negatively related to Chinese partners' possession of local knowledge. No significant links have been found between foreign partners' overall control and their technology levels and management skills. It also suggests that commonality of strategic objectives, cultural similarity, government support and mutual trust have a significant bearing on performance. The size of FDI, competition and technology and managerial expertise transfer are not significantly related to performance.

The results are compared with existing studies on control and performance of IJVs in China. Our distinctive results include the direct and significant effects of equity share and local knowledge on control, the direct and significant impact of common strategic objectives and mutual trust on performance, the insignificance of the size of FDI and competition and the non-existence of either single- or bi-directional control–performance relationships. The results from this study lend strong support to transaction cost economics and resource-dependence theory.

A systematic revealing of the Chinese managers' perceptions may help improve performance of EU–China IJVs. One critical area is JV objectives. It is essential to find commonality in each other's objectives for the formation of the IJV. Though the performance criteria used by JV partners appear to be converging (Osland, 1994), there is still a need for both sides to compromise in IJV objectives. Shared objectives will lead to better co-operation and higher performance.

Our study also suggests the importance of cultural similarity. Efforts need to be made to increase communications between the partners and enhance understanding of each other's cultures. The development of a complementary business culture in the JV is critical to JV success. It is desirable to win Chinese government support. While the Chinese economy is in transition from a centralized to a market economy, the Chinese government still influences JV performance significantly via its policies and its close connections

with Chinese business partners. For instance, because of the high initial production cost, the price of an EU–China JV in the sample was almost twice
as high as that of similar imported product. To help that JV, the superior
authorities of the Chinese parent firm provided price subsidies to the
venture and banks provided low-interest loans to buyers. In addition, one
province offered to become a 'trial base' for the product. With the help of
the Chinese government, the venture gradually overcame various problems
and became one of the top performers among all IJVs in China.

Though the above example highlights the importance of obtaining
support from the Chinese government, it would be misleading to conclude
that all IJVs can automatically obtain government assistance. The basic FDI
policy of the Chinese government is to encourage FDI in domestic markets in exchange for foreign technology. If the product is technologically
advanced and falls within the categories of FDI encouraged by the Chinese
government, the foreign partner should work with the Chinese partner
to pursue possible preferential treatment. Finally, mutual trust can be
enhanced via an increase in commonality in strategic objectives and cultural similarity, since the three are highly correlated. Increase in mutual
trust will lead to superior JV performance.

One important limitation of the study is its focus on the perspective of
Chinese managers. Ideally a 'bilateral approach' should be adopted – i.e.
the foreign partner's views on control and performance are compared.
Second, considering the large population of EU–China IJVs in China, the
sample size of this study is relatively small. A systematic assessment of the
determinants of control and performance and careful comparison of both
Chinese and foreign partners' perspectives using a larger sample would certainly provide further interesting results.

Note

1. We are obliged to an anonymous AIBUK reviewer for helpful comments on an earlier
   version of this chapter. The usual disclaimer applies.

16 Here We Go Round the Mulberry Bush: EU–China Trade in Silk

Jim Newton and Roger Strange

INTRODUCTION

This chapter is about the formation of trade policy in the European Union (EU) and, in particular, about the formation of EU trade policy regarding imports of finished silk products from China. In March 1994, the EU unilaterally announced quotas on the imports of certain silk products from China. Bilateral quota arrangements had been in effect between China and the main EU silk manufacturing countries for some time, but the creation of the Single European Market (SEM) had necessitated the introduction of an EU-wide arrangement. The quotas were to be administered by the European Commission. However, the quotas on many silk products announced for 1994 were far below the levels of imports for 1993, and were greeted with dismay by the European retail trade, particularly the large multiple store groups (Watkins and Phillips, 1994: 105). Eventually the Commission agreed to negotiate bilaterally with the Chinese authorities, and the quotas for 1995 and 1996 were significantly higher than those for 1994 – see Table 16.1. Furthermore, the responsibility for administering the quotas was passed over to the Chinese authorities (Islam, 1995: 52).

These observations raise a number of interesting questions about the formation of EU trade policy. The first is why the EU-wide quotas were initially set at such punitive levels in 1994. The second is why the EU quotas were initially introduced unilaterally without consultation with the Chinese authorities, in contrast to the bilateral approach adopted by the US government at roughly the same time. The third is why subsequently the EU engaged in bilateral discussions, and what prompted the Commission to revise the quotas upwards significantly in 1995.

The structure of the chapter is as follows. The first section provides background information about the production of silk, and about recent developments in the industry world-wide. Silk's share of total global fibre production is small, but it still generates a multi-billion dollar export trade and this trade is vital both to the Chinese economy and to localized sections of the European textile industry. The importance of China as a supplier of both raw silk and finished silk products will be established, as will the changing nature of the silk trade between China and the EU. The

248

Table 16.1 EU annual quotas for imports of non-MFA goods from China

Category	Type of article	Units	Imports 1993	Quantities 1994	1995	1996
ex 13	Underpants, briefs	'000s		150	616	634
ex 18	Singlets, vests	tonnes	450	98	759	793
ex 20	Bed linen, non-cotton	tonnes		10	33	35
ex 24	Pyjamas, bathrobes etc.	'000s		120	142	149
ex 39	Table linen	tonnes		10	322	337
115	Flax & ramie yarn	tonnes		450	979	1008
117	Flax & ramie woven fabrics	tonnes		450	466	480
118	Flax & ramie table linen	tonnes		950	1018	1059
120	Flax & ramie curtains	tonnes		63	401	417
136A	Woven silk fabrics	tonnes	1008	285	320	333
156	Knitted silk blouses pullovers etc.	tonnes	144	760	2588	2679
157	Various silk garments	tonnes	1829	5400	10250	10506
158	Silk blouses, dresses, shawls, scarves, ties etc, non-knitted	tonnes	4772	3020	3950	3990
160	Silk handkerchiefs	tonnes		n/a	44	45

Notes: Categories marked by 'ex' cover products other than those of wool or fine animal hairs, cotton or synthetic or artificial textile products.
Sources: *Textile Asia* (April 1994) p. 10; *Textile Asia* (April 1995) p. 11.

chapter will then explore the dynamics of silk production and trade from the days of the old Silk Road to the early 1980s. This will be followed by an analysis of more recent developments in the Chinese silk industry, and the effects of these upon trade with Europe. This then sets the scene for the discussion of the formation of EU trade policy. Finally we bring together some conclusions.

SILK PRODUCTION AND TRADE

The production of raw silk involves two principal stages (Ma, 1996: 331). The first stage is sericulture, which involves the cultivation of mulberry trees and the raising of silkworms and silk cocoons. Sericulture is very labour-intensive and time-consuming, and large areas of land are required for growing mulberry trees (Watkins and Phillips, 1994: 121). The second stage is silk reeling, when the silk cocoons are boiled and softened in water so that silk threads may be drawn out and reeled. Several threads of reeled silk may then be twisted together to form a stronger yarn for subsequent weaving into fabric. The silk processors then take this greige (or grey or loomstate) fabric, bleach it and, either by printing or dyeing, convert it into finished fabric. This finished fabric is then used to manufacture garments and other made-up goods (e.g. furnishings).

Silk has traditionally been considered a luxury item and has, for many years, been associated with *haute couture* garments. The use of silk for such garments still continues but, towards the end of the 1980s, a new middle-market for silk products emerged in the West. The catalyst was the development of 'sandwashed silks'. The sandwashing process was initially developed by a US company, Go-Silk, in 1982, but was subsequently refined and adapted for volume production in Hong Kong and China (Watkins and Phillips, 1994: 97–8). The process involves laundering the silks until the fabric becomes soft and supple, yet still remaining durable, and has the major advantage that it hides imperfections in the cloth so that sub-standard stocks may be treated and sold (at much lower prices). The result was that silk became a popular fabric for all kinds of daywear (both men's and women's), and was being incorporated in garments that had never before been made in silk.

The development of sandwashed silks enabled China to expand massively its domestic production of semi-finished and finished silk products. This expansion was accompanied by a huge increase in sericulture, though without any increase in productivity (Watkins and Phillips, 1994: 119), so there was not a shortage of raw materials either for domestic or foreign processors. Furthermore, these changes in the nature and composition of domestic production had consequent effects upon the structure of China's silk exports. China was, and still is, overwhelmingly the dominant contemporary producer of raw silk – see Table 16.2 – and currently has about a 90 per cent share of global exports. But the development of a domestic silk processing industry, aided by the policies of the China National Silk Import and Export Corporation (CNSIEC) (Hyvarinen, 1993: 46) – meant that exports of garments and made-up silk products accounted for about 70 per cent of the country's total silk export earnings in 1993. Indeed the silk industry had become an important source of foreign exchange for China, with earnings in 1993 of $3.76bn.

Western Europe has long been the most important location for silk processing world-wide, with the main industrial centres being Milan and Como in Italy, Lyon in France, and Zurich in Switzerland.[1] As little raw silk is now produced in Europe (see below), the processors are almost completely dependent upon imported supplies and these supplies come largely from China. Indeed, Western Europe has long been a major destination for China's exports of raw silk, being the recipient of about 40 per cent of total exports in 1990. In the decade from 1985, however, the composition of China's silk exports to the EU changed dramatically. In 1985, made-up goods only accounted for 3.5 per cent of the total value of the silk trade. By 1993, this figure had increased to almost 60 per cent reflecting China's move into silk processing – see Table 16.3 – whereas there had been a pronounced drop in raw silk imports.

Table 16.2   World production of raw silk, 1938–98

Year	Total	China	India	Japan	CIS	Brazil	Others
1938	56 500	4 855	690	43 150	1900	35	5870
1978	49 360	19 000	3 475	15 960	3240	1250	6435
1983	56 576	28 140	5 681	12 456	3899	1362	5038
1984	56 129	28 140	6 895	10 800	3999	1456	4839
1985	58 887	32 000	7 029	9 592	4000	1553	4713
1986	62 460	35 700	8 280	8 220	4000	1680	4744
1987	64 440	37 620	8 400	7 860	4000	1680	4839
1988	61 260	34 380	9 300	6 840	4000	1740	6322
1989	66 900	40 800	10 020	6 060	4010	1680	5206
1990	70 983	43 800	10 200	5 700	4009	1680	4699
1991	76 732	48 480	10 800	5 520	4000	2100	4940
1992	82 419	54 480	12 600	5 100	4000	2280	3783
1993	97 337	69 300	13 200	4 200	4000	2340	3750
1994	100 388	72 000	13 200	3 900	3000	2520	5800
1995	105 138	77 900	12 884	3 240	n/a	2468	n/a
1996	85 192	59 000	12 927	2 580	n/a	2270	n/a
1997	79 590	55 117	14 048	1 920	n/a	2120	n/a
1998	71 727	49 430	14 000	1 080	n/a	1821	n/a

Notes: All figures are in tonnes.
Sources: 1938–78 Hyvarinen (1993) from International Silk Association; 1983–85 Watkins (1997) from International Silk Association; 1986–98 Desco von Schulthess AG.

THE SILK ROAD IN HISTORY

The historical Silk Road was established at least 4000 years ago, and was essentially an all-purpose trading route between the Orient and the Middle East. It was about 5000 km in length, and stretched from Xi'an in China, across the stony wastelands of Central Asia, to Tyre and Antioch on the Mediterranean and to Rome. Silks were then transported to other parts of Europe by trading boats in the Mediterranean. Numerous commodities (e.g. tea, porcelain, rugs, cobalt, jade, Baltic amber, lapis lazuli) were traded along its length in addition to silks, but the route obtained its name because silk was the finest and most expensive of these commodities (Feltwell, 1991: 5).

The story of silk originates in China around 2600 BC,[2] and the art of silk production was an exclusive Chinese prerogative until AD 552 when two Persian monks smuggled some silkmoth eggs back to Constantinople (Feltwell, 1991: 9). Thereafter, silk production spread to many countries around the Mediterranean including Italy, Spain and France.[3] Notwithstanding the introduction of sericulture to Europe, Chinese silk was still imported through the Middle Ages because of its higher quality (Li, 1981: 4). Silk and tea were by far China's most important export

Table 16.3 EU imports of silk goods from China, 1985–98

Volume (tons)	1985	1986	1987	1988	1989	1990	1991	1992	1993	1994	1995	1996	1997	1998
Raw silk	5213	4963	4392	4500	5097	3402	2475	2792	2752	3944	3344	2985	3406	2642
Silk waste	978	1143	2058	1854	1943	1782	3149	2721	1556	2492	1556	1223	1476	1285
Semi-finished yarn	490	476	601	688	665	406	750	701	1051	1475	1036	808	893	824
Fabrics	1324	1717	1849	2593	2858	2401	1821	2155	2801	3043	2786	2778	2591	1976
Made-up goods	121	321	539	848	1181	1794	2900	3521	5080	4553	2670	2718	2677	2099
Total	8126	8620	9439	10483	11744	9785	11095	11890	13240	15506	11393	10511	11043	8826

Value (mn ecu)	1985	1986	1987	1988	1989	1990	1991	1992	1993	1994	1995
Raw silk	195.7	169.6	125.1	162.5	273.3	164.7	102.0	89.6	76.9	97.4	n/a
Silk waste	14.7	11.9	16.1	19.6	30.0	19.5	25.9	15.7	14.7	29.9	n/a
Semi-finished yarn	16.0	14.7	14.2	22.3	30.1	15.6	25.4	19.8	16.9	23.6	n/a
Fabrics	72.3	86.3	81.6	119.9	185.0	150.6	121.6	115.3	124.1	107.9	n/a
Made-up goods	10.8	20.9	26.7	42.2	79.9	127.7	223.0	237.6	332.1	268.8	n/a
Total	309.5	303.2	263.7	366.4	598.4	478.1	497.8	477.9	564.7	527.6	n/a

Sources: 1985–92 EUROSTAT, given in Watkins (1997) p. 62; 1993–98 EUROSTAT, reported by DESCO von Schulthess AG.

commodities after the opening of the treaty ports in the mid-nineteenth century. The tea trade declined drastically after 1887, but silk accounted for 30–40 per cent of the value of exports until just before the 1911 Revolution. World demand was kept high both by the rise of the US and French silk-weaving industries in the second half of the century, and by the spread of silkworm disease in Europe between 1854 and 1858 which devastated European domestic silk supply (Eng, 1984: 354). The importance of silk in Chinese exports declined gradually as China's trade became more diversified through the Republican period, but its share was still 16 per cent in 1930 (Li, 1982: 195).

Another notable aspect of the world silk trade at this time was the growing importance of Japan, both as a producer and as an exporter of raw silk (Park and Anderson, 1992: 27). Sericulture became widespread in Japan in the seventeenth century during the early Tokugawa period, and by the mid-nineteenth century the Japanese had caught up with the Chinese in silk technology (Li, 1982: 199, 205). The Japanese success was built upon more rapid modernization, and upon its ability to provide silk of consistent quality, even though the best Chinese silk was of superior quality. And, as with China, raw silk became, and remained until the 1930s, Japan's most important export commodity and a vital source of the foreign exchange needed to purchase the raw materials and machinery needed for industrialization.[4]

The commercial development of nylon in 1938, and the onset of the Second World War, precipitated the collapse of the world silk market. A substantial proportion of pre-war demand had been from manufacturers of silk stockings, but almost all stockings were made from nylon by the end of the war. Furthermore, pursuit of sericulture rapidly becomes unviable and uneconomic in a developing industrialized economy both because the labour-intensive nature of the activity meant that rising labour costs and income expectations had a significant effect upon the cost of raw silk, and because the land-intensive nature of the activity often conflicted with industrial expansion. The European silk-rearing industry had gone into decline in the nineteenth century, and Japan suffered likewise in the period after the war (Watkins and Phillips, 1994: 121).[5] In 1938, Japan accounted for over three-quarters of raw silk production world-wide (43 150 tons – see Table 16.3). By the early 1980s, production had fallen to barely one-third of this level, and accounted for less than 20 per cent of the world total. In contrast, China accounted for about 50 per cent of total world production.

THE MODERN SILK ROAD

Japan's dominance in silk production was thus relatively transitory given the long history of the fibre and, by the late 1970s, China was once again the world's principal supplier. As in the past, one of the most important destinations for Chinese silk was Europe. But the nature of the trade had changed significantly. In the last twenty years, the roles of producers at the two ends of the modern silk road have altered as Chinese firms have begun to produce fabric and garments that compete with those made in Europe. In the 1990s, the EU imposed quotas on Chinese finished goods in silk. The silk road was suddenly filled with potholes to the detriment, not only of Chinese producers, but also of European merchants whose modern caravans could no longer navigate the route to the market.

These changes raise a number of immediate questions. The first set concerns the causes of the locational and functional changes. Why did China re-emerge as – virtually – the world's monopolist in the supply of raw silk, and what were the processes by which Chinese firms began to compete internationally in finished goods? Secondly what was the relationship between these changes in the production structure, and the trade policy changes in the EU? This section addresses these questions as a prelude to raising wider issues concerning the dynamic of China–EU trade relations.

In order to understand the production changes, it is useful to identify again the four principal products that constitute the value chain, and which each require a different level of technical expertise. Raw silk is the basic raw material that forms the input to the weaving process. The second product is the woven greige fabric that then requires bleaching and printing and/or dyeing to create the finished fabric. Finally there are the made-up items which include furnishings but which are dominated by garments.

If we begin with a consideration of raw silk, the explanation for China's rising prominence is partly about Japan's decline. Part of the answer is provided by the relative cost – and particularly labour cost – structures of the two locations. However, political changes together with changes in the organization of production were also influential. In 1978, Chinese production of raw silk exceeded Japan's by a relatively small margin. In the next 15 years, however, Chinese production soared while Japan's fell drastically. In 1991, Japan produced only a little over a tenth of its 1938 peak whilst China produced ten times its pre-war output. This growth accompanied the political changes in China instigated by Deng Xiao Ping. As part of the modernizations, markets were permitted in certain areas and sectors, including silk. The central control previously exercised by CNSIEC, which had held a monopoly over the buying and distribution of silk, was relaxed, thus permitting the entry of private traders. An incentive for the new entrants was the exclusion of silk from the Multi-Fibre Arrangement (MFA) which had been signed in 1974. One of the first signatories to the agreement was Hong Kong, and Hong Kong has traditionally been among the largest buyers of Chinese raw silk. As China, too, became a signatory to the MFA, the incentive to expand exports of this quota-free fibre intensified.

China's modernization policies were also instrumental in the reorganization of fabric production. Beginning in the early 1980s, Hong Kong entrepreneurs were invited to form joint ventures with State-owned enterprises in Foshan, the principal silk-weaving city of southern China. The silk mills of Foshan had been operating for almost 100 years, but were handicapped by outdated machinery. As a result, the fabric was of a far poorer quality than the high-quality silks woven in Europe, and especially in Europe's major silk district, the Como–Milan region of Italy. The more forward-looking joint ventures (JVs) embraced European technology, upgrading both machinery and staff skills in a major investment programme. In a further relaxation of political control over the market, the Chinese government permitted a number of the JVs to have direct export status. By 1985, Chinese fabrics were beginning to compete on quality with Italian products on world markets, but at a far lower price. American fashion buyers were the first to recognize this major shift. They were led by Liz Claiborne, whose major market segment was the American professional woman. Italian buyers followed and Chinese exports of quality silk fabric began to soar.[6]

The combination of a sudden increase in foreign demand and looser control over suppliers in China disrupted the orderly functioning of the market. Speculation became rife, especially upstream at the point of cocoon production (Glasse, 1995). This led to the so-called 'Cocoon Wars' of 1986–8 which led both to a serious shortage of raw material for export, and to sharply rising prices (Watkins and Phillips, 1994). Further downstream in the production process, low-quality fabrics, produced by the mushrooming number of JVs in silk weaving, were being sold in export markets alongside the better-quality Chinese silks. While quality from these new entrants was low, prices were comparable thanks to the market conditions. Foreign buyers, especially those from Italy, suffered in the ensuing scramble for supplies and, as a result, demand fell sharply in 1989.[7]

But the soaring cocoon prices had stimulated a massive expansion in China's sericulture, leading to a huge increase in supply. Between 1985 and 1993 production of raw silk more than doubled, rising from 32000 tons to almost 72000 tons (Watkins and Phillips, 1994). At the same time, Western demand continued to fall, partly as a result of the recession of 1991 when the European processing industry imported almost 40 per cent less than the preceding year.[8] By 1993, raw silk imports were less than half those of a decade earlier (Watkins and Phillips, 1994). A glut began to appear in China from 1990, and this sparked two significant changes. The first was a resumption of State control, which covered exports of both raw silk and also silk fabrics and garments (Glasse, 1995). The second was the deliberate expansion of silk garment production in China, together with the widespread adoption of the newly developed mass production techniques for the manufacture of 'sandwashed' silk.

This had a major impact on the structure of the world silk market. China was producing at high volume and low prices. Silk was no longer the exclusive province of *haute couture*, but had moved into the department store. The fibre that was literally 'worth its weight in gold' at the time of the old Silk Road had gone from high fashion to the high street in a brief few years. This posed a number of threats to established Western interests. The first was a direct competitive threat to the garment industry. China was producing traditional lines such as blouses, dresses and shirts in conventional silk, but at prices that were only slightly above the cost of the equivalent yardage of greige goods, and hence was undercutting even the price at which Western manufacturers could buy finished fabric.[9] Secondly the new sandwashed silk was rapidly becoming competitive with other fabrics that had, traditionally, been used for casual wear items. The soft nature of sandwashed silk made it ideal for leisure wear, for sports attire and for smart casual clothing. The new fabric had one other critical attribute. It was washable, and hence easy to care for without the need for expensive dry cleaning. Whilst this opened up a new market for silk, it did so at the expense of cotton and other similar fabrics. Finally, the scale with which the markets were being supplied with silk threatened the high-class image that had for centuries been a part of its attraction.

This provoked a reaction in both the EU and the USA. Trade restrictions were imposed by both on this previously quota-free product. In the USA imports of silk garments had soared from US$900 million in 1991 to US$2600 million in 1993, thanks in part to selling prices that undercut cotton garments (Sung, 1994a: 6). American quotas were announced in February 1994, following the earlier annual negotiations covering the Sino–US bilateral Textile Trade Agreement (Sung, 1994a). The EU acted unilaterally, however, and introduced quotas on imports of finished silk products in March 1994.

EU TRADE POLICY TOWARDS CHINA

Although EU trade policy towards China has been documented in several earlier studies (see, for example, Strange, 1998), the processes and objectives that underlie the formation of these policies are often complex and not easily understood. In the case of silk, a number of factors require some explanation. The first is the punitive nature of the 1994 quotas. The second is the way that the quotas were imposed unilaterally, contrary to established procedures in the international textile trade. The third relates to why the EU subsequently agreed to bilateral negotiations, and to substantial increases in the quotas for 1995 and 1996.

In order to analyze these changes to trade policy, it is instructive to use the bargaining model proposed by Stopford and Strange (1991). Their work was principally concerned with the policy choices available for developing countries, especially with the potential for interaction with multinational enterprises, but the framework may also be extended to the present study. They contend that the way in which policy is formulated has changed over the years: 'The traditional players in the embassies are still in business, but they have been joined by members of other government ministries and by the executives of firms, both local and multinational. All are now involved in both bilateral and multilateral negotiation' (Stopford and Strange, 1991: 21) Thus, whereas traditional International Relations was confined to inter-governmental relations, the Stopford and Strange approach embraces three sets of interacting relationships. These include the original government-to-government relationship, but also include government-to-firm and firm-to-firm relationships. There is bargaining among States for power and influence. There is competition between firms over market shares, increasingly at a global level. Finally there is specific bargaining between States and firms as the latter seek to advance their wealth-creating interests, and States attempt to protect and advance their own objectives. In addition, the framework recognizes the potential for each of these bargaining relationships to be influenced by one or both of the others. For example, bargains struck between firms and government can affect the outcome of inter-governmental negotiations, and vice versa. The authors conclude that changes in each side of the triangle need to be taken into account if a satisfactory explanation is to be constructed.

In the context of EU trade policy, two additional sets of relationships should perhaps be included in the framework–'EU member state–Brussels' and 'foreign state–Brussels'. The form and outcome of negotiations is thus influenced by five sets of relationships, together with the range of potential agendas. Furthermore, with its emphasis on bargaining, the framework also suggests that outcomes may not necessarily appear rational, at least on first examination, but that even apparently irrational outcomes may be interpreted and understood in this wider context. An earlier study of the toy industry provides an excellent illustration (Newton, 1998). EU quotas were imposed on imports of Chinese toys largely to satisfy Spain's demands, but these were so damaging to UK commercial interests that the British government instigated legal action against the EU. EU trade policy would appear to be the result of bargains with individual EU member states that please some and anger others.

The silk case did not lead to legal action, but a similar pattern has emerged where policies that suited one member state were unsuitable for another. Italy, as the EU's remaining sizeable manufacturer of silk fabric and apparel, was clearly the major potential beneficiary of protectionist policies. Silk processing accounts for a large part of Italy's US$50 billion fashion business,[10] and employed 200 000 people in 1993, chiefly around Milan and Como. However other EU member states, including Germany and the UK, relied on imports of finished goods. Retailers such as Marks & Spencer were particularly affected. Hyvarinen (1993: 15) reports that a

> number of well known European and US fashion designers have a pro-
> portion of their collections of silk garments produced in China, in close
> co-operation with foreign technologists. Major department store groups,
> chain stores and mail order houses in the USA, Europe and Japan have
> also been co-operating closely with the Chinese in the production of silk
> garments and made-up goods for retail.

Thus a tightly linked supply chain had been developed, from the Chinese manufacturers through to the European retailers, that produced inexpensive silk goods to high-quality standards.

EU quotas on imported Chinese silk products were imposed in March 1994.[11] All national import quotas[12] should have been eliminated, or transformed into EU quotas, on 1 January 1993 as part of the new SEM regulations. But there was a delay because of strong differences between the 12 EU countries over a range of items including silk products. On 15 December 1993, the EU took the unprecedented decision to extend in principle the usage of quotas from textile items covered by the MFA to non-MFA textile items, and also to various non-textile items. But it was not until 8 February 1994 that the Council decided upon the specific products to be placed under restriction, and the size of the quotas. Meanwhile the USA and China had announced their new bilateral Textile Trade Agreement that provided, *inter alia*, for exports of Chinese silk clothing to the USA to be subject to agreed limits (Sung, 1994a). Apparently the European Commission had been prepared to negotiate a bilateral agreement on trade in silk, ramie and linen products, but the restrictions incorporated in the Sino–US Agreement (and the consequent fears of trade diversion) prompted the European side to include silk as one of the products to be placed under quantitative restriction.

The EU quotas on imported silk products were announced in the *Official Journal of the European Communities* on 10 March 1994, and took effect three days later (Sung, 1994b). Some form of quotas had been expected, but there were two surprising aspects. The first was the size of the 1994 quotas which were fixed by taking, on the one hand, the national quotas which had previously existed in countries such as Italy and France and, on the other, the actual imports for 1992 for those countries (e.g. the UK and Germany) which had no restrictions, 8000 tonnes were added to cover growth so that there were no cutbacks compared to 1992 (in contract for instance to the situations with regard to toys and footwear), but 1993 had been a boom year for Chinese exports. The quota levels were way below 1993 EU imports of many silk products – see Table 16.1 – let alone the contracted levels for 1994. For instance, silk dresses, blouses etc. (category 159) were allocated a quota of 3020 tonnes in 1994, whereas 1993 imports had been almost 5000 tonnes. Woven silk fabrics (category ex 136) were given a 1994 quota of 285 tonnes, against 1993 imports of over 1000 tonnes. And the 1994 quota for singlets, vests, etc. was only 98 tonnes against imports of 450 tonnes in 1993. The severe cutbacks caused serious problems for many EU importers who had already negotiated long-term supply contracts backed by irrevocable letters of credit, yet were unable to obtain the required import licences. UK industry sources suggested that the new levels were so low that the whole EU quota for silk shirts could be filled by a single UK importer.[13] The second curious aspect of the new quota system was the system for their administration. The MFA textile trade is regulated on an export-quota system, yet the new quotas were to be allocated by the European Commission, who had no previous experience of administering such a system. The quotas were to be allocated by Brussels on a 'first-come, first-served' basis, and this further fuelled suspicions of chaos.

So why were the quotas set at such low levels, why did the EU act uni-laterally and why did the Commission take on the responsibility for administering the quotas? One explanation for the low volumes could be that 'the EU seriously misjudged the size of trade flows',[14] and apparently 1993 import data were not available for all 12 EU countries when the quotas were fixed (Subhan, 1994). But this explanation does not tell the whole story. Rather it appears that the new quotas were a pure political compromise inside the Council of Ministers to obtain the agreement of France, Portugal and others at the end of the Uruguay Round of multilateral trade negotiations (Sung, 1994b: 11). This would also explain why the quotas were agreed in principle some time before their size and even the products to be placed under restriction were specified.

Furthermore there appears to have been an element of discrimination against China in that, even though new quotas were simultaneously introduced on imports from North Korea and the states of the former Yugoslavia, it was Chinese exports which bore the brunt of the new measures. Certainly this was the perception of the Chinese officials, who suggested that the quotas were deliberately set low as part of a longer-term trade negotiating strategy.[15] This is not implausible given the timing of the quotas, imposed as China's application to resume its membership of the GATT, and hence join the World Trade Organization (WTO) as a founder member, was being actively pursued (Strange, 1998: 32–6). Once China became a WTO member, any new quota protection would be prohibited unless extended as a temporary measure in response to 'market disruption'. But market disruption would be difficult to prove in the silk industry. So the quotas were introduced unilaterally and in haste before China could become a WTO member, as any pre-existing quotas could be maintained for some years after accession. One objective of this strategy was clearly the protection of the Italian and French silk industries. Also part of the agenda, it would appear, was the aim of further opening Chinese markets to European exports. Following China's anticipated accession to the WTO, such as bargaining strategy would be impossible.

The Chinese side were clearly angered by the quotas, and bilateral negotiations were subsequently conducted with the EU. Pressure was also brought by the European importers, many of whom were unable to satisfy their contracts. In July 1994, it was reported that

> China condemned recent quotas imposed by the European Union on its exports of products including toys and silk and warned yesterday that the curbs would immediately backfire. Mr Wu Jianmin, spokesman for the Chinese Foreign Ministry, speaking in Germany, said the EU restrictions did not send the right signals to China. 'If you want China to import more from Europe, then you should make it possible for China to export more to Europe . . . But if you introduce import quotas you will suffer ultimately.'[16]

After nine months of negotiations, a two-year bilateral Agreement on trade in non-MFA textiles was finally initialled on 19 January 1995 (Sung, 1995a: 10). The terms of the Agreement[17] provided for the system of uni- lateral import quotas to be changed into a system of bilateral export quotas. The administration of the system would be in the hands of the Chinese authorities rather than the European Commission. Furthermore, the agree- ment envisaged substantial increases in the 1995 and 1996 quotas over the levels announced for 1994 – see Table 16.1. For instance, the quota for silk blouses, pullovers, etc. (156) was raised from 760 tonnes in 1994 to 2588 tonnes in 1995, and the Agreement included special measures against fraud, including illegal transhipping through Hong Kong. Handing control back to China was a reversion to the norms under existing textiles and clothing bilateral agreements. There were, however, later accusations that China was still illegally transhipping through Hong Kong, taking advantage of the ter- ritory's exclusion from any form of quotas on silk,[18] though the accusations were hotly denied by the Hong Kong government.[19]

CONCLUSIONS

Three questions were posed at the start of this chapter. The analysis of the value chain in silk production has enabled considerable progress to be made towards providing answers, though further research is required on some of the detail. As regards the first question, it appears that the EU quotas were set at punitive levels in 1994 in a crude attempt to force the Chinese author- ities to open their markets to European exports. As regards the second question, it was partly the threat of retaliation from the Chinese side, and partly the protests of the EU retailers, that forced the Commission to raise the import quotas for 1995 even though such increases were contrary to the interests of the EU silk garment manufacturers. As regards the third question, it appears that speed and a desire to prevent circumvention of the quotas provide the answer to why the Commission only belatedly agreed to negotiate bilaterally with the Chinese authorities.

Two final points may be made. The first is to reiterate the importance of the silk industry as a source of foreign exchange for China. Furthermore, in contrast to much of Chinese manufacturing industry that is geared to export but which is dependent upon foreign capital and foreign supplies of parts, etc., both the technology and the inputs to silk production are largely Chinese, with the result that the *net* foreign exchange benefit is substantial. The second is to draw attention to another curious aspect of EU trade policy regarding imports of Chinese raw silk. In January 1980, the then European Community (EC) and China implemented an Agreement on bilateral trade in textile products. The Agreement permitted significantly increased access for Chinese textile products to the EC market, but also included a number of concessions to EC wishes including an undertaking by China (Article 11) to supply minimum guaranteed quantities of certain textile raw materials (such as raw silk, cashmere and angora) to the EC industry at the normal trade price (Strange, 1998: 68). The Textile Agreement has been subsequently amended, renegotiated and extended, but it still includes this *minimum* restriction on imports of raw silk. Why and how this requirement came to be enshrined in the Agreement, and if or how the negotiations on import quotas on finished silk goods are influenced by the existence of this requirement are questions for further research. The EU garment manufacturers clearly need supplies of raw silk from China, as China is to all intents and purposes a monopoly supplier, and this clearly puts a bargaining constraint on the process of establishing import quotas on finished garments.

Notes

1. About 70 per cent of the silk imported into Europe involves Swiss traders, either directly or indirectly. It may be bonded in Swiss warehouses, or invoiced in Switzerland even though delivered direct to buyers in other European countries (Hyvarinen, 1993: 26–7).
2. It was in China that the silkmoth and the white mulberry, the only food plant of the silkmoth, coexisted naturally (Feltwell, 1991: 8). Hyvarinen (1993: 9) reports evidence of a written Chinese symbol for silk as early as 2000 BC.
3. Hyvarinen (1993: 9) notes that 'by the 14th century, three Italian cities, Genoa, Florence and Lucca, had become important centres for silk weaving. By the end of the 18th century the French city Lyon had 1800 silk looms.'
4. The raw silk trade has been estimated as financing more than 40 per cent of Japan's

entire imports of foreign machinery and raw materials between 1870 and 1930 (Li, 1982: 197–8).

5. Hyvarinen (1993: 28) also suggests that an additional factor in the decline of raw silk production in Japan was that the post-war heirs to the cocoon farmers were unwilling to accept the harsh life of a silkworm breeder.

6. Industry sources in Hong Kong.

7. Ibid.

8. *Financial Times* (3 October 1991), p. 33.

9. Industry sources in Hong Kong.

10. *Financial Times* (18 April 1998), p. 10.

11. *Financial Times* (16 March 1994), p. 7.

12. Both Italy and France had in place national quotas that restricted Chinese silk imports.

13. *Financial Times* (16 March 1994), p. 7.

14. *Financial Times* (16 March 1994).

15. *Financial Times* (6 March 1995), p. 5.

16. *Financial Times* (5 July 1994), p. 6.

17. See the 'Agreement between the European Community and the People's Republic of China on trade in textile products not covered by the MFA bilateral Agreement on trade in textile products initialled on 9 December 1988 as extended and modified by the exchange of letters initialled on 8 December 1992', *Official Journal of the European Communities*, L104 (6 May 1995).

18. *Financial Times* (19 April 1995), p. 8.

19. *Financial Times* (3 May 1995), p. 20.

Bibliography

Adler, N. (1994) 'Competitive frontiers: women managing across borders', in N. Adler and D. Izraeli (eds), *Competitive Frontiers: Women in a Global Economy*, (Cambridge, MA and Oxford: Blackwell).

Adler, N.J. (1991) *International Dimensions of Organizational Behaviour* (Boston: PWS–Kent).

Adler, N.J. and Bartholomew, S. (1992) 'Managing globally competent people', *Academy of Management Review*, 6, pp. 52–64.

Adler, N.J., and Ghadar, F. (1990) 'Strategic human resource management: a global perspective', in R. Pieper (ed.), *Human Resource Management in International Comparison* (Berlin and New York: De Gruyter).

Adler, N.J., Dokter, R. and Redding, S.G. (1986) 'From the Atlantic to the Pacific centre: cross-cultural management reviews', *Journal of Management*, 12(2), pp. 295–318.

Adnett, R. (1996) *European Labour Markets: Analysis and Policy* (London: Longman).

Agarwal, S. and Ramaswami, S.N. (1992) 'Choice of foreign market entry mode: impact of ownership, location and internalization factors', *Journal of International Business Studies*, 23(1), pp. 1–27.

Aiello, P. (1991) 'Building a joint venture in China: the case of Chrysler and the Beijing Jeep Corporation', *Journal of General Management*, 17(2), pp. 47–64.

Ali, S. and Mizra, H. (1998) 'Entry mode and performance in Hungary and Poland: the case of British firms', in G. Hooley, R. Loveridge and D. Wilson (eds), *Internationalization: Process, Context and Markets* (Basingstoke: Macmillan), pp. 176–220.

Amin, A., Bradley, D., Howells, J., Tomaney, J. and Gentle, C. (1994) 'Regional incentives and the quality of mobile investment in the less favoured regions of the EC', *Progress in Planning*, 41(1).

Andersen, O. (1993) 'On the internationalization process of firms: a critical analysis', *Journal of International Business Studies*, 24(2), pp. 209–31.

Anderson, E. and Gatignon, H. (1986) 'Modes of foreign entry: a transactions cost analysis and propositions', *Journal of International Business Studies*, 17(3), pp. 1–26.

Antonelli, C. (1995) 'Technological change and multinational growth in international telecommunication services', *Review of Industrial Organization*, 10, pp. 161–80.

Auster, E. (1992) 'The relationship of industry evolution to the patterns of technology linkages, joint ventures, and direct investment between US and Japan', *Management Science*, 38(6), pp. 778–92.

Badaracco, J.L. (1991) *The Knowledge Link: How Firms Compete through Strategic Alliances* (Cambridge, MA: Harvard Business School Press).

Bae, J., Chen, S.-J. and Lawler, J.J. (1998) 'Variations in human resource management in Asian countries: MNC home-country and host-country effects', *International Journal of Human Resource Management*, 9(4), pp. 653–70.

Baglione, L.A. and Clark, C.L. (1997) 'A tale of two metallurgical enterprises', *Communist and Post Communist Studies*, 30(2), pp. 153–80.

Baird, I.S., Lyles, M., Ji, S. and Wharton, R. (1990) 'Joint venture success: a Sino–US perspective', *International Journal of Management and Organisation*, 20(1–2), pp. 125–34.

Bakhtari, H. (1995) 'Cultural effects on management style', *International Studies of Management and Organization*, 25(3), pp. 97–118.

Banco de Portugal various years *Relatórios Anuais* (Annual Reports).

Barnett, W.P. (1993) 'Strategic deterrence among multiple point competitors', *Industrial and Corporate Change*, 2, pp. 249–78.

Barney, J.B. (1986) 'Strategic factors markets: expectations, luck, and business strategy', *Management Science*, 32, pp. 1231–41.

Barney, J.B. (1991) 'Firm resources and sustained competitive advantage', *Journal of Management*, 17(1), pp. 99–120.

Barrell, R. and Pain, N. (1997) 'Foreign direct investment, technological change, and economic growth within Europe', *Economic Journal*, 107, pp. 1770–86.

Bartels, F. (1998) 'Strategic management interaction between French multinational enterprises and subsidiaries in sub-Saharan Africa', in P. Buckley, F. Burton and H. Mizra (eds), *The Strategy and Organization of International Business* (Basingstoke: Macmillan), pp. 36–54.

Bartlett, C. (1981) 'Multinational structural change: evolution versus reorganization', in L. Otterbeck (ed.), *The Management of Headquarters–Subsidiary Relationships in Multinational Corporations* (Aldershot: Gower).

Bartlett, C. and Ghoshal, S. (1986) 'Tap your subsidiaries for global reach', *Harvard Business Review*, November–December), pp. 87–94.

Bartlett, C.A. and Ghoshal, S. (1989) *Managing Across Borders: The Transnational Solution* (Cambridge, MA: Harvard University Press).

Bartlett, C.A. and Ghoshal, S. (1990) 'Managing innovation in the transnational corporation', in C.A. Bartlett, Y. Doz and G. Hedlund (eds), *Managing the Global Firm* (London: Routledge).

Beamish, P.R. (1993) 'The characteristics of joint ventures in the People's Republic of China', *Journal of International Marketing*, 1(2), pp. 29–48.

Beamish, P.W. (1984) 'Joint Venture Performance in Developing Countries', unpublished doctoral dissertation, University of Western Ontario.

Beamish, P.W. and Banks, J.C. (1987) 'Equity joint ventures and the theory of the multinational enterprise', *Journal of International Business Studies*, 18(2), pp. 1–16.

Beatson, M. (1995) *Labour Market Flexibility*, Research Series, 45 (London: Employment Department).

Beaumont, P.B. (1992) 'The US human resource management literature: a review', in G. Salaman (ed.), *Human Resource Strategies* (London: Sage), pp. 20–37.

Beekun, R.I. and Ginn, G.O. (1993) 'Business strategy and interorganizational linkages within the acute care hospital industry: an expansion of the Miles and Snow typology', *Human Relations*, 46(11), pp. 1291–318.

Beer, M., Spector, B., Lawrence, P., Mills, D. and Walton, R.E. (1984) *Managing Human Assets* (New York: Free Press).

Behrman, J.N. and Fischer, W.A. (1980) 'Transnational corporations: market orientations and R&D abroad', *Columbia Journal of World Business*, 15, pp. 55–60.

Berg, S.V., Duncan, J. and Friedman, P. (1982) *Joint Venture Strategies and Corporate Innovation* (Cambridge, MA: Oelgeschlager).

Birkinshaw, J.M. (1996) 'How multinational subsidiary mandates are gained and lost', *Journal of International Business Studies*, 27(3), pp. 467–95.

Birkinshaw, J. and Hood, N. (1997) 'An empirical study of development processes in foreign-owned subsidiaries in Canada and Scotland', *Management International Review*, 37(4), pp. 339–64.

Birkinshaw, J. and Hood, N. (1998) 'The determinants of subsidiary mandates and subsidiary initiative: a three country study', in G. Hooley, R. Loveridge and D. Wilson (eds), *Internationalization: Process, Context and Markets* (Basingstoke: Macmillan), pp. 29–55.

Birkinshaw, J.M. and Hood, N. (1998) *Multinational Corporate Evolution and Subsidiary Development* (London: Macmillan).

Björkman, I. and Forsgren, M. (eds) (1997) *The Nature of the International Firm* (Copenhagen: Copenhagen Business School Press).
Black, J.S. (1988) 'Work role transitions: a study of American expatriate managers in Japan', *Journal of International Business Studies*, 30(2), pp. 119–34.
Black, J.S., Gregerson, H. and Mendenhall, M. (1993) *Global Assignments* (San Fransisco: Jossey-Bass).
Blasi, J.R., Kroumova, M. and Kruse, D. (1997) *Kremlin Capitalism: Privatizing the Russian Economy* (Ithaca: Cornell University Press).
Blodgett, L.L. (1991a) 'Partner contributions as predictors of equity share in international joint ventures', *Journal of International Business Studies*, 22(1), pp. 63–78.
Blodgett, L.L. (1991b) 'Toward a resource-based theory of bargaining power in international joint ventures', *Journal of Global Marketing*, 5(1-2), pp. 35–54.
Blyton, P. and Turnbull, F. (eds), (1992) *Reassessing Human Resource Management* (London: Sage).
Boisot, M. and Child, J. (1988) 'The iron law of fiefs: bureaucratic failure and the problem of government in the Chinese economic reforms', *Administrative Science Quarterly*, 33, pp. 507–27.
Borensztein, E., de Gregorio, J. and Lee, J.W. (1995) 'How Does Foreign Direct Investment Affect Economic Growth?', *NBER Working Paper*, 5057.
Boseman, F.G. and Phatak, A. (1978) 'Management practices of industrial enterprises in Mexico: a comparative study', *Management International Review*, 18(1), pp. 43–8.
Boulton, L. (1994) 'Few rooms with views – building and managing hotels in Russia', *Financial Times* (7 January), p. 21.
Boxall, P. (1992) 'Strategic human resource management', *Human Resource Management Journal*, 2(3), pp. 60–79.
Boxall, P. (1993) 'The significance of human resource management', *International Journal of Human Resource Management*, 3(4), pp. 645–64.
Boxall, P. (1995) 'Building the theory of comparative HRM', *Human Resource Management Journal*, 5(1), pp. 5–17.
Brandt, K. and Hulbert, J. (1976) 'Patterns of communications in the multinational corporation: an empirical study', *Journal of International Business Studies*, 7, pp. 57–64.
Bresser, R.K. and Harl, J.E. (1986) 'Collective strategy: vice or virtue?', *Academy of Management Review*, 11, pp. 408–27.
Brewster, C. (1991) *The Management of Expatriates* (London: Kogan Page).
Brewster, C. (1993) 'European human resource management: reflection of, or challenge to, the American concept?', in P. Kirkbride (ed.), *Human Resource Management in the New Europe of the 1990s* (London: Routledge).
Brewster, C. (1995) 'Towards a "European Model" of human resource management', *Journal of International Business*, 26, pp. 1–22.
Brewster, C. and Bournois, F. (1991) 'Human resource management: a European perspective', *Personnel Review*, 20(1), pp. 4–13.
Brewster, C. and Harris, H. (1999) *International HRM: Contemporary Issues in Europe* (London: Routledge).
Brewster, C. and Hegewisch, A. (1994) *Policy and Practice in European Human Resource Management: The Price Waterhouse Cranfield Survey* (London: Routledge).
Brewster, C. and Larsen, H.H. (1993) 'Human resource management in Europe: evidence from ten countries', *International Journal of Human Resource Management*, 3(3), pp. 409–34.
Brewster, C. and Tyson, S. (eds) (1991) *International Comparisons in Human Resource Management* (London: Pitman).
Brewster, C., Tregaskis, O., Hegewisch, A. and Mayne, L. (1996) 'Comparative research

in human resource management: a review and an example', *International Journal of Human Resource Management*, 7(4), pp. 586–604.

Briggs, P. (1991) 'Organisational commitment: the key to Japanese success?', in C. Brewster and S. Tyson (eds), *International Comparisons in Human Resource Management* (London: Pitman Publishing), pp. 33–43.

Brouthers, K.D. and Bamossy, G.J. (1997) 'The role of key stakeholders in international joint venture negotiations: case studies from Eastern Europe', *Journal of International Business Studies*, 28, pp. 285–308.

Brouthers, K.D., Brouthers, L.E. and Nakos, G. (1998) 'Entering Central and Eastern Europe: risks and cultural barriers', *Thunderbird International Business Review*, 40(3), pp. 485–504.

Brown, R. and Raines, P. (1999) 'FDI policy approaches in Western Europe', in P. Raines and R. Brown (eds), *Policy Competition and Foreign Direct Investment in Europe* (Avebury: Ashgate).

Buck, T., Filatotchev, I. and Wright, M. (1996) 'Buyouts and the transformation of Russian industry', in F. Burton, M. Yamin and S. Young (eds), *International Business and Europe in Transition* (Basingstoke: Macmillan), pp. 145–67.

Buck, T.W., Filatotchev, I. and Wright, M. (1998) 'Agents, stakeholders and corporate governance in Russian privatized firms', *Journal of Management Studies*, 35(1), pp. 81–104.

Buckley, P.J. (1988) 'The limits of explanation: testing the internalization theory of the multi-national enterprise', *Journal of International Business Studies*, 19, pp. 181–93.

Buckley, P.J. and Casson, M.C. (1976) *The Future of the Multinational Enterprise* (London: Macmillan).

Buckley, P.J. and Casson, M. (1988) 'A theory of co-operation in international business', in F.J. Contractor and P. Lorange (eds), *Co-operative Strategies in International Business* (Lexington, MA: Lexington Books).

Buckley, P.J. and Castro, F.B. (1998) 'A time-series analysis of the locational determinants of FDI in Portugal', paper submitted to the annual conference of the Academy of International Business (Vienna, October).

Budhwar, P. (1997) 'Methodological considerations in crosss national human resource management research', *Management and Labour Studies*, 22, pp. 13–25.

Budhwar, P. and Sparrow, P. (1998) 'National factors determining Indian and British HRM practices: an empirical study', *Management International Review*, 38(2), pp. 105–21.

Burgers, W.P., Hill, C.W. and Kim, C.W. (1993) 'A theory of global strategic alliances: the case of the global auto industry', *Strategic Management Journal*, 14, pp. 419–32.

Burt, T. (1998) 'Assi Domain in Russia move', *Financial Times* (18 December), p. 23.

Burton, F. and Noble, D. (1996) 'European cooperative ventures between Spanish and UK firms', in F. Burton, M. Yamin and S. Young (eds), *International Business and Europe in Transition* (Basingstoke: Macmillan), pp. 109–21.

Bylov, G. and Sutherland, D. (1998) 'Understanding regional patterns of economic change in Russia – statistical overview', *Communist Economics and Economic Transformation*, 10(3).

Cainarca, G.C., Colombo, M.G. and Mariotti, S. (1992) 'Agreements between firms and the technological life cycle model: evidence from information technologies', *Research Policy*, 21, pp. 45–62.

Caligiuri, P.M. and Stroh, L.K. (1995) 'Multinational corporation management strategies and international human resources practices: bringing international human resources management to the bottom line', *International Journal of Human Resource Management*, 6(3), pp. 495–507.

Cameron, K.S. and Whetten, D.A. (1981) 'Perceptions of organizational effectiveness over organizational life cycles', *Administrative Science Quarterly*, 26, pp. 525–44.

Campbell, N.C.G. (1989) *A Strategic Guide to Equity Joint Ventures in China* (Oxford: Pergamon Press).

Casson, M. and Cox, H. (1997) 'An economic model of inter-firm networks', in M. Ebers (ed.), *The Formation of Inter-Organisational Networks*, (Oxford: Oxford University Press), pp. 174–96.

Casson, M., Loveridge, R. and Singh, S. (1998) 'Human resource management in the multinational enterprise: styles, modes, institutions and ideologies', in G. Hooley, R. Loveridge and D. Wilson (eds), *Internationalization: Process, Context and Markets* (Basingstoke: Macmillan), pp. 158–70.

Casson, M., Pearce, R.D. and Singh, S. (1991) 'Business strategy and overseas R&D', in M. Casson (ed.), *Global Strategy and International Competitiveness* (Oxford: Basil Blackwell).

Castells, M. (1989) *The Informational City* (Oxford: Basil Blackwell).

Castles, S. and Miller, J. (1993) *The Age of Migration – International Population Movements in the Modern World* (London: Macmillan).

Caves, R. (1996) *Multinational Firms and Economic Analysis* (Cambridge: Cambridge University Press) (1st edn 1982).

Caves, R.E. (1982) *Multinational Enterprise and Economic Analysis* (Cambridge: Cambridge University Press).

CEC (1995) 'Flexibility and work organization', *Social Europe*, Supplement 1 (Brussels: Commission of the European Communities).

Chen, M. (1996) 'Competitor analysis and inter-firm rivalry: toward a theoretical integration', *Academy of Management Review*, 21, pp. 100–34.

Chen, M. and Hambrick, D.C. (1995) 'Speed, stealth, and selective attack: how small firms differ from large firms in competitive behaviour', *Academy of Management Journal*, 38, pp. 453–82.

Cheng, J.L.C. and Bolton, D.S. (1993) 'The management of multinational R&D: a neglected topic', *Journal of International Business Studies*, 24(1), pp. 1–18.

Chi, T. (1994) 'Trading in strategic resources: necessary conditions, transaction cost problems, and choice of exchange structure', *Strategic Management Journal*, 15(4), pp. 271–90.

Child, J. and Lu, Y. (1990) 'Industrial decision-making under China's reform: 1985–1988', *Organisation Studies*, 11, pp. 321–51.

Chmelyev, A. (1998) 'Advice to foreign investors', *Russian Commerce News*, 6(2), pp. 1–6.

Clarke, C. and Varma, S. (1999) 'Strategic risk management: the new competitive edge', *Long Range Planning*, 32(4), pp. 414–24.

Clegg, J. (1996) 'US foreign direct investment in the EU – the effects of market integration in perspective', in F. Burton, M. Yamin and S. Young (eds), *International Business and Europe in Transition* (Basingstoke: Macmillan), pp. 189–206.

Coase, R.H. (1937) 'The nature of the firm', *Economica* (*NS*), 4, pp. 386–405.

Commumcations Week International (1997)

Commumcations Week International (1998), 27 July.

Commumcations Week International (1999), 15 November.

Contractor, F.J. and Lorange, P. (1988) *Co-operative Strategies in International Business* (Lexington, MA: D.C. Heath).

Cook, P. and Kirkpatrick, C. (1996) 'Privatization in transitional economies – East and Central European experience', in F. Burton, M. Yamin and S. Young (eds), *International Business and Europe in Transition* (Basingstoke: Macmillan), pp. 168–83.

D'Cruz, J. (1986) 'Strategic management of subsidiaries', in H. Etemad and L. Séguin-

Dulude (eds), *Managing the Multinational Subsidiary* (London: Croom Helm), pp. 75–89.

Davidson, W.H. (1987) 'Creating and managing joint ventures in China', *California Management Review*, 29, pp. 77–94.

Davis, J., Patterson, D. and Grazin, I. (1996) 'The collapse and reemergence of networks within and between republics of the Former Soviet Union', *International Business Review*, 5(1), pp. 1–21.

De Meyer, A. (1993) 'Management of an international network of industrial R&D laboratories', *R&D Management*, 23(2), pp. 109–20.

De Meyer, A., Nakane, J., Miller, J.G. and Ferdows, K. (1989) 'Flexibility: the next competitive battle', *Strategic Management Journal*, 10, pp. 135–44.

Deal, T. and Kennedy, A. (1982) *Corporate Cultures: The Rites and Rituals of Corporate Life* (Reading: Addison-Wesley).

Desatnick, R.L. and Bennett, M.L. (1978) *Human Resource Management in the Multinational Company* (New York: Nicols).

Dess, G. and Davis, P. (1984) 'Porter's (1980) generic strategies as determinants of strategic group membership and organizational performance', *Academy of Management Journal*, 27, pp. 467–88.

Dicken, P. (1988) 'The changing geography of Japanese direct investment in manufacturing industry: a global perspective', *Environment and Planning A*, 20, pp. 633–53.

Ding, D.Z. (1997) 'Control, conflict, and performance: a study of US–Chinese joint ventures', *Journal of International Marketing*, 5(3), pp. 31–45.

Döhrn, R. (1996) 'Direktinvestitionen und Sachkapitalbildung – Statistische Unterschiede und ihre ökonomischen Implikationen', *RWI-Mitteilungen*, 47, pp. 19–34.

Dong, H., Buckley, P. and Mizra, H. (1997) 'International joint ventures in China from a managerial perspective: a comparison between different sources of investment', in G. Chryssochoidis, C. Millar and J. Clegg (eds), *Internationalisation Strategies* (Basingstoke: Macmillan), pp. 171–91.

Douglas, S.P. and Craig, C.S. (1983) 'Examining performance of US multinationals in foreign markets', *Journal of International Business Studies*, 14(3), pp. 51–62.

Dowling, P.J. (1989) 'Hot issues overseas', *Personnel Administrator*, 34(1), pp. 66–72.

Doz, Y.L. (1976) *National Policies and Multinational Management*, DBA dissertation, cited in J. Roure, J.A. Alvarez, C. Garcia-Pont and J. Nueno, 'Managing international dimensions of the managerial task', *European Management Journal*, 11 (1993), pp. 485–92.

Doz, Y.L. and Hamel, G. (1998) *The Alliance Advantage: The Art of Creating Value for Partnering* (Cambridge, MA: Harvard Business School Press).

Dunning, J.H. (1958) *American Investment in British Manufacturing Industry* (London: George Allen & Unwin, 1958) (new revised and updated edn, London: Routledge, 1998).

Dunning, J.H. (1977) 'Trade, location of the economic activity and the MNE: a search for an eclectic approach', in B. Ohlin, P.-O. Hesselborn and P.-M. Wijkman (eds), *The International Location of Economic Activity: Proceedings of a Nobel Symposium held at Stockholm* (London: Macmillan), pp. 395–418.

Dunning, J.H. (1981) *International Production and the Multinational Enterprise* (London: George Allen & Unwin).

Dunning, J.H. (1988) 'The eclectic paradigm of international production: a restatement and some possible extensions', *Journal of International Business Studies*, 19, pp. 1–31.

Dunning, J.H. (1988) *Explaining International Production* (London: Unwin Hyman).

Dunning, J.H. (1993) *Multinational Enterprises and the Global Economy* (Wokingham and Reading, MA: Addison-Wesley).

Dunning, J.H. (1994) 'Multinational enterprises and the globalization of innovatory capacity', *Research Policy*, 19, pp. 392–403.

Dunning, J.H. (1994) 'Re-evaluating the benefits of foreign direct investment', *Transnational Corporations*, 3(1).

Dunning, J.H. (1997) *Governments, Globalisation and International Business* (Oxford: Oxford University Press).

Dunning, J.H. and Narula, R. (eds) (1996) *Foreign Direct Investment and Governments. Catalysts for Economic Restructuring* (London: Routledge).

Dunning, J.H. and Robson, P. (eds) (1988) *Multinationals and the European Community* (Oxford: Basil Blackwell).

Dussauge, P., Hart, S. and Ramanantsoa, B. (1992) *Strategy Technological Management* (New York: John Wiley).

Dyer, J.H. and Singh, H. (1998) 'The relational view: co-operative strategy and sources of interorganizational competitive advantage', *Academy of Management Review*, 23(4), pp. 660–79.

Economist (1993) 'The Enemy Within', (12 June), pp. 91–2.

Egelhoff, W.G. (1988) 'Strategy and structure in multinational corporations: a revision of the Stopford and Wells model', *Strategic Management Journal*, 9, pp. 1–14.

Egelhoff, W.G., Gorman, L. and McCormick, S. (1998) 'Using technology as a path to subsidiary development', in J.M. Birkinshaw and N. Hood, *Multinational Corporate Evolution and Subsidiary Development* (London: Macmillan).

Eisenhardt, K.M. (1989) 'Building theories from case study research', *Academy of Management Review*, 14, pp. 532–50.

Ela, J.D. and Irwin, M.R. (1983) 'Technology changes market boundaries', *Industrial Marketing Management* 12, pp. 153–6.

Eng, R.Y. (1984) 'Chinese entrepreneurs, the government, and the foreign sector: the Canton and Shanghai silk-reeling enterprises, 1861–1932', *Modern Asian Studies*, 18(3), pp. 353–70.

Ernst & Young (1997) *The Single Market Review: Impact on Manufacturing Motor Vehicles*, Subseries 1, Volume 6 (Luxembourg: Office for Official Publications of the European Communities).

Estrin, S. and Wright, M. (1999) 'Corporate governance in the former Soviet Union: an overview of the issues', *Journal of Comparative Economics*, 27(3), pp. 398–419.

Estrin, S., *et al.* (eds) (1995) *Restructuring and Privatization in Central Eastern Europe: Case Studies of Firms in Transition*, (New York: M. E. Sharp).

Estrin, S., *et al.* (eds) (1997) (Case Study Reports on Bulgaria and Romania), *ACE-PHARE Research Project*, 91-0381-R.

European Bank for Reconstruction and Development (EBRD) (1997) *Transition Report 1997* (London: EBRD).

European Bank for Reconstruction and Development (EBRD) (1998) *Transition Report* (November).

Evans, P. and Doz, Y. (1992) 'Dualities: a paradigm for human resource and organizational development in complex multinationals', in V. Pucik, N.M. Tichy and C. Barnett (eds), *Globalizing Management: Creating and Leading the Competitive Organization* (New York: Wiley).

Evans, P. and Lorange, P. (1989) 'The two logics behind human resource management', in P. Evans, Y. Doz and A. Laurent (eds), *Human Resource Management in International Firms: Change, Globalization, Innovation* (London: Macmillan).

Evans, P., Doz, Y. and Laurent, A. (eds) (1989) *Human Resource Management in International Firms: Change, Globalization and Innovation* (London: Macmillan).

Farris, G.F. and Butterfield, D.A. (1972) 'Control theory in Brazilian organisations', *Administrative Science Quarterly*, 17(4), pp. 578–80.

Faulkner, D. (1998) 'The management of international strategic alliances', in P. Buckley, F. Burton and H. Mizra (eds), *The Strategy and Organization of International Business* (Basingstoke: Macmillan), pp. 128–48.

Feltwell, J. (1991) *The Story of Silk* (New York: St Martin's Press).

Ferdows, K., Miller, J.G., Nakane, J. and Vollmann, T.E. (1986) 'Evolving global manufacturing strategies: projections into the 1990s', *International Journal of Operations and Production Management*, 6, pp. 6–16.

Ferner, A. (1997) 'Country of origins effects and human resource management in multinational companies', *Human Resource Management Journal*, 7(1), pp. 19–37.

Fiegenbaum, A., Hart, S. and Schendel, D. (1996) 'Strategic reference point theory', *Strategic Management Journal*, 17, pp. 216–36.

Filatotchev, I.V., Buck, T. and Zhukov, V. (2000) 'Downsizing in privatized firms in Russia, Ukraine and Belarus: theory and empirical evidence', *Academy of Management Journal*.

Financial Times (1994) *Survey of European Property* (11 March), pp. 22–4.

Flaherty, N. (1997) 'The billion dollar bait', *Corporate Location*, January–February, pp. 16–17.

Florkowski, G. and Nath, R. (1993) 'MNC response to the legal environment of international human resource management', *International Journal of Human Resource Management*, 4(2), pp. 305–24.

Fombrun, C.J., Tichy, N.M. and Devanna, M.A. (1984) *Strategic Human Resource Management* (New York: John Wiley).

Form, W. (1979) 'Comparative industrial sociology and the convergence hypothesis', *Annual Review of Sociology*, 5(1), pp. 1–25.

Forsgren, M. and Johanson, J. (1992) *Managing Networks in International Business* (Philadelphia: Gordon & Breach).

Foster, N. (1997) 'The persistent myth of high expatriate rates: a reappraisal', *International Journal of Human Resource Management*, 8(4), pp. 414–33.

Foster, N. and Johnsen, M. (1996) 'Expatriate management policies in UK companies new to the international scene', *International Journal of Human Resource Management*, 7(1), pp. 176–204.

Franko, L.G. (1989) 'Global corporate competition: who's winning, who's losing, and the R&D factor as one reason why', *Strategic Management Journal*, 10, pp. 449–74.

Freeland, C., Thornhill, J. and Gowers, A. (1997) 'Moscow's Group of Seven', *Financial Times* (1 November), p. 2.

Friedman, T. (1999) *The Lexus and the Olive Tree* (London: HarperCollins).

Gaddy, C.G. and Ickes, B. (1998) 'Russia's virtual economy', *Foreign Affairs*, 77(5), pp. 53–68.

Galbraith, C. and Schendel, D. (1983) 'An empirical analysis of strategy types', *Strategic Management Journal*, 4, pp. 153–73.

Garnier, G.H. (1982) 'Context and decision making autonomy in the foreign affiliates of US multinational corporations', *Academy of Management Journal*, 25(4), pp. 893–908.

Gates, S.R. and Egelhoff, W.G. (1986) 'Centralization in headquarters–subsidiary relationships', *Journal of International Business Studies*, 17(2), pp. 71–92.

Geringer, J.M. (1988) *Joint Venture Partner Selection: Strategies for Developed Countries* (Westport, CN: Quorum Books).

Geringer, J.M. and Hebert, L. (1991) 'Measuring performance of international JVs', *Journal of International Business Studies*, 22(2), pp. 249–63.

Geroski, P.A. (1982) 'Simultaneous equations models of the structure-performance paradigm', *European Economic Review*, 19, pp. 145–58.

Ghoshal, S. and Bartlett, C.A. (1988) 'Creation, adoption and diffusion of innovations by subsidiaries of multinational corporations', *Journal of International Business Studies*, 19(3), pp. 365–88.

Giddens, A. (1990) *The Consequences of Modernity* (Cambridge: Polity Press).

Gimeno, J. and Woo, C. (1996) 'Hypercompetition in a multimarket environment: the role of strategic similarity and multimarket contact on competitive deescalation', *Organization Science*, 7, pp. 322–41.

Glasse, J. (1995) 'Textiles and clothing in China: competitive threat or investment opportunity?', *EIU Special Report*, 2638 (London: Textiles Intelligence Ltd.).

Glen, T.M. and James, C.F. Jr (1980) 'Difficulties in implementing management science techniques in third world settings', *Interfaces*, 10(1), pp. 39–44.

Gnan, L. and Songini, L. (1995) 'Management styles of a sample of Japanese manufacturing companies in Italy', *Management International Review*, 35(2), pp. 9–26.

Gomes-Casseres, B. (1989) 'Ownership structure of foreign subsidiaries, theory and evidence', *Journal of Economic Behaviour and Organisation*, 11, pp. 1–25.

Gomes-Casseres, B. (1994) 'Group versus group: how alliance networks compete', *Harvard Business Review*, 72(4), pp. 62–70.

Gomes-Casseres, B. (1996) *The Alliance Revolution: The New Shape of Business Rivalry* (Cambridge, MA: Harvard University Press).

Graack, C. (1996) 'Telecom operators in the European Union. Internationalization strategies and network alliances', *Telecommunications Policy*, 20(5), pp. 341–55.

Grandori, A. and Soda, G. (1995) 'Inter-firm networks: antecedents, mechanisms and forms', *Organization Studies*, 16, pp. 183–214.

Granovetter, M. (1985) 'Economic action and social structure: the problem of embeddedness', *American Journal of Sociology*, 93(3), pp. 481–510.

Grant, R.M. and Baden-Fuller, C. (1995) 'A knowledge based theory of inter-firm collaboration', *Academy of Management, Best Paper Proceedings*, pp. 17–21.

Grubb, D. and Wells, W. (1993) 'Employment regulation and patterns of work in EC countries', *OECD Economic Studies*, 21, pp. 8–58.

Guest, D. (1987) 'Human resource management and industrial relations', *Journal of Management Studies*, 24(5), pp. 503–21.

Guest, D. (1990) 'Human resource management and the American dream', *Journal of Management Studies*, 27(4), pp. 377–97.

Gulati, R. (1995) 'Does familiarity breed trust? The implications of repeated ties for contractual choice in alliances', *Academy of Management Journal*, 38, pp. 85–112.

Hagedoorn, J. (1993) 'Understanding the rationale of strategic technology partnering: interorganizational modes of co-operation and sectoral difference', *Strategic Management Journal*, 14, pp. 371–85.

Hall, E.T. (1977) *Beyond Culture* (New York: Doubleday).

Hall, E.T. (1989) *The Dance of Life: the Other Dimension of Time* (New York: Doubleday).

Hall, E.T. and Hall, M.R. (1990) *Understanding Cultural Differences* (Yarmouth, ME: Intercultural Press).

Hamel, G. (1991) 'Competition for competence and inter-partner learning within international strategic IORs', *Strategic Management Journal*, 12, pp. 83–103.

Hamel, G. and Prahalad, C.K. (1985) 'Do you really have a global strategy?', *Harvard Business Review*, July–August, pp. 139–48.

Hamel, G. and Prahalad, C.K. (1994) *Competing for the Future* (Cambridge, MA: Harvard Business School Press).

Hannah, M.T. and Freeman, J. (1989) *Organizational Ecology* (Cambridge, MA: Harvard University Press, 1989).

Hanoaka, M. (1986) *Setting up a Hypothesis of the Characteristics of Personnel Management* (Institute of Business Research, Daito Bunka University).

Hardill, I. (1997) 'Gender perspectives on expatriate work: empirical evidence from Great Britain', paper presented at the Association of American Geographers, Globalization and Locality Sessions (Fort Worth, Texas, 1993).

Harrigan, K.R. (1985) *Strategies for Joint Ventures* (Lexington, MA: Lexington Books).

Harrigan, K.R. (1988) 'Joint ventures and competitive strategy', *Strategic Management Journal*, 9, pp. 141–58.

Harris, H. (1993) 'Women in international management: opportunity or threat?', *Women in Management Review*, 8(5), pp. 9–14.

Harris, H. and Brewster, C. (1999) 'International human resource management: the European contribution', in C. Brewster and H. Harris (eds), *International HRM: Contemporary Issues in Europe* (London: Routledge), pp. 1–28.

Harvey-Jones, J. (1988) *Making it Happen: Reflections on Leadership* (London: Fontana).

Harwit, E. (1995) *China's Automobile Industry* (London: M.E. Sharpe).

Hassard, J. and Sharifi, S. (1989) 'Corporate culture and strategic change', *Journal of General Management*, 15(2), pp. 4–19.

Haug, P., Hood, N. and Young, S. (1983) 'R&D intensity in the affiliates of US-owned electronics companies manufacturing in Scotland', *Regional Studies*, 17, pp. 383–92.

Hay, D.A. and Morris, D.J. (1979) *Industrial Economics: Theory and Evidence* (Oxford: Oxford University Press).

Hedlund, G. (1981) 'Autonomy of subsidiaries and formalisation of headquarters–subsidiary relationships in Swedish MNCs', in L. Otterbeck (ed.), *The Management of Headquarters–Subsidiary Relations in Multinational Corporations*, (Aldershot: Gower).

Heenan, D.A. and Perlmutter, H. (1979) *Multinational Organisation Development* (Reading, MA: Addison-Wesley).

Hendry, C. (1994) *Human Resource Strategies for International Growth* (London: Routledge).

Hendry, C. and Pettigrew, A.M. (1986) 'The practice of strategic human resource management', *Personnel Review*, 15(5), pp. 3–8.

Hendry, C. and Pettigrew, A.M. (1990) 'Human resource management: an agenda for the 1990s', *International Journal of Human Resource Management*, 1(1), pp. 17–43.

Hendry, C. and Pettigrew, A.M. (1992) 'Patterns of strategic change in the development of human resource management', *British Journal of Management*, 3(1), pp. 137–56.

Hendry, C., Pettigrew, A.M. and Sparrow, P.R. (1989) 'Linking strategic change, competitive performance and human resource management: results of a UK empirical study', in R. Mansfield (ed.), *Frontiers of Management Research* (London: Routledge).

Hendryx, S.R. (1986) 'Implementation of a technology transfer joint venture in the People's Republic of China: a management perspective', *Columbia Journal of World Business*, 21, pp. 57–66.

Hennart, J.F. (1982) *A Theory of Multinational Enterprise* (Ann Arbor: University of Michigan Press).

Hennart, J.F. (1991) 'The transaction costs theory of joint ventures: an empirical study of Japanese subsidiaries in the United States', *Management Science*, 37(4), pp. 483–97.

Hickson, D.J., Hunnings, C.R., McMillan, C.J.M. and Schwitter, J.P. (1974) 'The culture-free context of organization structure: a tri-national comparison', *Sociology*, 8(1), pp. 59–80.

Hill, C. (1990) 'Co-operation, opportunism, and the invisible hand: implications for transaction cost theory', *Academy of Management Review*, 15, pp. 500–13.

Hill, C.W.L., Hwang, P. and Kim, W.C. (1990) 'An eclectic theory of the choice of international entry mode,' *Strategic Management Journal*, 11, pp. 117–28.

Hill, S. and Munday, M. (1991) 'The determinants of inward investment: a Welsh analysis', *Applied Economics*, 23, pp. 1761–9.

Hirschhausen, C. and Hui, W. (1995) 'Industrial restructuring in the Baltic countries: large-scale privatisation, new enterprise networks and growing diversity of corporate governance', *Communist Economies and Economic Transformation*, 7(4), pp. 421–43.

Hofstede, G. (1980) *Culture's Consequences: International Differences in Work-related Values* (Beverly Hills: Sage).

Hofstede, G. (1991) *Cultures and Organizations: Software of the Mind* (London: McGraw-Hill).

Hollinshead, G. and Leat, M. (1995) *Human Resource Management: An International Perspective* (London: Pitman).

Holm, D., Blankenburg, D. and Johanson, J. (1997) 'Business network connections and the atmosphere of international business relationships', in I. Bjorkman and M. Forsgren (eds), *The Nature of the International Firm* (Denmark: Copenhagen Business School Press).

Hood, N. and Young, S. (1988) 'Inward investment and the EC: UK evidence on corporate integration strategies', in J.H. Dunning and P. Robson (eds), *Multinationals and the European Community* (Oxford: Basil Blackwell).

Hooley, G., Cox, A., Beracs, J., Fonfara, K. and Snoj, B. (1998) 'The role of foreign direct investment in the transition process in Central and Eastern Europe', in G. Hooley, R. Loveridge and D. Wilson (eds), *Internationalization: Process, Context and Markets* (Basingstoke: Macmillan), pp. 176–200.

Hoon-Halbauer, S.K. (1994) *Management of Sino-Foreign Joint Ventures* (Lund: Lund University Press).

Hrebiniak, L.G. and Joyce, W.F. (1985) 'Organizational adaptation: strategic choice and environmental determinism', *Administrative Science Quarterly*, 30, pp. 336–49.

Hu, A.M.Y. and Chen, H. (1996) 'An empirical analysis of factors explaining foreign joint venture performance in China', *Journal of Business Research*, 35, pp. 165–73.

Huang, T.C. (1999) 'The parent control of American, German and Japanese subsidiaries in Taiwan', conference proceedings of the Academy of International Business–UK Chapter, University of Stirling (April 1999).

Huczynski, A. and Buchanan, D. (1997) *Organizational Behaviour*, 3rd edn (London, Prentice-Hall).

Hughes, M. and Helinska-Hughes, E. (1998) 'FDI attraction policy in Central and Eastern Europe', *Conference Proceedings of the 25th Annual Conference of the Academy of International Business* (April), pp. 290–302.

Hunya, G. (1997) 'Large privatisation, restructuring and foreign direct investment', in Z. Salvatore (ed.), *Lessons from the Economic Transition: Central and Eastern Europe in the 1990s* (London: Kluwer Academic).

Hurdley, L.H. and White, P.E. (1999) 'Japanese investment and the creation of expatriate communities', *Euro Japanese Journal*, 2, pp. 17–21.

Hyakuya, J. (1994) 'Japanese automobile manufacturing in the UK: a Japanese perspective', paper presented at the Japan and the UK Economy: Opportunities and Challenges symposium, Coventry Business School (December 1994).

Hymer, S. (1960) *The International Operations of National Firms: A Study of Direct Investment* (Cambridge, MA: MIT Press).

Hyvarinen, A. (1993) 'Trends in the world silk market', *Textile Outlook International*, 47, pp. 9–59.

IBB (1996) *Review of Operations* (London: Invest in Britain Bureau, Department of Trade and Industry).

Inkpen, A.C. and Crossan, M.M. (1995) 'Believing is seeing: joint ventures and organizational learning', *Journal of Management Studies*, 32, pp. 594–617.

Institute for the Economy in Transition (1999) *Russian Economy: Trends and Perspectives* (Moscow: Russian Federation) (March), pp. 1–4.

International Bank for Reconstruction and Development (1996a) *From Plan to Market: World Development Report* (Washington, DC: IBRD).

International Bank for Reconstruction and Development (1996b) *Trends in Developing Countries* (Washington, DC: IBRD).

Islam, S. (1995) 'A new deal: European Union increases quotas for Asian exporters', *Far Eastern Economic Review*, 158(5), p. 52.

Jackson, S.E. and Schuler, R.S. (1995) 'Understanding human resource management in the context of organizations and their environment', *Annual Review of Psychology*, 46, pp. 237–64.

Jaeger, A.M. (1983) 'The transfer of organizational culture overseas: an approach to control in the multinational corporation', *Journal of International Business Studies*, 14(2), pp. 91–114.

Jamieson, I. (1980) *Capitalism and Culture: A Comparative Study of British and American Manufacturing Organisations* (Farnbourgh: Gower).

Jarillo, J.C. (1988) 'On strategic networks', *Strategic Management Journal*, 9, pp. 31–41.

Jarillo, J.C. and Martinez, J.I. (1990) 'Different roles for subsidiaries: the case of multinational corporations in Spain', *Strategic Management Journal*, 11, pp. 501–12.

Jego, M. (1997) 'L'Instabilité fiscale et la vie juridique freinenet les investissement étrangers', *Le Monde* (29 March), p. 2.

JETRO (1998) (Tokyo: JETRO).

Johanson, J. and Mattsson, L. (1988) 'Internationalisation in industrial systems – a network approach', in N. Hood and J. Vahlne (eds), *Strategies in Global Competition* (London: Croom Helm); reproduced in P. Buckley and P. Ghauri (eds), (1993) *The Internationalization of the Firm: A Reader* (New York: Academic Press).

Johanson, J. and Vahlne, J.-K. (1990) 'The mechanism of internationalisation', *International Marketing Review*, 7(4), pp. 11–24.

Johnson, J. (1994) *Should Russia adopt the Chinese model of Economic Reform*, Communist and Post Communist Studies, vol. 27, no. 7, pp. 59–75.

Johnson, Jr, J.H. (1995) 'An empirical analysis of the integration–responsiveness framework: US construction equipment industry firms in global competition', *Journal of International Business Studies*, 26(3), pp. 621–35.

Johnson, S., *et al.* (1996) 'Complementarities and the managerial challenges of state enterprise restructuring: evidence from two shipyards', *Economics of Transition*, 4(1), pp. 31–42.

Joynt, P. and Warner, M. (eds) (1996) *Managing Across Cultures: Issues and Perspectives* (London: International Business Press).

Kahraß, K. (1997) 'Investment down but competitiveness up', *Corporate Location*, July–August, pp. 48–51.

Kashani, K. (1990) 'Why does global marketing work – or not work?', *European Marketing Journal*, 8(2), pp. 150–5.

Keenoy, T. (1990) 'HRM: a case of the wolf in sheep's clothing ?', *Personnel Review*, 19(2), pp. 3–9.

Kerr, C., Dunlop, J.T., Harbison, F.H. and Myers, C.A. (1960) *Industrialism and Industrial Man: The Problems of Labour and Management in Economic Growth* (Cambridge, MA: Harvard University Press).

Keuning, D. (1998) *Management: A Contemporary Approach* (London: Pitman), p. 281.

Kidger, P. (1991) 'The emergence of international human resource management', *International Journal of Human Resource Management*, 2(2), pp. 149–63.

Killing, J.P. (1983) *Strategies for Joint Venture Success* (New York: Praeger).

Kim, W.C. and Mauborgne, R.A. (1991) 'Implementing global strategies: the role of procedural justice', *Strategic Management Journal*, 12, pp. 125–43.

Kim, W.C. and Mauborgne, R.A. (1993a) 'Procedural justice, attitudes and subsidiary top management compliance with multinationals' corporate strategic decisions', *Academy of Management Journal*, 36(3), pp. 502–26.

Kim, W.C. and Mauborgne, R.A. (1993b) 'Effectively conceiving and executing multinationals' worldwide strategies', *Journal of International Business Studies*, 24(3), pp. 419–48.

Kimberly, J.R. (1976) 'Organizational size and the structuralist perspective: a review, critique, and proposal', *Administrative Science Quarterly*, 21, pp. 571–97.

Knickerbocker, F.T. (1973) *Oligopolistic Reaction and the Multinational Enterprize* (Cambridge, MA: Harvard University Press).

Kochan, T.A., Batt, R. and Dyer, L. (1992) 'International human resource studies: a framework for future research', in D. Lewin *et al.* (eds), *Research Frontiers in Industrial Relations and Human Research*, (Madison WI: Industrial Relations Research Association).

Kochan, T.A., Katz, H.C. and Mckersie, R.B. (1986) *The Transformation of American Industrial Relations* (Cambridge, MA: Harvard Business School Press).

Kogut, B. (1985a) 'Designing global strategies: comparative and competitive value-added chain', *Sloan Management Review*, 26, pp. 15–28.

Kogut, B. (1985b) 'Designing global strategies: profiting from operational flexibility', *Sloan Management Review*, 26, pp. 27–38.

Kogut, B. (1988) 'A study of life cycle of joint ventures', in F.J. Contractor and P. Lorange (eds), *Co-operative Strategies in International Business* (Lexington, MA: Lexington Books).

Kogut, B. (1988) 'Joint ventures: theoretical and empirical perspectives', *Strategic Management Journal*, 9, pp. 319–32.

Kogut, B. (1989) 'The stability of joint ventures: reciprocity and competitive rivalry', *Journal of Industrial Economics*, 38(2), pp. 183–98.

Kogut, B. (1991) 'Joint ventures and the option to expand and acquire', *Management Science*, 37(1), pp. 19–33.

Kogut, B. and Singh, H. (1988) 'The effect of national culture on the choice of entry mode', *Journal of International Business Studies*, 19(3), pp. 411–32.

Kogut, B. and Zander, U. (1993) 'Knowledge of the firm, combinative capabilities, and the replication of technology', *Organization Science*, 3(3), pp. 383–97.

Koopman, K. and Montias, J.M. (1971) 'On the description and comparison of economic systems', in A. Eckstein (ed.), *Comparison of Economic Systems* (California: University of California Press).

Koser, K. and Lutz, H. (eds) (1998) *The New Migration in Europe – Social Constructions and Social Realities* (London: Macmillan).

Kotabe, M., Sahay, A. and Aulakh, P.S. (1996) 'Emerging role of technology licensing in the development of global product strategy: conceptual framework and research propositions', *Journal of Marketing*, 60, pp. 73–88.

Kuznetzov, A. (1994) 'Economic reforms in Russia: enterprise behaviour and change', *Europe–Asia Studies*, 46(6), pp. 955–70.

Kuznetzov, A. and Kuznetzova, O. (1996) 'Privatisation, shareholding and the efficiency argument: Russian experience', *Europe–Asia Studies* 48(7), pp. 1173–85.

Kuznetzov, A. and Kuznetzova, O. (1998) 'Corporate governance under transition and the role of the state: the case of Russia', *Conference Proceedings of the 25th Annual Conference of the Academy of International Business* (April), pp. 374–86.

Lado, A.A., Boyd, N.G. and Hanlon, S.C. (1997) 'Competition, co-operation, and the search for economic rents: a syncretic model', *Academy of Management Review*, 22, pp. 110–41.

Lall, S. (1980) 'Vertical interfirm linkages: an empirical study', *Oxford Bulletin of Economics and Statistics*, 42, pp. 203–6.

Lane, C. (1989)   *Management and Labour in Europe* (Aldershot: Edward Elgar).

Laurent, A. (1986)   'The cross-cultural puzzle of international human resource management', *Human Resource Management*, 25(1), pp. 91–102.

Lecraw, D.J. (1993)   'Bargaining power, ownership, and profitability of transnational corporations in developing countries', *United Nations Library on Transnational Corporations. Volume 3 – Transnational Corporations and Economic Development* (London: Routledge), pp. 374–95.

Lee, C. and Beamish, P.W. (1995)   'The characteristics and performance of Korean joint ventures in LDCs', *Journal of International Business Studies*, 33, pp. 345–69.

Legge, K. (1995)   *Human Resource Management: Rhetorics and Realities* (London: Macmillan).

Levitt, T. (1983)   'The globalisation of markets', *Harvard Business Review*, May–June, pp. 92–102.

Li, L.M. (1981)   *China's Silk Trade: Traditional Industry in the Modern World, 1842–1937* (Cambridge, MA: Council on East Asian Studies, Harvard University).

Li, L.M. (1982)   'Silks by sea: trade, technology, and enterprise in China and Japan', *Business History Review*, 56(2), pp. 192–217.

Likert, R. (1961)   *New Patterns of Management* (New York: McGraw-Hill).

Lin, X. and Germain, R. (1998)   'Sustaining satisfactory joint venture relationships: the role of conflict resolution strategy', *Journal of International Business Studies*, 29(1), pp. 179–96.

Lincoln, J.R. and Kalleberg, A.L. (1990)   *Culture, Control and Commitment: A Study of Work Organisation and Attitudes in the United States and Japan* (Cambridge: Cambridge University Press).

Littler, D. and Leverick, F. (1995)   'Joint ventures for product development: learning from experience', *Long Range Planning*, 28(3), pp. 58–67.

Lu, Y. and Burton, F. (1998)   'Reflections on theoretical perspectives of international strategic alliances', in P. Buckley, F. Burton and H. Mizra (eds), *The Strategy and Organization of International Business* (Basingstoke: Macmillan), pp. 149–72.

Lundvall, B.-A. (1992)   *National Systems of Innovation: Toward a Theory of Innovation and Interactive Learning* (London: Pinter).

Luo, Y. (1995)   'Linking strategic and moderating factors to performance of international ventures in China', *The Mid-Atlantic Journal of Business*, 31(1), pp. 5–23.

Luo, Y. (1997)   'Performance implications of international strategy: an empirical study of foreign invested enterprises in China', *Group and Organisation Management*, 22(1), pp. 87–116.

Luthans, F. and Hodgetts, R.M. (1996)   'Managing in America: recreating a competitive culture', in P. Joynt and M. Warner (eds), *Managing Across Cultures: Issues and Perspectives* (London: International Thomson Business Press).

Lyles, M.A. and Baird, I.S. (1994)   'Performance of international joint ventures in two Eastern European Countries: the case of Hungary and Poland', *Management International Review*, 34(4), pp. 313–29.

Ma, D. (1996)   'The Modern Silk Road: the global raw-silk market, 1850–1930', *Journal of Economic History*, 56(2), pp. 330–55.

Mabey, C., Salaman, G. and Storey, J. (eds) (1998)   *Strategic Human Resource Management: A Reader* (London: Sage).

Madhok, A. (1997)   'Cost, value and foreign market entry mode: the transaction and the firm', *Strategic Management Journal*, 18, pp. 39–61.

Mann, J. (1989)   *Beijing Jeep: The Short, Unhappy Romance of American Business in China* (New York: Simon & Schuster, reprinted 1997).

Marginson, P., Edwards, P.K., Martin, R., Purcell, J. and Sisson, K. (eds) (1988)   *Beyond The Workplace – Managing Industrial Relations in the Multi-Establishment Enterprize* (London: Blackwell).

Martinez, J.I. and Jarillo, J.C. (1991) 'Co-ordination demands of international business strategies', *Journal of International Business Studies*, 22(3), pp. 429–44.

Massey, D. and Allen, J. (eds) (1988) *Uneven Re-Development – Cities and Regions in Transition* (London: Hodder & Stoughton).

Matouschek, N. and Venables, A.J. (1998) 'Evaluating investment projects in the presence of sectoral linkages: theory and application to transition economies' (Unpublished manuscript).

Mattsson, L. (1987) 'Management of strategic change in a markets-as-networks' perspective', in A. Pettigrew (ed.), *Management of Strategic Change* (Oxford: Blackwell), pp. 234–56.

Mayhew, A. and Oriowski, W.M. (1998) *The Impact of EU Accession on Enterprise Adaptation and Institutional Development in the EU-associated Countries in Central and Eastern Europe* (London: European Bank for Reconstruction and Development).

McCarthy, D.J. and Puffer, S.M. (1997) 'Strategic investment flexibility for MNE success in Russia: evolving beyond entry modes', *Journal of World Business*, 32(4), pp. 193–219.

McFaul, M. (1996) 'The allocation of property rights in Russia,' *Communist and Post Communist Studies*, 29(3), pp. 287–308.

McGregor, D. (1960) *The Human Side of Enterprize* (New York: McGraw-Hill).

McKinsey (1998) *Driving Productivity and Growth in the UK Economy* (London: McKinsey Consultants).

Meyer, K. (1998) 'Multinational enterprises and the emergence of markets and networks in transition economies', Copenhagen Business School: Center for East European Studies, *Working paper*, 12, June.

Miles, M.B. and Huberman, A.M. (1994) *Qualitative Data Analysis* (London: Sage).

Miles, R. and Snow, C. (1978) *Organizational Strategy, Structure and Process* (New York: McGraw-Hill).

Miller, D. and Friesen, P. (1984) *Organizations: A Quantum View* (Englewood Cliffs, NJ: Prentice-Hall).

Miller, D. and Friesen, P.H. (1984) 'A longitudinal study of the corporate life cycle', *Management Science*, 30(10), pp. 1161–83.

Mjoen, H. and Tallman, S. (1997) 'Control and performance in international joint ventures', *Organisation Science*, 8, pp. 257–74.

Molle, W. and Morsink, R. (1991) 'Intra-European direct investment', in B. Burgenmeier and J.-L. Mucchielli (eds), *Multinationals and Europe 1992: Strategies for the Future* (London: Routledge).

Molony, D. (1999) 'Market strategies: new alliances key to operator plans', *Communications Week International*, 6, September.

Monlouis, J. (1998) 'The future of telecommunications operator alliances', *Telecommunications Policy*, 22(8), pp. 635–41.

Montagnon, P. (1997) 'The right skills are in the right location', *Financial Times*, 6 October.

Morgan, E. (1997) 'Industrial restructuring and the control of "concentrations" in the European market', in G. Chryssochoidis, C. Millar and J. Clegg (eds), *Internationalisation Strategies* (Basingstoke: Macmillan), pp. 91–112.

Morris, J. (1988) 'The who, why and where of Japanese manufacturing investment in the UK', *Industrial Relations Journal*, 19(1), pp. 31–40.

Morris, J. and Imrie, R. (1993) 'Japanese style subcontracting – its impact on European industries', *Long Range Planning*, 26(4), pp. 53–8.

Morrison, A.J. (1990) *Strategies in Global Industries: How US Businesses Compete* (New York: Quorum Books).

Mueller, F. and Purcell, J. (1992) 'The Europeanization of manufacturing and the decentralization of bargaining: multinational management strategies in the European automobile industry', *International Journal of Human Resource Management*, 3(1), pp. 15–34.

Naudet, J.-B. (1998) 'Le Kremlin met un coup d'arrêt au processus de privatisation', *Le Monde* (24 January), p. 2.

Naumov, A.I. (1996) 'Hofstede's measures in Russia: the influence of national culture on business management', *Menedzhment*, 3 (in Russian), pp. 70–103.

Negandhi, A. (1979) 'Convergence in organisational practices: an empirical study of industrial enterprises in developing countries', in C.J. Lammers and D.J. Hickson (eds), *Organisations Alike and Unlike* (London: Routledge & Kegan Paul).

Negandhi, A.R. and Baliga, B.R. (1981) 'Internal functioning of American, German and Japanese multinational corporations', in L. Otterbeck (ed.), *The Management of Headquarters–Subsidiary Relations in Multinational Corporations* (Aldershot: Gower).

Nelson, R. and Winter, S. (1982) *An Evolutionary Theory of Economic Change* (Cambridge, MA: Belknap Press).

Newton, J. (1998) 'Kid's stuff: the organisation and Trade of the China–EU trade in toys', in R. Strange, J. Slater and L. Wang (eds), *Trade and Investment in China: The European Experience* (London: Routledge), pp. 147–65.

Nickell, S. (1997) 'Unemployment and Labour Market Rigidities, Europe versus North America', *Journal of Economic Perspectives*, 11(3), pp. 55–74.

Nicolaidis, C. and Millar, C. (1997) 'National culture, corporate culture and economic performance: an interdisciplinary synthesis and implications for internationalisation strategy', in G. Chryssochoidis, C. Millar and J. Clegg (eds), *Internationalisation Strategies* (Basingstoke: Macmillan), pp. 113–31.

Nohria, N. and Garcia-Pont, C. (1991) 'Global strategic linkages and industry structure', *Strategic Management Journal*, Summer, pp. 105–24.

Nolan, P. (1995) *China's Rise, Russia's Fall: Politics, Economics and Planning in the Transition from Stalinism* (London: Macmillan).

O'Mahony, M. (1998) *Britain's Relative Productivity Performance, 1950–96: A Sectoral Analysis* (London: National Institute for Economic and Social Research).

OECD (1999) Conference on Corporate Governance in Russia (Moscow, 31 May–2 June), *Synthesis Note* (Paris: OECD Centre for Co-operation With Non-Members).

Oh, J.G. (1996) 'Global strategic alliances in the telecommunications industry', *Telecommunications Policy*, 20(9), pp. 713–20.

Oliver, B. and Wilkinson, N. (1992) 'Human resource management in Japanese manufacturing companies in the UK and the USA', in B. Towers (ed.), *The Handbook of Human Resource Management* (Oxford: Blackwell).

Osland, G.E. (1994) 'Successful operating strategies in the performance of US–China joint ventures', *Journal of International Marketing*, 2(4), pp. 53–78.

Osland, G.E. and Cavusgil, S.T. (1996) 'Performance issues in US–China joint ventures', *California Management Review*, 38(2), pp. 106–30.

Ostrovsky, A. (1997) 'Russia: emerging smoothly from the Mir mire', *Financial Times* (13 September), p. 2.

Ouchi, W.G. (1981) *Theory Z: How American Management Can Meet the Japanese Challenge* (Reading, MA: Addison-Wesley).

Oye, K.A. (ed.) (1986) *Co-operation under Anarchy* (Princeton: Princeton University Press).

Pang, K. and Oliver, N. (1988) 'Personnel strategy in eleven Japanese manufacturing companies in the UK', *Personnel Review*, 17(3), pp. 16–21.

Papanastassiou, M. (1995) *Creation and Development of Technology by MNE Subsidiaries in Europe: The Cases of the UK, Greece, Belgium and Portugal*, PhD dissertation, University of Reading.

Papanastassiou, M. and Pearce, R. (1995) 'Decentralisation of technology and organisation restructuring in the MNE group', University of Reading, Department of Economics, *Discussion Papers in International Investment and Business Studies*, 206.

Papanastassiou, M. and Pearce, R. (1996) 'R&D networks and innovation: decentralised product development in Multinational Enterprises', *R&D Management*, 26(4), pp. 315–33.

Papanastassiou, M. and Pearce, R. (1997) 'Technology sourcing and the strategic roles of manufacturing subsidiaries in the UK: Local competences and global competitiveness', *Management International Review*, 37(1), pp. 5–25.

Papanastassiou, M. and Pearce, R. (1998) 'Individualism and interdependence in the technological development of MNEs: the strategic positioning of R&D in overseas subsidiaries', in J. Birkinshaw and N. Hood (eds), *Multinational Corporate Evolution and Subsidiary Development* (London: Macmillan).

Papanastassiou, M. and Pearce, R. (1999) 'Host country technological and scientific collaborations of MNE subsidiaries: evidence from operations in Europe', in F. Burton, M. Chapman and A. Cross (eds), *International Business Organisation: Subsidiary Management, Entry Strategies and Emerging Markets* (Basingstoke: Macmillan), pp. 47–66.

Park, S.H. and Ungson, G.R. (1997) 'The effect of national culture, organisational complementarity and economic motivation on joint venture dissolution', *Academy of Management Journal*, 40(2), pp. 279–307.

Park, Y.-I. and Anderson, K. (1992) 'The experience of Japan in historical and international perspective', in K. Anderson (ed.), *New Silk Roads: East Asia and World Textile Markets* (Cambridge: Cambridge University Press), pp. 15–29.

Parkhe, A. (1993) 'Strategic alliance structuring: a game theoretic and transaction cost examination of inter-firm co-operation', *Academy of Management Journal*, 36(4), pp. 794–829.

Pearce, R.D. (1992) 'World product mandates and MNE specialisation', *Scandinavian International Business Review*, 1(2), pp. 38–58.

Pearce, R.D. and Papanastassiou, M. (1997) 'European markets and the strategic roles of multinational enterprize subsidiaries in the UK', *Journal of Common Market Studies*, 35(2), pp. 241–66.

Pearce, R.D. and Singh, S. (1992) *Globalising Research and Development* (London: Macmillan).

Pearson, M. (1991) *Joint Ventures in the People's Republic of China: The Control of Foreign Investment under Socialism* (Princeton: Princeton University Press).

Peng, M.W. (2000) 'Controlling the foreign agent: case studies of government–MNE interaction in a transition economy', *Management International Review*.

Pennings, J.M. (1981) 'Strategically interdependent organizations', in P.C. Nystrom and W.H. Starbuck (eds), *Handbook of Organization Design: 1* (New York: Oxford University Press), pp. 433–55.

Perlman, S. (1970) *The Theory of the Labour Movement*, 2nd edn (New York: Augustus M. Kelly).

Perlmutter, H. (1969) 'The tortuous evolution of the multinational corporation', *Columbia Journal of World Business*, 4, pp. 9–18.

Petersen, P. and Pedersen, T. (1997) 'Twenty years after – support and critique of the Uppsala internationalisation model', in I. Björkman and M. Forsgren (eds), *The Nature of the International Firm* (Copenhagen: Copenhagen Business School Press), pp. 117–34.

Pettigrew, A. (1985) *The Awakening Giant: Continuity and Change in ICI* (Oxford: Basil Blackwell).

Pfeffer, J. (1972) 'Merger as a response to organizational interdependence', *Administrative Science Quarterly*, 18, pp. 449–61.

Pfeffer, J. (1982) *Power in Organisations* (Marshfield, MA: Pitman).

Pfeffer, J. (1987) 'A resource dependence perspective on intercorporate relations', in M. Mizruchi and M. Schwartz (eds), *Intercorporate Relations. The Structural Analysis of Business* (New York: Cambridge University Press).

Pfeffer, J. and Nowak, P. (1976) 'Joint ventures and interorganizational interdependence', *Administrative Science Quarterly*, 21, pp. 398–418.

Pfeffer, J. and Salancik, G.R. (1978) *The External Control of Organisations: A Resource Dependence Perspective* (New York: Harper & Row).

Picard, J. (1980) 'Organizational structures and integrative devices in European multinational corporations', *Columbia Journal of World Business*, Spring, pp. 30–5.

Pieper, R. (ed.), (1990) *Human Resource Management: An International Comparison* (Berlin: de Gruyter).

Plakin, V. (1997) 'Foreign capital investment in Russia', *Problems of Economic Transition*, 39(12), pp. 43–54.

Poole, M. (1990) 'Editorial: human resource management in an international perspective', *International Journal of Human Resource Management*, 1(1), pp. 1–15.

Porter, M. (1991) 'Towards a dynamic theory of strategy', *Strategic Management Journal*, 12, pp. 95–117.

Porter, M.E. (1980) *Competitive Strategy: Techniques for Analysing Industries and Competitors* (New York: Free Press).

Porter, M.E. (1985) *Competitive Advantage: Creating and Sustaining Superiour Performance* (New York: Free Press).

Porter, M.E. (1986) 'Changing patterns of international competition', *California Management Review*, 28, pp. 9–40.

Porter, M.E. (ed.) (1986) *Competition in Global Industries* (Cambridge, MA: Harvard Business School Press).

Porter, M.E. (1986) 'Competition in global industries: a conceptual framework', in M.E. Porter (ed.), *Competition in Global Industries* (Cambridge, MA: Harvard Business School Press), pp. 15–60.

Porter, M.E. (1990) *The Competitive Advantage of Nations* (New York: Free Press).

Porter, M.E. and Fuller, M.B. (1986) 'Coalitions and global strategy', in M.E. Porter (eds), *Competition in Global Industries* (Cambridge, MA: Harvard Business School Press).

Powell, W.W. and Brantley, P. (1992) 'Competitive co-operation in biotechnology: learning through networks?', in N. Nohria and R. Eccles (eds), *Networks and Organizations: Structure, Form and Action* (Cambridge, MA: Harvard Business School Press), pp. 365–94.

Powell, W.W., Koput, K.W. and Smith-Doerr, L. (1996) 'Interorganizational collaboration and the locus of innovation: networks of learning in bio-technology', *Administrative Science Quarterly*, 41(1), pp. 116–45.

Prahalad, C.K. (1976) 'Strategic choices in diversified MNCs', *Harvard Business Review*, July–August, pp. 67–78.

Prahalad, C.K. (1995) 'Weak signals versus strong paradigms', *Journal of Marketing Research*, 23, pp. 3–6.

Prahalad, C.K. and Doz, Y.L. (1987) *The Multinational Mission: Balancing Local Demands and Global Vision* (New York: Free Press).

Prahalad, C.K. and Hamel, G. (1990) 'The core competence and the corporation', *Harvard Business Review*, 68(3), pp. 71–91.

Puffer, S., McCarthy, D. and Naumov, A. (1998) 'Russia, Central and Eastern Europe: business and management issues', *European Management Journal*, 16(4), pp. 373–7.

Raines, P., Döhrn, R., Brown, R. and Scheuer, M. (1999) *Labour Market Flexibility and Inward Investment in Germany and the UK* (London: Anglo–German Foundation for the Study of Industrial Society).

Rajagopalan, S. and Yong, S. (1995) 'Strategic alliances in the hospital industry: a fusion of institutional and resource dependence views', *Academy of Management Best Paper Proceedings*, pp. 271–5.

Ralston, D.A., Holt, D.H., Terpstra, R.H. and Kai-Cheng, Y. (1997) 'The impact of national culture and economic ideology on managerial work values: a study of the United States, Russia, Japan and China', *Journal of International Business Studies*, 28(1), pp. 177–207.

Rapoport, C. (1993) 'Japan to the rescue', *Fortune*, 128(9), pp. 30–4.

Reed, R. and DeFillippi, R.J. (1990) 'Causal ambiguity, barriers to imitation, and sustainable competitive advantage', *Academy of Management Review*, 15, pp. 88–102.

Reynolds, J. (1984) 'The "pinched shoe" effect of international joint ventures', *Columbia Journal of World Business*, Summer, pp. 23–9.

Ritchie, B. and Marshall, D. (1993) *Business Risk Management* (London: Chapman & Hall).

Robinson, A. (1997) 'Surge in capital flight from Russia', *Financial Times* (21 March), p. 2.

Robinson, R. and Pearce, J. (1988) 'Planned patterns of strategic behaviour and their relationship to business-unit performance', *Strategic Management Journal*, 9, pp. 43–60.

Robock, S.H. and Simmonds, K. (1983) *International Business and Multinational Enterprize* (Homewood, IL: Prentice-Hall).

Robson, M.J. and Kastsikeas, C.S. (1998) 'Determinants of international joint venture performance: an integrative review of the empirical literature', in C.J.M. Millar and C.J. Choi (eds), *International Business and Emerging Markets, Conference Proceedings of the 25th Annual Conference*, Academy of International Business – UK Chapter (London: City University Business School).

Robson, P. (ed.) (1993) *Transnational Corporations and Regional Economic Integration* (New York: UN TCMD).

Rodrik, D. (1996) 'Understanding trade liberalization and development', *Journal of Economic Literature*, 34(1), pp. 9–41.

Ronen, S. (1986) *Comparative and Multinational Management* (New York: Wiley).

Ronstadt, R.C. (1977) *Research and Development abroad by US Multinationals* (New York: Praeger).

Ronstadt, R.C. (1978) 'International R&D: the establishment and evolution of R&D abroad by seven US multinationals', *Journal of International Business Studies*, 9, pp. 7–24.

Rosenzweig, P.M. and Nohria, N. (1994) 'Influences on human resource management in multinational corporations', *Journal of International Business Studies*, 25, pp. 229–51.

Roth, K. and Morrison, A.J. (1990) 'An empirical analysis of the integration–responsiveness framework in global industries', *Journal of International Business Studies*, 21(4), pp. 541–64.

Roth, K. and Morrison, A.J. (1992) 'Implementing global strategy: characteristics of global subsidiary mandates', *Journal of International Business Studies*, 23(4), pp. 715–35.

Rudolf, R. and Hillmann, F. (1998) 'The invisible hand needs invisible heads: managers, experts and professionals from Western Countries in Poland', in K. Koser and H. Lutz (eds), *The New Migration in Europe–Social Constructions and Social Realities* (London: Macmillan).

Rugman, A.M. (1981) *Inside the Multinationals: The Economics of Internal Markets* (London: Croom Helm).

Rugman, A.M. (1985) 'Internalisation is still a general theory of foreign direct investment', *Weltwirtschaftliches Archiv*, 121(3), pp. 570–5.

Sachs, J. and Wu, W.T. (1994) 'Structural factors in the economic reforms of China, eastern Europe, and the former Soviet Union', *Economic Policy*, 9(18), pp. 102–45.

Sadler, D. and Amin, A. (1995) '"Europeanisation" in the automotive industry', in R. Hudson and E. Schamp (eds), *Towards a New Map of Automobile Manufacturing in Europe?* (Berlin: Springer).

Salt, J. (1991) 'Migration process among the highly skilled in Europe', *International Migration Review*, 26.

Salt, J. (1997) 'From relocation to the movement of expertise?', in CBI, Employment Relocation Report (London: CBI).

Salt, J. and Singleton, A. (1995) 'The international migration of expertise: the case of the UK', *Migration Studies*, 117, pp. 3–29.

Schneider, S. (1988) 'National vs corporate culture: implications for human resource management', *Human Resource Management*, 27(2), pp. 231–46.

Schuler, R.S. (1992) 'Linking the people with the strategic needs of the business', *Organizational Dynamics*, Summer, pp. 18–32.

Schuler, R.S., Dowling, P.J. and de Cieri, H. (1993) 'An integrative framework of strategic international human resource management', *International Journal of Human Resource Management*, 5(6), pp. 717–64.

Schuler, R.S., Dowling, P.J. and De Cieri, H. (1993) 'An integrative framework of strategic international human resource management', *Journal of Management*, 19, pp. 419–59.

Scullion, H. (1994) 'Staffing policies and strategic control in British multinationals', *International Studies of Management and Organisation*, 24(3), pp. 86–104.

Servan-Schreiber, J.-J. (1967) *Le Défi Américain* (The American Challenge) (London: Hamish Hamilton).

Service, R. (1998) *A History of Twentieth Century Russia* (London: Penguin), p. 384.

Shane, S. (1994) 'The effect of national culture and the choice between licensing and direct foreign investment', *Strategic Management Journal*, 15(8), pp. 627–42.

Shenkar, O. (1990) 'International joint ventures' problems in China: risks and remedies', *Long Range Planning*, 23(3), pp. 82–90.

Shlapentokh, V. (1996) 'Early feudalism the best parallel for contemporary Russia', *Europe–Asia Studies*, 48(3), pp. 393–411.

Siffin, W.J. (1976) 'Two decades of public administration in developing countries', *Public Administration Review*, pp. 61–71.

Simões, V.C. (1992) 'European integration and the pattern of FDI inflow in Portugal', in J.A. Cantwell (ed.), *Multinational Investment in Modern Europe* (Aldershot: Edward Elgar), pp. 256–97.

Simonin, B.L. (1997) 'The importance of collaborative know-how: an empirical test of the learning organization', *Academy of Management Journal*, 40(5), pp. 1150–74.

Singh, K. (1995) 'The impact of technological complexity and inter-firm co-operation business survival', *Academy of Management Best Paper Proceedings*, pp. 67–71.

Singh, K. and Mitchell, W. (1996) 'Precarious collaboration: business survival after partnerships shut down or form new partnerships', *Strategic Management Journal*, 17, pp. 99–115.

Slewaegen, L. (1988) 'Multinationals, the European Community and Belgium: the small country case', in J.H. Dunning and P. Robson (eds), *Multinational and the European Community* (Oxford: Basil Blackwell).

Smith, C. (1992) 'Trends and Directions in Dual-career Family Research', *Women in Management Review*, 7(1), pp. 23–8.

Smith, K.G., Grimm, C.M., Gannon, M.J. and Chen, M.J. (1991) 'Organizational information processing, competitive responses and performance in the US domestic airline industry', *Academy of Management Journal*, 34, pp. 60–85.

Sparrow, P.R. (1995) 'Towards a dynamic and comparative model of European human resource management: an extended review', *International Journal of Human Resource Management*, 6(3), pp. 481–505.

Sparrow, P.R. and Hiltrop, J.M. (1994) *European Human Resource Management in Transition* (London: Prentice-Hall).

Sparrow, P.R. and Hiltrop, J.M. (1997) 'Redefining the field of European human resource management: a battle between national mindsets and forces of business transition', *Human Resource Management*, 36(2), pp. 201–19.

Sparrow, P.R., Schuler, R.S. and Jackson, S.E. (1994) 'Convergence or divergence: human resource practices and policies for competitive advantage worldwide', *International Journal of Human Resource Management*, 5(2), pp. 267–99.

Springer, B. and Springer, S. (1990) 'HRM in the US – celebration of its centenary', in R. Pieper (ed.), *Human Resource Management: An International Comparison* (Berlin: de Gruyter).

State Statistical Bureau (1998) *China Statistical Yearbook* (Beijing: State Statistical Bureau).

Stopford, J. and Strange, S. (1991) *Rival States, Rival Firms* (Cambridge: Cambridge University Press).

Stopford, J.M. and Wells, L.T., Jr (1972) *Managing the Multinational Enterprise* (New York: Basic Books).

Strange, R. (1997) 'Trading blocs, trade liberalisation and foreign direct investment', in G. Chryssochoidis, C. Millar and J. Clegg (eds), *Internationalisation Strategies* (Basingstoke: Macmillan), pp. 19–42.

Strange, R. (1998) 'EC trade policy towards China', in R. Strange, J. Slater and L. Wang (eds), *Trade and Investment in China: The European Experience* (London: Routledge), pp. 59–80.

Subhan, M. (1994) 'Europe still protectionist', *Textile Asia* (December), p. 9.

Sung, K. (1994a) 'Pure silk is rough', *Textile Asia* (February), pp. 6–7.

Sung, K. (1994b) 'Foul play at Brussels', *Textile Asia* (April), pp. 10–13.

Sung, K. (1995a) 'The EU makes a U-turn', *textile Asia* (April), pp. 10–11.

Surlemont, B. (1996) 'Types of centers within multinational corporations: an empirical investigation', *Proceedings of the European International Business Academy* (Stockholm), pp. 745–66.

Taggart, J.H. (1996) 'Autonomy and procedural justice: a framework for evaluating subsidiary strategy', *Journal of International Business Studies*, 28(1), pp. 51–76.

Taggart, J.H. (1997) 'An evaluation of the integration–responsiveness framework: MNC manufacturing subsidiaries in the UK', *Management International Review*, 37(4), pp. 295–318.

Taggart, J.H. (1997) 'Autonomy and procedural justice: a framework for evaluating subsidiary strategy', *Journal of International Business Studies*, 28(1), pp. 51–76.

Taggart, J.H. (1998) 'An evaluation of the integration–responsiveness framework: MNC manufacturing subsidiaries in the UK', *Management International Review*, 37(4), pp. 295–318.

Taggart, J.H. (1999) 'US MNC subsidiaries in the UK: characteristics and strategic role', in F. Burton, M. Chapman and A. Cross (eds), *International Business Organisation: Subsidiary Management, Entry Strategies and Emerging Markets* (Basingstoke: Macmillan), pp. 29–46.

Taggart, J.H. and Hood, N. (2000) 'Strategy development in German manufacturing subsidiaries in the UK and Ireland', in C. Millar, R. Grant and Chong Ju Choi (eds), *International Business: Emerging Issues and Emerging Markets* (Basingstoke: Macmillan), pp. 200–20.

Taggart, J.H. and Taggart, J.M. (1997) 'Subsidiary strategies from the periphery', in B. Fynes and S. Ennis (eds), *Competing from the Periphery* (London: Dryden Press).

Tan, J. (1997) 'Chrysler's international operation: Beijing Jeep Company', in M.A. Hitt, R.D. Ireland and R.E. Hoskisson (eds), *Strategic Management* (New York: West).

Tavares, A.T. and Pearce, R.D. (1998a) 'Regional economic integration processes and the strategic (re)positioning of multinationals' subsidiaries: a conceptual investigation', *University of Reading Discussion Papers in International Investment and Management*, 11: Series B, 254.

Tavares, A.T. and Pearce, R.D. (1998b) 'The industrial policy implications of the heterogeneity of subsidiaries' roles in a multinational network', *Industrial Development Policy Discussion Paper*, 5 (Ferrara and Birmingham: Institute for Industrial Development Policy).

Tavares, A.T. and Pearce, R.D. (1998c) 'Economic integration and the strategic evolution of MNEs' subsidiaries in a peripheral European economy', in E.D. Jaffe, I.D. Nebenzhal and D. Te'eni (eds), *International Business Strategies and Middle East Regional Co-operation: Proceedings of the 27th Annual EIBA Conference* (Jerusalem).

Tayeb, M.H. (1988) *Organizations and National Culture: A Comparative Analysis* (London: Sage).

Tayeb, M.H. (1993) 'English culture and business organisations', in D.J. Hickson (ed.), *Management in Western Europe* (Berlin: de Gruyter), pp. 47–64.

Tayeb, M.H. (1994) 'Japanese managers and British culture: a comparative case study', *International Journal of Human Resource Management*, 5(1), pp. 145–66.

Tayeb, M.H. (1996) *The Management of a Multicultural Workforce* (Chichester: Wiley).

Tayeb, M.H. (1998) 'Transfer of HRM polices and practices across cultures: an American company in Scotland', *International Journal of Human Resource Management*, 9(2), pp. 332–58.

Tayeb, M.H. (1999) 'Transfer of HRM practices across cultures: an American company in Scotland', in F. Burton, M. Chapman and A. Cross (eds), *International Business Organisation: Subsidiary Management, Entry Strategies and Emerging Markets* (Basingstoke: Macmillan), pp. 97–111.

Taylor, S., Beechler, S. and Napier, N. (1996) 'Towards an integrative model of strategic international human resource management', *Academy of Management Review*, 21(4), pp. 959–85.

Teagarden, M. and Von Glinow, M. (1990) 'Sino–foreign strategic alliance types and related operating characteristics', *International Studies of Management and Organisation*, 20(1), pp. 99–108.

Teece (1986) *Profiting from Technological Innovation: Implications for Integration, Collaboration, Licensing and Public Policy*, Research Policy Vol 15. pp. 285–305.

Teece, D.J. (1981) 'The multinational enterprise: market failure and market power considerations', *Sloan Management Review*, 22(3), pp. 3–17.

Teece, D.J. (1983) 'Multinational enterprise, internal governance, and industrial organisation', *American Economic Review*, 75(2), pp. 233–8.

Teece, D.J., Pisano, G. and Shuen, J. (1997) 'Dynamic capabilities and strategic management', *Strategic Management Journal*, 18(7), pp. 509–33.

Thorelli, H.B. (1986) 'Networks: between markets and hierarchies', *Strategic Management Journal*, 7, pp. 37–51.

Thornhill, J. (1996a) 'Russia's unfinished revolution: with communists waiting in the wings, the country's market reforms depend on next month's election result', *Financial Times* (30th May), p. 2.

Thornhill, J. (1996b) 'Banker refused entry to Russia', *Financial Times* (26 June), p. 22.

Thornhill, J. (1996c) 'Desperately short of fuel: the risks of operating in Russia make foreign companies reluctant to provide much needed investment', *Financial Times* (20 December), p. 24.

Thornhill, J. (1997) 'The bear starts to lose its bugs', *Financial Times* (9 October), p. 25.
Thurley, K. and Wirdenius, H. (1989) *Towards European Management* (London: Pitman).
Todeva, E. (2000) 'Comparative business networks in Eastern Europe', *Journal of East–West Business*, 6(2).
Torrington, D. (1994) *International Human Resource Management: Think Globally, Act Locally* (Hemel Hempstead: Prentice-Hall).
Tüselmann, H.-T. (1995) 'Standort Deutschland – is Germany losing its appeal as an international manufacturing location?', *European Business Review*, 95(5), pp. 21–30.
UNCTAD (1997) *World Investment Report 1997* (Geneva: United Nations Conference on Trade and Development).
US–China Business Council (1990) 'Special report on US investment in China', *The China Business Forum*, Washington, DC.
Van de Ven, A. (1976) 'On the nature, formation, and maintenance of relations among organizations', *Academy of Management Review*, 1(4), pp. 24–36.
van Marrewijk, C. (1999) 'Capital accumulation, learning and endogenous growth', *Oxford Economic Papers*, 51(2), pp. 453–75.
Vanhonacker, W.R. and Pan, Y. (1997) 'The impact of national culture, business scope, and geographic location on joint ventures in China', *Journal of International Marketing*, 5(3), pp. 11–30.
Vernon, R. (1966) 'International investment and international trade in the product cycle', *Quarterly Journal of Economics*, 80, pp. 190–207.
Vernon, R. (1974) 'The location of economic activity', in J.H. Dunning (ed.), *Economic Analysis and the Multinational Enterprize* (London: Allen & Unwin).
Voss, C.A., Blackmon, K., Chase, R., Rose, E.L. and Roth, A.V. (1997) 'Service competitiveness – an Anglo–US study', *Business Strategy Review*, 8(1), pp. 7–22.
Warner, M. (1997) 'Management–labour relations in the new Chinese economy', *Human Resource Management Journal*, 7(4), pp. 30–43.
Watkins, P. and Pearson, P. (1994) 'Global Changes in the market for silk and silk products', *Textile Outlook International*, 55, pp. 93–127.
Watson, J. (1996) 'Foreign investment in the Russian oil industry', *Europe–Asia Studies*, 48(3), pp. 440–60.
Weber, M. (1930) *The Protestant Ethic and the Spirit of Capitalism* (London: George Allen & Unwin).
Weber, M. (1947) *The Theory of Social and Economic Organization* (New York: Free Press).
Welch, D. (1994) 'Determinants of international human resource management approaches and activities: a suggested framework', *Journal of Management Studies*, 32, pp. 139–64.
Welch, W. and Welch, S. (1997) 'Pre-expatriation: the role of HR factors in the early stages of internationalisation', *International Journal of Human Resource Management*, 8(4), pp. 402–13.
Wells, P. and Rawlinson, M. (1994) *The New European Automobile Industry* (London: St Martins Press).
Wheeler, H.N. (1993) 'Industrial relations in the United States of America', in G.J. Bamber and R.D. Lansbury (eds), *International and Comparative Industrial Relations*, 2nd edn (London: Routledge).
Whipp, R. (1991) 'Human resource management, strategic change and competition: the role learning', *International Journal of Human Resource Management*, 2(2), pp. 165–91.
White, M. and Trevor, M. (1983) *Under Japanese Management: The Experience of British Workers* (London: Heinemann).

White, R.E. and Poynter, T.A. (1984) 'Strategies for foreign-owned subsidiaries in Canada', *Business Quarterly*, 48(4), pp. 59–69.

Whitley, R. (1992) *Business Systems in East Asia* (London: Sage).

Whitley, R. (1992) *Business Systems in East Asia: Firms, Markets and Societies* (London: Sage).

Wiedersheim-Paul, F., Olsen, H.C. and Welch, L.S. (1978) 'Pre-export activity: the first step in internationalization', *Journal of International Business Studies*, 8, pp. 47–58.

Wiener, M.J. (1981) *English Culture and the Decline of the Industrial Spirit: 1850–1980* (London: Cambridge University Press).

Williamson, O.E. (1975) *Markets and Hierarchies: Analysis and Anti-trust Implications* (New York: Free Press).

Wilson, D.C. and Rosenfeld, R.H. (1990) *Managing Organizations* (London: McGraw-Hill).

Womack, J.P., Jones, D.T. and Roos, D. (1990) *The Machine That Changed the World* (New York and Oxford: Rawson Associates: Maxwell Macmillan).

Woodcock, C.P., Beamish, P.W. and Makino, S. (1994) 'Ownership-based entry mode strategies and international performance', *Journal of International Business Studies*, 21(2), pp. 253–73.

Wu, W.P. (1997) 'A study of EC firms' choice of entry mode into the Chinese market, licensing or joint ventures?', in G. Chryssochoidis, C. Millar and J. Clegg (eds), *Internationalisation Strategies* (Basingstoke: Macmillan), pp. 153–69.

Yan, A. and Gray, B. (1994) 'Bargaining power, management control, and performance in United States–China joint ventures: a comparative case study', *Academy of Management Journal*, 37(6), pp. 1478–517.

Yavlinsky, G. (1998) 'Russia's phony capitalism', *Foreign Affairs*, 77(3), pp. 67–79.

Young, S. *et al.* (1989) *International Market Entry and Development* (Hemel Hempstead: Harvester Wheatsheaf).

Young, S.N., Hood, N. and Dunlop, S. (1988) 'Global strategies, multinational subsidiary roles and economic impact in Scotland', *Regional Studies*, 22(6), pp. 487–97.

Young, S.N., Hood, N. and Peters, E. (1994) 'Multinationals and regional economic development', *Regional Studies*, 28(7), pp. 657–7.

Zhang, H.Y. and van den Bulcke, D. (2000) 'The restructuring of the Chinese automotive industry: the role of foreign direct investment and the impact of European multinational enterprises', in C. Millar, R. Grant and Chong Ju Choi (eds), *International Business: Emerging Issues and Emerging Markets* (Basingstoke: Macmillan), pp. 290–312.

Zloch-Christy, I. (1998) *Eastern Europe and the World Economy: Challenges of Transition and Globalization* (Cheltenham: Edward Elgar).

Name Index

Subject Index